The
Devil
and
Mr. Duncan

Portrait of Duncan by
Edward Curtis Studios

The
Devil
and
Mr. Duncan

PETER MURRAY

Sono Nis Press
VICTORIA, BRITISH COLUMBIA

Canadian Cataloguing in Publication Data

Murray, Peter, 1928-
    The devil and Mr. Duncan

Includes index.
Bibliography: p.
ISBN 0-919203-68-X

1. Duncan, William, 1832-1918. 2. Tsimshian
Indians - Missions. 3. Indians of North America -
Northwest coast of North America - Missions.
4. Missionaries - British Columbia - Biography.
5. Missionaries - Alaska - Biography. I. Title.
E00.T8D855 1985   266'.023'0924   C85-091190-7

First printing October 1985
Second printing April 1988

Published by
SONO NIS PRESS
1745 Blanshard Street
Victoria, British Columbia

Designed, printed and bound by
MORRISS PRINTING COMPANY LTD.
Victoria, British Columbia

To The Metlakatlans

Sources

EXCEPT WHERE OTHERWISE NOTED, the material for this book came from two sources of primary material. The first comprises Duncan's journals, notebooks, letter-books, correspondence received, and financial accounts. Now mouldering in a damp basement in Metlakatla, Alaska, these documents were microfilmed on 20 reels in 1964 by the Public Archives of Canada. Copies of the microfilm exist in the Archives in Ottawa, the University of British Columbia, the National Archives and Records Center in Seattle, and in Metlakatla, Alaska. The collection is unindexed but there is a rough outline of the contents of each reel. The second major source is the Henry Wellcome Collection in the Seattle Records Center. This massive accumulation of papers and documents relates primarily to Duncan's years in Alaska but also includes early biographical details and information relating to British Columbia. This collection is exhaustively indexed and cross-referenced.

Contents

Introduction

*Too many historians stumble on the missionary.
Nineteenth-century authors made him bigger than life, and
twentieth-century social scientists either underestimate or
confuse his very real humanitarian achievements.*

—Ted C. Hinckley,
The Americanization of Alaska, 1867-1897

FEW MISSIONARY CAREERS have had more mixed reviews than that of William Duncan. In Metlakatla, Alaska, he was described in 1982 by a young Indian, recently returned from studying computer science at a California university, as "that old pirate." Shortly afterward a respected village elder who remembers Duncan from his boyhood said he was "as close to a saint as anyone I've ever known."

The older man was echoing the sentiments of most of the village elders. They have been influenced by listening to their parents talk of the old days, and indirectly by two books written about Duncan during his lifetime. Henry Wellcome and John Arctander, two unlikely chroniclers, all but conferred sainthood on the sturdy little tannery clerk from Yorkshire. Their books also helped spread the fame of Metlakatla, a community of Tsimshian Indians which Duncan moulded on the northern coast of British Columbia and later moved to Alaska. Metlakatla was probably the best known Western Canadian place-name in British households. Over the years the little community commanded the attention of presidents, prime ministers, premiers, senators, governors and cabinet ministers.

The critical young man was expressing the view of those led to believe Duncan was a tyrannical rascal who manipulated the natives to serve his own ambitions and exploited their labour for personal gain. A campaign of vilification was started during his lifetime which alleged, among other things, that he was sexually promiscuous during his early years among the Indians and demented in his old age. This attitude has been strengthened by anthropologists and historians singling Duncan out as a leading agent of acculturation. He is accused of stripping the Indians of their identity by transforming them into replicas of dark-suited little Englishmen.

Most of the adulation for Duncan during his 30 years in British

Columbia came from outside the province. His combative nature and unwavering convictions created many enemies in B.C. among politicians, merchants and the high clergy of the Church of England. At the end of his life in Alaska, when he resisted the aspirations which he had helped create among the younger Metlakatlans, an aged and cantankerous Duncan was opposed by some of his own people. Most were reluctant rebels, however, too respectful of their mentor to openly criticize the embittered, beleaguered figure.

When Duncan arrived on the coast, in 1857, the disintegration of Indian society was already well under way. Nine tribes of Tsimshians had abandoned their winter and summer villages to cluster in a ramshackle settlement around the stockade logs of the Hudson's Bay Company's Fort Simpson trading post. It was a demoralized, squabbling and often violent community.

Three accoutrements of white civilization brought by the first traders—firearms, disease and alcohol—ensured that Indian society would not survive intact. Although guns and disease, particularly smallpox, claimed the most lives, it was liquor, previously unknown to the Indians, which split the fabric of their culture. The potlatch, idealized by whites who see Indians only in the guise of the "noble savage," was corrupted in many villages into a drunken orgy punctuated by gunfire.

To the vast majority of whites, who had come to this lonely outpost of empire only to seek their fortunes, the collapse of Indian society was a matter of small concern. They regarded the Indians as sub-humans with no meaningful role to play in the new society. If the Hudson's Bay Company treated the natives with a degree of decency, which was not always the case, it was only because they were essential to its business of acquiring furs—and a source of women for lonely Scotsmen far from home.

Enter the missionaries. They make easy targets. Assured, self-righteous, they arrived uninvited, bringing a new set of values and beliefs to a demoralized race. But generally overlooked is the fact that, misguided in many ways as they may have been, the missionaries were among the very few who *cared* about the Indians. Some regarded their mission as simply converting the Indians to Christianity and counted success in the number of baptisms they performed. But others, of whom Duncan was the most daring and innovative, could see that turning the Indians into nominal Christians was not enough. If they were to learn the skills needed to survive in the new world of commerce, it was essential that they be shielded from the rapacious white society in a temporary sanctuary. It was the implementation of that policy which brought Duncan into conflict with the colonial establishment. If missionaries in general annoyed the vested interests by meddling in affairs that were not supposed to concern them, Duncan goaded them to fury. They found much to dislike in him. He was often aloof, suspicious and vindictive. There seemed to be a war waging within him between compassion and cruelty, generosity and meanness.

The Catholic missionary and historian A. G. Morice, more observant and reflective than Duncan, described the explorer Alexander Mackenzie as a restless, impetuous and biased man who became stubborn and aggressive when crossed. "But his very defects were simply excesses of good qualities," Morice wrote, "and they admirably fitted him for the tasks he was so gloriously to achieve."

So too with Duncan. He was a flawed personality, beset by inner devils, but his weaknesses and faults should not obscure his accomplishments. They were considerable, despite efforts to diminish his historical importance. There has been a deliberate campaign by some in British Columbia, including the Anglican Church, to erase the memory of his work and the astonishing Tsimshian exodus which he led. The fact that more than 800 people felt strongly enough about their mistreatment to move to a neighbouring country is a stigma on the conscience of the church, the province and the nation.

For many years the historians of British Columbia ignored the Indian population as completely as the politicians. That has changed in recent years, but Duncan's role in the natives' struggle for recognition still is not sufficiently appreciated.

There are a number of reasons why his work deserves to be reviewed at this time. First, there is the issue of Indian land claims, which are being pressed with increasing vigour. Duncan was among the earliest to actively campaign for aboriginal rights in a province that recognized the principle even less than the Imperial and Dominion governments of the day. They at least made gestures in that direction. The refusal of the provincial government and courts to accede to the Tsimshians' demands for land tenure was the principal cause of the Metlakatlans' move to Alaska in 1887.

After more than a century of maladministration, there is a move now afoot to abolish the Department of Indian Affairs. Some have belatedly recognized that it is not too late to start treating the natives as individuals capable of managing their own affairs. Duncan was far ahead of his time on this question too, at least in theory. He warned repeatedly against making Indians wards of the state, shunting them off into reservations where they could survive only on whatever handouts governments were prepared to offer.

The stimulus of Metlakatla, its reason for being, was not as commonly believed an attempt to create a native Christian utopia. It was to show that Indians could become skilled tradesmen and help build the new frontier society. Above all, Duncan believed the Indians must have a sense of independence and self-respect to survive the trauma of cultural change. He did not force change upon them; once the white man took control of the area that was inevitable. His objective was to soften the blow. At first he encouraged the Indians to continue their seasonal pursuit of the salmon and oolichan, but he knew they would eventually have to live a more settled life so the young people could gain a proper education. The Indians also recognized that fact, and it was one reason they favoured the move from Fort Simpson to Metlakatla.

But the politicians, most of whom were deeply involved in speculative land ventures and depended upon the support of the other acquisitors who controlled the colony, did not heed the wisdom of a lone missionary. The Indians have often been betrayed. In 1871 Sir John A. Macdonald, who didn't care too much about the welfare of the Indians in any case, was so anxious to bring British Columbia into Confederation that he allowed the province in effect to opt out of the national policy which required treaties with Indian tribes. Some 110 years later another prime minister, Pierre Trudeau, was so desperate to have a new constitution approved that he gave way to demands by the provinces, led by British Columbia, to drop a clause guaranteeing aboriginal rights.

Although the proper role of missionaries is still being debated, there has been a growing awareness in this century that they should be concerned with improving the standard of life of the people they serve at least as much as "saving souls." Catholic and Protestant missionaries alike are now concentrating on providing the basic material needs of the poor of the undeveloped world. This trend is further proof that Duncan's approach was the correct one. Just as the new missionary is prepared to accept and help the non-believer, so was Duncan. It is not generally known that half the population of Metlakatla was not Christian. As long as the natives were prepared to accept the rules of the community, Duncan welcomed them. In fact, the conversion of the Tsimshians to Christianity was withheld by Duncan until he was satisfied the candidates were prepared to accept the gospel in their daily lives.

It is a sad fact that the largest Indian community in British Columbia in 1984—6,000 people, most of them young—existed within the boundaries of Vancouver's Skid Road. This melancholy statistic cannot be laid at the door of the missionary; we are all to blame. Fortunately the Indians, as described by the American historian Francis Parkman, are a rock-like people who cannot be easily shaped to our expectations and assimilated. And Canada, thankfully, is not a melting pot. There is room, and still time, for the Indians to take their rightful place in the country. To do that it is vital that we, and they, know more about their recent history, including the role played in it by men like William Duncan.

It is good to be often reminded of the inconsistency of human nature, and to learn to look without wonder or disgust on the weaknesses which are found in the strongest minds.

—Thomas Babington Macaulay

Chapter 1

Lonely Voyage

THE YEAR WAS 1856 and the legendary David Livingstone had just come home after 16 years to the day in Africa. In the midst of London's week-long celebration, four men huddled unnoticed in the winter evening chill on the platform of Paddington Station. Three were in their twenties, fellow students, and the fourth a middle-aged man in clerical collar. After handshakes and farewells, two of the students drifted off while the other pair boarded the train. The older man was the Reverend C. A. Alford, principal of Highbury Training College for Schoolmasters; the other William Duncan, one of Alford's prize pupils. They were bound for Plymouth, where Duncan was to board a Royal Navy ship as passenger on a six-month voyage around Cape Horn to the North Pacific coast. There he was to be the first missionary among the Tsimshian Indians in the Fort Simpson area between the mouths of the Skeena and Nass rivers.

Alford had come to see Duncan off. No members of his family were present, although it was understood they might not see him again. Duncan had picked up his written instructions earlier in the day from the Church Missionary Society headquarters in Salisbury Square. This was a historic occasion for the Church of England organization. With missionaries in Africa, India, Australia and China, the establishment of Duncan's mission would fill, in the phrase of a C.M.S. official, the missing link in the Society's chain around the globe.

Duncan and Alford arrived in Plymouth at 6 a.m. on the morning of December 23. The young man's 28 pieces of luggage, containing among other items, an axe, saw, shovel, rake, hoe and assorted carpentry and blacksmith's tools, as well as 100 family prayerbooks and six books of "selected homilies," were stowed aboard the newly commissioned steam-frigate H.M.S. *Satellite* by 9 a.m., though not to Duncan's satisfaction. He was aware of derogatory murmurs and curses from crew members about the accumulation of boxes and trunks. Nobody seemed to care where they were placed. Some were stowed in steerage, others went to a different deck.

The two men had breakfast in the wardroom, then strolled the decks waiting to meet Captain James C. Prevost, the man responsible for Duncan's impending journey. Three years earlier Prevost had been commander of the Royal Navy paddle sloop *Virago* when she was forced to beach for repairs at Fort Simpson. During his enforced stay, Prevost, a religious man, had been appalled by conditions in the Indian encampment surrounding the H.B.C. fort. More than 2,000 Tsimshians lived in what appeared to Prevost's disciplined mind to be a constant state of turmoil and squalor. Drunkenness and prostitution were rampant, and Prevost feared conditions would get worse as more white traders and miners moved into the area.

The Tsimshians at Fort Simpson were mostly middlemen in the fur trade, buying skins from neighbouring tribes and selling them to the H.B.C. Many had abandoned their summer and winter villages and lived year-round in the shadow of the fort. Others congregated there during trading season. Convinced of the Tsimshians' potential—"they manifest a great desire and aptitude to acquire the knowledge and arts of civilized life"—Prevost resolved to do something for them.

In the spring of 1856 while in England to take command of the *Satellite*, Prevost met the editorial secretary of the C.M.S., the Reverend Joseph Ridgeway, at a missionary meeting in Tunbridge Wells. He appealed to Ridgeway for support in establishing a mission at Fort Simpson. Protesting there was little money available for "a few sheep in the wilderness" of the northwest coast of America, Ridgeway was not encouraging. The Society already had its resources stretched thinly in more populated areas of the world, he said, and was not likely to launch a new undertaking, particularly in such a remote spot. The Society had been told as early as 1819 that the Indians west of the Rocky Mountains were a superior people likely to respond to missionary endeavour. Its workers were sent instead to the Red River area. They seldom ventured far beyond the plains.

Nevertheless, Ridgeway invited Prevost to describe what he had seen at Fort Simpson in the *Intelligencer*, a C.M.S. publication. Prevost wrote an impassioned appeal that caught the attention of the Society's secretary and guiding light, Henry Venn. The article also brought forth two donations totalling $2,500 for the proposed mission. Venn gave the go-ahead. A decision was required quickly because Prevost was due to return in December to deal with the San Juan Islands boundary dispute and had offered, with the approval of the Admiralty, free passage to a missionary. Prevost had expected an ordained minister would be chosen. Instead, the Society settled on Duncan, who had been attending Highbury after volunteering three years earlier for missionary service.

At first glance, Duncan, 24, seemed an unlikely choice for such an undertaking. His education was limited and his theological studies minimal. But what he lacked in formal preparation was compensated by experience in business and teaching that provided a practical rather than theoretical background. And his energy and zeal were boundless. Duncan was, in fact, fairly typical of the young men being dispatched at this time from England to foreign missions. Venn wanted missionaries who could take not only the gospel to the "heathen," but also the benefits of advanced western civilization, the fruits of the industrial and commercial revolutions. He was more concerned with encouraging the uncivilized races to establish and maintain their own independent churches than counting converts for the Anglican Church. Venn was in the forefront of the dominant Evangelical movement in the mid-nineteenth century. It emphasized the importance of trade and commerce in improving the lot of the natives, in addition to Christianity's less tangible benefits.

The government was a helpful ally in what it regarded as another arm of the world-wide embrace of Empire. Growing out of the anti-slavery campaign of the late eighteenth century, the English missionary movement spread steadily until about 1840, when it suddenly caught the imagination of the population. Support groups sprang up in every city and town, publications appeared extolling the exploits of devoted men in faraway lands, and money poured into the coffers of the half-dozen major societies. The stream of donations became a flood in the months following Livingstone's triumphant return—pennies from the poor and thousands of pounds from the wealthy.

It was the artisans and tradesmen, members of a new upward bound social group, who filled the missionary ranks in this period. Fired by a powerful social and spiritual drive for self-improvement, they sought escape from the lower classes. In an age that set a premium on individual initiative, missionary service offered a way of bettering one's esteem and station in life, while at the same time creating in the natives a new lower class which could be looked down upon. Thus, the motivation for offering oneself for missionary work arose from the new social currents as well as personal needs and ambitions.

Such was the case with William Duncan, who never did convincingly articulate the reasons for his commitment. First, there were the circumstances of his birth. He was born out of wedlock, not unusual in that era, but something that would be a matter of deep shame to a young man seeking religious salvation. His mother was Maria Duncan, nineteen-year-old daughter of William and Elizabeth Duncan of Beverley, Yorkshire. The place of birth was Bishop Burton, a nearby rural hamlet where Maria was likely working as a servant girl or inn-maid. The father is unknown. The boy was born April 3, 1832. The first official record contained in the baptismal book of the parish church, dated April 8, identified him as "William, illegitimate son of Maria Donkin." It is assumed Maria could not write and that when she gave her name to the minister, who did not know her, he mistook the spelling. There were a number of "Donkins" and "Duncums" and other variations in the area. Maria gave the baby the single name of her father, a tanner with a local firm which his grandson would later join. She was not in a position to look after her infant son and gave him to her parents to raise.

Duncan was always circumspect about his origins. In an interview late in life he said that because he had been moved to Beverley as a baby he had never seen his birthplace.[1]

"I was only told where I was born."
"What was your father?"
"I don't know. I know very little of him; he died when I was young."
"What was his occupation?"
"Farmer."

Beverley is a pleasant market town in East Yorkshire that dates its beginnings about 700 A.D. The name of the town comes from

[1] The interviewer was Henry Wellcome, in New Metlakatla during the winter of 1916-17. A verbatim transcript of the interview taken down by court reporter Charles Boren is in The Henry Wellcome Collection in Seattle.

"the beaver clearing in the woodland." The Hull River flowing around the town once harboured colonies of beavers which created the many ponds and meadows in the gently rolling countryside. By the time of Duncan's birth new industries had brought Beverley prosperity and a population of 12,000. Its most noted landmark is the magnificent Beverley Minster, which was built in the fifteenth century and rivals the better-known great Gothic cathedrals of England in size and grandeur.

The Minster and adjacent St. John's Chapel played an important role in Duncan's life and helped determine his career. The boy went to the National School in Beverley, where he was a bright student. His teacher, Jeremiah Self, was also choirmaster at the Minster and discovered that Duncan had an outstanding voice. When a vacancy arose in the choir, an audition was held which nine-year-old William won easily. From that day on he was increasingly involved with the church.

The choir was made up of six men and eight boys. "I was so little," Duncan recalled, "I could just get my chin or nose up to the desk where the book was... but I went up, up, up until I was the leading treble voice in the Minster for years. I sang the solos." His friend John Hall was the second treble-soprano voice. "He was just like a little brother to me. We were so fond of each other. We walked together in the choir... two by two, and we two were first, because we had to take the first places... and we walked into the church twice every Sabbath day for years."

Duncan's voice was said to be so remarkable that music lovers came to the Minster from great distances to hear him. He practised in the fields on the edge of town, pouring out hymns from memory at the top of his lungs. He ate apples diligently on being told they helped the throat. His voice did not break until he was 16, an advanced age for a boy soprano. William was then recruited by Reverend Anthony Carr of St. John's to teach Sunday School.

Carr had become the father figure missing in the boy's life. His mother had married a man named Botterill and William lived with them for a time, but was never close to either. Carr was the man he idolized and the one who awakened his religious yearnings. William never missed his sermons or Bible classes. It was Carr who inculcated the basic evangelical beliefs which Duncan maintained all his life. The two spent hours together discussing religious theory, how the basics of Christianity should be taught, and the schism over "high" and "low" practices in the Church of England.

William left school at 14 to take a special course in penmanship, then went to work as an errand boy for the tanning firm of George Cussons and Sons. He performed a variety of jobs for two years before beginning an apprenticeship as a bookkeeper. When he was 18 the firm's travelling salesman left and Duncan was promoted to his position. Office and warehouse chores were part of the new job, but he was now able to broaden his horizons by travelling to northern and midlands counties taking orders for the company's leather products.

It was an eye-opening experience. "My travelling threw me among a class of society which were above what I had been used to," he recalled in the journal which he began writing at the age of 21. "When seated in a beautiful room surrounded with comforts, and at a table covered with the good things of this world; when all my little wants were readily and eagerly supplied; and I mixed among a class of men far my superiors in education, rank and abilities, and was treated respectfully by them; Oh! I used to feel my heart overflow in gratitude, for God's wonderful love in thus elevating me, lifting me from the dunghill and raising my head, thus, in so little time; and so graciously and greatly surpassing my every expectation."

His family, a source of embarrassment to the ambitious young man, was part of that "dunghill." Mother, stepfather, uncles and aunts, even his two young half-sisters, were all "strangers to grace" in his intolerant eyes. Some, like his Uncle Peter, drank too much. None were regular church-goers. All were uninterested in the spiritual matters that concerned him. He was uncomfortable talking to them and wondered, "Why is not the salvation of my relatives as near my heart as the salvation of others?"

Duncan set out to rise above his family, but could not always meet the high standards he set for himself. "I perfectly abhor myself," he wrote in one of his earliest journal entries. "My weakness, my wickedness, my folly, my ignorance, and the madness of my heart are all in array before me." The insecurity, vanity and sexual stirrings of late adolescence, always unsettling to a self-conscious youth, were especially so in the Victorian era. "I have been much troubled this week with impure thoughts chiefly brought on by foolishly listening to our (tannery) men's impure conversation," he wrote. "This I resolve to avoid."

There were problems even in church: "I am afraid I am becoming proud of my appearance—young ladies seem to admire me so.

Tonight too I was showing off my vocal powers—singing to my own glory—because some near me at church appeared delighted." The pretty young women in their finery kept his mind off the sermon. Duncan tried to solve his problem by moving to a back pew where it was difficult to see and be seen.

It was in such a romantic, agitated state of mind that Duncan walked on a rainy November evening in 1853 to the quarterly Missionary Meeting in the girls' Sunday School room of the Minster. The speaker was the Reverend George Hodgson of York, who said the Church Missionary Society had money but not enough men. "What a great thing it would be if we could find some of our young men in Beverley that would volunteer to become missionaries!" Years later Duncan recalled his reaction. "It just struck me at the time I heard it, 'Well, that is a new idea. I think that is very good. I will think it over' and I did. Before I left the room I felt very much inclined to it. And I woke up that night and thought . . . what good is wealth . . . but if I can go and do good somewhere, that will be something worthwhile."

It was not the first such appeal he had heard—missionary recruitment and fund-raising meetings were commonplace, particularly in Yorkshire—but there had been no previous indication that Duncan was considering such a step. A desire to carry the gospel to the benighted souls of foreign lands had never been apparent, despite his claim to the C.M.S. in his letter of application that he was 18 when he "first felt a longing for the welfare of the heathen, accompanied by a strong desire to go and live among them." He had thought of going to "some foreign port," setting up in the leather business, learning the local language and then starting to preach.

It could not have escaped Duncan's notice that missionaries, at least those who survived the diseases and perils of tropical lands, were showered with adulation. The 1850's were the golden years of missionary fervour, Livingstone's exploits in Africa had captured the public imagination and created publicity for the whole movement. The glamour and excitement surrounding missionary work exerted a strong pull on the troubled young man.

The first to learn of Duncan's decision was his friend Stephen Hewson, a young pharmacist also active in the church who said he would join him. Carr was next to be informed of Duncan's intention. He was "much pleased and promised to further me all he could." Others were less supportive. His mother told William he should do what he thought best, but hoped he would continue in business where he was doing so well. He had recently saved enough money to build a small house for himself after lodging for four years following the death of his grandfather. His employer, George Cussons Jr., who had taken over the business from his father, was also reluctant to see Duncan go. He did not oppose the move, however, and was pleased when Duncan said he would stay on another six months. The elder Cussons, however, insisted Duncan would rue the day he left the firm.

If the younger Cussons believed Duncan, whose intelligence, hard work and adeptness in business assured him a successful and rewarding career, would have second thoughts, he was correct. After writing to Reverend Hodgson, Duncan was asked by the C.M.S. for an outline of his qualifications. He received the request December 5. A month passed and he had not replied. In the meantime, Hewson said he could not go with him after all. His mother, an aging widow whose health was poor, had pleaded with him not to leave and he had reluctantly decided he must stay. Although he had no close family ties to hold him back, Duncan now agonized even more over his decision. His diary reflected a mood of doubt and self-torment that brought him close to a nervous breakdown. He was weakened physically, too, from the effects of a persistent bronchitis. A medical examination disclosed he had a weakness in his right lung, but otherwise his constitution was strong.

Reverend Carr became ill that winter and Duncan was deeply concerned. Despite the difference in ages, William regarded Carr as "my nearest and dearest friend." When Carr died on February 9, 1854, Duncan grieved over "the greatest affliction that ever beset me in my life." Six days before his death, Carr had sent for him. After talking about missionary work and drafting together the letter to the Society, Duncan had promised to show Carr the finished version for approval before mailing it off. He had procrastinated too long and was distraught. "I learnt as I never learnt before, that delay is dangerous." Carr's death "seemed a direct judgement upon me for my sins." Rather than firming him in his resolve, the loss left Duncan even more confused. There was no one now he could turn to for advice. His letter remained unfinished.

Early in March, Duncan was called to London by his Uncle Sam, a man-servant to an army officer, to take charge of his money and valuables while he was in the Crimea. Duncan took advantage of the trip to deliver his letter at last to the C.M.S. offices. He was interviewed by three Society officials, who said they would advise him in two weeks whether he had been accepted. On March 22 a letter arrived informing Duncan he had been chosen to become a student at the Society's Highbury College.

There was one more temptation to overcome. A business acquaintance from a tanning firm in another city offered Duncan a job that would pay a minimum of $700 a year. "He set riches, lucrative positions and many honours, indeed a first-rate life before me... but all the vanities he offered made no impression, thank God." The final decision had been made and Duncan declared triumphantly in his journal: "I hope from this day to date a glorious career, and the commencement of a warfare which may end in the final overthrow of all my enemies." There was nothing in that ringing declaration indicating a passion to help the less-privileged members of humanity, but rather a disturbing tendency to view life as a battleground mined with "enemies."

Duncan arrived excitedly at Highbury, but was soon disenchanted. "The students are not good enough, rich enough, polite enough and intellectual enough for my pride. They do not reverence me as I was reverenced at home. My dignity is wounded at finding myself lowered in circumstance and class of acquaintances." In the arrogance of those words can be deduced the anxiousness and insecurity of a youth cast adrift in an alien environment. But Duncan was determined to make his mark at Highbury, to prove his superiority over the other students. It was not long before one of his teachers praised the clarity and intellectual vigour of Duncan's reports and told him he should be thankful for his intelligence. An older student said, "Duncan, your responsibility is very great. You are endowed with a great mind and you have nothing to do but to become a genius."

At the same time he was excelling scholastically, Duncan was experiencing religious doubts. "I do not see so clearly into spiritual matters as I used... I find there is a depth in knowledge, it is really wonderful." Concerned about these feelings of intellectual stimulation and the corresponding reduction in time spent at prayer, Duncan became an increasingly solemn and pompous young man. He was quick to find fault in others and sought to impose his own opinions. Any impulse toward fun was sternly suppressed.

These were not qualities that would endear him to his fellow students. As senior monitor he reported a number of them for minor misdemeanours and was subjected to taunts at the dinner table. "I'm held in abomination by some of the students," he confided to his diary. But "they walked in darkness," he added defiantly.

Duncan was also out of step with the other students in his lack of patriotic enthusiasm for Britain's battlefield successes abroad. When a school holiday was declared September 11, 1855, to mark the taking of Sebastopol, he stayed in his room writing letters while the others went off to London to join the celebrations. He expressed disapproval of the country's outpouring of self-glorification, "as though by our might this victory was achieved... *Rule Britannia* is not a song to please God or benefit a nation and is certainly not consistent with our position as a nation."

The Crimean campaign indirectly caused another, more personal crisis for Duncan. Six months after his Uncle Sam had left for Constantinople, Duncan wrote a friend in Beverley: "This money (entrusted to him by his uncle) I should have put into the bank but his letter informed me that he was likely soon to return so I kept it and passed the account of it into my cash book and began using it. A great part I lent and a small part I spent, but because I foolishly neglected to obtain of you before I left home what I needed to make it up, it follows that I must now trouble you to send it." Duncan asked for $100. He said he owed his uncle $350 altogether, but would try to make a deal with him. It was the first example, but not the last, of a casual disregard for bookkeeping principles and the misuse of funds.

On Monday morning, December 15, 1856, Duncan had just completed writing his final government examinations and was looking forward to a month's holiday from Highbury. After the Christmas break he was to return for another four months to take further studies in mathematics. But Alford called Duncan to his office to tell him the C.M.S. proposed sending him immediately to the North Pacific coast. Duncan expressed concern at having only three weeks to prepare, but told the principal confidently he was ready to go wherever he was needed. Then he fled to his room and wept. On Thursday Duncan learned the *Satellite* would actually be sailing in six days, not three weeks. There was time for only a quick visit to Beverley, where he stayed with his family overnight but dined with the Cussons, with whom he felt more comfortable. The farewells exchanged with his mother, stepfather and sisters were emotional, however, and accompanied by "many tears."

When Prevost's return to the *Satellite* after breakfasting with the Admiral was delayed, Reverend Alford left. Duncan felt lonely and apprehensive, especially when Prevost showed no interest in his young passenger as the ship prepared for embarkation. She sailed at 3 p.m. and Duncan brooded on how coldly he had been treated. It was his first taste of the "fearful amount of inhospitality" he was to encounter aboard the ship. As the *Satellite* plunged into heavy seas, he wandered morosely around the decks, worrying about the next six months. After nightfall, when the lights of England had disappeared below the horizon, the captain finally directed Duncan to the engineers' mess for his first food since morning. He was given tea, a herring and some hard biscuits, then assigned a hammock in steerage. But there was little rest for the next three days as the ship bucked and rolled. Duncan was miserably seasick. It was not a Christmas to remember.

Two passengers who had been sharing Prevost's quarters were dropped off at the Canary Islands and Duncan expected to be invited to move in. At a meeting with Venn and Duncan, the Captain had promised he would occupy a place in his cabin after the first week. But the invitation never came.

Duncan was uncomfortable eating with the engineers and listening to their "depraved conversation." When he complained to Prevost, the captain moved him in with the gunner, Mr. Moon, a surly man who mistreated his cabin boy and was no better than the engineers. Duncan also considered the charge for his food excessive, and bought some biscuits during a stopover in Rio de Janeiro.

On March 5 the *Satellite* reached the entrance to the Straits of Magellan, where Duncan had his first glimpse of aborigines. He was not impressed. After the long days at sea the sound of birds singing and the sight of wildflowers on the slopes above the beach inspired him to a burst of purple prose. "Where is he for whom all this outlay is made? Where is the ear these songs are to delight, eyes the flowers are to please... where is the tenant for whom this gorgeous palace is made? Ask these towering mountains... they will point you to a skulking, filthy creature. There he is creeping on the mountainside, ugly deformity. Gloom and vacancy sit with undisturbed security on his face."

Duncan went ashore at Fortune Bay and walked alone in the dark on the beach, reflecting on the "poor degraded beings." On his return to the ship he found that six Fuegian Indians—four men and two women—had been aboard during his absence and he had missed a closer look at these strange, dwarf-like creatures.

The ship arrived at Valparaiso in early April and stayed a welcome two weeks. Duncan spent much of his time on lonely excursions exploring the parched hills beyond the city. The elaborate Roman Catholic ceremonies over Easter "shocked and disgusted" him. He nervously accepted an invitation to preach his first sermon at the church of an American missionary, but was spared the ordeal when the ship left ahead of schedule.

Just before sailing, Duncan purchased a water-cooler, flask, some bottles of wine, and more bread and biscuits. For the remainder of the voyage he intended to be free of Mr. Moon and the ship's food and drink. He would "skulk away" somewhere to consume his bread and water. A bottle of wine was added each week to his water supply "to correct anything pernicious." For most of the day Duncan went to a dinghy suspended from davits over the stern of the ship. When he wanted to write he would sit on one of his trunks in steerage.

Next stop was the busy port of Callao, Peru, where a civil war was in progress and Prevost was asked by the government side to provide medical aid. Duncan visited the hospital. "I shall never forget the sight. Scores of men lay bleeding, groaning and dying. What a dreadful thing it was." The sheltered youth from rural Yorkshire was discovering a world he had only read about.

After leaving Callao, Prevost belatedly began to pay some attention to Duncan. The Captain gave up a corner of his cabin where he could read, write and pray. He was also befriended by the ship's doctor, and enjoyed the talk of an intelligent man after his long conversational drought. With less than a month remaining before they would reach their destination of Victoria, Duncan was invited to eat in the officers' wardroom. "This is human nature," he noted sourly, but accepted. Duncan was stirred to life by the sudden burst of attention he had craved, and attempted to introduce religion into the crewmen's lives. He organized a Bible class at which 14 men showed up. There was a congregation of 20 for a Sunday evening service he conducted in the Captain's cabin.

On the morning of June 13, 1857, the *Satellite* rounded Cape Flattery and started down the Strait of Juan de Fuca. The ship had not gone far when it was intercepted by a canoe with eight Indians aboard—Duncan's first sight of the race of people with whom he would spend the rest of his life. He was pleasantly surprised by this initial encounter. "Although in a pitiable condition, they were by no means so degraded in appearance as I expected to find them.

They showed a good deal of intelligence in what they did and their very beautiful canoe spoke their skills to be by no means small." Duncan noted the women appeared passive but took an equal share of the rowing with the men. A dirty blanket was their only clothing.

After towing the Indians' canoe for some distance, the *Satellite* cut them loose and proceeded toward Esquimalt naval base, where the anchor was dropped at 5 p.m.

Chapter 2

Victoria Interlude

WHEN DUNCAN AND CAPTAIN PREVOST stepped ashore next morning they were met by James Douglas, Chief Factor of nearby Fort Victoria and the senior H.B.C. official west of the Rockies. Douglas was also governor of Vancouver Island, the Company's Crown-granted colony.

Born out of wedlock to a Scottish trader and a British Guiana Creole, the burly Douglas had climbed rapidly in the company. During his early fur-trading days in the northern interior he had married the daughter of an Indian woman and an H.B.C. factor. Douglas was generally regarded to be more sympathetic than most toward the native population of his domain. But the interests of the company always came first. That loyalty continued, his critics claimed, even after he severed his H.B.C. ties in 1858 upon being named joint governor of the separate colonies of Vancouver Island and mainland British Columbia.

As the three men proceeded toward the home of Chaplain Edward Cridge, Prevost asked Douglas what ship would be taking Duncan the remaining 500 miles north to Fort Simpson. The governor was vague. He expressed surprise that the C.M.S. had picked Fort Simpson as the site of its first mission, apparently unaware that it had done so on the recommendation of Prevost. "There is no possible chance for you to do any good amongst them that we can see," Douglas told Duncan. His destination should be regarded as undecided. "Upon hearing which," Duncan noted, "the Captain rather abruptly assured him that was not the case. There was no doubt where the mission was to begin." The conversation was broken off when they reached Cridge's house. After introducing Duncan to the chaplain, Douglas and Prevost went off to the governor's house.

Cridge told Duncan that Douglas had written to the Society two months previously advising against sending anyone to Fort Simp-

son, and was now awaiting a reply. The governor had told the
C.M.S. it was too dangerous there, proposing that Duncan work
instead among the Indians in the Victoria area.

Douglas had more than Duncan's well-being in mind when he
sent the letter. Itinerant missionaries had previously created trouble in the company's fur-trading areas, and he sought to keep them
away from the frontier, restricted to settlements where they could
be closely supervised. Douglas wanted no interference in the trading patterns with the Indians which the H.B.C. had carefully
nurtured over the past half-century.

Cridge offered to take Duncan into his home while the issue was
being settled, but Prevost intervened. It was his duty to keep
Duncan on the *Satellite* until he had assurance of passage to Fort
Simpson, the captain said. If that was not forthcoming, he would
take him back to England.

Douglas invited Duncan to lunch to sound out his intentions. He
had no choice, Duncan told the governor, barring new instructions
from the Society, but to go to Fort Simpson. It emerged during
their conversation that Douglas, since he made most of the decisions in the colony, had expected to pick the site where Duncan
would settle. When he saw how determined both Duncan and
Prevost were, however, the governor reluctantly agreed to their
plan. Duncan would leave by the next boat north in September. In
the meantime he should learn as much of the Tsimshian language
as possible. With the *Satellite* due to leave Esquimalt shortly, the
governor offered Duncan a room in his house, but he elected to stay
with Cridge and his wife Mary.

Duncan spent the summer in Victoria, a pleasant three-month
interlude in which he regained his vitality after the sluggish months
at sea on a spartan diet. There were picnics and balls and numerous activities centred around Christ Church. Duncan put his
musical talents to use by organizing the church's first choir. He
also taught a Sunday school class and preached his first sermon, to a congregation of 50. The church warden, Joseph Despard
Pemberton, the colony's stiff-necked surveyor-general and a leader
in Victoria society, objected that Duncan should not have been
allowed in the pulpit because he was not ordained. Duncan also
conducted a funeral service for a woman he had comforted in
Cridge's absence while she was dying. He regretted his awkward-
ness during the service and inability to convey his true thoughts. "I
realized how a minister can become a mere mouthpiece, a sayer of
prayers."

The squalid Indian camps surrounding Fort Victoria reflected overcrowding and the easy availability of liquor. Great numbers of rival tribes converged on the town during the summer. In 1857 there were only about 200 whites in the area, but a year later there would be close to 4,000 transient miners in makeshift tent sites awaiting transportation to the newly discovered gold fields on the Fraser River. The diseases of prostitution became epidemic among the Indian women.

Returning from a church service at Craigflower one evening, Duncan came upon a party of Indians gambling in front of their huts. he found their rough appearance and guttural cries "truly horrible." Over the summer, however, he became more accustomed to the bizarre scenes and less apprehensive. In August, as he was travelling on horseback to Craigflower, he was confronted by a group of Indians on the road. Their faces were coloured with red dye and they were "bellowing" loudly. Duncan mused that if he had met such an alarming group under such circumstances a few weeks before he would have been terrified. He realized how fortuitous his unplanned stopover had been. "I believe if I had been sent direct to Fort Simpson without this time for reflection and preparation—I should have been prostrated in the work, an utter failure."

There was reason to fear the whites as well as the Indians. Returning from Douglas' house to the Cridges one evening, he was accosted by a drunken man who shot at him but missed. Duncan retreated to the nearby home of Dr. J. S. Helmcken as the man fired a second time. It was dark and the man apparently thought Duncan was an Indian. There had been several murders committed among the Indians recently and nearly all were now carrying guns or knives, causing the nervous whites to arm themselves in turn.

Although distressed by the wretched Indian camps, Duncan was impressed by what he saw and heard of the Tsimshians. They were generally regarded as being superior to the other tribes clustered around the town. A number found work as farm servants and were praised for their character and diligence. Duncan was introduced to a young Tsimshian named Wehawn to learn the language. Wehawn, whom he considered "very kind and intelligent," came to the Cridge house five nights each week for a dollar. He was always freshly scrubbed and wore a blue coat with brass buttons. "He quite understands my purpose and seems to feel very greatly honoured in assisting me." Wehawn assured Duncan he would be welcomed by the Indians at Fort Simpson. Others confirmed there was little to fear from the Tsimshians, but he was cautioned to lie low during intertribal warfare.

Among the friends Duncan made in Victoria was William John Macdonald, who had left the H.B.C. to open a general store. Later Macdonald was appointed postmaster, customs collector and gold commissioner before becoming a prosperous businessman and real estate speculator. Macdonald also went into politics, serving as mayor, member of the Legislative Assembly, and eventually Senator.

Duncan also came in contact with the underside of the hierarchic society created by the Hudson's Bay Company's feudal operation. On a visit to Douglas' farm he met the foreman of the property, who lived with his wife and son in miserable quarters. The woman was dirty and dressed in rags. "It struck me that the Indians would not be able to see much difference between their condition and the condition of the Scotchman and his family."

On September 13 Duncan received word that the H.B.C. coastal steamer *Otter* would be sailing within a week. Douglas agreed that although there still had been no reply from the C.M.S. to his letter, Duncan should proceed to Fort Simpson. The governor now seemed "exceedingly kind and affable." Douglas wrote a letter of introduction to William Henry McNeill, a former trader from Boston who sold his ship to the H.B.C. and was now Factor at Fort Simpson. Douglas told McNeill that Duncan, "a gentleman of pleasing manner and with every disposition to make himself agreeable," was to be placed under "your kind and special protection." Duncan should be given an apartment and "maintained at the Company's table in the same manner as any of the Company's officers."

The *Otter* sailed early September 25, docking at Nanaimo at 5 p.m. to take on coal. The few Indians Duncan saw there appeared "very wretched creatures in every way." One of the passengers was Alexander Dallas, an H.B.C. director not long out from England who the following year would marry one of Governor Douglas' five daughters. Dallas repeated Douglas' argument that Fort Simpson was the wrong place for Duncan to start a mission. The Indians at Victoria or Nanaimo were more likely candidates because they had more contact with whites, he said.

"This would have weight if *Christians* could be substituted for *Whites*," Duncan wrote Henry Venn. "The more I see of the Company's servants the less confidence do I place in their judgement. I see them actuated by but one feeling. They care not one straw for the bodies or souls of the Indians, it is the furs they want . . . and those places where the Indians cannot or will not procure them are just the places they would hand over to the missionaries."

Dallas also angered Duncan by telling him it was important to keep quiet about the low prices paid the Indians for furs. He didn't care about furs, Duncan replied, that was not his business. He later learned the company paid one coarse black blanket for 50 marten furs, a medium size white blanket for 30 furs, a forefinger's width of soap for one marten, one inch of copper for each mink skin (the copper was cut from a coil of wire and used by the Indians to make bracelets), and a quart-size tin cup painted in different colours for a bear skin or a land otter. The Indians also told him the company once gave a musket for a pile of mink furs reaching from the ground to the top of the barrel, then switched to guns with barrels two feet longer.

The next port of call was Fort Rupert, at the north end of Vancouver Island. Here Duncan saw his first large permanent Indian village, in contrast to the ramshackle collection of huts and tents outside Victoria. He noted the houses were built of huge cedar timbers at the edge of the beach. Their fronts were "most ludicrously painted." As the ship's party walked on the beach, hundreds of Kwakiutls sat on their haunches along the way, looking "grim and strong and intelligent." Some had painted their faces. Most were dirty, with only a blanket worn loosely around them. The women wore hats woven from bark and a few had caps, with their hair tied behind in a knot. "The first view of so many strange Indians all waiting and staring was a little alarming to me. Their smell was by no means agreeable. There was a constant clamour as we walked by—I suppose commenting upon *our* appearance."

Duncan made the acquaintance of Hamilton Moffatt, the H.B.C. factor at Fort Rupert for the past seven years. He found Moffatt to be an affable, intelligent man. Later, after he had been transferred to Fort Simpson as factor, an unlikely friendship developed between the two men, even though they had become business competitors. Both were independent minded, with an allegiance to their respective employers that was less than total and would eventually be broken.

When Duncan asked Moffatt about farming, he was told that corn would not ripen in the damp, grey Fort Rupert climate and Fort Simpson would not be much different. That was discouraging. The missionary movement was predicated on turning the nomads of the world into settled agriculturalists. In farming lay the path toward civilization and Christianity. It would take many years for Duncan to grudgingly accept that the Tsimshian could never be placed behind a plough, even if suitable land could be found. Why should they, when the natural products of the area were so bountiful? Their year-round needs could be collected in less than six months' time. They were one of the few aboriginal peoples in the world to build a stable, socially complex and artistically and culturally rich society as semi-nomadic hunters, fishermen and gatherers. They were nomads in the sense only that they had winter and summer settlements to shuttle between in harmony with the seasons.

Surprisingly, considering the abundance of wild berries, the Indians were also one of the few societies in the world that had not developed techniques for distilling intoxicating drink.[2] That explained why they were so susceptible to the liquor introduced by the white traders, and the home-brew they were later taught to make by soldiers and miners. They had no experience with alcohol, and it came into their lives at a time when other influences of the white men were already causing cultural disorientation.

At Fort Rupert Duncan walked along the beach to the house of Captain William Brotchie, the only white man living outside the stockade. Brotchie was a former seaman with the H.B.C. who had attempted to build up a business cutting spars, but the timbers proved too large for shipment and he soon gave up and returned to Victoria to become Harbour Master. On the way Duncan observed the intricately carved house-poles and was pleased to learn the carved images were not religious icons but family and clan symbols.

Further along the beach he came suddenly upon the scattered remains of three bodies. A party of Haidas had recently been attacked by the Kwakiutls in retaliation for an earlier raid in which one of their chiefs had been killed and four men taken prisoner. "How the land is defiled with blood," Duncan wrote feverishly in his journal. "Blood, blood from end to end. And here are none to come to the rescue—plenty who deplore the state of things—plenty

[2] Lemert, Edwin M. *Alcohol and the Northwest Coast Indians.* University of California Press, 1954.

who pour furious language upon the murderer—but none to rescue—none to guide the wretched creature to paths of peace and love."

The Kwakiutl were a fine looking people, superior to the southern Indians. Two chiefs he met seemed exceptionally wise and handsome. And the evidence of their skills was all about. The canoes were large and beautifully shaped, proudly displayed to him by an old chief. But the contradictions of their lives baffled Duncan. The atrocities they committed among themselves were horrifying. Slaves and other innocents were sacrificed for revenge. He thought how "truly immense" was the task confronting him in attempting to reshape their lives.

Not least of the obstacles was the attitude of many whites. When Duncan came to the defence of an Indian woman duped by Captain William Mouat of the *Otter* into paying more than the regular fare from Victoria to Fort Simpson, Mouat retorted, "she was only an Indian and not worthy of any better fate than skinning." In this way, Duncan wrote, the whites "vent their spite against a people whose energies they tax and whose simplicity they have taken away and whose women they have corrupted."

A conversation aboard the *Otter* with Harry McNeill, a wayward son of the Fort Simpson factor more interested in gold than furs, confirmed Duncan's impression that the H.B.C. officers were antagonistic to his mission because they feared interference in their trade. Young McNeill assured Duncan he need not be afraid of the Indians, who would receive him gladly.

Their talk was interrupted by Captain Mouat calling Duncan and Dallas to see a lunar rainbow in the passage leading to Milbanke Sound. Before entering that short stretch of open water, the *Otter* stopped at the H.B.C. trading post and Indian settlement at Bella Bella. "While I am writing we have just anchored ... and several Indians have come on board and are now peeping through the skylights down into the cabin watching me writing." Duncan was amused rather than alarmed, observing that the Indians appeared "robust, intelligent and good natured."

On October 1 Mouat advised they were within 50 miles of Fort Simpson. Duncan was apprehensive. "The nearer I approach the more stupendous does my work seem." He had been told that Factor McNeill was a hot-tempered man "who cannot bear being advised," a bit of information that did little to calm his fears.

Chapter 3

Fort Simpson

THE *OTTER* ARRIVED at Fort Simpson late in the evening of Monday, October 1, 1857. Duncan had reached his destination at last, more than nine months after leaving England. It was dark but the anchor had hardly been lowered before the Indians were clamouring in canoes under the gunwales. They had been alerted to the *Otter*'s coming by a blast of her steam whistle outside the entrance to the harbour. Duncan was rowed to the beach, where he was met by McNeill. The people crowded around, leaving only a narrow path to the fort. McNeill gave Duncan a quick tour inside the stockade, then ushered him to the two-room apartment that would be his home for the next four years.

The next morning Duncan got a look at his surroundings. He found the fort a "cheerful looking place—extremely neat and clean." McNeill had a reputation for running a tight ship, afloat and ashore. The buildings and stockade walls were freshly white-washed. Bright red paint set off the towering gates and roof ridges. The fort was 240 feet square, with bastions at the two waterfront corners each armed with four cannon. The buildings included a store, blacksmith's shop, fur warehouse and various dwelling places. The pickets were two-foot thick logs, 20 feet long, pegged and banded together.[3] Footings rotted rapidly in the sodden soil and the logs frequently needed replacing. A gallery four feet wide and 12 feet above the ground ran around the inside of the stockade. It provided a view of the harbour and 143 Indian houses strung along the walls and on a little peninsula jutting into the protected bay. A door was set in one of the gates just wide enough to admit one person at a time, indicative of the tension between the two com-

[3] Meilleur, Helen. *A Pour of Rain: Stories from a West Coast Fort.* Sono Nis, 1980.

munities. Inside the fort were 18 men employed by the Hudson's Bay Company and their families; outside, more than 2,000 Tsimshians.

The staff was made up of three company officers and 15 men— five French-Canadians, four half-breeds, three Plains Indians, two Hawaiians, and a Norwegian. Most, including McNeill, were married to or living with Indian women. There were separate houses for the officers and their families. The McNeills had an apartment in the "Big House," which also contained the officers' mess, social meeting hall, an office and bachelor apartments. The married men were not so lucky. They lived in small houses, more like huts, in which four families shared space.

Early in the new year Duncan visited each of the Indian houses over a two-week period. "Though I was not in a position to do them much good, still I thought I would at least go and see them all, and endeavour to win a little of their esteem and confidence." Another reason for the tour was to conduct a census. Duncan tallied 637 men, 756 women and 763 children. Most of the people were at home because it was winter, but he added a number who were away gathering firewood and arrived at a total of 2,325.

There were 27 Tsimshian-speaking tribes in all, nine at Fort Simpson, eight on the Skeena River, five on the Nass River, and another five scattered along 100 miles of coastline south of Fort Simpson. There were three distinct groupings of Tsimshians—the Nishga on the Nass, the Gitskan of the Upper Skeena and the Tsimshian proper on the coastal and lower reaches of the Skeena. Their total population is estimated to have been 8,500 at that time, dropping to 4,500 by 1885 following the ravages of smallpox and other diseases brought by the whites.

Counting the Indians was not a simple matter. A number had died in a measles epidemic after an enumeration some years before. They blamed the census for the tragedy. To compound the confusion in the crowded houses, some of the young people regarded it as a game. After being counted and sent to the opposite wall, they would slip back to the other side to be tallied again.

Duncan proceeded cautiously and nervously. "I confess that cluster after cluster of these half-naked and painted savages around their fires was to my unaccustomed eyes very alarming, but the reception I met with was truly wonderful and encouraging." On entering a house there was a chorus of "Clah-how-yahs," the Chinook trading jargon greeting. "This would be repeated several times; then a general movement and a squatting ensued, followed by a breathless silence, during which every eye was fixed on me."

What *they* saw was a pink-cheeked, sturdy young man with sandy-brown hair and beard. His head appeared large for his body. He was five feet, 6½ inches tall and weighed about 160 pounds.[4] His most striking features were bright blue eyes which could pierce or sparkle with gaiety. His compact, powerful body radiated energy, his voice was rich and sonorous. He had a commanding and charismatic presence despite his size.

What *he* saw were an animated people of about the same stature as himself, with black hair and dark eyes. Their broad features were more Oriental than other Indians he had seen and some could be mistaken for Japanese. The men were usually bow-legged from long hours in canoes. Their voices had a distinctive musical rhythm and tone.

After the initial greetings and examinations, several began nodding and smiling. "In some houses they would not be content till I took the chief place near the fire, and always placed a mat upon a box for me to sit upon. My inquiries after the sick were always followed by anxious glances and deep sighs: a kind of solemn awe would spread itself at once."

Duncan studied the Tsimshians closely during those first few weeks and formed some quick conclusions. They were a "fine, intelligent race but full of cruelty"; he was astonished at their skill in making utensils and art objects; they were more industrious than the natives he had seen around Victoria or at Fort Rupert. Their most serious problem was dealing with unscrupulous whites—and the white man's rum. Duncan was glad the H.B.C. was no longer using liquor in trade for furs, but the independent traders prowling the coast in their swift schooners continued the practice. The people were able to obtain as much rum as they could afford from the traders, and often prostituted the women to get it.

Duncan summed up his impression of Fort Simpson for the C.M.S. by declaring it was "just the place on the coast to begin the mission." There was only one drawback. "There is hardly any prospect of our ever being able to change the occupation of the Indians from their wild hunting to a more quiet life of farming. The land is densely forested, excessively rocky, uneven and mountain-

[4] Arctander, John W. *The Apostle of Alaska.* Revell, 1909.

ous. So much rain—grain can't ripen and barely allows some vegetables to grow." Wild hunting was not an apt phrase to describe the way of life of these fishermen, trappers, gatherers and traders.

On Sunday, October 11, Duncan held his first church service inside the fort. The H.B.C. steamer *Beaver* was in port at the time, and some of her crew members helped make up the congregation of 20. Most of the fort population was Catholic. The following Sunday, with no ship present, there were only seven at the service, including three young boys. Duncan noted that of the 16 men absent, one was sick, five had no excuse, five were Catholics "and five have scarcely any English (or anything else)."

Two days later he acquired some furniture and began school classes in his room, teaching in English to eight half-breed fort children ranging in age from 2 to 9. Duncan considered including some half-breeds from outside the fort but decided they had been deserted by their fathers for so long that any English words they might have known had been forgotten. Not long after the school started, Duncan was approached by a chief who wanted to know if he was going to give money to parents if they sent their children to classes. "I think I shamed him a little, at least I tried to do so, for entertaining such a selfish notion." Whenever the people tried to get something from him, Duncan told them he was not there to trade and explained the purpose of his mission as best he could. He also made a practice of telling all adult visitors he wanted them to help build a schoolhouse outside the fort as soon as he had a better grasp of the language.

Duncan began taking lessons in Tsimshian from a young man named Clah, who had first approached him to ask if he could attend school with the little boys. Although Clah was 26, Duncan wanted to include him but knew it would displease other Indians with whom he was unpopular. Clah spent much of his time inside the fort because he feared for his life. A few years before he had killed a woman. He thought her evil influence had caused a piece of wood being carried by some Indians to fall from their shoulders, seriously injuring one of his relatives. Although he had been paid 30 blankets in compensation by Clah, the slain woman's son was waiting his chance to avenge her death. Clah was no stranger to violence. His father had been shot and killed by his own brother, who was later killed himself. Clah's brother also died in a gunfight. His sister died of smallpox.

Clah had picked up some English as a teen-aged servant to the former factor of the fort, John Work, and acted as an interpreter for the company. When Duncan began their sessions in his room, however, he discovered Clah had been using mostly Chinook around the fort and knew less English than he had hoped. Although Tsimshian was considered the easiest of the coastal languages to learn, Duncan realized that acquiring a working knowledge would be more difficult than he had anticipated.

Clah started coming to his room for four hours each day. Duncan paid him $15 a month. Their sessions became mutual learning experiences, with each picking up the other's language. The lessons resembled a game of charades. When Duncan wanted the Tsimshian word for "cry" he would mimic crying. The same for "laugh." Other meanings were harder to convey, such as "try." Duncan described their routine: "I wrote his name on a slate. I said, 'you try' and he shook his head. So I took hold of his hand with the pencil in it and I shoved his hand along, and I had quite a job getting his big hard fist to make the outlines, 'C-l-a-h'. 'Now,' I said, 'you try' and I gave the pencil to him. 'Tumpahluh! Tumpahluh!' 'Oighack! Oighack!' he cried, which means 'right.' So I knew I had it. 'Pahl' is try. 'Tumpahluh' is 'I will try.'" Advancing in this laborious way, Duncan learned 1,500 words in the first month, which he combined into 1,100 sentences.

In late October, Duncan began a night school for the men in the fort. Thirteen showed up for the first lesson, but the prospects were not encouraging. He began with secular material, dropping in an occasional spiritual reference. He thought this was the best method, "considering the material I had to work with." His classes for the children were more rewarding. To mark the start of a short break, he staged one of the little ceremonies he favoured. "They came clean and nicely dressed, with hearts ever so joyful. The father of each boy, and another visitor or two, were present. We sang several hymns, and I then gave each of them a present, and after a little drilling they marched away. Their fathers seemed highly gratified. I did not let the little fellows read or repeat catechism (both of which they can do a little) as they were so excited. Thus I feel as though something has been done these last two months."

One of the Indians approached the gate-keeper to ask that Duncan visit his two young sons who were sick. He wanted the missionary to perform the same acts for them that a Catholic priest had done for him a few years before in Victoria. The priest had shown the man how to cross himself and he had got better. Duncan was indignant and determined to "show him the difference between a Christian and a Romanish priest." He was aware, however, that it was a risky matter to administer medicine. Whites had been murdered elsewhere when their attempted cures not only did not prevent death, but were blamed for it. The Indians believed their most serious ailments were caused by the spite of evilly-disposed people. Some individuals were said to have supernatural powers for conveying poisonous substances into the body. "It behooves me," Duncan wrote, "to be cautious in the face of such deep-rooted superstition."

Duncan, who had taken basic medical training for two years at Highbury, advised the people suffering a cough to keep warm, but they preferred to stay barefoot and half-naked. Only the chiefs and some members of their families wore smoked deerskin moccasins. Duncan tried to persuade the others to put on wooden clogs, but with indifferent success. Preventive measures were not part of their tradition. For body pains the medicine men applied a bag of hot ashes after first placing a damp cloth on the skin over the affected part. For severe headaches, switching with small spruce branches was prescribed. A gummy substance, probably pitch, was applied to the edges of wounds to keep them closed. The medicine men also had various salves which they used sparingly. The application of herbs as potions was usually left in the practised hands of old women.

When all else failed, the medicine men resorted to incantations, vigorously shaking over the patient a rattle shaped in the form of a bird or frog, with stones inside. Some illnesses were believed to be caused by the wandering of the soul from the body. It was up to the medicine man to catch the straying souls and bring them back. For this purpose they carried a hollow carved bone in which the souls were deposited when captured. Duncan noted that ailing natives received much sympathy and attention from friends and relatives, but those acting as nurses never washed their patients, who were soon covered in dirt. By proceeding carefully, emphasizing cleanliness and prescribing simple treatments, Duncan would gradually win over many to his primitive medical practice.

But the medicine men, who often amassed great wealth as the result of gifts showered on them by patients and their relatives, did not surrender their power willingly to the white shaman. Duncan later recalled a bizarre incident that occurred at Fort Simpson.

"One day I threw away one of my paper collars which had seen its day of service. The boy who cleaned out the ashes every day must have picked it up and gave it to a medicine man. He placed the collar in a tree and, dancing around it, put spells over me through this article of apparel. A nephew heard about it and taunted him. The medicine man took a gun to his nephew but the gun misfired and the nephew shot him in the chest and finished him off with an axe."

During one of his rounds of the sick, Duncan told an aged man of his desire to make the people happy and good. "He remarked that I was going to teach the Tsimshians not to shoot each other—as if that seemed to him to be the greatest boon I could confer." It was not surprising that Duncan was looked to for help. The carnage was all around. Following dinner one evening not long after he had arrived, a report circulated in the fort that an Indian had been shot just outside the gates. Duncan went to the gallery where he could dimly see several natives with muskets hovering over the dying man. Some fired at the still conscious victim as he lay on the ground with a gaping chest wound.

The assailant was the settlement's most powerful chief, Legaic, who was drunk after being taunted by some other chiefs. The victim was a young Haida trader who had been working in the fort for a few days. Legaic claimed a Haida of the same tribe had shot his brother 10 years before. This was one of the revenge killings Duncan so deplored. Now another man would have to be killed so that the chief under whose care the young Haida had been living could maintain his dignity. "Thus does one foul deed beget a never-ending strife among them."

It was inevitable that tension would develop between Duncan and McNeill in the claustrophobic atmosphere of the fort. The most contentious issue was observance of the Sabbath. Duncan was frustrated when church attendance declined because the men were engaged in sport shooting or some other activity he felt should be discouraged by the factor. The showdown came when McNeill planned to send four men on a Sunday to a spot some miles distant so they would be ready to start work gathering logs early Monday. Duncan was told by one of the disgruntled officers that it was an unnecessary step to save a little time. He promptly sent a note to McNeill declaring that in protest he would not conduct any service in the fort that Sunday. This was about 10 a.m., just as the men were preparing to leave. McNeill strode to Duncan's room. They had a "long talk," as Duncan described the heated exchange. "I told him that the H.B.C.'s desire, if not express command, was to observe the Sabbath."

The result was a signal victory for Duncan. The four men stayed in the fort until Monday and the service went ahead as scheduled. Duncan confided smugly to his journal later that whatever the outcome of the dispute, he intended all along to preach to the remaining men in his room.

In December McNeill turned to Duncan for the first time for help. The Indian wife of one of the fort men had been viciously beating her young slave and the factor feared the girl would be killed. He asked Duncan to speak to the woman. She was repentant, but said her husband had been mistreating her and she had seen whites deal with their servants in the fort in a similar manner.

Such was the atmosphere inside and outside the fort during Duncan's first Canadian Christmas. The company's custom of giving each man a pint and a half of rum after breakfast on Christmas morning did little to contribute to peace and goodwill. "Christmas and the beginning of the New Year have been times of dreadful riot and drunkenness here," Duncan wrote disconsolately in his journal.

He was more optimistic, however, in a letter to the C.M.S. McNeill had remarked to him how steady the men of the fort had become following his arrival compared to previous years. Duncan was also encouraged by Clah's report that the people were growing impatient waiting for him to explain why he was there. They besieged Clah with questions trying to discover what Duncan was saying to him. Some accused the fort residents of monopolizing Duncan's time in order to keep the Indians in ignorance. "They are *longing* for instruction," he wrote. "The presence of the whites and their own visits to the south have shaken their superstition and awakened inquiry ... there is a general belief amongst them that the whites do possess some grand secret about eternal things, and they are gasping to know it. This is the propitious moment."

Duncan's C.M.S. report was markedly different in tone from his journal entries, which included low-key and positive descriptions of some of the Indian customs. He transcribed the Tsimshian creation myths and praised their art. "The number of designs they have and the taste they display is truly surprising." But knowing his report would be circulated to a wide audience through the Society's publications, Duncan provided a frightening account of

42

his labours among a horde of blood-thirsty savages calculated to bring forth a flood of donations. He was mildly critical of the H.B.C. and the fort personnel, but saved his harshest language for the Indians. "The heathen people are notorious thieves and their word is never to be relied on." Treachery was so prevalent they never trusted one another. They lived in "dingy, smoky huts, content with their sloth and all its train of evils."

One incident that particularly upset Duncan that first winter was described in detail in his journal and report to the C.M.S. An old chief whose daughter had suffered a deep arm wound ordered a woman slave killed on the beach. Duncan understood the reason to be either that the murder would remove the "disgrace" of the wound, or that the chief did not think his daughter would recover and wanted the slave to be "sent ahead" to the next world to receive her. Duncan thought the former was most probable.

After she was slain, the woman's corpse was tossed into the water. "Presently two bands of furious wretches appeared, each headed by a man in a state of nudity. They gave vent to the most unearthly sounds, and the two naked men made themselves look as unearthly as possible, proceeding in a creeping kind of stoop, and stepping like two proud horses, at the same time shooting forward each arm alternately, which they held out at full length for a little time in the most defiant manner... besides this, the continued jerking of their heads back, causing their long black hair to twist about, added much to their savage appearance. For some time they pretended to be seeking the body, and the instant they came where it lay there commenced screaming and rushing round it like so many angry wolves. Finally they seized it, dragged it out of the water, and laid it on the beach, where I was told the naked men would commence tearing it to pieces with their teeth. The two bands of men immediately surrounded them, and so hid their horrid work. In a few minutes the crowd broke again into two, when each of the naked cannibals appeared with half of the body in his hands. Separating a few yards, they commenced, amid horrid yells, their still more horrid feast. The sight was too horrible to behold. I left the gallery with a depressed heart. What a dreadful place is this!"

Duncan was no doubt aware his vivid description and implication of cannibalism by the Tsimshians would create a stir at home. "Cannibal" was a word that raised goose-bumps and loosened pursestrings at missionary meetings all over England. Whether or not he knew then that the Indians were simply pretending to eat the flesh, Duncan spent the rest of his life trying to undo the impression left by his words. He always claimed that when he arrived the Tsimshians were a savage race, but as he grew closer to them over the years he sought to erase any notion that they were so depraved as to be capable of eating human flesh.

Some years afterwards, Duncan admitted he did not actually see what was being done with the corpse. The people vanished and left no trace of the murdered slave. "What became of the body I cannot tell you. We were expected however to believe that it was eaten." Later he was even less equivocal. In 1903 he protested to George Davis, the author of a little book on Duncan's work, about his reference to the Tsimshians as "a tribe of Indians who 50 years ago were degraded cannibals."[5] Duncan told Davis, "these words will, I fear, convey to your readers a condition of things *which did not exist*. The Tsimshian tribes on the coast of B.C. had secret sects of what we call Medicine Men, who on certain occasions publicly exhibited a barbarous custom of biting and tearing human beings, dead, or alive." It was, in short, a mime show that shocked unaccustomed eyes. Some anthropologists suggest, however, that the Indians sometimes actually bit and swallowed the flesh, which was immediately regurgitated.[6]

By the time the Indians began to disperse in mid-February, bound for Victoria or Puget Sound, Duncan had witnessed most of the traditional winter activities. He was especially disapproving of the potlatches and puberty rites in which the young were admitted to the secret societies. At his first potlatch Duncan witnessed a chief give away 480 blankets and hundreds of yards of cotton. He noted that 300 of the blankets had been contributed by the chief's tribesmen.

By spring Duncan had formed some further conclusions about the Tsimshian. "By far the most prominent trait of character of this people is pride." Revenge was their only means of adjusting wrongs. Sometimes vengeance was delayed until an opportunity presented itself, which might take 20 years. "It is astonishing what they will do or suffer in order to establish and maintain their dignity."

[5] Davis, George T. B. *Metlakahtla: A True Narrative of the Red Man.* Ram's Horn Press, 1904.

[6] Walens, Stanley. *Feasting with Cannibals: An Essay on Kwakiutl Cosmology.* Princeton University Press, 1981.

Chapter 4

Winning Converts

DUNCAN MADE STEADY PROGRESS in the language. By the end of May he was ready to tell the people for the first time in their own tongue why he had come to them. After completing the translation of his address, he sent word to the chiefs of the nine tribes that he wanted to deliver his message in their houses on Sunday, June 13.

At 10 a.m. on the appointed day, the usual time for an English church service, Duncan set out from the fort in the rain with Clah. Arriving at the house of the first chief, Neyahshnawah, he was dismayed to find no one else there. It was the first of many occasions Duncan would be frustrated by the Indians' unconcern for the white society's preoccupation with time. Within an hour, however, 100 people were rounded up and brought to the house.

They sat expectantly. "My heart quailed," Duncan wrote. Clah was told he might have to translate while Duncan read in English from a written paper. But Clah was so unnerved at that prospect, Duncan realized he would have to carry on by himself. The natives were solemnly attentive as he spoke and knelt at Duncan's instruction as he gave a prayer in English. Before leaving, Duncan asked whether they had understood his message and a woman replied, "nee, nee"—"yes, yes."

Duncan and Clah moved on to Legaic's house, where a canoe sail had been laid on the floor for him to stand on and a mat placed on a box for a seat. About 150 people were present, including a few from the fort to whom he spoke briefly in English before launching into Tsimshian. Duncan considered Legaic "a very wicked man," but the chief nevertheless admonished his people to behave while the missionary was speaking. Legaic likely felt compelled to make his house available to Duncan after the quick acceptance of Neyahshnawah, a rival for his power.

Duncan continued his rounds of the other seven groups, addressing a total audience of close to 900. The largest gathering was 200, the smallest 50. All gave him a polite hearing and seemed receptive to his words. His listeners included visitors in the chiefs' houses from outside points—Haidas from the Queen Charlotte Islands, Tlingits from the Stikine River, and Nishgas from the Nass. The Haidas and Tlingits understood the language from their trade dealings with the Tsimshians. Duncan got back to the fort at 5 p.m., exhausted by the strain of his day, but exhilarated by his apparent success. Two days later he delivered gifts of clothing to the nine chiefs.

There had been one tense moment. Despite his precautions to avoid any mistakes when speaking on spiritual matters, Duncan stumbled once. When he used what he thought was the Tsimshian word for "spirit," it actually translated as "ghost," which when spoken in the presence of a "cannibal" results in being bitten. But Duncan received nothing more than startled looks. A week before making his rounds, Duncan had begun work on a school outside the fort, five minutes' walk from the Indian houses. A dozen men were sent off in two canoes to get a raft of logs. After failing to get them to work for nothing, Duncan reluctantly gave some potatoes and tobacco in advance and cotton when they returned. He deplored the fact there were chiefs with the authority to make war, but not "to do good work." By the end of the month a drainage ditch had been dug around the site. Duncan had hoped to have the school up in a month but manpower was scarce. Another 20 canoes left July 1 for the fleshpots of Victoria.

While the school was being built Legaic offered his house for classes. Duncan started his first teaching outside the fort June 28 with 26 children in the morning and 14 adults in the afternoon. The children came almost exclusively from the families of the chiefs, whom Duncan was carefully courting. Some refused to send their children to Legaic's house, but said they would attend when the new school was ready.

While hauling logs up from the beach for the school, one of the natives dropped dead, apparently from a heart attack. There was great consternation among the others and the work was stopped. Duncan attempted to resume a few days later. He arrived first at the raft at 6 a.m. Thirty minutes later a half dozen men were standing around while others sat in doorways and watched. "I knew it was no use to push," Duncan wrote, "so I patiently waited." His tactic eventually succeeded when one man stepped forward and began working on the raft. Soon there were 40 men busily carrying logs amid a clamour of encouraging words and general excitement. They didn't want to stop for food but Duncan insisted. By 3 p.m. all the logs had been moved to the site.

The actual construction work started September 20. The men were fearful of an accident as they moved the big timbers around to fit Duncan's design. He worried too that something might go wrong. Before long, however, the natives became caught up in the job and even began to press for changes in the plans. Duncan had proposed putting on a bark slab roof similar to their own houses, but they persuaded him to use cedar planks for the roof and to cover the earthen floor.

The school was completed in mid-November and classes began immediately. At first the opposition of the medicine men caused many natives to be afraid to come themselves or to send their children. Eventually some who had attended classes at Legaic's began to show up. One banged a steel bar hung outside the school to attract the timid. Duncan started the day with just 15 students, but by noon there were almost 70. In the afternoon he had 50 adults and an equal number of children. The next morning 100 children and 40 adults came. A cleanliness examination was conducted each day, but the Indians were allowed to attend with painted faces and decorations such as nose rings.

Duncan detected resistance among many Tsimshians to the winter ceremonials. "Those tribes which still adhere to them are carrying them on exceedingly feebly, so much so that I am assured by all whom I speak to on the matter that what I now see is really nothing compared with what the system is when properly carried out." One chief told Duncan he felt ashamed when he came in contact with other chiefs carrying on the medicine work. Others said they were afraid to cast off all their customs so suddenly and would keep them going for another winter.

Duncan's hope that it would be the last winter of the ceremonials proved premature. It was not a simple matter for the people to cast off deeply held beliefs. One of the chiefs whose people had previously indicated they would give up medicine work told him they were beginning to regret their decision. Their conflict was symptomatic of the turmoil caused among the Indians by being exposed to another culture.

Early in December Legaic complained about the children running noisily past his house on their way to and from the school, disrupting the mystical rites within. He asked that classes be suspended for a month during the height of the ceremonies. Duncan refused and a power struggle began with the chief who had briefly been an ally. Legaic criticized Duncan and urged the others not to attend school. Five days before Christmas the medicine work reached a climax when Legaic's child "returned from above." The chief insisted there should be no school that day. Duncan was equally determined to carry on. When he arrived at the school Legaic's wife came and pleaded with him to close up, even for a short time. Duncan refused and went up the ladder himself to bang the steel. About 80 pupils soon appeared and classes began.

In the afternoon Legaic approached, leading a party of seven medicine men in full regalia. "The chief looked very angry," Duncan wrote. "I waited at the door until he came up." Shouting loudly, Legaic, who appeared to have been drinking, attempted to get the natives inside to leave. As the members of his party pushed their way in, Legaic was accosted by Duncan. He was not intimidated, despite being warned that the medicine men might try to kill him if school continued. The chief reduced his demand to two weeks' suspension of classes. Again Duncan stood firm, speaking to Legaic and his men "with more fluency, in their tongue, than I could have imagined possible." The parley went on for more than an hour just inside the school doorway. Some of the children fled. Natives from the village watched from a distance.

Urged on by his companions, Legaic pulled a knife and advanced menacingly on Duncan, who held his ground. Suddenly the chief, glancing over Duncan's shoulder, stopped in his tracks. Duncan feared Legaic was looking at one of his confederates who was about to attack him from behind. But Clah, alerted by the commotion, had come to the school and entered by another door. He was standing still, holding a pistol under his cloak. Legaic and his followers retreated in muttering disorder.

One of the students in the classroom throughout the incident was William Pierce, a half-breed boy from outside the fort who was Clah's nephew by adoption. Pierce later became a Methodist missionary and in his memoirs described the scene and its aftermath. "That revolver did the work and Mr. Duncan has often said that my uncle saved his life. All this time we boys were huddled together in a corner and locked in the room. We were crying through fear. After the Indians had gone, Mr. Duncan went back to his desk and cried for a long time; then he told us to take our seats and the lesson was continued."[7]

That evening another chief went to Duncan's room in the fort and told him Legaic had threatened to shoot anyone who passed his house on their way to the school. He offered the use of his house for classes, and Duncan readily accepted. Next day 100 showed up despite Legaic's gibes at the second chief.

Duncan was making progress with some of the people, particularly during his visits to the aged and the sick, to whom he administered equal doses of medicine and the gospel. He gained enough confidence to venture from the fort on his first night visit to a home where a woman was dying. He spoke to 20 of her friends and relatives gathered around. "Before I went away, one woman said that she and her people did not know about God, but they wanted to know, and learn to be good." Another man who recovered after being given medicine by Duncan began to talk against the ways of the medicine men.

Music was another means of breaking down barriers. "The Indians are exceedingly fond of the singing I am teaching them. I have got them to understand the difference between sacred and secular music, and they are particularly solemn when we sing hymns." Duncan led the songs with his concertina.

After the winter activities had subsided in February, Duncan moved back into the school building. He bought a canoe so the children living on the peninsula could paddle to school when high tides cut off their path. In mid-March many families began leaving for the oolichan run on the Nass River. They would be away about two months. Duncan suspended all classes during this period and urged parents to take their children with them. "I want to prove no hindrance to their procuring food as has been their custom." He welcomed the time to study, prepare lessons, and write booklets for his students.

Most of his school texts were in English, while books of religious instruction such as *Help For Christian Disciples*, which he had privately printed in Victoria, were written in Tsimshian. Soon he had a complete church service prepared in Tsimshian with three hymns comprising 14 verses, a prayer he had composed, a brief

[7] Pierce, W. H. *From Potlatch to Pulpit: The Autobiography of Rev. William Henry Pierce.* Vancouver, 1933.

catechism and 55 short, carefully selected scripture texts. He chose only those passages of the Bible that could be easily translated and were not likely to be misinterpreted. On one occasion when Duncan was reading from a scripture lesson book on the great flood, describing how Noah and his family offered up a sacrifice in thanking God for their deliverance, he was surprised when the natives related the story to their own flood myth.

In June of 1859 an old chief, Neesklakkahnoosh, urged Duncan to ask for a missionary to replace him so that he could take the children to some other place where they could be taught in peace. The chief, whose daughter attended Duncan's classes and passed on to him what she had learned, said many of the natives were willing to turn their children over to him to teach and bring up as he thought best. The adults would stay, however, because they "think it is good for them to die as they are."

The place suggested for the new settlement was known as Metlakatla. Situated 20 miles south of Fort Simpson on a twisting passage leading to the present city of Prince Rupert, Metlakatla was the former winter home of the tribes which moved to the fort when it was built in 1834. Nine separate encampments were located on both sides of the channel between the mainland and Digby Island. Duncan was told that one of Captain George Vancouver's survey vessels had passed by in 1793 and thought the villages were deserted because the bark roofs of the houses had been removed temporarily and taken to salmon camps on the Skeena. "Metlakatla" comes from the Tsimshian words "metla" meaning between, and "kah-thla," the word for salt, and indicates a passage between two bodies of salt water.[8] Duncan once rendered the translation as "an inlet with an outlet."

The site offered a number of advantages over Fort Simpson, where there was not enough beachfront for canoes and the land was difficult to cultivate. One reason for moving to the H.B.C. post had been to escape the recurring raids by Haida war parties. Another did not apply now that sailing ships had been replaced by steamers. The narrow passage into Metlakatla presented no problem for the new vessels, which were more easily manoeuvred. The Indians had been induced to leave their ancient home for the sake

---

[8] Walbran, John T. *British Columbia Coast Names*. Reprint, The Library's Press, Vancouver, 1971.

of trading with the fort, and now there was no necessity for them to remain that close. Duncan believed the importance of Fort Simpson as a central trading post had passed. Independent ships were already engaged in trade in the area, and Indians from other places did not gather at the fort as they once did. At Metlakatla there would be space for the people to spread out along the nine or ten sheltered beaches. The people were so crowded at Fort Simpson that when two tribes started fighting the others often became accidentally involved. There was also the consideration that while still only 3½ hours by canoe from the fort, the new community would be closer to six other Tsimshian tribes.

Duncan wrote the C.M.S. in July proposing the move and asking for a second missionary. The Society said there was no chance of sending an ordained minister but it hoped to find a layman to help, which would have been Duncan's choice in any case. The Committee also rejected his offer to pay his own expenses and accept a smaller salary, foiling Duncan's first bid for financial independence.

More violence in the fall confirmed Duncan's resolve to make a fresh start away from the fort. An Indian named Cushwaht, "a notoriously bad man," had sent his wife to the fort to get some salve for a leg wound he had suffered, and she had been turned away. Angered, and under the influence of rum, Cushwaht set out to revenge himself on the white men's property. He broke through the door of the school with an axe and smashed all the windows. When another intoxicated young native irritated one of the chiefs, who had also been drinking, the chief shot the young man's brother. That set off a series of shootings not far from the schoolhouse in which two more men were killed. A drunken quarrel followed in Cushwaht's house during which two women were shot to death, including his sister. "These murders and riots are all tending very powerfully to awaken the minds of those who have been under instruction," Duncan wrote, "and to wean them more from this place of darkness." More natives came forward to tell Duncan of their concerns and ask his advice.

But the riotous "rum feasts" continued as large quantities of liquor arrived from Victoria. "The camp seems maddened," Duncan wrote in despair. A five-year-old girl was found unconscious after drinking a bottle of liquor. In the school a week later, during a spell of cold weather, a sickly, scantily clad 10-year-old girl, neglected by her parents, toppled from her seat to the floor, dead. The winter ceremonies were in full swing again and some children were afraid to walk to the school. When one of the young men who had been assisting Duncan refused to participate, he was intimidated into throwing blankets as an offering to the medicine men as they passed his home. A rock slammed into the wall of the school while Duncan was teaching.

Yet Duncan was heartened that the ceremonies seemed tamer than in past years. Dog-eating had been given up and the rites now consisted of "mostly play and potlatch." Some of the people still adhering to the old customs did so to avoid shame. When Cushwaht's little boy showed up unexpectedly for school—his older sister had been a regular student for some time—Duncan concluded the father was feeling remorse for his violent deeds.

Three days after Christmas a "poor Mr. Denman" appeared at Duncan's apartment. Denman was an American civil engineer who had thrown over the traces to hunt for gold. He and 10 other fortune hunters were compelled to stay in the Indian camp over the winter because no one would take them to Victoria by canoe in the stormy months. Hamilton Moffatt, who had replaced McNeill as factor, refused to take them into the fort. Denman had been given shelter for a time by the chief of a Tongass tribe 15 miles to the north, but the natives there had taken most of his possessions and he was threatened with death in revenge for what an American had once done to the brother of one of the natives. Denman gave up all his remaining property to save his life and persuaded a native to take him to Fort Simpson. "He has now little else but what he stands in and he evidently will not want them long," Duncan wrote of the emaciated, dying prospector.

On December 29 when shooting erupted outside the school, Duncan and his pupils and a number of nearby adults ran for safety into the bush. It was Cushwaht again. A potlatch was being held in a house near the school and he sent his son for a share of the property. When the boy was turned away empty-handed, Cushwaht was enraged and began shooting at the house. The owner and his party fired back. Nobody was hit. The combatants were too drunk to shoot straight.

Duncan spent most of New Year's Day visiting the sick. He was forced to cancel his regular Sunday service when he was summoned to treat one of his pupils. A few days earlier the little girl had stubbed her toe on a rock. The injury did not heal and lockjaw set in. She died after two days of suffering and Duncan was deeply

52

moved. "I feel as though I had lost a little friend." He mused that when his grandfather had died 10 years previously he had "scarcely then felt even regret."

The weather stayed cold that winter and Duncan suffered increasing pain in his weakened right lung. After two natives had died of illness he wrote bleakly: "I live among the dying—and I am dying." On March 18 he trudged to the schoolhouse to find that during the night wind had blown snow through the roof smoke holes and the seats and floor were dusted white. He wiped them off, lit the fire and prepared for classes.

As Duncan's health worsened and his mood darkened, he took out his frustrations with a leather thong. "I had to give a severe flogging to one of my first class boys this afternoon—for his carelessness and obstinacy," he wrote on April 5. Duncan was tormented by his cruelty. "I feel I am not living and acting as a man of God ought to live and act." Four days later his fury erupted again. "Have had to give several severe floggings to my houseboy Alford tonight. I do not know whether I have done yet although I have strapped his bare back and marked it very much... I never flogged a boy so much before and I hope never to flog another like him. He seemed certainly subdued... after a long talk with him— he knelt down and I prayed with him."

Next day he was remorseful. "My heart has been in *much affliction* all day about my houseboy—whom I flogged so *unmercifully* last night. I have earnestly sought God's pardon and blessing. There is enough of human suffering in the world without my adding any more." Duncan thought the boy might have been innocent of his unspecified crime, "but even if he was guilty the severe and *very severe* flogging I gave him was disproportionate to his offence." It was a grim time, for lonely missionaries and frightened houseboys.

In early spring of 1860 Duncan decided to visit the Nass River to inspect the fishing camps of the Fort Simpson natives and the villages of the Nishga. As many as 5,000 Indians gathered on the river each spring for the oolichan harvest. A species of herring, the oolichan was a staple of their year-round diet. They were eaten smoke-dried or, after the white man came, pickled in salt brine. But mostly the "little fish" were valued for their oil. The extracted "grease" was bartered up and down the coast and inland as a coveted cooking ingredient or a dip for smoked salmon and berries. Oolichan are commonly known as candlefish because when dried and upended they were burned as candles. The oil was also burned for heat, greased the sawmill and cannery machinery, and was sometimes prescribed by Duncan as a medicine.

Because of their importance in trade and as a food staple, the oolichan were held in great reverence by the Tsimshian. "They called them 'chiefs,'" Duncan related, "and they had some sort of a cry they used when catching them, sort of an apology for taking them." The same reverence was shown when they were eaten—no one was allowed to breathe on the fish or drink while eating.

To extract the oil, fish which had been left long enough to become putrid were placed in a wooden box or bowl with water. Stones were dropped into the water after being heated in a nearby fire. The fish were then ceremoniously stirred while the people chanted. On the edge of the bowl, with heads looking downward inside, four fish would be placed "to see that there was fair play." After the fish had been cooked, the oil was extracted by the women. The men were not allowed to touch them, and the squeezing had to be done without using the hands.

"When I first saw them pressing out the oil I was horrified," Duncan recounted. "The fish were put on a board or table and the poor women pressed out the oil by leaning on the hot fish with their bare breasts." Duncan immediately set out to design a mechanical press. "It worked fine," he reported, "and in a few years they all adopted my press. They found out that the oolichans still came every year and were not insulted by using my style of press."

He left for the Nass April 16 in a large canoe provided by Moffatt. Camping overnight on a beach, Duncan noted two firsts. Since his arrival he had not been more than three miles from the fort, and it was the first time in his life he had slept outdoors. Duncan's crew was made up of two men and four youths. Three children went along for the ride.

Duncan arrived too late in the year to witness the arrival of the oolichan, an awesome annual display of nature. When the higher reaches of the river were still frozen and ice floes dotted the estuary, the first seagulls appeared in the western sky. A cry echoed from camp to camp along the riverbank that the great shoals of oolichan were approaching. They were trailed by salmon, halibut, cod, porpoise, seals and killer whales, all feeding on the oolichan or each other. And clouds of seagulls: "So many and so thick that as they moved to and fro, up and down, the sight resembled a heavy fall of snow," Duncan quoted one observer. Above the gulls soared eagles, overlooking all the other species in the hunt for prey.

54

The oolichan do not go above the tidal reaches of the river to spawn, so the fishermen congregated close to the estuary. In the bay they used canoes and nets. Up the river dip nets were dropped through holes in the ice. When Duncan arrived at the first camp the Indians crowded on the bank to greet him. A man waded out to the canoe and carried him piggyback to land. Others waded ashore with the baggage, which they took to the chief's house where Duncan was to stay. Two huge iron pots hung over the fire, one filled with salmon, the other with rice. Only men were present. They began singing and beating time with a stick, and Duncan brought out his concertina. Later he gave gifts of tobacco to the men.

Duncan did not venture far on this trip, but returned in September to visit Nishga villages further up the river. Along the way he witnessed his first seal hunt and marvelled at the natives' dexterity with a spear. He declined the meat, however, which he found greasy, and dined instead on fried duck. Moving up from the mouth of the river, he was awed by the towering mountains and his first sight of glaciers. The men talked to him about the myths which were linked to geographical features along the river. Duncan noted that the Son of God in their tales "occupies much the same role as in Christianity. The acts ascribed to Him are mostly acts of mercy or kindness."

Duncan was invited by the chief of one village to come to his house to witness native dancing and ceremonials. He declined on the grounds he had come on a solemn purpose and did not wish to join in their heathen practices. The chief's reply to this rebuff was: "Tell the white chief he must come; if he doesn't come to me I won't go to hear his word; but if he will come I will go and hear him." Duncan went.

"I was glad afterward that I did go. When I entered the house there was a person there ready to point out a seat for me. There was a bearskin spread over a box for me to sit on. The chief had all of his men placed around in different portions of the house, which was a very large one." A canvas sail had been hung as a curtain shielding part of the room. After some preliminary dances the chief leapt from behind the curtain dressed in a spectacular costume. His mask was inlaid with abalone shells and his headpiece ringed with porcupine quills. The top of his head was heaped with birds' down. Other natives clapped their hands and banged drums and sticks. As the chief shook his head to the rhythm, the down flew over him in a cloud.

"In the middle of the dance a man approached with a handful of down and blew it over my face, thus symbolically uniting me in friendship with all chiefs present and the tribes they represented." Although Duncan found the noise and excitement alarming, he observed that "the way they managed their several parts was truly imposing." Gazing upward through the smoke hole in the centre of the ceiling, the chief intoned a prayer declaring Duncan had come from heaven to bring them a message. He had made other tribes good and now he would make the Nishgas good. Duncan described the language of the prayer as "beautiful and eloquent." The people sat solemnly throughout, and chorused a form of "amen" at the end.

When Duncan turned back downriver the canoe moved swiftly with the current. He saw potato fields along the banks and salmon being smoke-dried for winter. Although he tried to be flexible among the strange new customs he encountered, Duncan's dogmatism created a domestic crisis in one village on the way home. After giving 10 chiefs a little gunpowder each, "I thought I would give the head chief's wife a bit of soap. I was reminded he had two wives. I knew it for they had just brought me a basket of potatoes each, and were standing still on the bank, but I handed one bit of soap and told them that I did not understand two wives... God made male and female and it was His law that one man should have one wife." This caused a stir. "One of the wives shouted out an affirmation of what I said and suggested that one of them be put away. I left them to decide as they could."

Chapter 5

Search for a Sanctuary

IN THE SPRING OF 1860 Duncan made his first trip back to Victoria. He had been asked by Governor Douglas to work for a time with the Indians in their camps there. The governor also wanted Duncan's suggestions on how the government might assist his work with the Tsimshian at Fort Simpson.

Duncan told Douglas he wanted to find a "home" for the Indians where they could be provided employment. "I confess my only hope of seeing the Indian races of this coast diverted from the destructive courses to which they are now so strongly tempted lies in the carrying out of some such plan...however small and insignificant at first such a place might be, I have no doubt of its ultimate growth and prosperity." The plans for Metlakatla were beginning to take shape in his mind.

Douglas reacted swiftly to this proposal. On February 18, 1860, he wrote to the Colonial Secretary in London, the Duke of Newcastle, referring to Duncan as "an exemplary and truly worthy gentleman, who has...been devotedly labouring with a wonderful degree of energy and perseverance." The governor said the plan to start a new settlement near Fort Simpson had his blessing. With Newcastle's approval he intended to reserve several hundred acres of land in the area. The facility with which Duncan had learned the native language and won the confidence and affection of the Indians, Douglas told Newcastle, was proof of "the good sense, kindness of heart, and talent which he has brought to the task." The governor hoped the Indians, through work like Duncan's, might be "rescued from ignorance, and assume a respectable position in British Columbia."

The governor was expressing the general view that the Indians' greatest task was to free themselves from their heathenish past, a belief to which Duncan at first subscribed. But now when Duncan spoke of protecting the Indians from "destructive courses," he was identifying their principal enemy as corrupt and avaricious whites. It was an attitude that would set him apart from most of his countrymen in the colony, who began to launch bitter attacks upon him.

Duncan had also gone to Victoria to meet Bishop George Hills, recently arrived to take over the newly created Diocese of Columbia. The diocese was financed by a $100,000 donation from English philanthropist Angela Burdett-Coutts. Cridge had appealed for help after preaching alone outdoors to thousands of miners passing through Victoria on their way to the mainland gold fields. Burdett-Coutts had taken a fancy to Hills, the handsome vicar at her church in Great Yarmouth, and saw to it that he was elevated to the rank of bishop for the new diocese.

Duncan and Hills could not have been more dissimilar, in appearance, manner, background and beliefs. The son of an admiral, Hills was over six feet tall and bore a patrician manner. His first home in Victoria was a typical small cabin. "The door at which people knock is the one of the room I sit in," he wrote in wonderment for an English audience.[9] "There is no 'hall' or 'passage.' So I open the door myself." Fastidious about his dress, Hills was referred to behind his immaculately tailored back as "Beau Brummel." When he travelled on horseback through the Cariboo to visit the outposts of his diocese, his reports reflected a smug self-consciousness, containing detailed descriptions of his rough apparel and the dust that settled rudely upon his stately presence. He liked to be addressed as "Your Holiness" and his first request to Duncan was to have the Indians make 500 hassocks for his cathedral congregation to kneel upon, a comfort which the abstemious Cridge had never thought necessary. During the 2½ months he remained in Victoria, and on subsequent visits, Duncan was never invited to dine with Hills, although he was often entertained by other prominent citizens such as Douglas and Chief Justice Matthew Baillie Begbie.

Not long after his arrival in the capital, Duncan bumped into his old nemesis Cushwaht on the street. For the first time, perhaps because they were away from the turbulent environs of the fort, the two men had a friendly conversation. Duncan urged Cushwaht not to allow his sister to follow the path into vice of other native women

[9] *Columbia Mission Annual Reports*, 1869-78. Christ Church Cathedral Archives, Victoria.

in Victoria. Cushwaht agreed, saying he had told her to live with a white man only if he would marry her.

It was only a few weeks before Cushwaht reverted to form. While Duncan was making the rounds of the Indian camps, a force of 150 men came ashore from H.M.S. *Ganges* to assist police in tracking down an Indian who had fired from a Haida camp at a schooner passing by. Duncan stayed with the Tsimshians during the search in order to pacify them, as they were "greatly alarmed at seeing the Red Jackets near." When the guilty man was eventually found he turned out to be not a Haida after all, but Cushwaht. Duncan interpreted during his trial, at which he was convicted, ordered publicly whipped and sent to prison for two months. Three days later two Haidas were arrested on suspicion of murder. On reaching the prison yard to be searched, the pair pulled knives on the police and were shot dead. The incidents reflected the tension in the capital created by the Indian camps.

In a letter to the Colonial Office, Governor Douglas revealed his lack of trust in the natives' abilities. He intended to withhold from them the power to sell or otherwise alienate the title of reserve property, "as they are yet so ignorant and improvident that they cannot safely be trusted with the management or control of landed estate, which if fully conveyed to them, would soon pass into other hands." Whatever truth there may have been in this observation, it served as a useful rationale for keeping control of Indian lands in case it might become desirable to use them for white settlements. Douglas recommended that reserves be conveyed in trust to the governor of the colony for the use of the Indians. Newcastle agreed.

While dining with Duncan in June, the governor described his problems with the Indians around Victoria and asked for advice. Duncan sat down the next day to draft a memorandum. Its main recommendations were to set aside a portion of waterfront on the Victoria reserve for each group speaking the same language; implement a register of Indian names with their movements to be entered as soon as they arrive; introduce a roll-call every night at 9; impose a $1 monthly tax to pay for police, medical aid and well-digging; appoint a native constable, preferably from an influential family, for every 500 adults; construct a log jail house in each camp with room to hold weapons taken from the Indians when they arrived; provide a combined school and place of worship, to be built for each tribe by public subscription; place any individual who refused to work in a chain gang, "until he has had enough";

and appoint a white man as general overseer of Indian affairs. Any tribes refusing to accept the regulations should be sent back to their villages.

Without waiting for Duncan's report, Douglas made an effort to drive all the Indians out of Victoria. When he toured the camps with Duncan the day after their dinner, the governor told them there was a serious measles epidemic on Puget Sound and they should consider moving out before it reached Victoria. He asked 60 chiefs to gather the next day in front of Government House, where he spoke harshly, with Duncan interpreting, about the people's behaviour. He told the chiefs the Indians would have to build permanent homes if they wanted to stay in the Victoria area. He agreed, however, to give Duncan's plan a trial.

On Sunday, July 1, Duncan preached to 200 Indians in one of the camps. The rest of the week he spent working with them clearing brush and preparing the site for a school. He also attended the first missonary meeting held in Victoria, which raised more than $300. A "Committee for the Improvement of the Indians" was formed at the meeting, with Duncan as treasurer. Douglas pledged $175 toward construction of the first Indian school in Victoria. It was agreed Duncan would organize the project and stay on to teach until someone could be found to replace him. When the *Satellite* sailed for England at the end of the month, Prevost said he would urge the C.M.S. to start a new mission in Victoria to take over the school.

When 27 canoes left for the north, Duncan decided it was time for him to return too. He proposed hitching a ride on H.M.S. *Alert*, but Douglas persuaded him to stay longer in Victoria. On August 1 a large contingent of Haidas arrived, raising the number of Indians around the capital to 4,000 and creating alarm among the white population. Douglas ordered a warship stationed at the entrance of the harbour as a show of force and to keep others away.

Gunboat intimidation was a regular tactic employed by the government against the Indians. In the spring of 1861 Victoria's *British Colonist* suggested a navy vessel be placed 200 miles upcoast at Seymour Narrows to turn back the Victoria-bound canoes. In a strident editorial headed "Invasion of Northern Indians," the newspaper said the influx of natives each summer was a "perpetual source of terror" to settlers at Nanaimo, Salt Spring Island and rural Victoria. Cattle were slaughtered by the Indians and white settler families forced to flee into the city. In florid language which bore the stamp of its colourful editor, Amor De Cosmos, the newspaper said feuds between the various tribes resulted in open warfare during which "human blood flows like water." It referred to the "thievish propensities" of the Indians and claimed the road to Esquimalt was too dangerous for travel. The outskirts of town had become a brothel, which the editorial naturally blamed on the Indian women and not their Victoria customers. The Indian camps were "a social ulcer" and their inhabitants a "moral pest from the north" who should be educated and civilized in their own areas and kept away from Victoria. De Cosmos lashed out at Douglas, who he said was supposed to be effective in controlling the Indians, but had accomplished little. At the same time, the editor praised Duncan for the progress he had made among the Indians while also protecting white traders.

In a reply to the editorial, Duncan was not swayed by De Cosmos' commendation. He argued that the proposal to keep all Indians away from Victoria would discriminate against those who were well-behaved. Such a ban was contrary to the constitution of the colony and would result in losing the goodwill of all tribes. "If strangers from every quarter of the world may come to Victoria, why not the Indians who are the aborigines of the country?" In his first public declaration of the principle of aboriginal land rights, Duncan declared: "It is his country, given him by the Maker and Governor of the Universe, which we occupy." The white man had corrupted the Indians; now he was trying to drive them from sight. Unruly natives who refused to observe the law should be dealt with in the same way as rowdy whites.

There was more to the colony than just the community of Victoria, Duncan pointed out. He asked what would happen when settlers spread out, as they inevitably would, to the more remote regions occupied by the Indians. He referred to the violence which had accompanied the opening of the frontier in the United States, where the Indians had been driven off their lands instead of being taught to adapt to the white man's ways. "Let the Governor simply carry out what he has pledged to do, and what the Indians have been led to expect from his hands and all will be well."

On August 8, 1860, the Reverend and Mrs. Lewen S. Tugwell arrived in Victoria, sent by the C.M.S. to assist Duncan at Fort Simpson. He was more anxious than ever now to return north, and approached H.B.C. officer Roderick Finlayson seeking free passage for himself and the Tugwells on the company vessel *Otter*. Finlayson responded coldly, complaining that the company received only abuse for all its good deeds. Duncan got the same answer from other H.B.C. officials. Chief Factor Dugald McTavish said company officers had once felt a duty to help missionaries in their work among the Indians, but now that they had been reduced to "just merchants" in the colony they did not feel the same obligation.

Duncan left on the *Otter* August 13 with the Tugwells and a pair of goats the new missionary had acquired in Victoria. He gave the couple their first Tsimshian language lesson, but felt he didn't have Tugwell's full attention. When he went ashore at Nanaimo Tugwell went with him, "but I could see that his wife was so engaging his thoughts that he could enjoy to join in nothing. His eyes were ever toward the ship when he had left her but an hour or so." In Duncan's eyes it was a more serious affliction than mere newly-wed infatuation. "I see that wives after all may be a great hindrance to a man in diverting his mind from the work before him." His diary entries also indicate jealousy of the Tugwells' marital bliss. He was even irked by the little things they did together, such as fishing over the side of the *Otter*.

A few days after their arrival at Fort Simpson, H.M.S. *Alert* pulled into the bay. Duncan interpreted for Captain William Pearse when he addressed the assembled chiefs. Pearse told them the Indians must start obeying British law, which meant an end to slavery and taking revenge on the innocent to settle grievances. After his address, Pearse proposed offering the chiefs a conciliatory glass of wine, but Duncan objected so forcefully to the gesture that the captain dropped the idea.

Next day the people, no doubt at Duncan's prompting, confronted Pearse and demanded that he deal harshly with whites selling liquor to the Indians in Victoria. They blamed troubles among themselves and with whites on drunkenness. Duncan spoke heatedly to the natives against liquor and prostitution, and worried afterwards that he had been "too angry." But the people were so moved by his outburst they demanded "pledge papers." Forty promised to abstain from alcohol.

Duncan decided to put on a show for Pearse, the ship's officers and the Tugwells to display the progress made by the natives under his tutelage. Rounding up 40 children and an equal number of adults from the few who were not away salmon fishing, he had them sing hymns and read from their copy-books. "The Captain had tears in his eyes," Duncan recorded. "He had long believed that nothing good could be done with Indians." On Sunday Duncan conducted his first service with Tugwell present. Legaic arrived with his hair cut short, a significant act because long hair was associated with medicine work and the winter ceremonies. Tugwell expressed surprise at the apparent devotion and understanding of the Indians. As they left the schoolhouse and strolled back to their houses in their Sunday finery, Mrs. Tugwell said it looked just like England. To her, there could be no greater tribute to Duncan's work.

Not long after arriving back at the fort, Duncan received a letter from the Reverend Alexander C. Garrett in Victoria informing him that he was now working as a C.M.S. missionary among the Indians in that area and there was no need for Duncan to return. He was relieved that he could stay with the Tsimshians, 100 of whom arrived in six canoes September 19 after waiting in Victoria for his expected return. They had thought he might stay there and wanted to be with him.

Plans went ahead during the winter for the move to Metlakatla. Some of the natives were eager that the new community be established soon. "Take away our children with you to Metlakatla," one man told Duncan, "and we will follow you as birds follow their young." Duncan had made his first inspection of the site shortly after returning from the Nass in May. He was ecstatic at what he saw when his canoe entered the passage: "A narrow, placid channel, studded with little promontories and pretty islands with a rich verdure, a waving forest, backed by lofty but densely wooded mountains." Some of the old houses were still standing just beyond the high-tide line. Others had been knocked down and chopped up for firewood. The promontories had been cleared and would be suitable for gardens. All around was a profusion of wild berry bushes in bloom. The natives with Duncan told him they wished to return to this home of their ancestors in order to begin anew. He looked forward to providing better schooling, especially industrial training which would give them the skills they needed to find work.

In late September, Duncan, Tugwell and nine natives from five tribes, including two chiefs, made a scouting trip to Metlakatla, arriving at 6 p.m. on the evening of the 25th. "Beautiful, beautiful," Duncan exclaimed. Tugwell was equally impressed. On the journey home, however, they paddled in a cold rain and Tugwell, who was proving too frail for the climate and diet, later became ill. He missed a number of church services in the schoolhouse, which were now attended by as many as 200 natives, but had recovered sufficiently by November to join, with his wife, the first Metlakatla work party.

Duncan and the Tugwells set out with eight natives. Ten others followed a few days later. Trees were felled and ditches dug to drain a boggy area. The rain fell in torrents each day, all day, keeping the Tugwells in their tent most of the time. Duncan laboured on in the miserable conditions. He paid each man a shilling's worth of cotton a day—30 yards—for 10 days. "They worked hard and I told them I was pleased." They shot geese, ducks and a big buck deer which was overtaken swimming across the channel. Legaic came by and gave the party a goose and some cranberries. Duncan gave him some powder and shot in return. He ate his first meal of boiled seaweed dipped in oolichan grease and pronounced it "very wholesome." He was adapting to the country and some of the Indian ways.

But his background stayed with him. For the New Year's Day party Duncan taught the children such English schoolboy games as hunt the hare, sheep and goats, sack-racing, keeping a prisoner in the ring, cat and mice, and blindfolded boys running to catch the boy with a bell. He also introduced them to physical drills and gymnastics, which they took to eagerly. A climbing pole was erected on the school ground and the only boy to reach the top was rewarded with a handkerchief. Afterwards Duncan distributed gifts and prizes, including 80 magnifying glasses, combs, scissors and needles. He divided five gallons of molasses which the children took home instead of eating on the spot as he intended. For the feast on the clear, cold day Duncan borrowed eight big kettles from the fort in which he boiled 50 gallons of soup from two deer, 100 pounds of rice, potatoes and meal. The children arrived early and watched the cooking.

Later in the day he entertained 40 adults, including a few of the older boys, in a room at the fort provided by Moffatt. After the meal Duncan played his concertina and performed a number of gymnastic stunts which the natives eagerly attempted to imitate. "I began by showing them that we could be happy and play without quarrelling. God wants us to be happy."

After the games Duncan spoke to the people about the evils of prostitution. Two days later he applied his strictures more directly. A schooner manned by three whites was anchored in the harbour. The wife of a chief went aboard. Next day the chief asked Duncan to help him collect blankets which one of the men had refused to pay for the enjoyment of his wife. Instead, Duncan rebuked the chief for allowing his wife to sell her body. "As I told him, had the man owed any lawful debt I would of course have interfered, but with this matter I would have nothing to do."

When the winter rituals and drunken feasts continued unabated into the new year, Duncan closed the school for three weeks and held a series of meetings in the chiefs' houses. "I find many of the old people have settled in their own minds to shut their eyes and walk on as they had been used to do. Some gave the reason for their drunkenness and prostitution—'we get so little for our furs and are poor and want property'—and the women are strongly tempted to prostitute themselves and almost forced, and thus the evil had come to its present magnitude." Others were becoming disillusioned, however, with the continual round of potlatches which often left families destitute and seemed to benefit only the chiefs.

At that time Duncan was planning to visit the Nishgas again in the fall, then spend the winter in Fort Simpson while Tugwell moved to Metlakatla with a few natives. He did not expect many would join the new community at first. Some who would have gone a year ago, now wanted to stay at the fort to profit from the Skeena-bound miners who were expected to winter there. Duncan was aware of the risks involved in his plan. "Though this move will be attended with much difficulty, and will make the Mission to be apparently doing less good, at least for a time, as the numbers will be much reduced who are immediately under its influence; yet I feel assured . . . that it is the best step to be taken."

Duncan's plans also included establishing a mission at Fort Rupert, where he would work among the Kwakiutls. According to Moffatt there were 30 tribes comprising 12,000 Indians in that area speaking the same tongue. "I like the character of the Fort Rupert Indians very much," Duncan wrote. "They are exceedingly anxious to receive instruction. It is a pity the mission was not first begun there, I think."

Duncan had three construction projects on the go in the spring of 1861. After deciding to move the schoolhouse to a location farther away from the disruptions of the settlement, he sent some men off to get logs and began tearing down the old building to retrieve planks and desks. He also started building a cottage for himself outside the fort, adjacent to the new school. At the same time, he was involved with the Tugwells in planning their house at Metlakatla, although he had become dissatisfied with the couple. "I do not enjoy much spiritual communion with my two fellow labourers," he wrote. He tried to persuade them to reduce the size of their Metlakatla house, which they insisted must be large because they intended to adopt some orphaned Indian children. Duncan opposed this idea as impractical and unnecessary in view of the natives' kinship support system.

Later that spring Duncan recorded that Captain John Swanson of the H.B.C. steamer *Labouchere* had been trading liquor for marten skins in the village. He was unsure whether Swanson did so with the approval of the company, but "from the shy way which Capt. Swanson looks at me I am led to think he suspects I have heard about his selling rum to the Indians."

Duncan suffered his usual spring bout of bronchial congestion, coughing up blood and writing in his journal, "I often think I shall die young." He decided to go to Victoria for a holiday, to buy some furniture, and see what progress had been made in the Indian camps there. He was disappointed during his two-week stay to find that Douglas had not carried out his detailed organization plan.

Before returning north he wrote to the C.M.S., asking for 10 more missionaries for the coast and funds for a mission schooner. He bluntly told the Society it was "ignorant of many things" about his mission and suggested he travel to London to give a full report on conditions. The committee was not receptive to any of these proposals. Its resources and manpower pool had been severely depleted by the deaths of many missionaries in Africa. Duncan's idea of returning to England to generate public enthusiasm and more workers for his mission was politely but firmly rejected. The committee felt he was doing more good among the Indians than could be gained by going before the public. Instead of looking for more English missionaries, Duncan was told, he should develop native converts who could preach to their own people. That was the policy Henry Venn had attempted to implement, with mixed success, in the C.M.S. foreign missions.

Duncan agreed with the principle of self-help, but on a more rudimentary level. He told the children they must contribute toward the cost of the new school. Since they had no money he proposed they send dishes, spoons, mats, masks and baskets to Victoria to sell as "curiosities." He got one of the older women to teach the girls how to make the traditional conical cedar-root hats. The most helpful students, some of whom brought mats to decorate the walls of the school, were rewarded with bars of soap.

Duncan tried to rid the children of superstitions learned from the elders. By teaching science, telling them about wind, tides and astronomy, he hoped to eradicate such beliefs as tides being caused by a great hole in the sea, eclipses a sign that a chief was about to die, and dragging a fish at the stern of a canoe would excite the wind to follow.

July 26, 1861, was a historic day for Duncan. The first seven adults, four men and three women, were baptized by Reverend Tugwell. The first name on the list was Shooquahnaht, a young man in line to become a chief who had run away from home when his father disapproved of him becoming a Christian. Older than most of the others, Shooquahnaht was an eager student at the first school and became a favourite of Duncan. At the time of the baptism ceremony Duncan was reading a biography of Samuel Marsden, one of the most famous C.M.S. missionaries, whose name he bestowed on the young convert. Samuel aspired to be a preacher and helped Duncan in the classroom and Sunday school, although Duncan occasionally became impatient with his slowness to learn.

In October the Tugwells returned to England. They were unsuited physically and mentally for the rigours of frontier life. Duncan was not unhappy to see them depart, but his relief was tempered by an acute sense of loneliness. "When I returned to the house and saw and felt that they had actually left me all alone I felt very strange." He picked up his concertina and paced back and forth in his room, singing a hymn to raise his spirits. His gloom was deepened a few days later when he cut his hand and accidentally spilled acid on the wound, causing it to become painfully swollen. "I find it very trying to be without a white friend near me," he wrote. "The Indian boys cannot help me much."

Duncan persuaded the Tugwells not to take their two adopted Indian children to England and the girls were left in his care. He was not always a loving foster parent. When an aunt of one of the girls arrived from Victoria dressed in expensive garments which indicated the wages of sin had been remunerative, she brought back presents for her niece. "Yesterday the little girl came to church decked out with garments got by sin, and I rebuked her sharply for accepting such presents when she knew how they had been got." By afternoon the child, shamed for something she did not understand, had cast off the ill-gotten clothing worn earlier with pride. The incident showed an unbecoming meanness of spirit in Duncan. He could be tolerant about some matters, but whenever sexual misconduct was involved he became almost irrational.

After many delays, the new combined school and mission house was opened on December 8. It had been frustrating work. The men, who were paid for their labour with cotton, tobacco, shoes, blankets and molasses, carried heavy logs up the hill on a rough roadway knee-deep in mud. On one occasion when they were ready to give up, Duncan told them they should be ashamed of their laziness. He would carry the logs himself. But one man stepped forward to help and the others followed. Six chiefs were present at the opening ceremony, and 53 students, including 18 adults, showed up for classes. Duncan hired Charles Ryan, "a useful and quick young man" about 20 who had recently been baptized, to assist in the school and help around his cottage.

It was a difficult winter. There was a resurgence of the traditional ceremonies such as Duncan had not seen since his arrival. The medicine men waged a strong campaign against his work, warning him a number of times to abandon the mission. He began to fear he was losing the struggle. Again the journal reflected a dark mood of depression, referring to his loneliness and the "want of ordinary comforts of home and proper food." Despite his difficulties, Duncan was careful not to antagonize the chiefs. Although his converts had given up potlatches, he told them it was not necessary to stop supporting the chiefs by traditional means of taxation.

On February 15 the *Labouchere* arrived with supplies from the C.M.S. for the school. There was a small printing press, a magic lantern, books, maps, school texts and slates. Three months later Duncan began dismantling the school to raft it to Metlakatla, where some natives were already cutting support timbers for the new building. They also planted some potatoes to harvest in the fall.

Plans for the move gained new impetus on May 17 when a canoe arrived from Victoria bearing news of a smallpox epidemic which had already taken the lives of 30 Tsimshians. Many more Indians were on their way north, forced to disperse along the coast by the frightened authorities at Victoria. When a number of canoes arrived on the 19th, Duncan noted how different it had been a year ago when the home-coming craft were decked in flags and there were drunken shouts and laughter. "Now all is still."

The camp was plunged into a state of alarm and more people indicated their wish to go to Metlakatla. Duncan used the plague as a means of exhorting the Indians to follow him. They had been warned by "the hand of God," he told them. In a heavy downpour on May 27, he began supervising the loading of canoes. As others emerged from their houses and sat in a semicircle watching the proceedings, 50 men, women and children prepared to set off in six canoes on a short but momentous voyage.

"On that day every tie was broken; children were separated from their parents, husbands from wives, brothers from sisters; houses, land and all things were left," Duncan wrote. Others promised to follow soon. The little flotilla set off in late afternoon. "Their hearts seemed to bound with delight when they saw that their long longed-for flight was actually begun and it was no longer talk but that I was in the canoe with them."

The party camped that night only three or four miles from the fort. Happy, excited, but also fearful, the natives sang and prayed around the campfire in the rain. In the morning they were joined by another canoe carrying 10 people. With 10 men already at Metlakatla, clearing, building and planting potatoes, that made a total of 70 Tsimshians involved in the initial move. At 2 in the afternoon of May 28, 1862, the group arrived at their new home.

Chapter 6

A Hard Beginning

THE BEGINNINGS OF the new village were not auspicious. Duncan's terse journal entries for the first week tell a tale of raincoast frustrations: "Thursday—Rain. No work. Look for timber. Friday—Rain. Sharpen axes and make axe handles. Saturday —Rain, but cleared a bit. Sawed. Sunday—Rebuked Indians for wasting time by strolling and talking. Monday and Tuesday— Men go back to Fort Simpson for goods and food. Warned not to stay in their old houses because of smallpox. Wednesday—More rain. No building. Thursday—Work despite rain. Drenched."

On Friday a fleet of 30 canoes arrived, bringing two chiefs and 300 members of one Fort Simpson tribe who had locked up their houses and left their possessions behind. With a population now close to 400, the hastily erected meeting house was already too small for evening prayer gatherings. But on Sunday the sun came out at last, lifting spirits as only it can do in sparkling northern air cleansed by rain, and Duncan preached outdoors. He described the day as the first real Sabbath for the Tsimshians. When the *Labouchere* arrived en route to Fort Simpson, the Union Jack was raised over the town for the first time. Each evening thereafter the whole community, "a happy family," assembled for singing and prayer.

The natives paddling back to the fort to retrieve their belongings found ravages of the smallpox plague everywhere. The sick were left untreated and the dead unburied. The survivors were forlorn. Some, mostly relatives of those already there, decided to join the exodus to Metlakatla. Among the new arrivals was Legaic, who had been sheltering in Duncan's cottage because there was smallpox in his own house. "That deceitful, drunken murderer and liar who has threatened my life to my face if I persisted in going on with my work, came after prayer and asked to be baptized with his wife and child." Duncan told Legaic they must wait to be sure of their commitment.

In early July the plague struck Metlakatla. After studying his medical books and receiving a shipment of vaccine from Victoria, Duncan worked at a frantic pace to inoculate the population. Edward Cridge, who had managed to secure the vaccine, advised Duncan to use either a needle or a penknife to puncture the skin. Some of the natives had to be re-injected two or three times before the inoculation took.

A special house was built for the stricken, but some refused to move into it. During his rounds of the sick children, Duncan learned of an ailing girl who was suffering alone after telling her grandmother to leave because she was sure she was going to die. The girl had crept into the bush and lain down under a tree to wait for death. "I stood on the rocky beach and called aloud," Duncan wrote. "After some time the poor girl responded with a deadly voice and her grandmother made an appearance. The poor old creature said she was very much afraid." When the grandmother shouted for the girl to come out, "she obeyed and when I could see her she was spitting blood and pus continually. Her face was a sad sight. How sudden a change in a few days." The girl did not survive.

The death that touched Duncan most was that of Stephen Ryan, who had been among the first group of Tsimshians baptized. "He died in a most distressing condition, as far as the body is concerned, away from everyone whom he loved, in a little bark hut on a rocky beach, just beyond the reach of the tide, which no one of his relatives dared approach, except the one who nursed him."

There were only five deaths at Metlakatla, three of which resulted from caring for infected relatives who had come for help. It was a far different story at Fort Simpson, where 500 died, one-fifth of the remaining population. The story was the same all along the coast.

The epidemic contributed to the decline of the medicine men. When the natives saw their lack of effectiveness in stopping or healing smallpox, they began to lose faith in traditional sorcery. The white man's medicine—vaccine—was the only thing that seemed to protect them. "Many of the heathen came crying to me in great fear, but for the safety of those with me I was obliged to be very cautious in receiving any fresh comers, and some I could not admit at all." The people clung to Duncan like timid children. "Death stared us in the face on every hand." That was not just a rhetorical flourish.

Fear of the plague affected the whites too. Duncan was asked in July to go to the fort to attend McNeill, who had come back to replace Moffat for two years and was said to be gravely ill. He found the factor "in a most wretched state of mind," crying and afraid he was going to die. An examination disclosed the tough old sea-dog was suffering from rheumatism in his hip.

To encourage the house-building program at Metlakatla, Governor Douglas gave a grant of $250 which Cridge, on Duncan's instruction, used to purchase 600 pounds of nails and 150 window sashes. On June 19 the foundation was prepared for the mission house. A month later the ground was measured for 25 houses with 50 feet of beachfront each. The population was growing steadily. On July 13 there were 400 at Duncan's Sunday service. That same month one more was added by the first birth in the village, "a fine little son." At the beginning of August Duncan estimated there were 600 living in Metlakatla.

Duncan had a difficult time persuading the people to accept his plan for the town, which had the houses set in a row 100 feet beyond the high-tide line, with a road between them and the beach. "They liked to have their houses on piles, on the shore, partly to enable them to get their luggage in and out of canoes easily, and partly because they enjoyed the noise of the waves."

A sudden outbreak of violence in the area during the summer of 1862 caused Duncan concern. A blood-spattered whaleboat was found not far from the village containing the bodies of two white men, miners returning from the Stikine River gold rush. One man had escaped and said he could identify the killers. He claimed they were Tsimshians, three men and a woman. A short time later a canoe carrying more miners was attacked and plundered. Duncan reported the two incidents to the governor, and complained about whisky traders lurking in schooners near the settlement. He asked for a gunboat in the area.

Douglas wasted no time in dispatching H.M.S. *Devastation*, under Commander John W. Pike, to Fort Simpson. Pike declared he was there to deal with the recent "daring and unbridled conduct" of the north coast Indians. In the official manner of the day, he blamed the whole race for the crimes of a few. He warned that strict measures would be taken to bring the offenders to justice, "and to teach the natives that these lawless acts cannot be committed with impunity." What Pike meant by strict measures was to burn down the village outside the fort unless the offenders gave themselves up.

72

On October 10 Duncan received an urgent message from McNeill. Pike was poised with the torch because the murderers had not surrendered. Duncan was afraid. He knew he would be called upon to act as interpreter for Pike and as the only white man in Metlakatla he would be a likely victim of native revenge if the Commander acted rashly. He prudently decided it would be unsafe to travel to the fort in the small canoe sent by McNeill. If he was waylaid and taken prisoner en route, Pike might be incited into taking vengeance upon the Indians. He went instead in a large canoe escorted by 18 men.

For three tense days Duncan acted as both interpreter and mediator. The navy survey ship H.M.S. *Hecate* had also arrived, adding to the fears of the fort Indians. Duncan accompanied Pike aboard the *Devastation* to nearby Dundas Island, where shots were exchanged by some Indians and the bluejackets. Two natives were taken prisoner and a number of hostages seized, including an ailing old chief. Under Duncan's guidance the Metlakatlans drew up a petition pleading for release of the chief. It was presented to Captain G. H. Richards of the *Hecate*, who replied to Duncan: "I beg you to assure (the Indians) that in capturing the chief and sending him to Victoria as a hostage I chose the course which I believed would be the least oppressive and would entail the least amount of suffering on the innocent section of the tribe. To have destroyed their village and canoes and food at the commencement of a season would have been a heavy punishment."

Captain Richards found the atmosphere and appearance of Metlakatla such a refreshing contrast to Fort Simpson, however, that he granted the petition and let the chief go free. In the meantime he and his men surveyed the channel for the first time and officially bestowed the name Metlakatla upon the village. Until then it had been uncertain; Duncan had even written to the governor asking him for suggestions on what to call the new settlement. Richards was so impressed by the peaceful manner of the Metlakatlans that he invited them all to visit his ship. They crowded around in canoes and clambered up on the decks in relays. The *Hecate* also donated a bag of clothing and $71 for the mission, half of which was collected from the crew. After giving a plum-pudding feast on shore for the children, Richards wrote to Douglas in praise of Duncan's work and recommended that he be appointed a magistrate.

His tougher-minded colleague, Pike, also softened after the

children sang for him at a special concert. Pike sent 30 of his men ashore to raise a flagstaff and help construct the mission house. Before leaving he swore in 10 natives as special constables and presented them with ornate belts which Duncan had previously purchased. In return, the Indians distributed "curios" among the crew. The two navy ships then left with the two murder suspects and the hostages. A short time afterwards, a native came out of hiding and told Duncan he was one of the suspects, but insisted on his innocence. Duncan was convinced by the man's manner he was guilty, but did not turn him in.

He was worried about the approaching winter. Metlakatla had been the only community on the coast to escape the smallpox plague relatively unscathed, but the people were demoralized. They lost their enthusiasm for building, and most of the houses begun in the summer were unfinished by the time the fall storms began. The people had also failed to gather and preserve the food they would need. The strain of his responsibilities began to tell on Duncan. "I have not a moment I can call my own. Helping builders—settling disputes—giving advice—seeing the sick—preparing for teaching—paying goods out to Indian workmen." There was no time for rest or reflection and his temper became frayed. By October Duncan was already ailing from the chest weakness which usually did not afflict him until spring. There was pain in his lung and he was spitting blood again. He applied a mustard plaster to himself as the doctor in Beverley had advised. His handwriting, usually firm and clear, became shaky and almost illegible. He suffered another bout of depression and went a month without making any journal entries.

The work went ahead despite the bad weather and Duncan's difficulties. "I have scarcely a man with me who knows how to use a tool," he complained. Nevertheless, the first permanent house was completed on October 29 by Robert Hewson. By the end of the year 30 homes had been finished. The rest of the people spent the winter in bark huts. During a spell of fair weather in early December the combined church and school, designed to seat 600, was rushed to completion. When the first Sunday service was held in the new building four days before Christmas there were almost 500 in the congregation. School classes started for 100 adults, who were taught by Duncan about geography, astronomy, natural history and morals.

There were other cheering developments. In mid-October Duncan harvested the first crop of potatoes from his garden. The four bushels planted for him in the spring had yielded 30 bushels. But more significant was his conversion of Quthray, the young "cannibal chief" who conducted the ceremonial murder and dismemberment of a slave woman on the beach at Fort Simpson. Duncan received word in October that the chief was dying and wanted to see him. He had been visiting Quthray for some time to treat a severe cough which had caused his lung to hemorrhage. Quthray had moved to Metlakatla with the second group and seemed to have undergone a "change of heart" before his illness. Now he wanted to be baptized, but there was no one to perform the rite reserved for ordained clergymen. Others were waiting for baptism too and Duncan had asked Bishop Hills to send a minister as soon as possible, but none came. As Duncan explained in a letter to the C.M.S., "being thus left alone I was obliged to act a little out of order." Quthray had expressed in such clear terms his repentance for his sins that Duncan promised he would baptize him before he died if a minister didn't arrive in time from Victoria. "I had no fear but that I was doing what was pleasing to God in administering that sacred rite to the poor dying man as no officially appointed person was within several hundred miles of him."

There had not been time for Quthray to build a house and he was living in a bark shed when Duncan visited him. As the young chief lay on a couch, Duncan performed the baptism, bestowing on him the Christian name Philip Atkinson. Quthray died the next day and a Christian burial service was held on a little island about a mile from the village.

Duncan met in the fall with the chiefs and constables to consider the rules or "civil laws" he had drawn up for the new community. They were discussed for three hours, then approved unanimously. Duncan later described his method of guiding the Tsimshian to the position he desired. "I never took a step with them for their improvement until I had first educated them up to it before it was taken. When I planned to make another improvement, I first called them together. If they did not think well of the proposition, I would say, 'All right, put it aside.' By and by I would call another meeting, and some of them in the meantime had been thinking matters over, and they would then agree to take the step. Thus, inch by inch, they were educated, and thus we took each fresh step, and slowly we improved."

Duncan called frequently on the chiefs to help settle disputes but also worked through the women. He found them more pliable because they suffered most in the chaotic conditions that followed the arrival of the white men. At the same time, Duncan helped break down some of the barriers against women in the male-dominated culture. Tsimshian society was matrilineal but not matriarchal, and Duncan did not attempt to diminish the political control of the men. Socially, however, he persuaded them to abandon such customs as the all-male feast. When the relatives of newly baptized Charles Ryan gave a rice feast, Duncan persuaded them to invite women for the first time.

There were 15 basic rules which each prospective Metlakatla resident had to agree to before acceptance. They must not participate in the winter ceremonies; call in conjurers when sick; gamble; give away property for display (the potlatch); paint their faces; drink liquor. They must rest on Sundays; attend religious instruction; send their children to school; be clean, industrious and peaceful; be liberal and honest in trade; build neat houses; and pay the village tax.

Each new applicant for admittance was required to have the approval of the town council. After a period of probation they were publicly welcomed at a general mass meeting on New Year's Day. Each candidate was required at this ceremony to make a declaration giving his reasons for seeking admittance, and solemnly pledge to observe the laws and regulations. After each had spoken, they were addressed by council members with words of encouragement. The new members were inducted by lot into one of 10 "companies" into which the community was divided. Duncan's aim was to have every Indian who joined the settlement be assigned a responsibility. If they did not become church elders, council members or constables, they were encouraged to join the fire brigade or brass band. After being presented with a metal badge, they were formally welcomed by acclamation into the company. The companies were named by their respective colours and the appropriate badge worn on the chest. The badges were inscribed with the words "faith, love, loyalty," encircled by "United Brethren of Metlakatla." Each company included three council men, two elders and two constables. It was the kind of organization and ceremony that Duncan, ever the schoolmaster, used again and again with the Indians.

On New Year's Day the council was chosen, 20 by "ballot" and another 10 older men chosen for life. Duncan devised a voting system in which only he knew how each man voted. After the men stood in a line with their backs to him, he told them to open their hands for a "yes" vote and keep them closed for a "no." Another 20 were elected elders of the church. Their duties were to watch over the moral and religious affairs of the community—spotting offenders and making them conform—as well as conducting religious services on fishing and hunting expeditions. After the election of the elders, the voters were called upon to pick 20 constables, with two serving each week in rotation as watchmen. Occasionally they paraded through the town during the day, but were on duty mostly at night. A curfew bugle was blown at 9:30.

The first Christmas in Metlakatla was a time for celebration. Because the people had little food, Duncan supplied everything for the feast. He set 10 men baking bread in the morning in the public ovens he had installed, and provided rice, molasses, cakes and tea for 250 adults. On New Year's Day, after a feast given by the chiefs with provisions donated by Duncan, the first taxes were collected —$2.50 or one blanket from each adult male and $1.00 or a shirt from those approaching manhood. Of the 130 eligible to pay tax, only 10 defaulted and they were excused for poverty. Revenue from the first year amounted to 96 blankets, 17 shirts, a pair of trousers, one dressed elk skin, and $7. The fund was divided, half to the chiefs for their services to the community, and half to public works such as a new road around the village, which was started in February. Other projects planned by Duncan included construction of two guest houses for natives who came to trade, so as to avoid interference with family domestic arrangements, as well as canoe storage racks on the beach. Tracks were laid for launching at low tide. Some 100 garden plots had been marked out on cleared ground along the channel. More public wells and pumps were installed.

Duncan talked to the people at this time about the advantages of buying a schooner to provision their own stores and extricate themselves from the clutches of the white traders. He proposed that 100 men put up $5 each to buy the vessel. In a letter to Governor Douglas, Duncan said the Tsimshian were eager to have a direct means of transport with the Victoria market for trading furs, salted and smoked fish, oolichan grease and dried berries. Ownership of the schooner would give the Indians a deeper interest in business matters, while manning her would provide employment. Profits would come back to the village. But Duncan admitted the main reason behind the plan was his desire to avoid trading with "those barbarous class of men who are employed in running the smaller vessels of the coast." He identified the worst offenders in selling liquor to the natives as the *Kingfisher, Eagle, Petrel*, and *Langley*. "Their visits are marked by murder and riot."

Six months later he turned to Douglas for help. The Indians had been unwilling or unable to put up the money for the schooner and Duncan suggested the government might do so instead. He proposed that $1,000 be advanced to be divided into 200 shares worth $5 each. Ten shares would be given to each chief and one to each adult male in the settlement. The shareholders would be obliged to repay the whole amount to the government within two years. Douglas took no immediate action on the request.

Later, Duncan asked for a $100 grant to start manufacturing soap and wooden clogs, as well a further $150 for window sash, nails and garden seeds. He also sought $250 to provide a "simple uniform" for three chiefs and 20 constables.

In support of his requests, Duncan pointed out to Douglas the positive effects Metlakatla was already having on neighbouring tribes. The settlement was looked to for inspiration and leadership. In the first 10 months of its existence, there had not been one case of drunkenness. (Some had succumbed on visits to Fort Simpson, however, and two had been banished from the community after their guilt was admitted). It was vital to the success of Metlakatla, Duncan said, that profitable employment be available to the people so they could be kept away from "labour markets which have temptations too strong." If his plea for government assistance was turned down, "I see no possible way of keeping the Indians at their own houses but by armed forces . . . the Indians will continue to rush in large bands to the settlements of the whites and thus become more and more demoralized, victims to any low vice." The threat of more Indians descending on Victoria was effective. He received a grant of $1,000 within a month.

Adding to the new community's woes that first winter was what Duncan described as an "invasion" of hungry wolves. He borrowed Legaic's sword to defend himself against them when he made a patrol around the village at night. When a slave girl ran away from Legaic's house into the woods behind the village she was attacked and killed. Duncan encouraged the natives to set traps—to eliminate the wolf menace, obtain their furs, and help preserve the deer population, which was in danger of being wiped out. To protect the goat herd started by the Tugwells and now numbering about 50 animals supplying milk and meat for the village, Duncan set out strychnine pellets. When the Indians balked at skinning a poisoned wolf, he made a charcoal breathing mask for them. They also became upset when a number of ravens were found dead after feasting on a poisoned carcass left in a garden.

Late in 1862 Duncan was informed by the C.M.S. that a missionary was on his way to replace Tugwell. He had asked for someone more robust than Tugwell, and Robert Cunningham more than met that requirement. An ex-prizefighter, the Irishman had turned to religion after losing a number of teeth in the ring. He had little education, was unordained, and it is not clear why the Society considered him suitable for the posting. His appointment turned out to be another of the numerous errors of judgement made in Salisbury Square.

Chapter 7

Independence

In APRIL 1863, H.M.S. *Devastation* anchored off Metlakatla, bearing bluejackets and a bishop. The bluejackets, led by the intrepid Commander Pike, were hunting Indian murderers and white whisky traders. Bishop Hills had come to baptize more natives, most of whom were away netting oolichan. When Pike decided to go off to the Nass in pursuit of the schooner *Langley*, Duncan and Hills went with him to call the people back from the camps for the baptism services.

After questioning the candidates carefully, the bishop admitted 56 adults—33 men and 23 women—to the church, as well as baptizing 13 infants. During his week-long stay he also performed three marriages. Describing the ceremonies later, Hills emphasized the simplicity of Duncan's makeshift church: "There were no external aids...to produce or increase the solemnity of the scene. The building is a bare and unfinished octagon of logs and spars—a mere barn—sixty feet by sixty, capable of containing seven hundred persons...a simple table covered with a white cloth, upon which stood three handbasins of water, served for the font, and I officiated in a surplice. Thus there was nothing to impress the sense, no colour, or ornament, or church decoration, or music." Hills left little doubt he favoured the more elaborate surroundings of the "high church" Anglicanism which Duncan regarded as "popery."

Duncan never wavered in his policy of sticking to the basics of religion with the Indians, who could not be expected at that stage to comprehend the subtleties of church symbolism. They tended "to regard in a superstitious sense every rite and ceremony of the church, and to attach undue importance to the powers of those who are serving them in God's name." The Catholics and Methodists, Duncan was convinced, acted irresponsibly in baptizing the Indians without adequate instruction in order to record an impressive number of converts. These natives, he said, regarded baptism as a charm—the white man's way of warding off sickness and death. He kept each candidate under his instruction and observation for three years before baptism. Duncan wanted to be sure they knew what Christianity was, and were incorporating it into their lives. He once indelicately compared baptism to the label on a tin of salmon—each represented a guarantee the contents were good.

The most prominent of those baptized by the bishop was Legaic, who kept his tribal name as a surname but was given the Christian name Paul. Much has been made of Legaic's conversion, but in his case the motive might have been Tsimshian politics as much as devoutness or Duncan's persuasive powers. Anthropologist Homer G. Barnett suggests Legaic was in an "intolerable situation" in 1862, when Duncan offered him a way out.[10] According to Barnett, before Duncan's arrival there had been a tribal dispute at Fort Simpson over the succession to a dead chief. The struggle was between a younger brother of the dead man and Legaic, a nephew. Legaic eventually won out, mainly because he had the support of the young men, who favoured his plan for a raid on the Haidas in revenge for killing a number of their tribe. The proposal to attack was abandoned, however, and there was discontent with Legaic's leadership. He came under heavy pressure from the disgruntled uncle and his followers. A volatile, vindictive man, Legaic was subjected to a sneering campaign that made him increasingly mean and unpopular. It was under these circumstances, says Barnett, that Legaic turned to Duncan. Whatever his motives, Legaic's conversion was a major coup for Duncan.

The last adult baptized before the bishop ended his week-long stay was Neshaki, the Nishga wife of Captain McNeill. She was given the Christian name Martha. McNeill's first wife was also a native, an Alaskan Haida who had died before his posting to Fort Simpson. Neshaki was a remarkable woman. Her father was the highest chief of the Nishgas. After her marriage she continued to maintain a home on the Nass which she used as the base of a lucrative fur-trading business. She was a controversial figure. When Duncan heard she had been selling liquor to Metlakatlans on the Nass he summoned her for a lecture. Moffatt once described

---

[10] Barnett, Homer G. *Innovation, The Basis of Cultural Change.* McGraw-Hill, 1953; *Applied Anthropology in 1860,* an article in Applied Anthropology, 1942; *Social Forces, Personal Conflicts, and Cultural Change,* an article in Social Forces, 1941.

her as a "beast" in a letter to Duncan. "She is a *lying, drunken whore* and I shall not fail to let Capt. McNeill know all when next I write," Moffatt added.

After Sunday church service Hills and Duncan strolled along the shoreline. The bishop asked if he intended to apply for ordination, a move Hills clearly favoured. Duncan said no, giving a number of reasons, none entirely convincing. In the first place, he did not feel "called" to take ordination. He had not become a missionary to enter the church "but to be useful to men," and would rather be a "thorough schoolmaster than half a clergyman." And he would feel "trammelled" in secular matters if in holy orders. Hills was not persuaded. He was concerned that Duncan's refusal might damage the future of the mission by lowering the ministry in the eyes of the Indians. Duncan assured the bishop he was prepared to leave Metlakatla and start another mission elsewhere on the coast whenever an ordained man was ready to take his place. Duncan was apparently sincere at this time in his offer to move, but when the question came up again in later years there was always a reason why he must stay.

Duncan's dogged refusal to accept ordination remains one of the mysteries of his life. His religious beliefs were deeply held, but it is possible that his scorn for the trappings of the church prevented him from submitting himself totally. There was also his awareness that the business undertakings he envisioned with the Indians were not compatible with a clerical collar. One thing is certain: if Duncan had been as power-hungry as his critics claim, ordination was the best step he could have taken.

On April 20 the *Devastation* returned to Metlakatla with her catch, the schooner *Langley* and sloop *Petrel*. The *Langley* was carrying 36 gallons of alcohol and two casks of mixed spirits in her hold. Although the *Petrel* had no liquor at the time of her capture, Commander Pike claimed to have strong evidence both vessels had traded spirits among the Indians. There had been a drunken outburst of shooting on the Nass following a visit by the *Petrel* which resulted in the deaths of three chiefs. The *Langley* had landed 221 gallons of liquor at Kitimaat Village, Pike said, and cached some on the way north in bush near Alert Bay.

These incidents confirmed Duncan's belief that Metlakatla should have its own schooner. Leaving Cunningham in charge of the mission, he set out for Victoria on May 16 with $424 in cash, 46 marten and 57 mink skins collected from the natives toward the purchase price of a ship. On the way south Duncan picked up another $25 from H.B.C. officers aboard the *Labouchere*, including $10 from Captain Swanson. A missionary meeting at Nanaimo added $14 to the fund.

After a month in Victoria Duncan found a suitable vessel for sale. She was the *Carolena*, a trim and swift 45-foot schooner owned by a colourful Welsh-born seaman, Captain James "Jemmy" Jones. The *Carolena* had been employed mainly in trade between Victoria and Puget Sound since her launching five years before.

Duncan paid $1,500 for her. He wrote a cheque for $1,000 on C.M.S. funds, which he advised the committee he was "borrowing" for a short time. The balance was paid with $250 from the sale of the natives' furs and $250 from public donations augmented at meetings in Victoria. The government had previously pledged $500 toward the purchase and Duncan hoped to raise the balance by subscription to pay back the C.M.S.

He told the Society his goal was to stimulate the Indians to greater industry and provide profitable labour for them away from the vices of Victoria. With their new habits and tastes in clothing and other products of white civilization, the Indians would be demanding more consumer goods. The schooner would enable them to buy at fair market prices. Duncan would also be able to sell furs in Victoria for higher prices than he could obtain at Fort Simpson. Knowing this would result in an H.B.C. protest to the C.M.S. against competition from one of its missionaries, he did not mention it in his letter to the Society.

The *Carolena*, which not long before had run aground on the little island off Victoria that still bears Jones' name, was in need of repairs. Duncan sought help at the Esquimalt naval base and Admiral John Kingcome obligingly provided six seamen and two carpenters for a week's work scraping, painting and building a forecastle with berths for the native crewmen.

Duncan wanted an experienced white seaman to take command of his new vessel. There were plenty of applicants in Victoria, but few could meet his demand for a teetotaller. Eventually he found a suitable man, recorded only as a "Mr. Patterson," and loaded the ship for the voyage north with $3,000 worth of trade goods bought on credit and a $1,500 C.M.S. draft. He also discussed with Victoria merchants the products to be sent south by the natives—furs, oolichan oil, dried fish and berries, yellow cedar lumber, red cedar shingles, mats and native handicrafts.

There were other matters to deal with while Duncan was in the south. He appealed to Douglas to establish a land reserve around Metlakatla, commission him as a magistrate, and release a suspect jailed in the miners' murder case. Douglas agreed to all of Duncan's requests, although he did not deal specifically at that time with the land reserve.

The potential conflict in his position as law enforcer, business-man and father-figure to the natives apparently did not concern Duncan. The C.M.S. had a standing rule that its missionaries could not serve as magistrates, but made an exception in Duncan's case. "We could easily understand that you had sufficient reasons for undertaking the office," Henry Venn wrote him.

At 5 a.m. on July 29, two months to the day after he had arrived in Victoria, Duncan set sail aboard the *Carolena* for Metlakatla. Patterson was at the helm. Four natives, including the freed murder suspect, made up the crew. Duncan knew nothing about handling a schooner, the crew were experts only at canoeing, and Patterson had never seen the intricate "Inside Passage," sheltered between the coastal islands and the mainland. The charts of the day were incomplete and often erroneous. Hidden rocks and swift tides were a constant danger. The schooner hit a reef near Savary Island but managed to slip free. Progress was slow as winds and tides always seemed to be against them.

When they reached Fort Rupert, Duncan was gratified by the Indians' surprise that the vessel was owned by the Tsimshians. He was not so happy, however, to learn that the *Otter* had just delivered two Catholic priests and a layman to begin a mission there. The H.B.C. had agreed to sell the church some of its land. Declaring there was no "social advancement" at Catholic missions, Duncan told the natives Bishop Hills would be sending a Protestant missionary to Fort Rupert that winter. He noted scornfully that the priests were wearing black cassocks and metal crosses, and that one had a brass musical instrument which he was "endeavouring to play." So much for Catholicism. Duncan was careful, however, not to display sectarian differences before the Indians. When a Nawitti chief asked him a few days later about the Catholic priests at Fort Rupert, "I spoke of course very cautiously."

Captain Swanson gave the *Carolena* a 20-mile tow behind the *Otter* toward the entrance to Queen Charlotte Sound. Just as the two vessels were about to part, the southbound *Labouchere* arrived. Duncan went aboard to plead with Captain H. G. Lewis to lend him an experienced pilot to guide the *Carolena* the rest of the way. He said Patterson was "in continual fear about the way and keeps me in continued anxiety and fear for our safety by his many mistakes." Lewis responded coolly to the request from someone he regarded as a rival for the Indians' trade. But he could not refuse when Duncan convinced him the schooner's crew was in danger. Lewis gave up a man named McKay to take command.

Sailing up Grenville Channel the *Carolena* met the schooner *Thorndyke* with two tipsy crew members. One recognized Duncan and called out, "How do you do Mr. Duncan. You have a good deal of whisky on board by all appearances," a reference to the *Carolena*'s heavy load of freight. "That's a damn sight better trade than preaching."

On August 29 they were met by a canoe sent out to look for them, and arrived at Metlakatla on the afternoon of September 1 after taking more than a month to make the 500-mile voyage. It was an emotional homecoming. There was a gunshot salute as the men and women lined up in separate rows on the beach. Duncan shook hands warmly with everyone. A meeting was held that night at which he patiently told them about his activities in Victoria, the eventful voyage home, and his plans for the future.

Anxious to get the community to work on some of the tasks he had set out, Duncan was annoyed when interrupted by the arrival of the gunboat H.M.S. *Grappler* under Lt.-Commander Edmund Verney, with the Reverend R. J. Dundas aboard. They stayed two weeks, during which time Dundas baptized 37 adults and several children, and performed a number of marriages. Verney and Dundas were more sophisticated, worldly men than Duncan and wanted to socialize while eating and drinking aboard the ship. But the master of Metlakatla had no time for such diversions. Another winter was drawing near.

The *Grappler* left November 6 after taking the schooner *Eagle* into custody for selling whisky. Duncan had set a trap by using native John Tait to make a purchase. After fining the owner $200, Duncan asked Governor Frederick Seymour of the mainland colony for permission to use the money for public works. He was told that half the fine must be forwarded to the colony's treasury. When Duncan asked permission to burn the *Eagle* on the beach at Metlakatla to demonstrate the government's determination to stamp out the liquor trade, he was refused. Seymour said the collector of customs had already accepted an offer for her.

By mid-November Duncan employed fifty men to saw boards, split shingles, build roads and erect a protective embankment around the mission building. He had a difficult time convincing them they should work hard like the white men to acquire wealth and property for their own use instead of giving it away. When he visited their homes he told the people he could see they needed many things, such as stoves, tables and chairs, clocks, wallpaper and matting for the floor. To obtain these benefits of civilization, he exhorted them, would require unremitting toil. But the Indians were reluctant converts to incentive capitalism. When Duncan put the lumber cutters on contract—a penny a foot—they balked and asked for a flat 50 cents a day. "But I would not yield, and so they have."

Duncan was presented with another problem that winter. After work one afternoon, John Tait asked if he would see six young men in the church that evening on an urgent and confidential matter. Their plight, they disclosed at the meeting, was that there were not enough young women in Metlakatla eligible for marriage. They wanted Duncan's permission to marry girls from outside the community. He attempted to reassure them it was only a temporary problem. If they "had to suffer privation" then God would recompense them. Duncan did not explain how. He told them of the evils involved in union with a heathen woman and the benefits of marrying a Christian. They were not forbidden to take brides from other tribes, but told that if they did, the women must first be placed under his instruction. He would rule if the marriage could take place.

Samuel Marsden had found the girl of his choice in Metlakatla —Catherine Tugwell, one of the former missionary's two adopted children—but he was even more frustrated than Tait and the other young men. Catherine, the star pupil at Duncan's boarding school, was not ready to marry him. She was still a teen-ager and Samuel was considerably older. There may have been another obstacle. The evidence is strong that Duncan had picked Catherine to become his own wife. Whenever Samuel came to him to tell of his troubles, the cryptic entries in Duncan's journal reveal an inner conflict. He did not know what to tell Samuel. He could not indicate his own interest in Catherine, and felt guilty giving Samuel any counsel. For a while Samuel became a live-aboard crew member of the *Carolena* so that he could "drown his misery."

Duncan wrote in his journal on February 7, 1864: "I had great pain on being constantly reminded of the great disaster that has lately come on my house—the case of Catherine and Samuel Marsden.'' This was clearly a matter causing him deeper concern than the simple problem of two star-crossed Indian lovers. It is known that Duncan at one time seriously considered marrying a native girl. In Metlakatla, Alaska, some of the older natives say they were told by their parents that Duncan had selected one to be his bride, but she had backed out at the last minute and married a Tsimshian. The responsibilities of marriage to the white leader were more than the young woman was prepared to endure. Whether or not this girl was Catherine Tugwell is not certain.

Chapter 8

Tightening the Reins

DESPITE DUNCAN'S PROGRESS at Metlakatla, the hold-outs at Fort Simpson remained a troublesome group. They clung tenaciously to the old ways while exerting pressure on their kinfolk who had become Christians. The chiefs were angry at Duncan for dividing the village, breaking down the traditional rites, and usurping their powers and privileges. The Christians from Metlakatla who went back to visit relatives were pressured to return.

At the start of 1864 Duncan decided to meet the problem head-on by inviting the chiefs and leading figures of Fort Simpson—about 100 in all—to visit Metlakatla for a few days. A number of feasts were given in their honour at which Duncan employed both cajolery and power politics. He pointed out that he was the only one among them teaching school; the only one who had a sailing ship; the only one training native constables. What, he asked, would they get by clinging to their present way of life? Knowing the chiefs were afraid more of their people would leave and further reduce their power, he played on those fears. "The chiefs will sink to the rank of common man," he warned them, "without authority, influence or support." As an inducement to win them over, Duncan indicated he would take only chiefs into his trading business. They way they could retain some of the privileges lost by giving up their traditional practices.

After the chiefs had left, Duncan turned to his budding enterprises. A number of natives he considered capable of participating were called together. They were enthusiastic, but their naive questions worried Duncan. He decided they were not up to the task. He would have to manage the business affairs himself, despite already feeling overwhelmed by paper work and constant demands on his time. He took a hand in much of the menial work himself. When Legaic saw Duncan salting and smoking a shipment of oolichan for Victoria, he expressed amazement. Under the old ways, Legaic told him, no chief would undertake such menial work.

To encourage more business from nearby tribes, he made store prices the same for everyone, removing special privileges extended to Metlakatla residents, including credit. It was not long before some began to complain about his tight-fisted business methods. When one of the critics was identified, Duncan gave the man a tongue-lashing for "speaking ill of Metlakatla—attributing dishonesty to me in trade—and complaining about my plan with regard to the schooner." The incipient revolt had to be nipped. A meeting was called of everyone who had put up money toward the purchase of the *Carolena*. When a few argued they should be able to travel free of charge and not pay freight for packages, Duncan denounced their "nonsensical talk." Anyone dissatisfied with his management was challenged to turn in his shares. Duncan's boldness carried the day, as usual.

He was tightening the reins of his power, as he confirmed in a report to the Society. "I deem it necessary that I must for a time be everything to the settlement, and the Indians naturally . . . look to me to be everything to them and thus I have placed myself at the head of their trade." Duncan defended his operation of the schooner, which the C.M.S. had made clear it opposed. The society pressed Duncan to shift some of his secular duties to the Indians. He admitted it might appear out of place for him to engage in such business activities, but was confident the ship would prove a great benefit to the mission. At the same time, he looked forward to withdrawing from the trade management by setting up a native company to take over. In the meantime the only aspects of his work being neglected as a result of the added business duties were keeping a detailed record of village events, and teaching. The children must wait, he said.

Only eight older girls boarding in the Mission House with him were receiving lessons each day. He had taken them despite earlier concerns about the propriety of such a step expressed by Douglas, Cridge and Hills. The C.M.S. promised financial support after Duncan insisted the arrangement was "absolutely necessary" to preserve the girls' virtue.

Chafing under Duncan's tight control, a few natives expressed a wish to go into trade or storekeeping for themselves. Charles Ryan bought a small schooner, *Wild Wave*, the first rigged ship owned by an Indian on the coast. But rather than let Ryan go off on his own,

Duncan engaged this enterprising Tsimshian to work for him procuring furs in exchange for store goods. Legaic was trapping in the Interior and planned to set up a trade shop there. Later the chief had six natives working under him trading on the Skeena.

Duncan was unhappy with the operation of the *Carolena*. Patterson had been replaced as skipper by Alexander McKinnon, who was now about to be fired because he was "not altogether the man I want." Duncan's ideal captain was a married Christian abstainer, and there weren't many of those waiting around the docks of Victoria for a low-paying job on a mission ship. So he decided to put his own people in charge. On McKinnon's final voyage to Victoria, first mate Sam Pelham was to learn the ropes as captain. John Tait would replace him as mate.

Duncan was also dissatisfied with the prices he was getting for furs in Victoria. Some of the independent natives, notably Clah, had negotiated higher prices for themselves than he had received on his last shipment. He asked his new agent in the capital, Siffkin Bros., to get better quotes for the current shipment. Duncan, who purchased most of the skins from the natives for resale, also told Siffkin that the Indians on board the *Carolena* would "be very desirous to know what you get for the furs and what you gave for the goods you purchased—please do not satisfy them." He was not willing to confide his profit margin on either skins or store goods, even though the money was supposed to be ploughed back into the community. He also ordered Siffkin not to hand over the crew's wages while they were in Victoria. He didn't want them wandering the streets of that sinful city with money in their pockets.

It was not easy being Duncan's agent. Siffkin was bombarded by complaints about the prices negotiated for furs and the cost and quality of store goods shipped on the *Carolena*. More than once Duncan returned food he said had spoiled during the slow voyage up the coast. When Siffkin attempted to explain that fur receipts on one shipment were low because the mink skins were inferior, Duncan angrily retorted that the agent should not have had them appraised by semi-retired H.B.C. factor Dr. W. F. Tolmie, who he said could not be an impartial judge of Metlakatla furs because of his continued loyalty to the company.

Despite his business worries, Duncan still found time for games with the Indians. He built a playground for the children, and Queen Victoria's birthday was celebrated there in 1864. Duncan taught the boys to stand on their heads and introduced them to

90

football, played on the beach at low tide with more enthusiasm than skill. He organized canoe races and foot races, giving a dollar to the winners and 50 cents to the runners-up.

In July a new worker for the mission arrived on the *Carolena*. Arthur W. Doolan was a graduate of Caius College, Cambridge, and ordained as a deacon, a step below priest in the church hierarchy. After only two weeks to get his bearings, Doolan was sent off to the Nass with Robert Cunningham. The rush was prompted by a report that two Catholic missionaries were in the area, and Duncan told the C.M.S. he could not go because the trading business made him indispensable at Metlakatla. Before leaving, Doolan baptized the dying son of Paul Legaic and, more happily, united in marriage Sam Marsden and Catherine Tugwell after Duncan had some "long and serious" talks with Catherine. Samuel went back to work as his school assistant and also helped in the store.

In mid-August Duncan received a note from Hamilton Moffatt complaining about drunkenness at Fort Simpson following the arrival of some liquor-trading schooners. Five constables were dispatched to arrest the master of the *Random* and bring him and his vessel to Metlakatla to face charges. After the summons had been served, the schooner left the fort with the native policemen aboard. About four miles out the *Random* suddenly changed course to the north. When the constables protested, the three whites aboard started shooting. One Indian was killed and three others wounded. The injured men and one unhurt survivor were dropped off with a canoe at Dundas Island. They made their way home but the schooner escaped.

After writing to the Colonial Secretary about the "horrible tragedy," Duncan decided to go directly to Governor Seymour to lodge a formal protest. Cunningham was summoned from the Nass to supervise affairs at Metlakatla, and Duncan set out in a small boat with three Indians and four homeward-bound miners.

When he arrived in Victoria Duncan discovered that not everyone shared his outrage. Publisher Alexander Bell of a new daily newspaper in Victoria, the *Vancouver Times*, claimed the *Random* was outside Duncan's jurisdiction when apprehended. He also questioned the propriety of employing Indians to arrest whites. Accusing Duncan of "recklessness," Bell's editorial said "it may be gravely doubted whether this gentleman showed that prudence and thought, which ought to have been exercised, when he sent a canoe full of savages to seize a distant sloop." Bell did not approve of Indian constables decked out in red shirts, Christian or not. They were "insolent and domineering," he wrote. In a parting shot at Duncan, Bell said it had been shown in England that clergymen made the worst possible magistrates. They could not draw the distinction between a crime and a sin, or appreciate the difference between "a legal wrong and an honest evil." Duncan should be stripped of his commission as a justice of the peace, the editorial concluded.

Because Seymour was based in the mainland capital, Duncan spent much of his time travelling back and forth between Victoria and New Westminster. He begged the governor to provide better protection along the coast against the whisky sellers. The traders often anchored in Russian waters near the mouth of the Stikine and sold liquor to the natives with impunity. Others who were more bold anchored close to a village and invited the chiefs for a drink to get the fur-trading transactions started. Duncan proposed to Seymour that the government obtain a small steamer manned by six or eight men to patrol the coast. As well as looking out for the white whisky dealers, it could report to the government on the moves of the various Indian traders, many of whom were involved in the liquor business themselves.

When he returned home in late September aboard H.M.S. *Grappler* under Commander Verney, Duncan was accompanied by naval surgeon Dr. David Walker, who was to treat the wounded constables. The *Grappler*'s desultory effort to track down the *Random* was contrasted bitterly by Duncan with an incident earlier that year when 19 white men building a road from the head of Bute Inlet had been massacred by Chilcotin Indians alarmed about the impending loss of their lands. In that instance, two large-scale expeditions were mounted to bring the guilty Indians to justice, at an estimated cost of $80,000. But at Metlakatla, the government spent a mere $600, which it gave the wounded men for medical expenses and compensation for injuries.

The following year, however, Seymour dispatched H.M.S. *Clio* to scour the bays and inlets of the north coast. Duncan had pleaded for the man-of-war because of the "clouds of trouble" threatened at Fort Simpson by the presence of whisky traders. But the actions of the *Clio* in seizing three schooners at Duncan's request, and the penalties he imposed on their owners, brought more criticism on the head of the missionary-magistrate. Although no liquor was found on the vessels, Duncan was not deterred in his prosecution of the case. He sent the *Clio* to pick up Indians who testified that the captains of the *Eagle* and *Nonpareil* had sold them liquor at one time or another.

On this shaky evidence, some of it a year old, Duncan, holding court aboard the *Clio*, imposed a find of $4,000 or eight years' hard labour on W. J. Stephens of the *Nonpareil* and $3,000 or six years on John Knight, master of the *Eagle*. Crew members and three Indians involved in the trade received lesser penalties. Duncan also ordered the vessels and their cargoes seized, to be sold at public auction in New Westminster.

The harsh frontier justice caused an outcry in Victoria. Stephens wrote an angry letter to the *British Colonist* protesting that Duncan had acted as prosecutor, interpreter and judge. The Indian witnesses had all been "prompted," he said. Stephens' cause was eagerly taken up by editor Amor De Cosmos. It was a clear case of "the overstraining of authority in the endeavour to punish," De Cosmos wrote. He agreed with the traders that they should not be subject to entrapment by natives set up to offer them $50 for a bottle of whisky. Duncan was "thoroughly ignorant of the powers and jurisdiction of a magistrate." His zeal had outrun his discretion, and it was time to curb his autocratic powers. De Cosmos also concluded that missionaries were "the most incompetent as well as the most dangerous persons to be entrusted with magisterial powers and responsibilities."

Prodded by the newspaper, the merchants of Victoria collected money for an appeal. Appearing before Chief Justice Begbie at New Westminster, the prisoners were released after posting $500 bonds. Attorney-General Henry Pellew Crease advised Duncan the men had to be released because he had sent improper depositions in all but one of the cases. Convictions must be supported to ensure imprisonment, Crease lectured the neophyte magistrate.

Duncan was taken aback by Crease's letter. Admitting his personal inclination to show the convicted men no mercy, he insisted the sentences were within the terms of the law. Captain Nicholas Turnour of the *Clio* had urged him to give 10-year prison terms to each of the "scoundrels." Turnour had taken an active role in the trials and had not raised any objections about the proceedings, he added. Letting the liquor traders go free would convince the Indians of "the hollowness and imbecility of our law in dealing with evil men."

Duncan pointed out to the attorney-general that he had received little instruction in the preparation of depositions. "It surely cannot be expected for me to know and carry out all the technicalities of law as if I was a London magistrate and had nothing else to do but mind such duties." He could only act with a stern sense of justice, "with unflinching firmness and as far as possible according to common sense."

There was a second case about the same time which also brought Magistrate Duncan into conflict with Crease and the law. The affair began in June of 1865 when three canoes of Kitimaat Indians passed by Metlakatla en route to Fort Simpson to sell their cargo of liquor. Four constables were dispatched to seize the whisky. But not, it should be noted, until they had thoroughly checked the kegs to see if they indeed contained the genuine article. "I am sorry to say," Duncan ruefully observed in his journal, "three of the four tasted and one of the three did more than taste the contents and was nearly intoxicated when he arrived back." Two constables were fired and the others subjected to severe reprimands.

In August Duncan learned that in revenge for the liquor seizure a Metlakatla boy had been seized by the Kitimaats from a Skeena River fishing camp and killed. Duncan was able to restrain the vengeance-bent parents of the boy, but an uncle killed an innocent Kitimaat at Fort Simpson. Duncan asked Captain Turnour to go to the Kitimaats' village and demand that the guilty men be given up. When they were not forthcoming, Duncan, though lacking evidence, issued warrants for the arrest of five suspects. They were sent down on the *Clio* with the liquor traders to be imprisoned. Crease ordered them released. "The arrest of perhaps innocent men to facilitate the capture of others is in law...an arbitrary abuse of judicial and magisterial power," the attorney-general said.

Duncan conceded the five had been arrested to set an example. If the tribe refused to turn over the offenders then all became accomplices in the crime, he asserted. It was a dubious policy, but one that had been employed for years by the navy and colonial authorities to control the Indians. In the officially sanctioned reprisals everyone suffered in the villages placed under attack. An example was furnished by the *Clio* on her voyage south when she stopped at Fort Rupert and was greeted by clamouring, hostile natives. A chief was promptly seized, the houses cleared and the ship's guns trained on the village. The natives sheltered behind the fort as their houses were splintered by cannon balls in front of their eyes. They raised a white flag, but the fusillade went on. A party of seamen was sent ashore to put the battered houses to the torch. Food stored for the winter was destroyed, and 100 canoes wrecked in the wanton attack, which was applauded by the *Colonist* for providing the Indians with "a wholesome dread of the law."

In contrast, Duncan's method resulted in only five men being victims of injustice. To Duncan it was a matter of degree. Fundamental legal principles were foreign to him. "I never allowed myself to stumble over a law," he conceded late in life, "when something good was to be accomplished."

The H.B.C., which earlier had kept out of the liquor trade, now decided to take it up again because it was losing business to the independent schooner merchants. Hamilton Moffatt admitted as much in an indignant letter to Duncan. Moffatt was angry at Robert Cunningham for asking him if it was true that he sold rum to the Indians or gave a bottle with every 11 marten skins traded. "It was very foolish of him to ask Indians, who always lie," Moffatt protested. "I really did not think that Mr. Cunningham, after being hospitably received at an H.B.C. post, would go round prying into their private affairs."

Unknown to Moffatt, Cunningham's own private affairs were being subjected to an intense prying. It had begun soon after his arrival when Duncan discovered the rugged Irishman liked to gamble and had an eye for the attractive Tsimshian maidens. His method of keeping Cunningham away from the temptations of Metlakatla was to exile him aboard the *Carolena*, where he was to supervise the natives, including Samuel Marsden, and learn the language. Duncan told the C.M.S. Cunningham lacked self-control, seriousness of purpose and spirituality. "It would not be proper to allow him to commence spiritual work until he becomes a married man." That happened much sooner than Duncan expected.

When he returned to Metlakatla in September with Commander Verney he had been met by shocking news. Cunningham was married. "Poor Cunningham," Duncan lamented. "Poor, poor fellow. How he astonished me and the Commander when he announced to us that he was going to introduce us to Mrs. Cunningham." The next unpleasant surprise was that he had taken for his bride one of Duncan's most trusted girl boarders, Elizabeth Ryan. There was still worse to come. Sam Marsden wrote Duncan a letter telling of Cunningham's "unfaithfullness and sin"—he had been sleeping with Elizabeth before asking Doolan to marry them. Duncan complained bitterly about the marriage being carried out in haste while he was away.

Despite Cunningham's misdeeds, the C.M.S. decided that since it had no replacement to send out as a helper for Doolan, he should remain in the service for the time being. But his days as a missionary were clearly numbered. Duncan's unforgiving nature was not likely to bend in the case of one of his associates raiding his most cherished institution—the girls' boarding school under his own roof.

In January of 1865 Doolan wrote from the Nass that a girl born prematurely to Elizabeth had died after three days. The mother had suffered a severe cough during her confinement during the bitterly cold Nass winter. Doolan, contrite because he had performed the marriage in Duncan's absence, expressed compassion for Cunningham but agreed he was "very weak, and easily led to sin."

Cunningham decided to leave his wife on the Nass and proposed to Duncan that he be allowed to take command of the *Carolena*. He was refused. Not long afterward, Doolan reported that on the previous night Elizabeth had "broken through all bounds and I hear she was very drunk, and going about the camp singing." Duncan wrote again to the C.M.S. and this time it was agreed that Cunningham should be dismissed. He joined the H.B.C. and later became an independent trader at the mouth of the Skeena. He and Duncan remained bitter enemies.

When Cunningham joined the H.B.C. he was placed in charge of the store at Fort Simpson, where Duncan publicly accused him of "pandering to the lust" of Captain Daniel Pender of the company steamer *Beaver* by providing him with a room in the fort and supplying Indian girls. Duncan also lured Cunningham into giving a bottle of gin to an Indian in exchange for furs, assumed his magistrate's power to convict him, and imposed a stiff fine. Some years later Duncan exacted further vengeance by denying an application for a public house licence renewal by Cunningham and his partner Thomas Hankin while extending the licence of their Port Essington rival, William Woodcock.

When Elizabeth returned to Metlakatla, Duncan showed a rare compassion and forgiveness towards his fallen boarder, although she had been drinking heavily and was suspected of having contracted venereal disease from her husband. Duncan took the unusual step of pleading with Governor Seymour to make a special provision for divorce in such cases. "In a new community like this it seems cruel that Indians should be bound by laws of which they cannot know the nature. There should be some facility to escape from those laws when they become oppressive." The governor turned the matter over to Attorney-General Crease, who advised Duncan it would be impossible to have a special law for mixed marriages because of the difficulty of classifying part-blooded Indians. "I do not see any way of effecting that object," Crease declared, "without a general divorce law—applicable not only to the Indians but to white people."

The shooting of the constables and the unpleasantness with Cunningham put Duncan in an ugly mood that winter. The weather was cold and many were sick. At a Sunday service after being repeatedly interrupted by coughs and crying children, Duncan angrily demanded silence from the congregation. The following Sunday he was too sick himself to conduct the service, a rare occurrence.

Despite impatience with his workmen, Duncan succeeded in completing the church roof before Christmas. More than 700 slabs of bark had been fitted into place. On December 24 Duncan sent bags containing four turnips, a cabbage and some salt to 30 of the poorest families. On Christmas morning crowds gathered at his house to shake his hand, but Duncan did not emerge because it was a Sunday. He announced later in the day he would greet everyone on Boxing Day morning. Four hundred showed up, despite their earlier rebuff. There was a Christmas box for each—two biscuits for the children, powder and shot for the young men, tobacco, pipe and matches for both the older men and women. Younger and middle-aged women received a small handkerchief, a small pair of scissors and a piece of soap.

The first Sunday service in the new church was held on January 11, 1865. The bell was installed just in time to toll for the annual midnight election meeting at which Duncan again shook hands with all the townspeople. He was not satisfied with the voting this year, which had resulted in some men being elected whom he did not consider true converts and loyalists. Duncan blamed the result on pre-election grumbling stirred up by Legaic, who was chafing at some of the new restrictions and threatening to return to the old ways.

Despite his ambitious new business enterprises, Duncan had

97

never taken out the trade licence required by the government. "I do not consider myself a trader," he told the Colonial Secretary ingenuously, "any more than a schoolmaster who teaches bookkeeping considers himself a clerk." The inference was that he was merely teaching the Indians the principles of trade and intended later to place the whole of the Metlakatla trading operations in their hands. In the meantime he was receiving no personal benefit from the trade, Duncan claimed. In the same letter, Duncan responded to Governor Seymour's request for his advice on a proposed lease of land to white entrepreneurs near the mouth of the Nass. Firmly opposing any alienation of traditional Indian lands, he said the natives were jealous of their right to the oolichan run. They would not peacefully submit to being displaced by a few white men. This marked the first time in correspondence with the government that Duncan claimed the Indians' right to certain lands and resources. It was an argument not often heard or well received in the colony at that time. But Duncan cagily added that the Nass grease trade provided employment for Indians who would otherwise be making their way to Victoria. It was proving an effective tactic. The lease was turned down.

The Colonial Secretary also informed Duncan that Governor Seymour had extended the reserve around Metlakatla to a distance of five miles on each side of Mission Point and five miles inland from the shoreline. "His Excellency has also directed that the two acres of land known as Mission Point is to be held in trust by the Government for the benefit of the Church Missionary Society." There was no objection from Duncan. He had no idea then how contentious that clause would become.

Chapter 9

Brother Workers

ONE OF THE MYTHS grown up about Duncan is that he could not work with others. It is said that missionaries sent out to help him, forbidden to question his methods or make suggestions, were driven out of Metlakatla to other outposts in the area. The twisting of events to support this charge was started by historians of the Church Missionary Society and the Anglican Church after he had left both organizations. Numerous other writers have picked up and embroidered upon the accusation, but the facts do not bear them out.

First to arrive were the Tugwells, neither of whom were strong enough to cope with the demands of frontier mission life. They lasted only a year before returning to England. Next came Arthur Doolan, an honest, naive but sincere bachelor who formed a close and lasting friendship with Duncan. After establishing the first mission on the Nass under Duncan's instructions, and working with him at Metlakatla, Doolan also returned to England after two years, discouraged by his inability to master the Tsimshian language. Unsure of his faith and commitment to the work, he too had resisted the bishop's pressure to be fully ordained.

The rawness of life around him was unsettling to Doolan's gentle nature. He once described to Duncan how a Nishga girl had been thrown by her drunken father into a boiling box of oolichan grease and water. "She saved her head by putting out her arms, which are frightfully burnt. Her moans are very piteous." Doolan was a softer man than Duncan, more generous and indulgent. After taking back into the fold a native woman who had strayed, he told Duncan that "we are commanded to forgive not seven times, but seventy times seven," a biblical injunction too seldom observed by the implacable ruler of Metlakatla.

Duncan often sought Doolan's advice and it was freely given, even in the area of personal matters. "I should strongly advise you to marry a native," Doolan wrote from England in January 1870. "In fact, I much doubt if you would find a European suitable to take charge of the station. Are you certain the Society would object? I fancied not from what some said, when speaking to them on the subject on my first arrival in England." He pursued the matter again in 1872. "My dear Brother, why do you not marry a native? They are better adapted for strengthening your hands than a European female—the world cannot say that you took the step all in a hurry for the years you have lived alone would deny this." After his return to England, Doolan took on the task of special agent for Metlakatla, receiving financial contributions and using his home as a depot for donated books and clothing.

The next couple appointed to Metlakatla were Frank B. Gribbell and his wife Lise, who landed in Victoria in the fall of 1865. Duncan eagerly awaited their arrival, but it was not until the following March that Gribbell advised him by letter that the trip north had been postponed because of his wife's health. She was expecting a baby and had suffered severe seasickness on the voyage from England. Doolan observed when he visited Victoria in the spring that she appeared very delicate. At last, on June 20, the couple reached Metlakatla, but their stay was brief. A few days later the Gribbells were on their way back to Victoria for the birth of the baby.

When they returned in September, the signs were not promising. Watching them unpack, Duncan was upset to see cases of liquor among their baggage, although he occasionally drank a little wine himself. He was scornful when Mrs. Gribbell had to ask her husband how to cut off the neck of a goose, and some Indian women how to make stuffing. She could not bake bread. The couple also adopted a rude and condescending manner toward the faithful Doolan. After an uncomfortable month, Gribbell told Duncan he was leaving the mission because of his wife's health. They were gone the next week, much to Duncan's relief. He had determined neither was suited to the work. During the 10 months they were in Victoria, the Gribbells had made no effort to learn Tsimshian. It also became obvious they had received an unflattering picture of Duncan and the mission from Bishop Hills and others. After Gribbell returned to Victoria, Hills employed him as a preacher in the area.

The next candidate proved even more unsuitable. Henry Burnard Owen, accompanied by his wife and servant, landed two years later in Victoria, where he met the Gribbells. Before Owen reached Metlakatla, Duncan had been advised that he too had been prejudiced against the mission. When the couple arrived, after leaving the servant in Victoria, Owen insisted his wife was not required to teach or do any work for the mission. Although they had no children, he also demanded that an extra room be built on his house.

The bumptious Owen, not realizing his C.M.S. instruction to spend time at the mission before seeking ordination had been issued at Duncan's request, attempted with Hills' encouragement to circumvent it. The bishop persuaded him that ordination would lead to quicker advancement. Owen's "impudent" attitude caused Duncan to consider sending him back on the next ship, but Cridge, who had accompanied him north, intervened. Eventually it was decided that Owen and his equally ambitious wife should return to Victoria to discuss the situation with the bishop. He left the employ of the C.M.S. and, like Gribbell, was hired by Hills in the Victoria area. By this time Cridge had taken a strong dislike to Owen and to show his displeasure, boycotted his ordination ceremony in Christ Church Cathedral. Owen did not stay long. He was dismissed by Hills for unspecified reasons and left for Nova Scotia under a cloud.

Earlier in 1867 another missionary of a different mould had come to Metlakatla. After Gribbell left, Duncan had written the C.M.S. asking for "men of a peculiar stamp, simple and hearty, hardy and daring—men who are able and willing to endure rough work." Duncan had other criteria. He believed that a missionary should be physically strong in order to command the respect of the Indians, and not consider any labour beneath him. "If the man's dignity is in the way he is not the man for this place and he will do us no good." Robert Tomlinson measured up to those standards as Tugwell, Gribbell and Owen had not.

Born in Dublin in 1842, Tomlinson had inherited stubbornness and an independent streak from his father, an Anglican clergyman in Catholic Ireland. After a spartan childhood, he worked as a livery boy and tutor to get into medical school, but left to join the C.M.S. before graduation. He reached Metlakatla on May 20, 1867, as a passenger aboard the schooner *Kate* from Victoria.

His arrival was not auspicious. Duncan noted in his journal that "Mr. Tomlinson astonished Mr. Doolan and myself by announcing that he could not reside in the Mission House as he did not think it right." Tomlinson objected to the presence of the girl boarders, whom he had heard about in Victoria. He delivered a stern lecture on what he considered the impropriety of the arrangement. "We had a long talk," Duncan wrote, "I must say very distressing to our feelings." Duncan said if Tomlinson would accept responsibility, the girls would be moved out of the house. Duncan added that he would go away himself "as soon as possible." If Tomlinson was to remain at Metlakatla, Duncan said, he could not live apart from Doolan and himself. Faced with such an ultimatum, Tomlinson reluctantly agreed to stay in the Mission House with them and the boarders, but said he would let the Society know of his feelings. He would ask to be moved to some other place, "where he could carry out *his own plan* of missionary work," Duncan noted increduously, adding: "I must say neither Mr. Doolan or myself are very favourably impressed with our new fellow labourer."

Tomlinson left with Doolan on June 4 to reopen the Nass mission at Kincolith. He had decided he wanted to go to the Queen Charlotte Islands to work among the Haida, but changed his mind in July when Doolan decided to leave and suggested Tomlinson replace him on the Nass. By the following April Duncan was writing affectionately of his new worker: "Dear Tomlinson started today for Victoria in a canoe to fetch up a wife." She was Alice Woods, a niece of Archdeacon C. T. Woods who Tomlinson had met when he first arrived in Victoria and stayed at Woods' home. She was only 16 then and her father, Richard Woods, told the young missionary to go up the coast alone and return in a year for his daughter's hand if he was still inclined. They were married on April 24, 1868, after Tomlinson had come south by canoe with a party of Nishgas. The next day they began paddling upcoast. After a month-long voyage the couple spent three days at Metlakatla before proceeding to Kincolith.

It did not take Tomlinson long to prove his worth. His letters to Duncan from the Nass revealed a clear-thinking, capable mind. He was quick to size up a situation and soon picked up the language. And Alice had been a good choice, quickly becoming proficient in the skills required for survival in their harsh and lonely little outpost. At first only five Indian families made up the community, which had once been known as the "place of scalps" because it was where the Nishgas had displayed the trophies of their slain enemies on posts. There seemed to be a constant supply of liquor from the trading schooners and frequent outbreaks of violence along the river between the Nishgas and coast Tsimshians. Discouraged, Tomlinson told Duncan he wanted to develop a new site further up the river. He was urged to hang on because such a move would be "like succumbing to the enemy."

So the couple stayed, hacking out brush and forest along the river bank for a vegetable plot. The meagre crops were often lost to winter frosts. The Tomlinsons built the first hospital on the northern coast, with three rooms able to hold 10 patients. The Indians were afraid to use the beds because of the space underneath where evil spirits could lurk, and brought their own bedding so they could lie on the floor.

Sickness and disease were ever-present. The hardships were made vivid in a poignant letter dated July 10, 1871, advising Duncan that while suffering from typhoid fever Alice had given birth prematurely to an infant which had lived only a few hours. "Born, baptized and buried in one day," Tomlinson grieved. As husband, father, minister and doctor he had presided at all three.

Duncan gained such confidence in his new co-workers that only a few months after their marriage he felt able to leave the Tomlinsons in charge of Metlakatla for a few weeks while he went to Victoria. In the capital he was subjected to considerable abuse by the H.B.C. and its friends in Victoria who were outraged by Duncan's defaming of Captain Pender and his vendetta against Cunningham. He encountered stiff resistance to his proposals for sweeping the coast clean of liquor traders. Crease was particularly unwilling to risk offending the H.B.C. Governor Seymour seemed "incapacitated in mind and body." In fact, the entire government appeared in a state of disarray. "Such weakness, such shuffling and inconsistency in . . . those who are supposed to uphold justice in the land."

On his return to Metlakatla, bonds of mutual respect and friendship grew between Duncan and Tomlinson. Although he could be even more intractable and rebellious against authority than Duncan, Tomlinson sometimes was a restraining influence. Expressing regret that Duncan had gone out of his way to avoid Hills while in Victoria, Tomlinson wrote that "he is our Bishop and there are many always ready to catch at such things and cast them in the teeth of the Society." Duncan frequently asked for and received Tomlinson's advice on both personal and policy matters.

He urged Duncan to reconsider his proposal to bring his sister Maria out as the chatelaine of Metlakatla. "Were she one who was coming out as your wife I would have nothing to say, but your sister is in a different position . . . supposing you marry at home? Or more important still, as you still entertain the possibility of union with a native, what will be your position then?" Tomlinson advised Duncan not to warn Maria of the dangers or trials involved—"for there is a sort of romantic heroine stirred up by such recitals"—but rather to point out "the dull monotony, the little cares and the perpetual worry."

To Duncan's request for his opinion on whether he should accept ordination, Tomlinson responded: "You know I always wished it. I could appreciate your reasons for postponing it when you were thinking of it before. But I see no valid reason why you should not. It seems to me like a soldier fighting among his comrades without his regimental stripes." He felt he could speak freely to Duncan on the matter, "because you know how I hate high church doctrine."

Despite such advice, and much to the annoyance of Bishop Hills and the C.M.S., Tomlinson resolutely refused ordination himself. Just as Duncan put forward the argument that becoming ordained would be incompatible with his business activities, so Tomlinson claimed holy orders would interfere with his medical practice. The fastidious Hills did not care for Tomlinson's forthright manner, which he considered "Irish fanaticism."

Governor Seymour had made his first visit to Metlakatla in the summer of 1867. He told the assembled natives that as long as they behaved the government would assist them. But if they transgressed the law, "no more mercy shall be shown you than to the white man." In May of 1869 Seymour made a return visit on the *Sparrowhawk*. He did not come ashore the first day, and on the next Duncan observed that the governor seemed exhausted after a stroll through the village. Their meeting on this occasion was not cordial. Duncan angered Seymour by his blunt complaints about his administration. Later he learned that the ailing governor had died on the warship off Bella Coola during the return voyage. Ironically, the man who had failed to support Duncan's fervent anti-liquor crusade was a victim of acute alcoholism.[11]

About this time Duncan had a falling out with Clah, the young native who taught him at Fort Simpson to speak Tsimshian.

[11] Akrigg, G. P. V. and Helen. *British Columbia Chronicle, 1847-1871*. Discovery Press, 1977.

Because of his poor standing with the other natives, Clah had not joined the move to Metlakatla. He became a trader on the Nass and Skeena Rivers and, to Duncan's disgust, began paying for furs with liquor. Clah also extended credit to his native customers, another practice Duncan disdained. "I can only account for this daring step on the ground that Clah relied upon his own power to intimidate and his power to seize the property of the Nass Indians when they came to the coast." Before they became estranged, Duncan had appointed Clah constable at Fort Simpson, but was compelled to strip him of his badge when he abused his power over the other Indians. Clah had his own little jail in which he locked up anyone who offended him. Although they had become enemies, Duncan later forced Clah's debtors to pay up, a principle which he attempted to uphold whatever the circumstances.

When the Collins overland telegraph line was being pushed toward the upper Skeena area, where it was soon abandoned, a number of Metlakatlans were employed hauling freight. Clah decided to get in on the action. "I was on friendly terms with all the Indians," Captain James L. Butler of the contracting firm wrote Duncan, "and had no trouble till Clah happened to pass like an evil cloud." Butler accused Clah of persuading the natives not to carry any more goods for the company. He concluded that Clah acted out of jealousy because the others were making money, and described him as an "underhanded, double-dealing rogue."

Estranged from Duncan, Clah decided he might as well join the Methodists, who had established a beachhead at Fort Simpson by wooing the chiefs who had refused to go along with Duncan. He was given the Christian name "Wesley," later changed to Wellington, and he became known as Arthur Wellington Clah. His haughty manner led some scornful whites to call him "the Duke of Wellington." Clah kept a daily journal in English for many years while carrying on his dubious trading activities. In his old age he moved to Victoria in poverty and poor health. By this time Duncan had forgiven him and sent money to help.

As his work load and demands on his time increased, the number and length of Duncan's journal entries began to decline. He was becoming less introspective and did not agonize over his failings as before. One milestone he did record was the death in May 1868 of Paul Legaic at the age of 45. Following his conversion, Legaic worked under Duncan for seven years as a trader, mainly on the Nass. He was outfitted with up to $650 worth of goods each season to trade for furs. The arrangement worked well except for the occasional falling out caused by his own and his wife Lydia's aggressive and outspoken manner. Duncan stuck with Legaic through a number of crises because he was determined to demonstrate to other reluctant chiefs there was a special place for them in his regime.

On April 29 Legaic wrote from Fort Simpson that he was dying and asked Duncan to look after his wife and daughter Sarah. He instructed that his tools, coppers, coat, hat, swords, double-barrel gun and revolving pistol be sold to help support them. Prized possessions not to be disposed of included two cannons, two blunderguns, 11 carved boxes, a clock and a watch. Legaic sent Duncan a second letter May 5 saying, "I always remember you in every moment... you showed me the ladder that reached heaven. I am on the top of that ladder now." Later that day he wrote again. "Dear Beloved Friend in the Lord, this is my last words to say I am very happy to say that I am going to rest from trouble, trial and temptation. I am not afraid to meet my Lord."

Later that year, Duncan sold the *Carolena* for $1,000, which he used to pay off the government loan. He made the decision when the H.B.C., eager for the lost Metlakatla trade, raised prices for furs and lowered them on store goods. When it also offered new rates to carry goods to and from Metlakatla, Duncan accepted. He warned the company, however, that if it attempted to return to its former prices he would go back into the shipping business.

After dithering for some time whether Metlakatla could get along without him for a few months, Duncan finally decided in January of 1870, after 13 years away, to visit England. The Indians were agitated about his impending departure, afraid he might not return. They had written a letter pleading with him not to leave: "Because you are like a father to us... we do not know what we going to do if you went away... we know that it is very difficult for you to live amongst us, but it is more difficult for us if you leave us."

On the evening before he was to depart, Duncan went to every house in the village to say good-bye, spending as usual most of his time with the aged and sick. At the end of his rounds Duncan spoke to a group of natives who had assembled in the Mission House. Some sat there throughout the night and Duncan stayed up with them. There was much sobbing.

The emotional leave-taking continued in the darkness next morning when Duncan walked to the wharf at 6:30 a.m. The constables fired a salute, while the women lined up to shake hands once more. Duncan was accompanied by 10 canoe-loads of natives as he was rowed to the *Otter*. On board he said good-bye to Tomlinson, who was to remain on the Nass but check up periodically on William Rudland, who Duncan put in charge of Metlakatla during his absence. Rudland was a white man, married to an Indian woman, who Duncan had hired to run his store. He had once been rebuked by Duncan for his "impatient and unkind way of treating Indian customers."

Duncan sailed from Victoria to San Francisco, where he caught the train for New York. During a stopover there Duncan wrote to Vincent Colyer, appointed the previous year by President Ulysses Grant to head a special commission studying Indian problems in the U.S. During a tour of Alaska the commission visited Metlakatla. Colyer wrote Duncan at that time: "The fame of your mission has gone all the way up and down our coast, and everyone said to me: 'if you want to see what can be done with the Indians you must visit Mr. Duncan's mission.' Well, I have seen it and you well deserve your hard-earned reputation." Colyer hoped Duncan would not allow anything to deflect him from his work. "I know from sad experience how weak is the flesh and how easily Satan can use it as a power to overturn any good work which he hates," he wrote. "He has had his own way for so many years over the poor Indians that he must hate your mission—and seek to turn you aside or discourage you in it."

Duncan learned from Colyer that steps were being taken to improve the lot of the natives of Alaska. It was a pity, Duncan said, that missionaries had not preceded the soldiers there. Military rule over the Indians had bred the troubles it was intended to check. "The accounts I have received from time to time of the conduct of the soldiers in the Indian camps of the coast of Alaska are truly shocking."

Duncan boarded the S.S. *Calabria* on March 2, arriving in Liverpool 10 days later. He went directly to London, where he was reunited with Arthur Doolan and met C.M.S. officials. He then made an odd return to Beverley. Duncan went directly to the Great Hotel and did not let anyone know of his arrival. He strolled round the town, looking at tombstones in the Minster yard and walking past the homes of his friends. The next day, Saturday, Duncan went through the market, recalling how as a boy he had carried clay pots for the potters. He saw some of his old friends but did not approach them. None guessed the identity of the bearded missionary who had been away so long.

After attending a Methodist service on Sunday where he knew he would not be recognized, Duncan decided to make his presence known at last. He called first on the Cussons family. On Monday he went to see his mother and sister Jane. Cussons accompanied him "to break the ice." He had been criticized earlier by a family friend for failing to keep in touch with his mother, who had to be content with extracts from his letters to others. His mother wept uncontrollably after her son appeared unannounced on her doorstep. Though greatly aged, she seemed well. Duncan learned that his stepfather had died. He visited with his relatives for the next few days, taking time to make a carriage journey with Cussons to his birthplace of Bishop Burton.

The following weeks were taken up by fund-raising speeches at missionary meetings in a number of cities. At the Castle Hotel in Richmond, Duncan shared a platform with Samuel Crowther of Nigeria, the first black Anglican bishop. After speaking to the St. Mary's Mission Army in Brighton, he received $3,000 in goods for Metlakatla. Duncan also visited a number of factories to learn about weaving, rope-making, the manufacture of leather shoes, wooden clogs and brushes, all of which he hoped to introduce among the Indians. In the meantime he sent instructions back that all house-building be stopped until his return. He wanted to start a new "model village" instead of adding on to the old town.

In Ireland Duncan bought a weaving machine which he learned to take apart and reassemble. Then he boarded a steamer for New York. He had to wait almost a week in San Francisco for a ship to Victoria, but made good use of his time by learning a new technique for dressing deer-skins, and visiting another spinning mill. He also took music lessons on a brass band set donated in England for the mission. A quick learner in both mechanics and music, he grasped enough about each instrument to teach the natives the basics.

When they first saw the instruments the Indians thought they were magic. Their only music apart from drumming consisted of a "croaking noise," as Duncan described it, made by blowing into an animal bladder, as well as the sound made by blowing on blades of grass. Otherwise, the men chanted and the women clapped hands. "I took a cornet and played a tune they knew, God Save the Queen," Duncan recalled. "They were all amazed and looked at one another in surprise. I took the instruments down off the wall and gave one to each and told them to go out in the bushes and blow. It was bedlam." But the Indians had a flair for music and it was not long before they were playing enthusiastically and well. A music teacher was imported from Victoria for two months to give advanced training. A brass band was formed, the first on the coast. It became a trademark of Metlakatla. Duncan later acquired some old U.S. army uniforms from Alaska for the bandsmen to wear. They polished the brass buttons as brightly as their instruments.

Chapter 10

A Growing Feud

DUNCAN SPENT A FEW WEEKS in Victoria before boarding a steamer crowded with miners bound for the Omineca, site of a new gold rush. He disembarked at the mouth of the Skeena, where he was picked up by canoe, arriving in Metlakatla February 27, 1871. He had been away 13 months. Musket and cannon fire celebrated his homecoming. A church service was held almost immediately at which Duncan performed 13 marriages held up for his return. In the evening he met with 50 natives in his house for a discussion of his trip and future plans for the community.

The biggest project was the church Duncan had been planning since first moving to Metlakatla. He was forced to work through Bishop Hills because much of the money was being raised by the bishop's Columbia Mission fund. Hills had hired Victoria entrepreneur and architect Edward Mallandaine to draw up the plans. Mallandaine sent preliminary drawings to Metlakatla in the fall of 1867. Duncan was dissatisfied. "Your design is altogether too grand and your working plan quite unintelligible to an amateur like myself." Duncan wanted a plain, strong building "free of complications of grandeur which the building you have designed presents." He wanted to be told simply the number and size of each kind of timber to be used. "The bare circumstances of a remote Indian village should have been sufficient for you to guard against extravagance in your work." It was a classic architect-client dispute. Duncan returned the drawings and refused to pay the "unreasonable" fee.

He decided to take over the project himself, undaunted by his inexperience and the size and complexity of the job. With typical thoroughness he drew up eight different sets of plans, which he sent to Tomlinson for an opinion. At last a design was decided upon and work began. On August 13, 1873, Lieutenant-Governor Joseph Trutch laid the foundation stone. He had been accompanied to

Metlakatla by H.M.S. *Scout* and H.M.S. *Boxer*. The ships' officers expressed scepticism at the scale of the project for a primitive Indian village, but donated ropes and pulleys to lift the huge beams into place. Admiral A. A. Cochrane walked into the carpentry shop where a number of natives were busy at workbenches and exclaimed in surprise, "I say these men are not Indians. They are white men." It was the highest praise he could bestow.

The sawmill stepped up production of cedar timbers and planking. To obtain more waterpower, Duncan supervised the blasting of a channel from a lake in the hills to the sawmill stream. Weary at the end of a full day in the bush, he would return to the village in the evening to be excitedly besieged by natives describing everything that had happened during his absence. It was a busy, happy time in Metlakatla.

Duncan had been joined by William Henry Collison and his wife Marion from Cork, Ireland. Collison, more stoical and less mercurial and stubborn than his countrymen Cunningham and Tomlinson, was a schoolmaster when he heeded the call of the Church Missionary Society. He had wanted to be ordained before going to the North Pacific but the C.M.S. once again acceded to Duncan. "My advice is that he should come out unordained and be willing to help in school work while learning the language—say two or three years—and then he can preach in the native tongue in formal attire of priest; he should be ordained and take full charge of the church here. By that time... there will be a native able to take up the school and I should be free to start a new mission on Queen Charlotte Island... I could occasionally visit Metlakatla till they learn to do without me." The C.M.S. was confident Collison was "exactly suited" for such a program.

There was one stipulation. As Collison put it, "The secretaries intimated to me that, as there was no lady missionary at Metlakatla, it would be advisable that I should find a wife to accompany me to the field."[12] His choice was a nurse, Marion Goodwin, who had served on the battlefield during the Franco-Prussian war and worked with smallpox victims in Cork. The Collisons arrived in Metlakatla on a stormy November Sunday, and were given an enthusiastic welcome by Duncan and the natives. Duncan had rare praise for the new bride. "Mrs. Collison proved herself a brave

[12] Collison, W. H. *In the Wake of the War Canoe*. Edited and annotated by Charles Lillard, based on 1915 edition. Sono Nis, 1981.

woman by the way she maintained the attack upon her nerves at the first landing." He was pleased to see they both cheerfully tackled whatever jobs were at hand and quickly undertook to learn the language.

On Christmas Day, 1873, more than 700 attended church service outdoors in the campground, the largest congregation in the history of the community. Twenty-one canoes had brought 250 relatives and friends from Fort Simpson for the festivities. Four big feasts—separate ones for the Christians and the unconverted—marked the festive season and Duncan recorded that "the village looked very gay and all seemed very happy."

A year later the impressive new church was ready for the Christmas service. It seated 1,200 and was said to be the largest church north of San Francisco and west of Chicago. The solid sawn timber walls were five inches thick, lined inside and out with planed tongue-and-grooved planks. The total cost was close to $12,000, of which half had been raised by Duncan in England.

One of the Collisons' shipmates on the voyage to Metlakatla had been the Reverend William Pollard, on his way to establish a Methodist mission at Fort Simpson. It had been a matter of some contention that Duncan had neglected the settlement after founding Metlakatla. He obviously hoped the rest of the people would be more inclined to follow if Metlakatla prospered and Fort Simpson declined as the H.B.C. operation wound down. Trusted natives such as Thomas Gilbert, Sam Pelham and Ed Mather were sent to preach at the village. Fourteen young men specially trained by Duncan went to Fort Simpson in pairs each Sunday to conduct services, while Mary Rudland spoke to the women. Shortly before Pollard's arrival 300 persons attended one of these meetings.

But Duncan underestimated the hostility of the chiefs who had refused to give up their prestige and power to join him. They not only remained, but were influential in keeping many with them who wished to adhere to the old ways. When one threatened to seize the old schoolhouse because he had not been recompensed for the seizure of ancestral land at Metlakatla, Duncan sent a party to dismantle the building and raft it to the new settlement. In this instance Duncan, one of the first champions of Indian land claims, became one of the first targets.

Anxious to have an established church in Fort Simpson to help keep the unruly natives under control, the H.B.C. invited the Catholics, who declined. The company then turned to the Methodists.

Duncan was annoyed that Pollard did not come ashore at Metlakatla to pay a courtesy call, but was smugly pleased when told by Collison the Methodists were moving in partly in retaliation for Bishop Hills encroaching on their missions in the south. The bishop blamed Duncan for creating an opening for the Methodists. Hills again raised the issue of Duncan's refusal to receive ordination. Pollard would not have entered the area had there been someone at Metlakatla in holy orders, the bishop said. Although he resented the intrusion in his territory, Duncan was not as concerned about the Methodists as were the Victoria Anglican clergy. He was surprised that Archdeacon Woods worried more about Methodists than Catholics.

Duncan and Pollard had "a painful discussion" when the Methodist missionary called in at Metlakatla on his way south after turning over the new mission to Thomas Crosby in March of 1874. Duncan accused the Methodists of ignoring thousands of other Indians on the coast who needed a missionary more than the people of Fort Simpson. He also criticized Pollard for baptizing 124 children within a few hours of arriving.

Pollard told Duncan bluntly that he had neglected Fort Simpson for the last 12 years; the Indians were afraid of him because he was a magistrate rather than a minister; and his main interest in attempting to lure more Indians to Metlakatla was to satisfy his greed as a trader. Pollard also claimed Metlakatla was Duncan's own property and the Indians did not feel they could have legal land tenure there. The accusations had been made to Pollard by the chiefs and disgruntled natives of Fort Simpson who had run afoul of Duncan's anti-liquor crusade, and expressed the bitter views of his many critics. Pollard paid unwitting tribute to Duncan's work, however, by boasting that the Methodists had subscribed $1,000 for their new mission and would soon have a sawmill and steamboat to rival Metlakatla's.

As the feud between Duncan and Bishop Hills increased in bitterness, the Church Missionary Society found itself in an increasingly difficult position. Although it had a measure of autonomy as an independent missionary organization, its officials and workers, both lay and ordained, were at least nominally Anglican. In a communication to all its missionaries in 1867, the C.M.S. blamed the growing ritualistic movement in the church for diverting funds to ceremonial purposes which might otherwise have been spent on missions abroad. The letter referred to a "spiritual stagnation" in mission work. It was becoming difficult to attract good men, and those in the field were overwhelmed by a multitude of secular duties. For this reason, said the Society, it was vital that more day-to-day work be turned over to the most capable natives.

But Duncan did not believe the Indians were ready to take over even such basic work as schoolteaching. Before Collison's arrival in 1873 he had tried some native help in the classroom, but told the C.M.S. his experience had convinced him it would take more time and training. The natives were satisfactory as occasional teachers but lacked endurance and stability for permanent work. Their energies flagged if left long at one thing. And the natives themselves preferred white teachers over members of their own race.

If Duncan had encouraged native talent he would have cemented his position with the C.M.S. and by accepting ordination might have defused his struggle with Hills. But by his persistent refusal to accept holy orders and failure to bring a native along into the clergy, Duncan became engaged in a battle on two fronts that he could not win. As long as Henry Venn was the guiding force of the C.M.S., Duncan had leeway. After Venn's death in 1873, when the Society's policy began to shift away from its evangelistic origins toward the ritual wing of the Church, a showdown became inevitable.

The Society was diverted about this time by a clerical controversy in Victoria which presaged Duncan's rupture with the C.M.S. and the Anglican Church. At the centre was his friend and evangelistic ally, Edward Cridge. Cridge and Hills had seemed destined for conflict from the time of the bishop's appointment. Believing he had been more entitled to fill the position, Cridge resented the aristocratic newcomer. To his credit, Hills was aware of these bruised feelings and tried to maintain good relations with his Dean. His peace-making attempts were not reciprocated. The stolid, humourless Cridge made little effort to get along with his new superior.

When the bishop offered Cridge a promotion in 1868 as arch-deacon of Nanaimo, it was turned down. Cridge felt it was an attempt to move him out of the way. His roots were in Victoria and he knew that in a showdown he could count on the support of many influential citizens, especially members of the H.B.C. old-boy network. The Cridges were charter members of Victoria society. Mary Cridge ran a private school for girls, taught Sunday school, and was a founder of the Protestant Orphans' Home. Prudish and

114

sanctimonious, the Cridges condemned card playing, dancing and reading novels as "worldly amusements" to be shunned. They had nine children, four of whom died in infancy. The survivors seemed emotionally deprived. Richard was a drifter and social outcast. Maude, who corresponded with Duncan, became a sickly spinster. Nevertheless, the family was more popular than the Hills. The bishop was considered snobbish and his wife aloof.

Their battle erupted on the evening of December 5, 1872, during a special consecration service opening the new Christ Church Cathedral. The congregation included Lt.-Governor Trutch and ex-governor Douglas. In the pulpit was Archdeacon William Reece of Vancouver, who had been invited by the bishop. To Cridge's dismay, Reece spoke out in praise of ritualism and ceremony in the Anglican service. Despite the solemnity of the occasion, when Cridge came forward to announce the hymn after the sermon he burst out in agitation. He told the congregation as pastor he felt it was his duty to protest what they had just heard. "During the 17 years that I have officiated as your pastor in this spot this is the first time Ritualism has been preached here; and I pray Almighty God it may be the last. So far as I can prevent it, it shall be." A number of worshippers, including Mrs. Hills, stalked out. But most supported the rebel Dean. The *British Colonist* said Reece's sermon was "indiscreet and in very bad taste."

The bishop could not ignore such an unseemly outburst and asked for an apology from Cridge, who refused. Since Cridge was thus guilty of "canonical disobedience," Hills felt compelled to pronounce "grave censure" upon him, a sentence considered lenient but not conciliatory. Cridge was being more conscientious than stubborn, but his self-righteous manner alienated many. In that, he had a lot in common with his friend Duncan.

Over the next 18 months the bishop and his recalcitrant Dean, instead of getting together to talk out their differences, exchanged a total of 50 letters. It was the manner of the times, and succeeded only in escalating the level of bitterness. In July of 1874 Cridge provoked another crisis by refusing to allow a regular "visitation" to the cathedral by the bishop. This act of insubordination led to a church trial which resulted in Cridge's licence to preach being revoked. Hisses from the public gallery greeted Hills' reading of the verdict. The bishop then went to Supreme Court to ask Chief Justice Begbie for a civil court order removing Cridge. A friend of both men, Begbie was reluctant to hear the case. His attempt to bring about a reconciliation failed, however, and he had no choice but to uphold the bishop's authority.

Cridge left the Anglicans to build a breakaway church, and subsequently became a bishop of the Reformed Episcopal Church, based in the U.S. Most of his Cathedral congregation followed him and were generous with their support, especially Douglas, who donated the church site, $10,000 in cash and a new organ. The wealthy but tight-fisted W. J. Macdonald gave a paltry $500.

A student of the affair has concluded that Cridge "essentially, was not an Anglican."[13] It is an apt observation and one that in the light of subsequent events could be equally applied to Duncan.

The dispute was followed closely in Metlakatla. Duncan used the controversy to reinforce his theories about how best to conduct an Indian mission. The natives identified with Cridge. They had come in contact with both the dean and his bishop and did not need Duncan's persuasion to be convinced that Cridge was a better friend.

Duncan expressed his outrage to the C.M.S. over the bishop's actions, accusing Hills of exercising "ecclesiastical tyranny to crush a man of God from raising his voice in defence of the truth." It was impossible now, he said, for Tomlinson or Collison to accept ordination from such a man.

Meanwhile, Duncan was also embroiled at this time in a dispute with the dominion and provincial governments over Indian affairs, particularly land policy. After Douglas' departure as governor, Duncan's advice was not often sought by his successors. His views were too much at odds with the prevailing prejudices, especially after more settlers arrived and the power of the H.B.C. waned. But in 1873 Duncan's views were solicited by Dr. Israel Woods Powell, the new federal Commissioner of Indian Affairs for B.C. Powell was a pioneer Victoria doctor whose credentials for the post were not apparent. It was considered to be his reward from Sir John A. Macdonald for supporting union of the two colonies into a single province to join Confederation.

Duncan divided his recommendations to Powell into categories for "civilized" Indians and the rest. Urging that "ample reserves" of land be set aside for each uncivilized tribe, he said the greatest need for civilized natives was to keep out whites and lawless

[13] Dickinson, Susan. *Edward Cridge and George Hills, Doctrinal Conflict, 1872-74.* Unpublished B.A. essay, University of Victoria.

Indians. Each family should be allotted 10 acres, which could not be sold except to members of the same village. Civil authority would gradually be handed over to a native council.

Duncan firmly opposed financial assistance for individual Indians. "In no matter affecting the Indians can the government do more good or harm than in the matter of gifts," he told Ottawa in 1875. "Money may be spent to a large amount upon the Indians and yet tend only to alienate, dissatisfy, and impoverish them if wrongly applied; whereas a small sum rightly administered will yield much good both to the Indians and the country at large. The policy of dealing out gifts to individual Indians... is both degrading and demoralizing. To treat the Indians as paupers is to perpetuate their baby-hood and burdensomeness. To treat them as savages, whom we fear and who must be tamed and kept in good temper by presents, will perpetuate their barbarism and increase their insolence." Duncan urged that money be spent on public works to benefit the community as a whole.

Over the next few years Duncan's views on Indian policy crystallized. He made numerous suggestions to the Dominion government, which was more willing than the province to recognize him as an authority on the subject. He was among the first to suggest that Indian reserves be based on language groupings. There were 10 or 12 separate language areas in the province, he told Powell, that should be granted large reserves away from white settlements, each with its own superintendent. When Indians speaking the same language were widely scattered, as in the case of the Tsimshian, the policy should be adapted to their needs by creating two or three reserves. The government should also hold in trust for each tribe favourite fishing stations which whites would not be allowed to pre-empt.

He complained that the Department of Indian Affairs in Ottawa was too remote from B.C., and fought against the early appearance of red tape in Indian affairs, a disease that would reach epidemic proportions long after he had given up the battle. As a schoolmaster, Duncan received detailed instructions from the Department: "You will call the roll twice in the course of the day—at noon and before dismissal in the evening—at the former time marking those present by a diagonal line across the column and at the latter by another, crossing the first; and making a cipher to denote the whole day's absence." The forms were to be filled out in triplicate, and Duncan was forced to comply in order to receive a small amount of financial aid for his school.

In the dispute between B.C. and the dominion government over Indian policy following confederation, Duncan more often than not was on the side of Ottawa, for it soon became apparent the new province had the most backward policy in the country. In the original resolution on union passed by the Legislative Council in Victoria there was no reference to Indians. Jurisdiction went almost by default to Ottawa.

The dominion order-in-council of May 16, 1871, setting out the terms of union, declared Ottawa would follow "a policy as liberal as that hitherto pursued by the British Columbia Government." In view of the province's past record, that wording was regarded by many as a grim joke. Ottawa obviously didn't know what had been going on in the far west for the last quarter of a century. An example of British Columbia's attitude toward its indigenous population was the provincial budget of 1869, in which a mere $500 was allocated for the Indians out of a total expenditure of more than $600,000, although they contributed a quarter of the Treasury's funds through taxes and tariffs.

Commissioner of Lands Joseph Trutch, later to become lieutenant-governor, was particularly critical of missionaries. He had spent time in Oregon before moving to B.C. and had acquired the common American frontier scorn for Indians. He had never met a Christian native, Trutch said. The work of the missionaries was useless. He accused them of inciting the natives to demand rights they otherwise would not have cared about. "The Indians have really no right to the lands they claim, nor are they of any actual value or utility to them, and I cannot see why they should either retain these lands to the prejudice of the general interests of the Colony, or be allowed to make a market of them either to the Government or to individuals."

Trutch was the most prominent but by no means the only influential Victorian who believed the Indians would disappear if ignored long enough—and who were willing to wait. The views of Dr. J. S. Helmcken, Speaker of the Assembly, were typical. When Ottawa expressed fears the Indians in B.C. might resort to violence if land disputes were not settled, Helmcken declared there was no danger, "if misleaders and agitators did not put their own cranky, socialistic, untenable, impracticable, and unlawful notions into Indian heads." He left little doubt who he thought most fitted that description.

Chief Justice Begbie seemed to support aboriginal rights for a time, but he too ended up opposing the principle of Indian title. As early as 1860 Begbie was urging Douglas to take prompt action to extinguish Indian claims. "Separate provision must be made for it, and soon," he wrote. But Begbie's position changed over the years. In an 1878 letter to the deputy minister of justice in Ottawa dealing with the question of reserves, he made no mention of aboriginal title. Like many others in Victoria, his views had hardened after a visit to the province by Governor-General Dufferin.

An outspoken Irishman noted for his rhetoric and wit, Dufferin did not avoid controversy in Canadian politics despite his supposedly neutral role.[14] He was especially attracted to Western Canada, where the vast spaces and unlimited possibilities appealed to his romantic disposition. He liked the convivial John A. Macdonald, and cared little for the dour Liberal leader, Alexander Mackenzie.

In 1876, concerned by growing discontent in British Columbia over Mackenzie's failure to carry out construction of the transcontinental railroad as pledged by Macdonald, Dufferin decided to travel west as a peacemaker. After a pleasant 10-day social whirl in Victoria soothing ruffled feelings with their Irish charm, Dufferin and his wife set off aboard H.M.S. *Amethyst* to tour the coast. On August 29 they arrived at Metlakatla. During a long interview aboard, Duncan found the governor-general to be "a most pleasant, unassuming and kind-hearted, clever man."

Duncan spared no effort to impress his visitor, the most prestigious to set foot in the community. When the Dufferins came ashore the following day they were greeted by a cannon fusillade as well as the usual rifle salute from the constables. A little Indian girl who had been taught to curtsy by Marion Collison presented Lady Dufferin with a bouquet of poppies and sweet william. The governor-general praised the new church as "a monument of the way in which you have profited by the teachings you have received." During an official inspection, each member of the vice-regal party left a $20 gold piece on the collection box table after discovering the slot was too small to take the outsized coin.

Because the Indians were not represented in Parliament, Dufferin said, he felt a responsibility to "watch over their welfare with especial solicitude." The dominion government recognized the

[14] St. John, Molyneux. *The Sea of Mountains: An Account of Lord Dufferin's Tour Through British Columbia in 1876.* London, 1877.

Indians as the "ancient inhabitants" of the country. "The white men have not come among you as conquerors, but as friends. We regard you as our fellow-subjects, and as equal to us in the eye of the law as you are in the eye of God, and equally entitled with the rest of the community to the benefits of good government, and the opportunity of earning an honest livelihood."

On his return to Victoria Dufferin repeated these remarks, but to a much less enthusiastic audience. Before 200 of the city's leading citizens gathered at Government House, he was direct: "We must all admit that the condition of the Indian question in British Columbia is not satisfactory." The provincial government, he said, had refused to recognize Indian title. "In Canada this has always been done; no government, whether provincial or central, has failed to acknowledge that the original title to the lands existed in the Indian tribes and the communities that hunted or wandered over them."

The governor-general overstated the case, but his point was well taken. British Columbia *was* treating its native population badly, and the reaction of his audience showed that Dufferin had hit a sore spot. Dr. Helmcken said it was true the Plains Indians needed land, but B.C. natives wanted only "sea-water." Chief Justice Begbie considered the vice-regal comments "blarney for the mob," as the newspapers later paraphrased his views in a court case involving Metlakatla and a claim of aboriginal title.

Begbie ruled in the case that Dufferin's speech, brought forth as supporting evidence by the lawyer for the Indians, future premier Theodore Davie, was not relevant. When Davie also sought to introduce the views of the Dominion minister of justice on the subject of Indian land rights, Begbie was equally dogmatic. The views of federal ministers could be discounted, he said, because they were usually acting "on compulsion of politics," as if the whole issue, not to mention the case being heard, was not wrapped in politics.

Until they were given the vote, Begbie decreed, the Indians had no rights whatever, "except such as the grace and intelligent Benevolence of the Crown may allow, and has always allowed them." Which, in British Columbia, was not much. Begbie deplored Dufferin's expression of "views which were certain to come to the eyes of the Metlakatla Indians and well might . . . possess great authority with them, and lead them, or confirm them, in most disastrous expectations and actions."

In the same judgement the Chief Justice summarily dismissed Edward Cridge's assertion that the law should be on the Indians' side because "their fathers and nobody else have dwelt there and hunted there." Replied Begbie: "Though at first sight (Cridge's) language seems much more humane, more equitable, more philanthropic, a very little consideration will show that his view is utterly unreasonable, utterly mischievous all round and (fortunately) impossible." The Chief Justice summarized his new-found belief: "I assume that the right of a civilized power—England, France, the U.S.—to occupy and settle in a country utterly barbarous, inhabited only by a sparse population of separate petty tribes more or less nomadic without any approach to any formal government, will not be disputed." Certainly not by the government of British Columbia.

Such were the views of Sir (he had by now been knighted) Matthew Baillie Begbie, supposed friend of the Indian. Begbie's biographer finds his turnabout on aboriginal rights "inexplicable."[15] The reason is not hard to surmise, however. Like most of the leading politicians and jurists of the day, he had become a major land-owner, with holdings in Victoria, New Westminster, Richmond, Yale and elsewhere in the province. Since the Indians were claiming some of the choicest land, these powerful real estate speculators who controlled B.C. affairs were not especially sympathetic to their cause. They wanted those lands for their own gain.

If Dufferin's remarks outraged some, they also spurred the missionaries and a few other supporters of the Indian cause to greater efforts. But it soon became clear that the province, while nominally accepting the principle of large reserve blocks, intended to exclude prime agricultural land, giving up only wild areas and ignoring Indian claims to ancestral sites and burial grounds. The two governments decided to set up a joint three-man commission to seek a compromise solution. Duncan was Ottawa's first nominee, but he was rejected by the province.

As a result of all this political bickering, the Indians became confused about their rights and who they should turn to for redress. It is not surprising the natives regarded the missionaries as their only allies.

---

[15] Williams, David R. "... *The Man for A New Country": Sir Matthew Baillie Begbie.* Gray's Publishing, 1977.

The C.M.S., meanwhile, decided to send more help to Metla-katla. Despite taking lessons in the Haida tongue and preparing himself for a move across Hecate Strait to the Queen Charlotte Islands, Duncan decided once more that the affairs of Metlakatla demanded his presence. Collison proposed to the Society that he be allowed to go instead, and his offer was accepted, leaving Duncan short-handed once again.

Schoolteacher Henry Schutt arrived with his wife and their two young children in October 1876. A fellow Yorkshireman, Schutt had some knowledge of medicine and also took part in Duncan's musical evenings on the harmonium.

Duncan now turned his attention to Fort Rupert. The area was ripe for the Anglicans, he felt, as it had been abandoned by the Catholics and the Methodists had passed it by. The C.M.S. reluctantly supported the proposed expansion. The Society agreed Schutt was not the right man for such an important post, and Duncan determined to take it on himself. He sent John Tait ahead to make contact with the Kwakiutl chiefs. Tait returned with two natives from whom Duncan began taking language lessons. He told the Society he intended to go there for a month, then leave a native teacher in charge. "Thus I hope to divide my time between Metlakatla and Fort Rupert, gradually increasing the proportion given to the latter place."

Once again, that idea was soon dropped. Metlakatla was just too important for him to leave. He quoted a Fort Simpson chief as saying, "a rope has been thrown out from Metlakatla which is encircling and drawing together all the Indian tribes into one common brotherhood." Fort Rupert would require only mission-ary work, while caring for Metlakatla involved vital secular duties. The community was at a critical point, he wrote, needing more home industries to avoid scattering the people in search of work. The worst threat to the progress already made, especially among the young people, would be to let them mix with the itinerant gold seekers. Duncan characterized them as "rolling stones and reckless gamblers."

At the same time, Tomlinson was pleading for more help to maintain his little mission at Kincolith. The medicine men and chiefs, he told Duncan, were trying "to close the door of every house against us." There was a reason. "The chiefs say that they were prepared to give up fighting and liquor drinking and to observe the sabbath, and to open their houses for the spreading of the Gospel—but since in addition to this they will have to abandon giving away of property, they don't do it." Tomlinson said he had made steady progress, however, winning over three chiefs and gaining 38 new settlers. Now he wanted to organize the population in companies like those in Metlakatla.

Tomlinson was also in hot water with the bishop. During a visit to Victoria he had taken part in a service at Cridge's new church and was publicly criticized by the embattled Hills, who also revoked Tomlinson's licence to preach. The C.M.S. expressed concern to Duncan over the bishop's action, but hoped he would "agree with us in the importance of maintaining the Church of England character of the mission." The Society's new Secretary, Henry Wright, asked Tomlinson to bear in mind the difficult position of the C.M.S. No cause should be given for charging the Society or its missionaries with disloyalty to the Church of England. Tomlinson had told the Society he was seriously thinking of leaving the Church bcause of "creeping ritualism."

Chapter 11

Peacemaker from Athabasca

IN ENGLAND, another man was preparing to join the growing corps of missionary workers based at Metlakatla. This one was going to arrive in holy orders, as the C.M.S. decided to override Duncan's objections. James Alfred Hall was attending the Islington Training School. The Society assured Duncan that "few students have raised such universal respect and affection as he has done." Arthur Doolan had met Hall at the Tugwells and confirmed the Society's assessment, although in less glowing terms. "He seems a quiet, commonplace, young man... no foolish pride in him and he will accommodate himself to circumstances." Doolan added, however, that Hall seemed "afraid of doing anything to prejudice the bishop against him." Significantly, during his stopover in Victoria Hall failed to make the customary call on Edward Cridge that Duncan expected of all the new arrivals.

Reverend Hall arrived in Metlakatla August 6, 1877. Unaccountably, Duncan departed for Victoria five days later without instructing him how to conduct a church service for the natives. Schutt was nominally in charge of the mission, with Tomlinson keeping watch from Kincolith. Despite his long-standing concern about a young ordained preacher who did not speak the language, Duncan in this case dropped his guard. It proved to be almost the undoing of Metlakatla.

Impetuous and emotional, the young minister became carried away while preaching an evening sermon, his fourth of the day, to a raptly attentive congregation. He decided the natives were "not sufficiently under the power of the Gospel" and it was his duty to launch a revival among them. Hall succeeded beyond his wildest hopes. His voice rose in excitement until he was almost shouting. The natives, accustomed to Duncan's low-key, conversational sermons, were astonished at this passionate new voice among them. They became caught up in Hall's fervour and, in Duncan's words, "soon a fire raged which defied all control."

Duncan, delayed in Victoria, first learned of the bizarre events that followed Hall's fateful sermons from fragmentary accounts in the Victoria newspapers. He returned as quickly as possible, to find the press reports were essentially accurate but did not convey the seriousness of the situation. Everyone, including Hall and Schutt, was reluctant to tell him the details, but Duncan was able to piece together the story.

As the religious excitement had spread, the natives began holding meetings of their own to discuss their experiences and dreams. Worst of all in Duncan's eyes, the sexes were allowed to mix as they never were under his tight rules, wandering "about the village and in the bush at all hours of the night." The event which "cut them all quite adrift" occurred when five men entered the church after midnight. They heard a murmuring sound near the communion table. Not finding anyone in the church, they were awestruck. One man fainted and the others ran through the village declaiming that the Spirit of God had visited the church and the voice they heard was His voice. The people all rushed to the church at 3 a.m.

At dawn 60 men left in six canoes to spread the word to neighbouring villages. "As might be expected, Fort Simpson readily accepted the delusion and soon imparted to it fresh vigour," Duncan wrote. While the men were away, a party of young girls who had been roaming in the bush throughout the night announced early in the morning that they had discovered the Cross of Jesus. Crowds rushed off to behold the wonder, which turned out to be an oddly-shaped, rotten tree branch. Nevertheless, they tried to set it up on the church and were stopped only by the quick action of Hall, who by this time was thoroughly alarmed at the crisis he had provoked.

When the men arrived back from Fort Simpson they seemed possessed, claiming to have seen angels. One of the native teachers set out to exorcize them. There was little Hall or Schutt could do to restore order until the fervour began to abate a day or two before Duncan returned.

Duncan decided his best course was to deal first with the congregation as a whole before calling in the worst offenders. On the second Sunday after his return he cancelled the regular morning service and called 300 men to a meeting in the school house, where he spoke for an hour and a half. The session did not go smoothly. Some of the men attempted to dispute Duncan's authority. He patiently brought them around to his position. The next day he sent for the five Elders he felt had betrayed his trust. Only four showed up. Their encounter, which lasted six "painful" hours, was stormy. The most outspoken of the group quoted scripture to Duncan to justify their behaviour. Only when Duncan threatened excommunication did they reluctantly repent. The "rebellion" was over. Special Bible class meetings were conducted by Duncan every night for the next few weeks "to expound the Scriptures they had misunderstood and perverted."

There was still the indignant report to be written to the Society. That was a task Duncan took up with relish, for had not the recent events dramatically borne out the wisdom of all his warnings not to send out an ordained priest who did not know the Indian character, customs or language? Hall had played into his hands at a most opportune time, and he was going to make the most of it. "Your sending out Mr. Hall young and inexperienced yet in full orders as pastor of this flock . . . was no doubt well meant and even necessary in an ecclesiastical point of view, but God has seen fit to rebuke the step and I verily believe that it is to his premature ordination Mr. Hall's bold conduct is attributable. No doubt his heart is right but his judgement is very far from a sober one." Surprisingly, Duncan did not write Hall off as he had Gribbell and Owen, but suggested to the C.M.S. that he be posted to Fort Rupert to make a fresh start.

It would be wrong to regard the incident as one only of sweet vindication for Duncan. He *was* seriously alarmed by what he found on his return to Metlakatla—the potential for disintegration of all his work. It was not *he* who was mistaken about the form of Christianity best suited for the Indians. He had soon learned at Fort Simpson that his converts tended to regard the rites and ceremonies of the church in a superstitious sense. They also attached great importance to the powers of the preacher. That was why Duncan spoke from beside a table instead of a pulpit, and dressed in plain clothing rather than the colourful robes of the priesthood. That was why he avoided in his services any reference to the Holy Ghost or direct revelation of God's word.

As for Holy Communion, it went without saying that one didn't perform a ceremony relating to the Indians' former cannibalistic rites. And how could wine be served when it was so firmly forbidden in all other instances? Most of all, the incident explained why Duncan insisted on thoroughly preparing the natives before baptism and admission to the church. That way he could be sure they would not slip back to the old customs, as they did in so many cases where the missionaries were more concerned with numbers they could flaunt than in making true converts.

In Duncan's case, the problem was that the rituals were important to the bishop and the numbers to the Society. Neither was prepared to let him proceed in his own way at his own pace. He was equally convinced of the rightness of his policy and unwilling to compromise.

In 1876 the bishop criticized Duncan for publicly supporting Cridge's breakaway church. The C.M.S. had asked Hills to go to Metlakatla to ordain both Tomlinson and Collison, but the bishop felt it would be "more convenient" to hold the services in Victoria. No doubt at Duncan's prompting, the Indians had written Hills telling him to stay away from Metlakatla until he had made peace with Cridge. Duncan then threw fuel on the flames by accusing the bishop of collecting money in England in the name of Metlakatla which had not been turned over to the mission. In the face of such opposition, Hills recommended to the Society that it send Bishop William C. Bompas of Athabasca to Metlakatla to set matters right.

An avowed evangelist and reluctant bishop, William Carpenter Bompas was happier tramping the brush and scrub forest of his vast diocese than performing the rituals required of his office. His clothes were usually tattered and he bedded down wherever nightfall found him.[16] During a brief stay with Collison at Masset, he declined his host's offer of a bed and spread his blanket on the floor. "To sleep on a bed in a bedroom would tend to unfit me for my future itinerary in the forest," he told the bemused Collison. After meeting Bompas at Kincolith, Tomlinson told Duncan he was "one to love and respect, one we know and see feels with us and for us. I feel sure when you see more of him you will think as I do."

The bishop arrived at Metlakatla November 24, 1877, more than six weeks after leaving his Peace River base by canoe. A shaggy beard and torn shirt resulted in his being mistaken for a miner when he landed at the mouth of the Skeena. Bompas liked what he found at Metlakatla and got on well with Duncan, despite an underlying

---

[16] Cody, H. A., editor, *An Apostle of the North: Memoirs of Right Reverend W. C. Bompas.* Musson, 1908.

tension caused by the nature of his task and the fact his visit to Metlakatla was instigated by Bishop Hills. Duncan's guard had also been raised when Bompas wrote earlier in the year that he was sure it would be "a source of great encouragement to you when the clergy of your mission are in full orders and able to administer the Sacrament regularly."

Soon after his arrival the bishop baptized 67 adults and 64 children, and held confirmation service for 124. Because of the recent outburst of fanaticism, Bompas agreed it would not be wise to administer the sacrament to any members of the congregation and he reprimanded Hall for his provocative conduct.

Bompas spent Christmas in Metlakatla and wrote a glowing account of the celebration for the Society. Carollers paraded through the streets on Christmas Eve and after the church service 600 villagers shuffled through the Mission House to shake hands. "On Christmas morning the first sight which greeted us was that of the constables lengthening to its full height the flagstaff on the watch-house, to hoist the flag for Christmas, and all the village street was soon gaily dressed with flags. The constables then marched about the village to different houses to shake hands and make Christmas peace with all whom they had been called to interfere with in the course of the year."

On Boxing Day visitors from neighbouring settlements spending the holiday at Metlakatla were invited to the mission hall, where Duncan spoke and distributed gifts of soap, apples, sugar and tobacco. The next day was set aside for the school children, with Duncan entertaining 200 at his cottage, girls first and then the boys. Each received sugar plums and apples, as well as articles of clothing such as a cap or cloak. On December 28 all the men of the village, about 300, assembled in the Market House to be addressed by Duncan and receive a half-pound of sugar and six apples. There were copy-books, pencils and tobacco for the older men. Next day the Schutts entertained the widows, 60 in all. On December 31 some 300 women gathered in the Market House, where they were given apples, soap and rice.

When the year-end festivities ended, Bompas set to work seeking a compromise that would satisfy Duncan, the C.M.S. and Bishop Hills. It was a daunting task, since Duncan seemed intractable. Bompas insisted the Society was bound by its principles and association with the Church of England to maintain a fully ordained minister at Metlakatla. Duncan was equally adamant that the placing of a clergyman in spiritual charge of the mission would require him to leave.

Bompas went to Fort Simpson to determine how the C.M.S. should respond to the Methodist incursion, and also visited Masset and Kincolith to consult with Collison and Tomlinson. He met Crosby at Fort Simpson, was not impressed, and resolved not to have any more dealings with him. Shortly before this encounter Crosby had been forced by bad weather to stay over at Kincolith with Tomlinson, who tried to work out an amicable agreement for their rival missions on the Nass. "Our interview proved a stormy one and finally he left the house in a temper," Tomlinson told Duncan.

Bompas saw no need for the C.M.S. to have a mission at Fort Simpson, which he said was close enough to be serviced from Metlakatla. He felt the Society's agents should be more widely dispersed. Bompas did not believe the Methodist mission at Fort Simpson was harmful to the C.M.S. "The fact that Mr. Crosby is rather crusty only gives us more room for the exercise of Christian forbearance and forgiveness."

Duncan had suggested an ordained minister be stationed at Fort Simpson instead of Metlakatla, but Bompas saw through that as a means by Duncan of avoiding interference. "I doubt whether this would be a manly, straightforward Christian course either as regards yourself or others," he bluntly told Duncan. Bompas added that Duncan's threat to leave if his leadership was challenged by an ordained minister conflicted with his previous declarations that a missionary should not consider his own comfort, convenience or dignity, but only the work.

If the criticism was harsh, Bompas' attitude was not. "If you think you can induce the C.M.S. to take a different view of this question why not attempt it?" he told Duncan, suggesting he visit England to present his side. There had already been too many conflicting letters on the subject, the bishop said, and he wanted to avoid a "paper war" with Duncan.

Bompas was confident that having Collison in charge of the Metlakatla church would cause "no inconvenience or annoyance" to Duncan, but that was for him to decide. He also believed Duncan could reach an agreement with the Society on a new position that could be "more useful to the work of the Gospel than even your present one." Under the burden of Metlakatla, Bompas said, Duncan had become a "slave" to the natives. They were too dependent upon him and in the event of his sudden illness the whole project might collapse. Duncan wanted Metlakatla to be a model Christian village, Bompas said, but refused to acknowledge that could not happen without the presence of an ordained Christian minister.

Bompas made a number of proposals on the placement of personnel. Tomlinson should open a new mission up the Skeena, and Schutt join Collison on the Nass. Bompas said there was not enough firm evidence against Schutt to expel him from the mission as Duncan and Tomlinson had urged. Schutt had angered them by asking the C.M.S. for a bigger salary and allegedly becoming romantically involved with Catherine Ryan at Kincolith, a charge both she and Schutt denied. Duncan was disappointed with Schutt because "he loves ease and his own comfort too well and his work too little."

Bompas urged Duncan to give up the store for a year on a trial basis, but rejected Duncan's proposal that a Victoria merchant take it over temporarily. The H.B.C. would be better for the village, he said, a suggestion that squelched the idea as far as Duncan was concerned. Bompas also urged that Duncan or someone else take on the task of translating the Bible into Tsimshian, which Duncan had resisted in the past.

To carry out all these plans it was essential that Duncan be relieved as soon as possible and Collison be ordained. Tomlinson had been Bompas' first choice, but he continued to refuse ordination. After being examined for a week by the bishop at Kincolith, the oath admitting Collison to both deacon's and a full priest's orders was administered March 17, "a good day for an Irishman" as Tomlinson put it. But the seeds of future conflict between Duncan and Collison had been sown.

Tomlinson and Collison accompanied Bompas up the Skeena to the trail-head for his long journey back to the Peace. He told them he regretted not having time to study the Metlakatla system more thoroughly so that he might copy it at his own mission.

Duncan had been courteous to Bompas throughout the winter even though the bishop had left little doubt what he would be recommending to the C.M.S. The time required for Bompas to get home and write his report gave Duncan the opportunity to reach the Society first. "I am afraid," Duncan wrote after Bompas left, "he will prove not a safe counsellor to the Society about the work here." The bishop's Indians were so different from those on the coast that he could not be expected to understand Metlakatla. "No doubt from his standpoint we have too little of the ecclesiastical element and too much of the secular. What has ever struck every other visitor . . . the energy and the industry of the place, has failed to win his sympathy. It strikes me it would be well for the poor wanderers in Athabasca if they had some friend who would teach them in temporal matters as well as teach them catechisms." There was truth in Duncan's remarks, but they were unfair to Bompas, who worked under conditions far more difficult than those Duncan enjoyed. The bishop had shown himself to be a reasonable man.

As for the translations, Duncan said he had been working on some and would soon have a new litany in Tsimshian. His progress was slow because of the pressing demands of other, more important tasks. "The progress the Indians are making in English will make it quite unnecessary to translate the Scripture into their tongue. They prefer reading in English and a translation would not be read if presented." This was a doubtful claim, since English was neither as widely used nor understood as Duncan wanted others to believe.

Some of Bompas' recommendations dealing with personnel were implemented without awaiting C.M.S. approval, which was always slow in coming. Hall went to Fort Rupert, reporting to Duncan that as he arrived at the fort entrance, "the Romish priest walked out of another and I trust he will not walk in again." The H.B.C. had provided a house beside the old Catholic school which he planned to repair. Hall was being assisted by George Hunt, a young native respected by the other Indians and who later gained recognition as the gatherer of a vast amount of material on Kwakiutl customs for anthropologist Franz Boas.

Hall had 150 people at his first Sunday service, out of the Fort Rupert population at that time of 200. There were 20 other Kwakiutl villages with a total population of 5,000 in the area south of Queen Charlotte Sound, on Vancouver Island and the mainland inlets and neighbouring islands. Although smaller than the surrounding villages, Fort Rupert had 21 chiefs who existed on the proceeds of potlatches at the expense of their neighbours. There were feasts and dancing every night, and Hall complained of the incessant drumming. Nevertheless, he wanted the C.M.S. to let him stay. Otherwise, he said, the Catholics would move back.

In May the C.M.S. sent instructions to Duncan based on Bompas' report. Hall's transfer to Fort Rupert was confirmed, as was the planned move by Tomlinson to the upper Skeena. Collison was to be "associated" with Duncan at Metlakatla, not only in the administration of the mission but also as joint secretary of the Society's North Pacific operations. The C.M.S. hoped Duncan would stay on under these terms, because the natives needed him. But he should also make greater efforts to visit the surrounding tribes and develop more young natives as paid assistants for church and school work. This admonition was reinforced in another letter from Secretary Christopher Fenn later that year to all C.M.S. missionaries. "The observation and experience of 11 years as a missionary and 14 years as a secretary," Fenn wrote "have produced in my mind the absolute conviction that in all missions without exception the tendency acting irresistibly in almost every missionary is to undervalue the strength and the worth of Native Christian activity." Duncan was proof of that dictum.

Meanwhile, Duncan focused his attention on the secular affairs of Metlakatla, perhaps to take his mind off the impending ecclesiastical storm. But he was also convinced that Metlakatla was at a critical point in its development. It was essential that more industries be established to keep the people from scattering in search of work. He was thinking of canning salmon for the European market and developing a hand-loom weaving industry. Capital was needed for such projects, but Duncan was confident he could get it from Victoria businessmen. He was concerned, however, that independent speculators might gain a grip on the community's future. The profits should be kept in Metlakatla.

In the six years since Duncan's return from England a number of new industrial and building projects had been undertaken. More money was being advanced by the federal and provincial governments. In 1874 there was a $500 grant from Ottawa toward an industrial training school for older boys. The following year $400 was approved in Victoria for a new jail after Duncan complained that his original little blockhouse could not hold more than one or two prisoners. He had occasionally been forced to use his own home to hold the overflow. Now he wanted a four-cell building with a guard room. The same year Ottawa sent $750 for new housing and $250 to encourage the trade of barrel making. A cooperage was built and a man brought in from Victoria to teach the techniques. The experiment was not entirely successful, however. The natives were unable to seal the casks tightly for shipping oolichan grease and Duncan eventually switched to tins.

In the fall of 1877 the Metlakatla economy was stagnant. The natives had lost money the past two years on the oolichan fishery, and salmon stocks were already being depleted by the first canneries on the coast. Duncan was not sending as many furs to market because there were so many new traders in the area. As late as 1874 there had been only 50 whites on the 50 miles of coast between the mouths of the Skeena and Nass Rivers; now the number was much greater, especially in the summer salmon season.

Duncan was one of the first to raise his voice on behalf of the Indians against the depredations of the new canneries. It was a pity, he said, that the Indians should see the wealth of their fishery taken away by outside speculators, "and not be able to reach out and get at least a share of the bounty." In August of 1876 Duncan warned the superintendent of the Northwestern Commercial Company that its white fishermen were encroaching on traditional Indian fishing grounds. "As the Indians here are very numerous, and salmon is their chief article of food, it is hardly to be expected they will yield up any of their ancient rights and privileges to white men without a struggle." Duncan suggested that if the firm was unable to secure enough salmon from its allotted fishing grounds, it should purchase additional fish from the Indians.

As a result of hard times that summer, a party of Metlakatlans paddled north in search of work and picked up a wood-cutting contract at Wrangell from the U.S. Army. The natives' efficiency and strict observance of the sabbath made an impression in the turbulent Alaska settlement and prepared the way for a future mission there. The men evangelized while wood-chopping, and after the job was completed one of them stayed behind to carry on the religious work.

That was not the only link between Metlakatla and Alaska. The village became widely known as a "city of refuge" on the coast for runaway Indian slaves, and received a number of Tlingits and Alaska Haidas. One woman paddled 150 miles alone to escape her owner and find sanctuary with Duncan. A man was freed after 30 years of slavery. A fund of $5,000 was set up in Metlakatla to recompense owners for the loss of their slaves, but some chiefs were not satisfied with compensation. Edenshaw of the Haidas travelled to Metlakatla from the Queen Charlottes to ask Duncan for the return of an escaped slave, but was refused.

Because of a shortage of funds, only 12 new houses had been built in the new townsite plan, even though Duncan was selling lumber from the sawmill to the people below cost. To bring in more money, he intended to start exporting salmon. He planned to begin with salting and smoking, which required less initial investment. Duncan hoped to provide jobs for "hundreds" later with a cannery. He estimated his capital requirements at $5,000, and asked the dominion government to set up an industrial loan fund that could be paid back in five years. There would be no more than ordinary business risk for the government, Duncan said, and he would superintend the operations without salary.

It seemed a reasonable proposal considering the showcase progress already made at Metlakatla, but Commissioner Powell turned it down. If he gave a loan to the settlement, he said, all the other Indians in the province would want one. Powell offered instead to increase support for the industrial school as was done in the other provinces. He did not acknowledge Duncan's argument that there was no point training the Indians for jobs that weren't there. There were other causes of friction with Powell.

In May of 1877 Duncan received a letter from Attorney-General A. C. Elliott concerning a petition from some white residents of the Nass complaining of "insolent and offensive" behaviour by armed native constables from Metlakatla. Duncan conceded his policemen might have been overly aggressive while making an arrest, but said they were angered by one of the whites living with and forcibly detaining a half-breed girl who had been under Tomlinson's care. The protest was instigated by the man's employer, J. Johnston Robertson, who owned a fish company on the river and was also a justice of the peace for the area. One of his business partners was none other than Dr. Powell, who might be considered to have had a conflict of interest if such business activities by government officials had not been so common in those free-wheeling times. Tomlinson alleged Powell was involved in Robertson's money-losing camp "to the tune of some thousands of dollars."

If true, Powell could afford the losses, since he had been busily buying up land during his government service, including some valuable property on the site of the future city of Vancouver. He owned large farms at New Westminster, Saanich and Cowichan, as well as a number of mining properties. Senator Macdonald complained that through men like Powell the dominion government's efforts to help the Indians were being "thwarted by the selfish indifference of subordinate agents, who may be too much occupied with their private business to attend to that for which they are paid."

In any case, Elliott told Duncan the government would appoint a white constable for Metlakatla, and there would be no further need for Indian policemen. And so another of Duncan's innovations was thwarted by officialdom, although he continued to use the constables in an ex-officio role in the community. Before Elliott's decision, Duncan had urged the provincial government to ensure that constables in all Indian villages were natives. The results might not be satisfactory at first, he admitted, but it would be good training for the men and serve to enlist support for the law.

On the Nass, Tomlinson was preparing to move after 10 years of frustrating labour. He told Duncan the Methodists were having even less success winning the people over. "There is a deplorable deadness among the Nishgas. Their chief object seems to be to hold back until they see where they are likely to obtain the greatest worldly advantages." In mid-May 1878, Tomlinson and Collison began preparing a new mission site a short distance from Skeena Forks at Ankitlast, near Kispiox.

It was a bad time for Duncan, discouraged by the slackening growth at Metlakatla and concerned about the future under the new C.M.S. policies, which he found so at odds with his own. His infrequent journal entries complained of feeling physically weak. With Tomlinson farther away than before up the Skeena, Collison back in the Charlottes, Schutt in Kincolith and Hall at Fort Rupert, he was alone again. His ablest native helper, David Leask, had gone to help Collison at Masset. As a young boy, Leask had been in Duncan's first class in Fort Simpson in 1858 and was the first native-born preacher on the mission staff.

A few months in Fort Rupert had taken away much of Hall's initial optimism. Attendance at his church services had dropped from 150 to 70 as the chiefs began holding feasts on Sundays to keep the people away. The winter ceremonials were even more discouraging. Early in 1879 Hall wrote Duncan: "On Christmas morning all my people cleared out to attend a distribution of property at Alert Bay and since that day I have not seen the Fort Rupert Indians except a few stragglers returning for provisions. I had prepared my Christmas address, and some of them wished to wait—however they had a favourable wind and away they went."

At Metlakatla, the picture began slowly to brighten. Work was proceeding on a number of projects which Duncan hoped would lead to the mission becoming self-supporting. New workshops with a total floor space of 6,000 feet were erected, keeping the sawmill, now managed entirely by the natives, operating at full capacity. A large wing had been added to the school, increasing its capacity to 200 students. By the beginning of March 1879, some 30 new homes were completed and work was ready to start on another 25. Each Indian starting to build was given a 100-pound keg of nails and eight window sashes. By the end of the year 88 houses were under construction as the townsite plan was filled in.

The jail had been empty all year and there was a noticeable improvement in the spirit of the townspeople. One hundred men volunteered to construct a new section of the shorefront road and install 50 new gas streetlights donated by Admiral Prevost. They finished the job in two weeks. Prevost also bought 50 fruit trees in Victoria and shipped them to the village. "Our main road is now over half a mile long and the lamps being placed at nice intervals made us look very grand at night," Duncan wrote. "The first night the lamps were lit a lot of the old men became so elated . . . they persisted in parading the village to enjoy the sight."

Two visitors to Metlakatla in the summer noted the happy atmosphere of the place. One was the Reverend Sheldon Jackson, who stopped over on his way to Sitka. Jackson, who was to become an influential figure in Alaska affairs, was intrigued by Duncan's methods and vowed to introduce some of them in the new Presbyterian missions in Alaska. The other visitor was A. C. Anderson, now an Indian Commissioner for the federal government. He described the community in a report to the *British Colonist*.

The sawmill was on a small stream falling into the bay a mile away, Anderson wrote. It had a large circular saw driven by a water wheel and a turning lathe. A regular street system included oil lamps on the main thoroughfare. The school children were clean and decorous. The women were neatly dressed, some in black, others in varied colours. There was a public reading room and discussion area, but most of the people could only browse through the picture books for amusement. Anderson noted the adults spoke English better than they read it, but said the room was humanizing and beneficial. Carvings of crests had been gathered for a relics museum, proof that the traditional arts had not been obliterated by Duncan. Service in the store was prompt and diligent. Anderson said Duncan's dual role of missionary-magistrate had led to resentment in the past but now he had other magistrates in the area to call upon in difficult cases. There was no apparent attempt at coercion. Each man's labour was his own, which contributed to the general feeling of independence and self-reliance.

Chapter 12

Bishop Ridley Arrives

THE STRAIN OF MANAGING the affairs of Metlakatla took its toll on Duncan. He told the C.M.S. at the end of 1880 that he had been unable to focus on bookkeeping and his accounts were temporarily in arrears. He also apologized for not providing the Society with more information. "I have been going to write an account of mission work but have been too busy and now I am afraid I cannot remember detail enough to make it worthwhile."

Although he could not find time to keep the Society fully informed, Duncan's regular reports to Dr. Powell during this period show the community was steadily expanding in prosperity and population. In the fall of 1880 the first blankets were turned out on new looms which had been made at Metlakatla with the aid of a weaving expert brought in from Victoria. Besides rough blankets, the women made shawls and skirts for their own use after carding and spinning the wool.

By the following summer 100 new homes had been completed with government aid. Each had two storeys, were 18 x 36 feet, with two rooms on the ground floor and three bedrooms upstairs. They were connected by a common middle room if the adjacent families were related. These connecting rooms had an open Indian fire and accommodation for visitors. The lots were all 60 x 120 feet fronted by 50-foot wide roads. Each was fenced in with a small front flower garden and large backyard for domestic berry plants and vegetables. There were also separate garden plots outside the village.

The house-building had kept the sawmill humming and stimulated the manufacture of furniture, window sash and doors. There was now a telephone line to the mill from the village. A blacksmith's shop was installed. The natives began to make their own bricks. They were also encouraged to maintain traditional carving skills and the new village hall was almost entirely Indian in style and structure.

In his 1881 report to Powell, Duncan said the population of Metlakatla had reached 1,100. Not all residents were Christians, however. Many were relatives who chose to live there because of its prosperity and peacefulness. They agreed only to abide by the community's rules. Duncan said his Christian teaching had taken such hold on the whole community, it had become easy to enforce the law.

The 10 "companies" of citizens had been expanded to include two church elders, two constables, three town councillors, two musicians, 10 firemen and a captain—20 community workers in all. On New Year's Day the companies assembled for church service, then paraded in a large circle singing the national anthem. Each body of officials was brought into the circle and cheered. A final hurrah for Metlakatla ended the ceremony. Duncan stressed the value of such displays. "These measures tend to destroy all tribal animosities, afford a useful position for the chiefs, secure the sick a visitor and the erring a monitor, uphold the law, bring suitable bylaws into operation and provide pleasure for all and promote the safety of the village, and not least, a general feeling of brotherhood is fostered, prompting each man to assist his fellow in time of need."

The cannery was the biggest project, and Duncan was not able to obtain financing until January of 1882 when 48 natives put up $100 each for shares. They advanced half in cash and borrowed the balance from Duncan. He charged them 10 per cent interest on the loan just as if it were an ordinary business transaction. One of his first actions after forming the company was to inquire of the cannery manager at Inverness on the Skeena what wages he intended to pay during the coming season, pledging not to alter the scale without first consulting him. The canning business should be placed on a "sensible footing." What Duncan meant was that he didn't want the workers playing one firm off against another to drive up wages and salmon prices. It marked his first tentative step into the cannery cartels that had already begun to dominate the industry along the coast of B.C. and Alaska. He was too much of a loner and his operation too small, however, for him ever to become a full-fledged member.

Describing the progress of the mission to Powell, Duncan said there was no doubt of the capability of the Indian to become a skilled and honest workman. Changes in sanitation habits and morals had raised the general level of health. Babies were more likely to survive and the children were more robust. The Indians themselves were struck by the improvement in their lives. Many couples decided to have just one or two children despite the better medical care now available to them.

Duncan wanted a resident doctor to serve Metlakatla and the surrounding tribes, who were constantly asking for medicines or bringing people to him for treatment. They came from as far as 30 miles away. He and the Indians pledged to raise $1,000 a year toward a doctor's salary if the government would put up the remaining $500 and provide a house. Money now spent on medical care along the coast was not being put to good use, Duncan told Powell. But his request was turned down, presumably on the overused excuse that other Indians in the province would ask for doctors too. Duncan hired a doctor for a short time by paying his salary out of his own and community funds. Then Dr. James D. Bluett, who was to stay with Duncan for 12 years, arrived in 1882. Bluett, 32, had independent means and served without salary. Another new worker, George Sneath, was also added to the staff at this time. Sneath had trained as a carpenter before going as a missionary to Africa, where the heat had proved too much for him and he was re-posted to the North Pacific.

While steady progress was being made on the secular side, all was not well with the administrative affairs of the mission. The trouble started with a letter from C.M.S. Secretary Henry Wright dated March 21, 1879, which disclosed that a proposal by Bishop Hills to divide his diocese into three had been accepted. Hills had suggested such a step as early as 1862 but it had never been acted upon. Now the C.M.S. had agreed to select and support a bishop for the new northern diocese of Caledonia. Hills was to retain the diocese of British Columbia (Vancouver Island) and the third diocese of New Westminster (the mainland) would be headed by Reverend A. W. Sillitoe. At last Hills had succeeded in getting Duncan out of his well-coiffed hair. Caledonia was to take in all the Indians of the coast north of Fort Rupert. The man selected to oversee this vast territory was William Ridley.

It came as a surprise when Ridley was named first Bishop of Caledonia; no one had expected he would rise to such rank. Ridley had never been considered a man of exceptional ability, and some of his fellow C.M.S. missionaries were sceptical about the appointment. One explanation offered was that he was a close friend of C.M.S. Secretary Christopher Fenn, a former colleague in India who was now in charge of the Society's North Pacific operations.

Ridley would not have been the choice of the Anglican hierarchy. He was selected by the C.M.S., which insisted on its right to name the new bishop when the church asked it to pay his annual $2,000 salary.

Ridley was the son of a Devon stonemason and worked as a carpenter before enrolling in the C.M.S. Islington Training School.[17] In 1866, at the age of 30, he was posted to the northern Indian province of Peshawar to work among the Afghans. It was a testing assignment. In the previous three years fever had claimed the lives of three missionaries and three others were invalided home. Within three years Ridley was repatriated too, broken in health and spirit.

Ridley spent the next two years in parish work before becoming vicar of a Huddersfield church. Even that proved too much of a strain. Ridley advised the C.M.S. in 1878 that he had suffered "a very serious breakdown from working beyond my strength and have been warned against a renewal of it by the doctor." He asked for a less onerous position. "I should like a small charge near a large population with a railway station at hand—so that I may be able to devote a great part of my time to the Society cause without neglecting my parochial duties." Instead, after being consecrated bishop on July 25, 1879, he was dispatched to Metlakatla.

Ridley arrived with his wife Jane on October 14 in Victoria, where he was met by Duncan, who accompanied them on the voyage north. Duncan was coolly courteous to his new superior. After one of his first Sundays in the village, the new bishop wrote in wonder: "The church bell rings, and from both wings of the village, well-dressed men, their wives and children, pour out from the cottages, and the two currents meet at the steps of the noble sanctuary their own hands have made."

Ridley then jumped to a conclusion which has been widely repeated. "It would be wrong to suppose that the love of God alone impelled them all. All, without reasonable cause to the contrary, are expected to attend the public services. A couple of policemen, as a matter of routine, are in uniform, and this is an indication that loitering during service hours is against proper civil order... at present one strong will is supreme. To resist it, every Indian feels, would be as impossible as to stop the tides. This righteous autocracy is as much feared by the ungodly around as it is respected and admired by the faithful..." After Duncan and the C.M.S. parted

[17] Stock, Eugene, *The History of the Church Missionary Society*. 1899.

company, the Society's official historian, Eugene Stock, carefully excised Ridley's curious, ameliorating conclusion: "Thus are law and Gospel combined with good results."

In this way the erroneous impression was created by Ridley in the first instance, and later by a selective editor and other critics, that Metlakatla's great church was filled only by the menacing presence of jack-booted constables. The C.M.S. and its parent, the Church of England, had begun its campaign of distortion to discredit the man who had defied their edicts. Stock also claimed the Metlakatlans had become totally absorbed in their new world-ly possessions. When Duncan was about to break away and sought the Indians' support, they were, Stock wrote, "no longer poor wandering Indians, but a thriving community with considerable investments in Victoria, and they owed it to him."

Just what those "investments" in Victoria consisted of was never explained. Though better off than other Indians on the coast, the Metlakatlans were scarcely in a position to participate in the financial affairs of the capital. Indeed, Duncan had a difficult time persuading them to part with their small savings to invest in the little industries at home.

Ridley's alliance with Bishop Hills, founded on their common dislike of Duncan and agreement on ecclesiastical issues, was cemented six months after Ridley's arrival when Cridge naively invited him to preach at his church. Cridge, mistakenly believing Ridley to be a supporter of the evangelical wing of the Anglican church, invited the new bishop while he was in Victoria to speak out on the subject at the Reformed Episcopal Church. The bishop regretted that he was too busy, but let Cridge know exactly where he stood. "The people of this town have rightly concluded from what I have spoken in the Cathedral pulpit that my sympathies are with those who interpret the Book of Common Prayer in its strict form."

Duncan's attitude toward the Anglican communion service went beyond what he regarded as its unsuitability for the Indians. He believed observance of the Lord's Supper was a Roman Catholic ritual which had divided Christianity by being "shame-fully abused and corrupted." Duncan felt so strongly on the matter, Ridley claimed, that he had told him he regarded the Church of England as "an utterly corrupt organization, to which he owes no kind of allegiance." Allowing for Ridley's fondness for hyperbole, these were close to Duncan's views at the time, embittered as he was at the actions of Bishop Hills. He called the diocese-splitting manoeuvre a "spiteful coup d'etat."

Duncan was not alone in his opposition to ecclesiasticism in missionary work. The Church of England journal *The Rock*, published in London by an evangelical group, ran an article in its November 1879, edition under the heading, "Do Lord Bishops Help or Hinder Foreign Missions?" Answering its own question, the journal declared "missionary bishops" went into the field not to work but to represent and set up as close an imitation as possible of the High Anglican church with all its paraphernalia. "Let us have them without the baubles and ecclesiastical frippery that surrounds them at home," *The Rock* urged. Its ideal missionary was pious, intelligent, and laborious, which happened to be Duncan's virtues.

These views were echoed by William Healey Dall, a pioneer American explorer in Alaska and the Yukon, who asked why "intelligent men still go on talking three or four times a year to Indians on doctrinal subjects, by means of a jargon (chinook) which cannot express an abstract idea, and the use of which only throws ridicule on sacred things, and still call such work spreading the truths of Christianity?" In other words, what good was a missionary in the North Pacific, in Duncan's phrase, who could apply the sacrament but not a mustard plaster? Dall also observed that Indians were fond of tobacco, "and for a pipeful apiece you may baptize a whole tribe."

Duncan told Ridley the new Metlakatla church had been deliberately situated outside C.M.S. property so that he could avoid "sectarian" demands in any showdown with the Society. He was planning to introduce a modified version of the communion service to the Indians, Duncan said. It was to be a simple, emblematic form of an evening meal or social feast and would not be administered by a priest. Neither Ridley nor the C.M.S. was receptive to the idea, however. There was another disagreement with Ridley over Duncan's reluctance to preach to the natives in their own tongue. The bishop declared his intention to quickly learn Tsimshian so that he could translate the Book of Common Prayer.

Soon after arriving at Metlakatla, Ridley complained about the dangers of canoe travel and launched a public appeal for funds to purchase a small vessel to visit the mission's outports. Collison told him he should have it built in Metlakatla, but Ridley insisted on placing his order in Victoria, where the *Evangeline* was launched in August of 1880 with suitable fanfare. Bishop Hills' wife broke the traditional bottle of champagne across the bow. The *Evangeline* proved to be underpowered, however, and could not be used on the rivers. She had sails for auxiliary power at sea.[18]

Meanwhile, Duncan asked W. J. Macdonald to raise a $6,000 loan from his businessmen friends in Victoria so that *he* could purchase a small steamer, an all-purpose vessel for the cannery and other mission chores. "They may be as sure of their money returning as they can be of any business transaction in the world," Duncan wrote confidently. Macdonald was now acting as Duncan's business representative in Victoria following the bankruptcy of his agent for 15 years, J. Englehardt, who was accused of fraudulently misusing mortgage funds. Duncan also alleged that Englehardt had misappropriated $4,000 of the mission's secular fund which had been forwarded to purchase goods but were deposited instead in the agent's own bank account. He was never able to recoup the loss, despite a number of bitter, threatening letters to Englehardt.

The agent was partly a victim of the times, which were hard in Victoria in 1880. The capital was losing out to the new trade patterns. Steamers from San Francisco now went directly to New Westminster with freight and passengers. Unemployed men in Victoria left with their families to find work in the mines or on the railroad. There were many empty houses in the city.

England was also in the grip of a recession, and the Society informed its missions that funds were low. It was able to find $2,000, however, for Ridley to build a new house at Metlakatla. Duncan tried to persuade the bishop to make his headquarters in Fort Simpson, but without success. In addition to his house grant, Ridley received a salary almost three times that of Duncan. In 1880 he was paid $2,000; Tomlinson and Collison received $1,200, which included allowances for a wife and children; Hall and Schutt got $1,000; while bachelors Duncan and Sneath were paid $750.

Hall was ready at last to admit defeat at Fort Rupert. During the two years he had spent there, the natives had been away a total of 14 months, leaving him with little to do. The people all seemed poor. Hall said George Hunt agreed with him that Alert Bay, as the central gathering place for the area tribes, would be a better site for a mission. There was a good beach, lots of firewood, and the

---

[18] Ridley, William. *Snapshots from the North Pacific.* Longmans, Green, 1904.

Nimpkish River opposite was full of salmon. He proposed to the C.M.S. that it buy 160 acres there.

Duncan claimed Hall had wanted to establish a Metlakatla-type mission at Fort Rupert but had been overruled by Ridley, who supported the move to Alert Bay. The bishop had been taken in by the "flatteries and promises" of the white traders. Duncan's prediction that it would prove a poor site for a mission proved correct. Hall had a difficult time for the next 30 years.

Relations between Ridley and Duncan were increasingly strained as the bishop began exercising more control over mission affairs. The tension spread through the staff. "Disturbing causes are at work for our mission staff are not working happily or harmonious-ly," Duncan wrote in his journal in August of 1880. Sneath was stung by criticism from Ridley and returned to Masset in a huff. Tomlinson was so outraged at Ridley's order to leave Ankitlast and set up a new mission at Skeena Forks that he left for England to lodge a protest with the C.M.S. Schutt was left in charge of Kincolith, where he was discouraged by the lack of unity among the Nishgas.

Collison grudgingly went to Skeena Forks to hold the ground temporarily against the invading Methodists. He complained to Duncan that Tomlinson had acted impetuously in rushing off to England, and should have started to build on land near the Forks which had been offered by merchant Thomas Hankin. Collison said he did not blame the Methodists for expanding into the area because "every village up the Skeena is open and unoccupied." In November Ridley bought four acres at the Forks for $500, a price which the Society protested was too high. The committee informed him that high-level discussions were to be held in England with the Methodists in an effort to reach a "mutual understanding" on their respective areas in the province.

In a surprising move, the committee upheld Tomlinson's protest and told him to return to Ankitlast and carry on with his farming, which the C.M.S. naively hoped would lead to an "agricultural Metlakatla." Another ordained missionary would be sent to the Forks. The committee also told Tomlinson that any land he acquired near Ankitlast should be purchased with C.M.S. funds and become the Society's property. It objected to a missionary having large land holdings for his own use. Later, when Tomlinson was on his own, he acquired a 999-year lease on 200 acres which he vainly tried to transfer to his native converts.

The Society decreed that in future the Metlakatla mission should be governed by a committee of staff workers chaired by Ridley and a separate finance committee headed by Duncan. The first committee meeting in July of 1881 was to decide the future of the mission. Present were Tomlinson, Collison, Hall, Schutt, Duncan and Ridley. After the latter two withdrew, the others voted to ask Duncan to stay on. In a secret ballot it was also decided to advise the C.M.S. to leave Metlakatla as a lay mission under Duncan without clerical supervision. One of the missionaries, presumably Tomlinson, cast a vote in favour of Metlakatla being given complete independence from any church authority.

Backed by this vote of confidence, Duncan wrote the Society a few weeks later with a detailed defence of his position, particularly his opposition to the communion service for the natives. "A missionary should study the people amongst whom he labours (and) have nothing whatever to do with the ranks, dignities or adornments of ecclesiasticism." His duty was to "give his people a clear and intelligent view of the fundamental verities of the Gospel." Duncan was concerned that, through impatience or outside pressure, the missionaries might "prematurely introduce them to higher religious profession than their religious experience and intelligence would warrant." He insisted that exposure to the "externals" of religion would lead them to fanaticism, followed by apathy and indifference after the novelty had worn off. Since it was difficult to determine which natives were ready to receive communion, it would be better to defer it altogether. To restrict the service to some would cause disunity in the community, Duncan said.

Four years later Duncan expanded on his reasons for withholding communion from the Indians. "I believe I know more about the Indians than (the C.M.S.) do and that I know what is suitable and what is not suitable for the Indians in public worship," he wrote. The law treated the natives as wards of the government who could be fined for drinking the smallest amount of wine. "Does not this suggest at least adopting a wise precaution before admitting the Indians to the Lord's Table?" The church offers them the very thing the law forbids them to take, and "this anomaly stares the Indian in the face." Duncan's point was well taken, but it was yet another example of his selectivity in invoking the laws which suited his purposes. At the same time he was insisting that the Indian Act did not apply to the Metlakatlans because they were civilized, he was hiding behind it.

Duncan told the C.M.S. he realized the Church of England and the Society could not sanction the simplicity of style and method that he favoured and that was why he had suggested to the recent staff meeting that the Metlakatla church be free to work out its own destiny. The natives should be trusted to establish their own church organization, he said, glossing over the fact that it was actually *his* organization and he had done little to develop independent native preachers.

Under the proposed arrangement, Duncan said, the mission would retain a "sympathetic relationship" with the Society but there would be no financial ties. Metlakatla was in the unique position among C.M.S. missions of being able to fund its own activities. "The industries I have already started and others now developing will secure ample provision in the future for all expenses connected with religion."

Duncan followed this letter with another in October in which he said he did not want to have anything more to do with Ridley, "for I have come to consider him an enemy to Metlakatla . . . I cannot trust him." He then restated his own religious views and lectured the C.M.S. against interfering when it did not know the facts. Missionary societies should not have an "over-weening confidence" in their own church system, he said. Sectarianism had become the bane of Christianity, and there were special reasons at Metlakatla for deviating from the usual procedures.

When the C.M.S. received a report of the local committee's vote for Metlakatla remaining a lay mission, its answer was a firm no, coupled with an invitation to Duncan to come "home" to discuss the situation. It did not understand that home for Duncan now was not England but Metlakatla. The Society wrote Ridley at the same time informing him of its decision, and enclosed a letter of dismissal to be given Duncan if he refused to go.

Duncan was in Victoria in early 1882 when his letter from the C.M.S. arrived. He had instructed the post office to intercept his Metlakatla mail and deliver it to the Cridge household, where he was staying. He promptly wrote the Society that he was too busy buying equipment for the new cannery and could not leave until it had been assembled at Metlakatla, possibly in late spring or early summer. He was somewhat offhand in his reply because he correctly surmised the Society would not yet have received his long letter written in August outlining his position. He assumed that when it had been studied there might be no need for a conference in London.

146

Ridley, meanwhile, received his C.M.S. letter with its fateful enclosure thinking Duncan would not get his letter until he returned to Metlakatla. Excited by the prospect of Duncan's ouster, he met the boat from Victoria and accosted Duncan on the beach while he was supervising the unloading and before he would have a chance to go through the mail. The bishop demanded a meeting. Duncan curtly brushed him off and went on working. After about an hour he went coolly to the Mission House where he found Ridley pacing about. Duncan told him he had already advised the Society he could not come at that time, but the bishop replied that he had not been invited but "summoned" to London. When Duncan disdainfully refused to change his mind, Ridley thrust the C.M.S. notice at him. "With the deepest pain and sorrow," it read, "the Committee has come to the conclusion that, in such a contingency, they have no course to pursue, but to take the necessary steps for dissolving your connection with the Society."

When all the mail was sorted that day it was found there were other letters bearing on the tense situation, but any chance for compromise had been lost. The C.M.S. had received Duncan's long defence of his policies and felt there might still be time to work out a solution. Ridley found too late a letter from the Society telling him to withhold the letter severing its ties with Duncan. Belated attempts to rescind the dismissal failed. The final rupture had taken place. The Society's clumsiness and Ridley's impetuousness could not be undone. Duncan was now on his own. The final battle for control of Metlakatla had begun.

Chapter 13

Scandalous Charges

WHEN DUNCAN TOLD THE INDIANS what had happened, they quickly rallied to his support. A house was prepared for him in the village and his possessions were moved from the Mission House within a few hours. Ridley also packed that afternoon and left in the evening on the steamer's return journey to Victoria. Concerned that he might have acted too hastily, he had decided to go to London to present his story to the C.M.S.

Fewer than 50 of the more than 1,000 residents of Metlakatla stayed with Collison, left in charge by Ridley as the official C.M.S. representative. Duncan dismissed them as relatives and supporters of three "would-be-chiefs" jealous and humiliated over the influence the Church Elders had acquired in the community. The group was now attempting, through Collison and the Society, to regain lost power. The C.M.S. was allied with "self-seeking malcontents" against him, Duncan declared.

On their own initiative, the natives nailed boards over the doors and windows of the church to keep Collison out. They were determined now to build up an independent Christian church with Duncan and invite neighbouring tribes to join. It was also decided not to use the C.M.S. school building for the time being, but to hold classes in a native house. A new teacher, a Mr. Chantrell, stayed with Duncan, although he had been offered a salary increase by Ridley.

Duncan told the Society in March of 1882 it never occurred to him that the proposal to travel to England for a conference was a summons and not an invitation. He had informed Ridley of his letter to the committee on the matter, but this information was disregarded by the bishop. "He threw the letter at me with so much apparent self-satisfaction and triumph as if he had been dealing a last deadly blow to an enemy." Under the circumstances, Duncan said, he had no choice but to follow his present course.

Secretary Charles Fenn said the Society regretted Duncan had "opted" for breaking away, ignoring the fact he had been dismissed. Fenn tried to explain the letter mix-up and Ridley's rash action, but was not convincing. He also objected to Duncan's reference to Ridley as an "enemy" of Metlakatla. "He has always written in the kindest tone of yourself and your work." The secretary then proceeded to seal the issue by declaring the C.M.S. was bound to the Church of England form of communion and could not accept Duncan's modified version. This was one point on which Duncan was determined never to compromise.

Duncan's next step was to consult a lawyer in Victoria on the legal aspects of separation. Could the C.M.S. claim possession of the church if it was not on its property or built with its funds? The church had never been consecrated or formally turned over to the Society. The lawyer said that under the 1880 Indian Act, reserve land and buildings upon it, including a church, were vested in the Crown for the benefit of the Indians. Therefore the C.M.S. could not claim it. Duncan asked about his store. Since there was doubt whether the building was on reserve or Society land, the lawyer said, it should be moved onto the reserve.

Collison, meanwhile, made his unhappiness apparent by asking the C.M.S. to send him to the Nass or anywhere else it thought fit. "Perhaps you may know of a better plan," he added plaintively. "If so I will be happy to adopt it if only it will tend to promote unity, peace and concord." He was caught in the middle of a fight between two dogmatic, stubborn men.

Dr. Powell received a complaint that native constables were parading around the village armed with guns, threatening Ridley supporters. He urged Duncan to put a stop to the intimidation. The constables must be warned they would lose their jobs if they abused their position, Powell said.

Duncan attempted to maintain business as usual. He hired a cannery manager from Oregon and ordered tins, labels and machinery for the coming salmon season. The first shipment of Metlakatla canned salmon was loaded on the *Otter* in August of 1882 and transferred in Victoria to a ship bound for England.

Senator Macdonald was still acting as business agent in Victoria, but Duncan's prickly manner and determination to squeeze the last penny from every transaction put a strain on their friendship. It almost broke when Duncan attempted to cancel a sale of furs that Macdonald had negotiated. He complained the price was too low because Macdonald had been misled by an H.B.C. appraisal which had caused him to sell to a freelance buyer. The furs fetched $1,700 and Duncan insisted they were worth at least $500 more. He threatened a lawsuit against the buyer but Macdonald said it was too late because the shipment had already left the country. The senator was also concerned about the publicity that would arise from such a court action. "However strongly I might be convinced that I was right—I certainly would not for the sake of $500 allow you to go into court, where I would be obliged to give testimony in opposition to yours." He would rather make up the difference himself, Macdonald said in a rare expansive gesture.

In August a petition was presented to Collison asking him not to use the school building. He had insisted it was C.M.S. property despite being on Indian land. Duncan said it was his duty as magistrate to inform Collison that the situation was "more serious than you imagine—and if once a breach of the peace occurs there is no saying what sad result will follow." Duncan was clearly abusing his position as magistrate, but Collison gave way. It was left to the provincial cabinet to decide which faction should have the use of the school.

Tomlinson remained at Ankitlast throughout the spring and summer before coming down the Skeena in August to see Duncan. He intended leaving the C.M.S. within a year. "The line of action they have taken at Metlakatla if continued settles that question as I could not even silently acquiesce in it." Tomlinson was concerned, however, about surviving with no income to support a growing family. Ridley told the C.M.S. Tomlinson was in debt to Duncan over the sawmill at Kincolith, but it had been transferred to him at no cost.

After his return to Ankitlast, Tomlinson reported to the C.M.S. that Metlakatla appeared calm. Ridley and Collison still had no more than 40 or 50 supporters hoping for "worldly gains." Tomlinson denied that Duncan was manipulating the Indians. The natives' expressions of regret at the separation were genuine, he said, and their desire to form their own church was in line with previous C.M.S. policy. They should not be stopped by a minority supported by the Society. The majority were native Christians who did not have to be communicants. Tomlinson said Duncan's stand against administering the Lord's Supper to the Indians was proper. It was not a matter of the Tsimshians' ignorance, but of their immaturity. Otherwise, Tomlinson asked, why did the church wait until children were 15 or 16 before letting them receive the sacrament? He denied the Metlakatlans had not been well instructed in religious matters. Bishop Bompas admitted he had never seen such intelligent use of the Bible in other missions, Tomlinson said, and the Indians did not need written translations.

Tomlinson's letter expressed deeply held convictions and reflected the man—eloquent, passionate, sincere. Critical of the new C.M.S. leadership, he said it was easy to sit in a Salisbury Square office and issue directives for a faraway place the deputies knew nothing about. Tomlinson invoked the name of Henry Venn, who he said had encouraged Duncan in his unique methods. Duncan always kept the Society informed of his progress and never worked in secret. Tomlinson ended his letter to the Society bitterly. "You have nearly succeeded in accomplishing what neither hardships, trials, difficulties or disappointments could do—you have nearly killed my missionary zeal."

Nearly. Despite the hardships at Ankitlast, Tomlinson was prepared to go it alone next spring. He was butchering all his livestock for meat to last the winter. Tomlinson considered leaving his family in Victoria while he returned to Ireland to get a medical diploma, but that was not to be.

Powell informed Collison in the fall the school building appeared to be the property of the C.M.S. because it was erected with Society funds. He said Ridley's faction could use the school, but it might be necessary to apply to a magistrate (presumably someone other than Duncan) for protection. Although the government continued to pay the salary of Duncan's teacher, a Mr. Chantrell, Powell told Duncan his people would have to put up their own building on the reserve if they didn't want to go to Ridley's school. The provincial cabinet expressed regret over the feud splitting the community but said it would not intervene except to protect people and property, ignoring the fact that possession of property was a key issue in the dispute.

Cridge and Macdonald visited Metlakatla in July and the senator told a Victoria audience on his return that Ridley was "useless" there. Addressing Cridge's congregation, Macdonald said it had been a mistake to send a bishop to Caledonia, where there were so few whites. Church dignitaries, he observed, were "generally fonder of power and authority than of performing simple missionary work." Ridley's offer to grant Duncan a trade monopoly at Metlakatla—which in effect he already possessed— was an insulting attempt at bribery, the senator said.

Angered by Macdonald's attack, Ridley said Macdonald was not a disinterested observer of Metlakatla, but had a large financial stake in the community's future. He was the main source of capital for Duncan's business enterprises, the bishop said. When Macdonald retorted he had nothing to do with Duncan's trade, "more than helping all I can, without fee or reward," the bishop called on Collison to show the senator was straying from the truth. "I am prepared to state on oath," Collison said, "that Mr. Duncan's accounts show that he has been borrowing thousands of dollars from Mr. Macdonald at 12 per cent, and the same books show that this interest was duly paid." Macdonald admitted later to the C.M.S. that he had lent Duncan money "to finish some useful work."

Ridley also dashed off a vitriolic privately-printed 12-page pamphlet which said Duncan was no longer an ornament to the missionary cause.[19] "Instead of developing the noble work he reared, he is damaging it," he wrote. The status-conscious bishop also referred disparagingly to Duncan's "common day school education" and career as a mere tannery clerk.

But the pamphlet became a notorious document not for these petty attacks, but because Ridley went on to portray Duncan as a sadistic man with a whip who presided over a town seething with sexual shenanigans. Metlakatla had at times been referred to as "the sacred city." Ridley's little scandal sheet made it seem a frontier Peyton Place.

The pamphlet's full title was deceptive: "Senator Macdonald's Misleading Account of His Visit to Metlakatla Exposed by the Bishop of Caledonia." The real target, of course, was Duncan. Ridley put into print for the first time the innuendos circulated by Duncan's critics. Presiding as house-master of a bevy of Indian maidens, and his open use of corporal punishment, had made the pious Duncan an inviting target for gossip. Ridley now attempted to give the rumours credibility.

To Macdonald's description of Metlakatla as a "happy village," Ridley snorted: "Happy village indeed, where men and women have been publicly flogged for sins the flogged retorted on the flogger! Happy village! Where men and women have been forced

---

[19] Ridley, William. *Senator Macdonald's Misleading Account of His Visit to Metlakatla, Exposed by the Bishop of Caledonia.* Victoria, 1882. Provincial Archives of B.C., Victoria.

to marry against their will, and at the conclusion of the dark ceremony the terror-stricken bridegrooms torn from the brides and thrust into horrid prison cells! When after weeks of unlawful imprisonment, they were released and went home, the home was empty. Before their own release, constables had escorted their brides into the magistrate's presence, and they were hurried in the darkness, without warrant or trial, into the very cells from which, a quarter of an hour before, their husbands had been set free." Such cruelty was so common, said Ridley, it caused no surprise or outrage in the village.

The pamphlet contained allegations of sexual misconduct by the Indians as well as Duncan. Noting that Macdonald's report of "many of the prominent men" making speeches during his visit to Metlakatla, Ridley commented: "This was in the church, and the most prominent was known to Mr. D as a notorious seducer, one of his acknowledged paramours being that paragon of excellence who 'never did anything wrong.'"

Ridley even implied that Macdonald and Duncan were giving liquor to the Indians to win their support. A number of Haidas from Masset had visited Metlakatla during Macdonald's stay and "feasted" at his expense. "I found them all drunk and loud in their praise of Mr. D. . . . I do not think anyone grudges him his drunken sympathizers, but everyone will cry shame on the man depraved enough . . . to set the heathen against the only persons able to send and support teachers among them."

Among other crimes, Duncan was accused of working on Sundays at his cannery while objecting to others doing the same on the Skeena; improperly seizing C.M.S. funds before he left the Society and hiding his action by slicing out 12 pages of the account books; deliberately keeping the natives in ignorance; lowering the office of magistrate by imposing arbitrary processes and penalties; and holding out the "pleasure" of inflicting cruel punishments to win the loyalty of the constables.

It was a stunning litany of misconduct. Ridley claimed to have confronted Duncan "on his inhuman cruelty, of which he seemed unconscious." And out of loyalty, the bishop said, Collison had tried to conceal the scandals.

At first, Duncan and Macdonald replied in angry generalities. Ridley had written the pamphlet "for the purpose of trampling me in the mire," Duncan sputtered. In an agitated letter to the C.M.S. in November of 1882, he fired off all the epithets in his well-stocked arsenal. The pamphlet was monstrous, cruel, untruthful, libellous, spiteful. Ridley was hypocritical and unscrupulous. Duncan wondered why, if he had behaved as ruthlessly as Ridley claimed, so many natives from surrounding tribes had moved to Metlakatla over the years, raising the population from 50 to 1,100.

His policy toward prisoners, he said, was to "restore and save the person while punishing the sin." For a long time the people were reluctant to help him discipline wrongdoers because they feared becoming victims of revenge. Gradually, however, they came to appreciate the peace and security which the laws and village regulations provided. Duncan said nearby tribes which copied many of the Metlakatla rules were more severe in their punishment of violators. The means adopted to suppress vice had grown up naturally, Duncan insisted, and had not been enforced cruelly or vindictively. There had been no bloodshed in the 20 years of Metlakatla's existence. One reason for this remarkable fact was that marital problems, particularly adultery, were dealt with peacefully. There was no community in the province of the same population with so little crime or need for a jail, Duncan said.

Duncan was contradictory in his attitude toward the Indians' treatment of their young. Often he would criticize parents for being too cruel, for throwing children roughly to the ground when they misbehaved. At other times he complained the children were indulged and parents did not punish enough.

When he attempted to deal with the matter of corporal punishment, Duncan's admissions and evasions did not serve him well. But it must be remembered how common was the use of the rod and whip at that time. As Duncan pointed out, flogging was prevalent everywhere in the world, "and is not yet obsolete in the Bishop's own enlightened country." Sailors in the Royal Navy were whipped for such minor offences as stealing a pocket handkerchief. He had seen a sailor flogged "with a very cruel kind of whip on board one of Her Majesty's ships and by the order of a very humane captain now an admiral and for much less an offence than were the offences for which the Indians received a few lashes with a rope end."

Corporal punishment was certainly not unusual in the colony. James Anderson of Victoria, the son of A. C. Anderson, described in his memoirs watching as one of the fort employees was flogged on the H.B.C. jetty. The man was stripped, bound to a post and lashed on his back with the cat-o'-nine-tails. Anderson looked on, "not for a moment thinking it cruel, accustomed as we were to the cruel."[20]

Although Duncan used the term "flogging" in his journal to cover both forms of punishment, he made a distinction between whipping with the flayed end of a half-inch manila rope and administering the switch or strap to errant house-boys, school children and the teen-age boarders. He had nothing similar to the infamous cat-o'-nine-tails.

He had used the rope on only five men, Duncan said, three of them convicted of attempted murder and two of adultery. There was no cruelty or bloodshed involved in the punishment, he insisted, "but we would make him sing. We made him smart." In the adultery cases the cuckolded husbands would accept no lesser punishment, he said. In common with most whip-wielders, Duncan claimed his victims later expressed their gratefulness to him for his efforts to "save them," and they were now "warmest friends."

In one instance a man convicted of attempted rape threatened to kill the man who whipped him. Duncan ordered the man blindfolded and told his constables not to talk. He then pointed to one of them to start whipping, but the constable was so afraid he began to whimper. Duncan promptly picked up the whip, told the prisoner he was about to administer the punishment, and did so. The father of the victim had wanted to kill the man, Duncan said, so he had actually spared his life.

As to Ridley's accusation that women had been whipped, Duncan said this was an old slander, "too sensational for the Bishop to reject so he revives it." Duncan admitted only that 16 years previously he had punished two girls with a strap for stealing from the Gribbells. One had been guilty of a previous offence. The strapping had been carried out in Doolan's presence. Duncan blamed Gribbell for the false report that the girls had been "flogged on their naked backs."

Duncan concluded firmly: "I never did attempt to take the life of a fellow creature, I have never cohabited with any woman married or single in my life, I have never robbed anyone of anything that I am aware of since I arrived at the age of intelligence."

If Duncan was upset by the pamphlet, Macdonald was outraged. "What an unscrupulous black-hearted dog he is," the senator said of Ridley in a letter to Duncan. He was also frustrated because the

---

[20] *Diary*, the unpublished memoirs of James Anderson. P.A.B.C.

155

bishop refused to debate his allegations. Macdonald's angry notes to the newspapers went unanswered.

In the same letter, however, Macdonald referred to the interest owing on a loan he had given Duncan and said he needed it now because of his poor financial position. He also suggested that Duncan switch the loan to the firm of Turner-Beeton, presumably for the sake of appearances in the wake of the Ridley accusations. Turner-Beeton had taken over as Duncan's agent in Victoria.

Ridley was not the only one spreading salacious tales about Duncan. Early in the new year Kate Macdonald, wife of the senator, wrote Duncan that Mrs. Collison had been mischief-making in Victoria. "She has been telling me most mean gossiping yarns as when she saw you with her own eyes—whipping a poor Indian girl in the open square until you could hardly stand over her." Marion Collison must have known she would set the teacups rattling in Victoria's drawing-rooms with that kind of chat. "They are a low vulgar set," Kate Macdonald sniffed, "coarse in their speech and ways."

Whatever Mrs. Macdonald thought of Duncan's accusers, their allegations of sexual misconduct were to haunt him all his life, and beyond the grave. Ridley's nasty little pamphlet was so much a factor in tarnishing Duncan's reputation it must be examined closely.

First, the accuser. Over the next five years, the impetuous, excitable Ridley proved to be a most unreliable witness. His descriptions of incidents and events were shown on a number of occasions to be exaggerated and untrue. He was willing to believe everything anyone told him about Duncan, and became so consumed by hatred he lost all perspective. Duncan, on the other hand, who could be so suspicious and exasperating in his dealings with others, behaved with comparative restraint toward Ridley. He was confident the bishop would discredit himself by his excesses.

It is impossible to know whether Duncan was celibate all his life, although that is strongly indicated. It is most unlikely, however, that he fathered any illegitimate children or had a sexual relationship with a native girl or woman. He could not have retained the respect and confidence of the Indians, particularly the converts to Christianity, if he had behaved improperly himself. His rigid attitude toward sexual misconduct made it impossible for him to transgress the rules without losing his standing.

The Tsimshians were a sensuous people but not especially

promiscuous. A study of British Columbia Indian mores concluded, "although the rules regarding sex had wider areas of permissiveness than the rules of sex in middle-class Victorian England, they also had wide areas of absolute prohibition and in general husband-wife fidelity was the standard."[21] The authors say it was "unfortunate" for the Indians that they came in contact with the whites at that particular time in history. "In other centuries the two groups of cultures would have been much closer in some of their values related to sex." But because of the Indians' lack of puritanical restraints on sex compared to Victorian-era standards, the women became the prey of white men who could find few unmarried women of their own race. The missionaries, besides trying to impose their own rigid sexual standards on the natives, also felt responsible for protecting them from the depredations of their European countrymen.

In this regard, Duncan was more zealous than his counterparts elsewhere in the province. The circumstances of his own life were obviously a factor. The humiliation of being born out of wedlock was something that a religious man with a deep sense of sin could never forget. It also probably explains why Duncan remained a bachelor. This background, compounded by the puritanical standards of the day, made Duncan uncomfortable, almost irrational, on the subject of sex. Repressing his own needs with great difficulty, he expected others, especially the young, to do likewise.

Duncan was concerned most about the teen-age girls. He told the C.M.S.: "Those most in danger from the coming flood of profligate miners are the big girls... I deem it my duty to take them under my special care. I see no better plan than taking a number into my house, feeding, clothing, and instructing them, until they find husbands from among the young men of our own party."

This was the decision that resulted in the first gossip about Duncan and led to the widespread opinion that he was immoral. The rumours soon got back to Duncan, but he was determined to carry on. When he first heard of whispering by some of the natives, Duncan called them together to speak about "the evil and slanderous reports I have heard respecting me." After his stout denials of wrongdoing, they begged him to forget what he had heard, Duncan said.

[21] Hawthorn, H. B., Belshaw, C. S., and Jamieson, S. M. *The Indians of British Columbia.* University of Toronto Press, 1960.

In 1867 Duncan complained to the Society about its failure to appoint a female missionary to Metlakatla and expressed regret over the problems he had encountered with the wives of the married men. "It is not the matter of household management which calls so loudly for a married lady to come here, but rather the fact of my being unmarried; but whatever may be thought or said by the outside world disparagingly on that score, in the mission itself nothing of the kind is thought or heard of. I have the full confidence of the Indians around me, and especially of the parents of the children I protect." There is no reason to doubt that claim.

Duncan's object in taking the girls under his wing was not restricted to preserving their virtue in the face of threats from ardent village youths and unscrupulous whites. As early as 1859 he began sewing classes for the girls at Fort Simpson. His goal was to make them good homemakers and desirable Christian wives for the most upstanding young men. He saw this as an effective way of winning more converts to his cause.

Duncan also undoubtedly gained vicarious pleasure from having the girls in his home. Their gaiety, songs and laughter offered relief from the drabness of his life. In an article written for a missionary publication, Edward Cridge described the happy atmosphere in the Mission House brought about by the girls' presence. Duncan had told them a story about a man with a permanently twisted neck who had fallen and hurt himself. A friendly stranger helped him up and tried to straighten his neck, to which the man cried out, "Hold hard there! Born so, born so!" A few evenings later a guest made a remark about the Indians' peculiar gait, which Duncan interpreted to the girls for their amusement. One exclaimed, in English, "Born so!", which was immediately taken up as a chant by the rest, some of whom jumped up and caricatured their walk.

Duncan held tea-parties at which he would entertain the girls with scientific tricks, shows, jokes and riddles, as well as his melodious voice and concertina. The attention, admiration and giggling flirtation gratified his vanity if not his lust. He had not changed much from the self-conscious young man in Beverley, anxious to have the shy glances of the "young ladies" in church, but afraid of intimacy.

Duncan's journals reveal the torments of repression—rages and black moods of despair which frequently led him to pick up the whip. The beating of his houseboy at Fort Simpson and the contriteness that followed became a pattern. But Duncan was more restrained with the girl boarders and the lurid scene described by Mrs. Collison was an obvious exaggeration. For one thing, a strap was used on the girls and not the rope whip. The strap *was* used often, however, especially in the decade starting in 1865 when Duncan took the first female boarders into the Mission House with him.

On an October Sunday after church service in 1865, Duncan spoke to the older boys and girls, separately of course, on the evils of fornication. In November he placed one of the 15 boarders, Margaret, in "prison" for two days and a night for pilfering, and added a "severe beating." In this instance prison meant confinement in a large cupboard in the Mission House. The following journal entry appeared January 10, 1866: "I had to flog Rebeckah very severely last night, and after I had flogged her she very piteously cried 'Thank you Sir'. Her offence was sending a message to a young man in Legaic's house and calling him to speak to him— unknown to me. She seems truly sorry and has been crying very much yesterday and today." Rebeckah had also been visited by her father and aunt, who "both talked severely to her."

On March 17, 1866, Duncan sentenced the first jail prisoner to a whipping, 20 lashes for a former slave who had attempted to rob the store at Fort Simpson. He also talked to him about the biblical story of Joseph and the slave.

One of the bigger boys was "severely flogged" June 5 for an undisclosed offence. The punishment was administered in front of other boys and the "young scamp" was left tied to the post all day before being confined to his house for a week. June 8: "I had to flog two girls very severely—one for 'sin' and the other for being an accomplice and confidante. They were also confined to the mission house for a few days." June 25: "Had to flog six children today— three boys for playing on Sunday—two girls for playing and quarrelling in school after I went out—one girl for neglecting to watch the flock and permitting a young deer to hide itself."

In a case involving a man who had threatened someone with a gun, the town council voted on his punishment. It was a hung jury—14 wanted the man whipped and 14 favoured taking the weapon away and placing him on probation. Duncan cast the deciding vote for probation, which was to be supervised by three men. He also felt it necessary to lecture his constables on their duty to serve the public and save the offender. "I find I have to guard them against too great severity on the culprit."

159

Duncan devised another way of bringing sinners to heel, less severe than flogging but effective in its own way. It involved raising a black flag on the village pole, signifying that someone was violating the rules. If they didn't already know who the culprit was, the villagers would make inquiries and soon everyone was whispering his name. The offender usually left town. That was the course taken by Lequeenesh, one of Duncan's most troublesome natives, after the black flag was hoisted because he was "living in sin" with Hannah.

The people constantly besieged Duncan with their problems and domestic troubles. The smallest digression was confessed to him and he patiently listened and offered advice. He persuaded one man not to take revenge on someone who had wronged him. The man promised Duncan he would not resort to violence but would wait for compensation in property. Duncan noted approvingly that the natives possessed "a great tenderness of conscience." He showed his tolerant side a few weeks later in reuniting a native couple. He could not marry them because they were not Christians, but counselled them "and they promised to live well and truly together."

In cases of wife-beating, Duncan put the husband in jail until the wife asked for him to be freed. The wife had to cook his meals while he was imprisoned and have them delivered by their children. Sometimes Duncan would have a constable lock a child up with the father for a time. It was a crafty but apparently effective means of bringing about a reconciliation.

When one of his star boarders, Eliza, was married to Andrew, Duncan was as proud as a parent. During the Christmas holiday he gave a party for his 14 boarders and 10 "graduates" of the preparatory school for brides. He recorded his pleasure in his diary. "The old boarders have now 7 children all healthy and strong. The 24 tonight round the fire present a spectacle very cheering—very compensative for all the trouble and slander one has endured for their sakes." A year later there was another party with eleven ex-boarders and their eight infants. Again Duncan was ecstatic. "It was a glorious sight to me to see those healthy happy young wives and mothers all around me." The strappings evidently had not diminished the girls' affection for their teacher.

Duncan at age 20.

Duncan in middle age, around 40.

An older Duncan, about 80.

Church at Old Metlakatla.

Court house and jail at Old Metlakatla.

Metlakatla, British Columbia in 1881, looking west toward Mission Point, church and cannery.

Row of houses, Metlakatla, British Columbia, west of Mission Point.

Corps of constables, Metlakatla, British Columbia.

Councilmen, Metlakatla, Alaska. Top row, left to right: Fred Verney, Charles Brendible, William Duncan, Jacob Scott, Frank Allen. Centre row, left to right: James Leask, Paul Mather, Benjamin Haldane, Edmund Verney. Bottom row, left to right: Sam Auriol, Sidney Campbell, Mark Hamilton, Adolphus Calvert, Henry Ridley, Sr.

First bandstand at Metlakatla, Annette Island, Alaska.

Brass Band at New Metlakatla.

Robert Tomlinson

Edward Marsden

Henry Wellcome

Duncan, right, and Sheldon Jackson, front, with boys bound for Sitka school.

Hilda Minthorn with two Indian girls.

Panoramic view of New Metlakatla.

First huts at New Metlakatla with Tlingit totem in foreground.

William Duncan, late in life, exhibiting to friends for photographing the canvas, hammock, clock, water bottle and accordion used by him on his voyage to Victoria, B.C., in 1856-57. On back of photo: "Taken during 1916-17 visit of H. S. Wellcome by B of K."

William Duncan, about 84 years old. Man on the left is Henry Wellcome. Duncan's cottage in background, 1917.

Loving Cup presentation in 1917.

Duncan in the office/study of his cottage at New Metlakatla.

Last picture of Duncan four days before his death in 1918.

Funeral procession for William Duncan. Sidewalk in front of church. On left: Brendible. Centre: Harry Lang, Jenkins, Van Marter, John Hudson, Thomas Hanbury. On right: partial view of Marsden.

PHOTO CREDITS: Robert Tomlinson, P.A.B.C. (No. 41743); Edward Marsden, courtesy Graduate Theological Union Library, San Anselmo, California; two views of Metlakatla, B.C. looking toward church and cannery, and row of two houses, also corps of constables, all by Edward Dossetter, courtesy Department Library Services, American Museum of Natural History; all other photographs courtesy the Henry Wellcome Collection, National Archives and Records Center, Seattle.

Chapter 14

A Bitter Struggle

THE YEARS 1882 TO 1887 form an unhappy chapter in the history of Metlakatla. If the issues had not been so crucial to the Indians of British Columbia, it could be regarded as a five-year farce. Two English-born churchmen—one a self-important, excitable bishop, the other a sanctimonious, scrappy little missionary with an aversion to authority—locked in a strutting and posturing war of words.

Almost ten to one in support of Duncan, the Tsimshian became so agitated and belligerent at times that he had trouble exercising control. It is commonly assumed that the Indians were manipulated throughout this period by Duncan and Tomlinson for their own purposes. It was not so. The Metlakatlans had their own militant leaders now who could see that the outcome of the struggle would affect their future and that of other tribes.

This was only superficially an ecclesiastical fight. What was involved was the first real battle in the province over Indian rights, particularly land tenure. It was unfortunate that the principal combatants were a pair of prickly churchmen who gave the politicians an excuse to dismiss the whole affair as a tempest in a teepee.

The Indians were growing more aware of the lowly regard in which they were held by the province. Senator Macdonald reported to Duncan in 1882 that some native witnesses and constables sent to Victoria from Metlakatla to testify in a trial had been treated like the prisoners. They were forced to sleep in a jail cell with drunks being held for the night, and fed on the floor like dogs.

Despite the tense situation, Duncan was busy in the summer of 1882 with the cannery and other business concerns. Weary and discouraged, he mused in his journal: "Shall I go on with the cannery or shall I go away?" His salary had been cut off by the

Society; but he noted defiantly that he had never regarded himself as a mere "hireling." Resolving to stay and fight, Duncan took comfort from the fact that it was the church congregation which, unanimously, had asked him to carry on. He knew Ridley and Collison could never receive such an overwhelming vote of confidence.

A barrage of letters containing accusations, ultimatums and threats flew between the two camps. Ridley complained that Collison's house had been barricaded by armed men who shadowed him whenever he stepped out. The bishop also claimed to have heard of threats that his own throat would be cut and the Mission House, which Duncan had evacuated, set afire. Ridley opened a general store on the C.M.S. property and started selling goods at cost, ordering his own people not to shop at Duncan's store. Duncan charged this was an attempt to starve him out.

In late November Duncan's Indians posted a notice on the doors of the jail and the church—a choice of locations symbolic of the whole affair—declaring their intention to establish a new "Christian Church of Metlakatla." No other church would be allowed on the reserve. Buildings belonging to the village were to be removed at once from C.M.S. ground. "Unless you promise to remove your school house from our reserve to the ground granted to the Society by the Government, we shall undertake to take it down and remove material and place the same on the Society's grounds," the notice read.

Ridley and Collison answered that volley with a missive of their own to Duncan. "We have been publicly notified that it is the intention of certain evilly disposed persons to damage the buildings standing on the CMS land. We hereby inform you that we do and shall hold you responsible for any damage that may be done." Later that day, Duncan accused Ridley of standing watch over the schoolhouse during the night with a rifle. "I sincerely beg in the interests of peace that you will not repeat the conduct of carrying firearms during the present excited state of the public mind here. Should you disregard this warning I am afraid that in spite of all I can do to prevent it, the Indians too will arm themselves and angry passions will be then encouraged."

The bishop contemplated that threat for a few days before assuming the stiffly formal stance he favoured: "Bishop Ridley refuses to enter into any pledges or to answer any questions, and he considers you or the Indians have no right to ask what use the

162

Committee intends to make of their buildings." Ridley also fired off a petition of his own signed by 25 followers protesting Duncan's supposed plan to erect a new store on the reserve. Duncan huffily denied such intentions and condemned the "enmity and ingratitude" of his former followers. "If I had wanted to buy land at Metlakatla I could have done it years ago. Instead I secured land for you but you would refuse me a few square yards to erect a building for the benefit of the village if I needed it."

Meanwhile, Senator Macdonald sent a copy of Ridley's scurrilous pamphlet to the C.M.S., protesting the bishop's conduct and the Society's support for him. "We do not at present see our way to quit Metlakatla," the committee answered, "and therefore must defend our position there." The C.M.S. pleaded for efforts "to cultivate a friendly and fraternal spirit between the two congregations, each party taking the most charitable view possible of the motives and conduct of the other."

There was little evidence of either fraternity or charity in Metlakatla as the verbal exchanges escalated to push and shove. When Ridley let it be known he intended to turn the schoolhouse into a church, Duncan and his people took direct action. First they emptied the store and put the goods in some of the native houses, then dismantled the building and markethouse. As the store was being knocked down, Ridley and Collison read the Riot Act. The Indians kept working in the rain.

Ridley sent to Fort Simpson for Magistrate Robert H. Hall, who was not anxious to become involved in the Metlakatla dispute. "I feel convinced that the fault lies not with the Indians," he had written Powell, "but with their leaders, by whose promptings they are led, I fear, into turmoil and acts they would never think of if left to themselves." Hall was also concerned about the effect of the power struggle between Duncan and the bishop on nearby tribes. When the call came from Ridley, he made himself unavailable. Two other magistrates in the area also refused to deal with the bishop's complaint, but came and talked to Duncan. They concurred that there was no riot and also, according to Duncan, agreed the Indians were justified in demanding the school be left unoccupied until the provincial cabinet had made a binding decision, something it had shown no inclination to do.

Hall started out on the short voyage a few days later but almost lost his life when driven into Alaska waters by a winter storm. On eventually reaching Metlakatla he told Ridley he had been wrong in attempting to turn the schoolhouse into a church, but also criticized the Indians for taking the law into their own hands by dismantling the school. The natives were eager to finish the job with their axes and crowbars, however, and Duncan was able to hold them back only by saying he would give Powell all the details of the dispute and ask for a ruling.

The truce was short-lived. A dispute over a drum began innocently enough but soon got out of hand. A group of about 10 young Duncan supporters had bought the drum jointly. Some did not pay their share at the time and one of the co-owners sold it to the bishop's group, which Duncan mocked for "trying hard to raise a little music." The other owners tried to retrieve the drum. Duncan asked Collison to intervene but while the bishop procrastinated and there was no ruling forthcoming on ownership, the drum was still being used. When a young boy in the bishop's faction, caught up in the excitement of Christmas, marched down the village road banging away, tempers flared. Two men seized the drum. Ridley, recently and unwisely named a magistrate by the provincial government, issued warrants for the men. Then, without a hearing, he put them in prison for a week.

Duncan's Indians demanded the pair be tried or freed on bail. If refused, they said they would break open the jail and let the men out. On their way to see the bishop, the delegation met him walking on the road with his wife beside the churchyard. After heated words were exchanged, Ridley struck out at Paul Legaic, a constable and nephew of the late chief, and took a fighting stance. Legaic turned away but two of his companions challenged the bishop, who flailed at them. They hit back. As the Indians milled around, Ridley was pulled away by Collison. The natives ran to the jail and freed the two prisoners.

The bishop's loss of composure in the encounter was condemned by Duncan. "He surely must have been either insane or drunk to have done such a thing at such a time." After sending for Magistrate Hall, who bluntly refused to come this time, Duncan began gathering evidence and vowed to settle the matter on his own. On New Year's Day he mounted a display of force. More than 200 men—councillors, constables, elders and firemen, accompanied by the brass band—marched slowly round the village. The bishop's group spent the day clustered around a small cannon which they fired periodically during the parade and church service.

Meanwhile, Ridley laid charges of assault against the men who had jostled him and sent an urgent plea to Victoria for help. He implied Metlakatla was in a state of anarchy and his life was in danger, as well as those of his wife and some visiting clergymen and their wives. The government could hardly ignore such a plea from a bishop of the Church of England. Since there were no navy vessels available for the relief of Metlakatla, Premier Robert Beaven sent an unprecedented request for assistance to Captain Louis N. Stodder of the U.S. Revenue Cutter *Oliver Wolcott* based at Port Townsend in Washington Territory. After obtaining approval from Secretary of the Treasury Charles Folger, Stodder left for Victoria en route to Metlakatla. As the *British Colonist* fulminated against the use of foreign vessels in domestic disputes, Stodder told Beaven he would not use force "except to repel attacks imminent against white people, and then only at the written request of provincial officers." Boarding the *Wolcott* at Victoria were Indian Superintendent Powell, Fisheries Commissioner Anderson, both empowered as magistrates, and Charles Todd, Superintendent of the Provincial Police.

The *Wolcott* arrived at Metlakatla on January 18. In his report to Folger after the incident, Stodder said he found the Indians greatly agitated. They asked him to take Bishop Ridley away, but Stodder explained to them he had no authority to remove anyone, that his mission was only to protect white people.

Anderson began hearing the case on the 19th. Legaic testified that Ridley struck him when he asked about the two men in jail. The bishop countered that Legaic had been threatening from the beginning and hit him across the face with a stick. Ridley said the blow caused him great pain and kept him in bed for three days. To add insult to physical injury, after the two men had been released from the jail, Legaic removed his hat and made a low sweeping bow of derision toward the bishop. Mrs. Ridley submitted an affidavit to the magistrates in which she said native Daniel Auriol had pushed his hand in her husband's face. Then Legaic had seized the bishop by the shoulders and pushed him back. A "mob" of 150 Indians was milling about, Mrs. Ridley testified. Robert Hewson "savagely struck" the bishop on the arm. Ridley, momentarily forgetting the biblical command to turn the other cheek, hit back at Hewson. At this point the wife of one of the visiting clergymen exclaimed, "They are going to kill the bishop!"

The magistrates were not convinced of the seriousness of the affray. They fined Hewson and Auriol $10 each for assault and decreed that the two prisoners should remain free because their conviction and imprisonment by Ridley had not been preceded by a legal trial.

Captain Stodder was asked by Anderson and Powell to keep the *Wolcott* around until it seemed certain there would be no further trouble. He agreed, but Ridley still was not reassured. The bishop sent a message to Stodder on the 22nd: "I am sorry that it is my humiliating duty to seek from you a place of refuge for the wives and families of British missionaries. I will not enter into the causes of their terror at the prospect of being left behind here on the departure of your vessel. It will be enough for a gentleman and an officer of a chivalrous nation to know that gentlewomen and tender children can look to him alone as able to rescue them from ever accumulating horrors."

Terror, horror, chivalry—it was the prose of a man imagining himself the hero of a Victorian romance. Stodder replied coolly. "I am astonished to learn that you consider the situation dangerous to yourself and colleagues. I had thought that all difficulties of a serious nature had been settled and that the Indians had become quiet." Stodder said Anderson and Powell had assured him there was not the slightest danger. He offered to take the women and children to Ridley's mission house at Fort Simpson. Ridley declined because the house was unfinished and unfurnished, requiring considerable preparation to be made comfortable. He had hoped, he told the captain, to send the ladies to hotels in Victoria. Stodder politely said sorry, but he was not authorized to carry families farther than to a place of safety. In any case, there was no provision for ladies aboard the *Wolcott*.

"We will hope our apprehensions are unfounded," Ridley replied. Stodder sailed from Metlakatla on the 24th, no doubt with a sense of relief at departing such a strange place with its strange inhabitants, both dark and light skinned.

On his way north the captain had told Premier Beaven the B.C. government would be expected to pay for a coastal pilot, fuel costs and mess bills of the *Wolcott*'s officers. On his return, however, Stodder was advised by the U.S. consul in Victoria that when H.M.S. *Osprey* had been called in by the Americans on a peace-keeping mission to Sitka, she had supplied her own fuel and he should do the same. The bill for the other costs, paid by the province, totalled $7,000.

Powell and Anderson dealt with the Metlakatla situation in

their annual reports. Powell said the voluntary departure of either Ridley or Duncan, or both, appeared the only solution. Since Duncan had nine-tenths of the community behind him, "the withdrawal of the Agents of the Society to more congenial headquarters would I think be greatly in the interest of all concerned."

Although Duncan and Senator Macdonald considered Powell to be on Ridley's side, the Indian Commissioner was a grudging admirer of Duncan's accomplishments. In a letter to Sir John A. Macdonald after returning to Victoria on the *Wolcott*, Powell said Duncan's departure "would be a calamity to the residents—the fruit of his many years of marvellous energy and industry would be entirely destroyed and the Indians deprived of a worker whose like, in all probability, they will never see again."

Anderson was among those who blamed Duncan for goading the Indians into demanding ancestral fishing and land rights. His main concern was the economic impact of the dispute on the expanding Skeena River salmon canning industry. "An important fishing and transport trade has been established, all of which will be affected and perhaps imperilled, should the defiant stand of late taken by a party at Metlakatla be suffered to continue," Anderson wrote in his report.

Duncan seemed to have more problems than usual that spring with his native workers. He found them indifferent and careless. When a boom of logs for the sawmill broke apart, he could not rouse the men to chase the drifting timber. They left mailbags untended on the dock. While they were unloading tinplate over the side of the cannery steamer *Princess Louise* to a canoe, one of the cases fell through a woman's hands and landed on other boxes in the canoe, which split apart. Eighteen cases of tea were lost and Duncan was furious.

Duncan complained to Powell that Collison was handing out certificates permitting natives to go to Victoria, after he had attempted to discourage such travel. It was part of Ridley's plan, Duncan said, to gain popularity by criticizing his restraints and promising greater freedom to any natives who switched sides.

Spring put Duncan in a better mood. Powell wrote to say an assortment of garden seeds was on its way by steamer. There was an encouraging letter from George Sneath, who had left the C.M.S. and gone to work for the Presbyterians in the U.S. "You are on the side of truth and equity," he told Duncan. Sneath had seen a copy of Ridley's pamphlet and commented: "I always thought Bishop Ridley very wanting in judgement, but I did not think he was so utterly void of all Christian love as to be able to write such a blackguard production as that." Senator Macdonald wrote that former lieutenant-governor Joseph Trutch, who was close to Sir John Macdonald, had declared that Ridley must leave and he would advise the bishop to do so. Tomlinson reaffirmed his support. "I have no wish to have any conference or correspondence with the Bishop about anything," he wrote. Soon after, Tomlinson moved to Metlakatla to be with Duncan.

Duncan was active with his pen that spring on behalf of the Indians. He appealed to Powell for a government loan to help the natives become shareholders in the Metlakatla cannery. "It is sad to see the Indians as a race are being made mere hewers of wood and drawers of water with the fate before them of soon being little more than mute witnesses of the grasping energy of the white man." Duncan said all the white help he had employed had failed him and he wanted the Indians to take on more responsibility. Powell agreed on the desirability of providing more jobs for the Indians near their homes, but did not commit himself on the loan.

Duncan wrote an open letter to gold miners on the Skeena River, with a copy to Provincial Secretary John Robson, pointing out that the area where gold had been found was the ancient hunting and provision ground of three Tsimshian tribes. "The chiefs and members of these tribes are in no sense opposed to white men mining in their country provided that the Indians who wish to mine are allowed equal liberty and privileges with white men." Duncan said the Indians claimed a special right to mine in the area because one of them had helped a white prospector discover the gold. On the particular creek where mining was about to begin, three or four native families had held exclusive rights. The Indians accepted that some of their privileges would be lost, Duncan said, but they looked to the government for compensation. So far there had been no benefits of any kind for the Skeena Indians that might have reconciled them to encroachments on their ancient preserves. A sum of money "judiciously spent upon these reluctant natives" would ease their irritation and give proof of the government's goodwill, paternal care and justice. It might also smooth the way for settlement of future difficulties, Duncan said. But no one was listening.

In April Duncan was advised his resignation as magistrate and coroner, tendered in January, had been accepted by the government. The attorney-general's department had previously told Duncan and Ridley not to act as magistrates in any matter connected with their dispute. Duncan said Trutch and Anderson had both advised him not to resign, but he decided it would be best. Retired fur trader James McMillan told the government it was making a mistake in cancelling the commission of the "only magistrate who really enjoyed the respect of the natives and commanded their confidence."

When Tomlinson went to Victoria in mid-May to look after some mission business matters, Duncan missed his colleague's support as he wrestled with cannery problems. There were 70 women making nets for the upcoming season to supervise, as well as 150 natives in the cannery and another 42 men out fishing. He was making plans to can clams for export, and there was the ongoing fur trade to look after. When the salmon market dropped sharply in Britain after a botulism scare caused by a faulty tin from the J. H. Todd cannery, Duncan's agent switched to the Eastern Canada market.

If trade was down with England, travel was not. W. J. and Kate Macdonald left London just as Ridley was arriving. They reported to Duncan that Salisbury Square was abuzz with conflicting opinions on how to resolve the Society's festering rebellion in the North Pacific. The committee told Macdonald it planned to send out two men to investigate the situation. One of them was to be Admiral Prevost, who was taken aback when the outspoken Kate declared he was biased in favour of Hills and Ridley. Kate also started to read some of the more lurid passages of Ridley's pamphlet, but the flustered committee members cut her off.

An uneasy calm held for more than a year in Metlakatla. It was broken in September of 1884 with the arrival of a government surveyor, Captain E. E. Shearburne, who had come at Ridley's request. The bishop intended to assert the Society's right to Mission Point by officially surveying the two-acre plot. The Indians protested this attempt "to surreptitiously deal with our property," and warned Shearburne not to proceed. He quickly abandoned the work.

Emboldened by this success, Duncan's supporters advised the bishop he would no longer be allowed use of the schoolhouse. Ridley became alarmed once again and appealed for protection to Andrew Elliott, the former attorney-general and premier who was now both a magistrate and Indian Agent for the district. Elliott proceeded to swear in a number of special constables from the bishop's faction to protect C.M.S. property. Elliott advised Victoria that "a very dangerous state of things exists not only among the Indians of this place, but among those of the entire coast."

There had been a skirmish between Indians and miners at Lorne Creek on the Skeena, and a new C.M.S. church was set afire at Kitkatla. These incidents, coupled with the increasing Indian assertion of land rights, prompted the government in October to launch a formal inquiry into "the causes and sources" of the disturbances at Metlakatla and elsewhere on the northern coast. The three commissioners named were Elliott, Attorney-General Theodore Davie, and Henry Maynard Ball, a former magistrate and gold commissioner.

The commission began its hearings November 12 in Fort Simpson. Robert Hall, the H.B.C. agent and magistrate, testified that the troubles had begun in the winter of 1878. Duncan invited the Fort Simpson Indians to a feast and raised the issue of land rights. Hall said the boundaries of the Tsimshian peninsula reserve adjacent to Metlakatla at first seemed satisfactory to the natives, but they had recently begun to ask for more land. "A few years before that much less would have satisfied them as they did not know anything about it." The message was clear: Duncan was to blame for putting ideas in the Indians' heads.

After hearing Hall, the commissioners moved on to Metlakatla, where they told the Indians assembled in the schoolhouse they had come because "somebody has told the government that the Indians of Metlakatla have been behaving badly, and that other Indians say they will do the same as Metlakatla." The commissioners left no doubt where they stood. Without hearing any evidence, Attorney-General Davie declared the government did not believe the Metlakatla Indians were bad themselves. "The government think the Indians may have had bad teachings; that the Indians would not do bad things unless they had bad teachings." This seemed to confirm Senator Macdonald's warning to Duncan that the government believed the Indians were acting under his direction.

Davie also spelled out the government's policy on Indian land claims. "We are told the Metlakatlans say all the lands belong to the Indians. This is not true. White men who teach this are false to both Indians and whites." All the lands belonged to the Queen, said Davie, but She had told the dominion and provincial governments to be very generous to the Indians. "The reserves are very many and take in the choice of the best lands all over British Columbia." Most Indians were satisfied, the attorney-general said.

The first witness in Metlakatla was Joseph E. White, manager of the cannery at Inverness on the Skeena. White said he had been in the village on business a month before when the natives presented a notice drawn up by the town council addressed to all white men. It warned they would not be allowed to remain until their purpose had been approved. This took place a few days after Captain Shearburne had attempted to survey Mission Point for the bishop, and now all strangers were suspect, White said. He had attended a council session at which the matter was discussed and Duncan spoke out on the sensitivity of the land issue. He quoted Duncan as saying there were only three ways of acquiring property—finding it unused, buying it, or stealing it. The government had not purchased the land from the Indians, Duncan said, it did not find it uninhabited, and did not acquire it by right of conquest, so it must have been stolen. Duncan had warned that the Indians would not allow one inch of their land to be taken away from them. "They would all be hanged first."

Tomlinson's brother-in-law, Charles Woods, was also accused by White of inciting the Indians. Woods had posted notices on several creeks along the Skeena warning the white miners the streams belonged to the Indians and they should leave. The next witness, miner C. W. D. Clifford, said there had been no trouble between Indians and miners in the Peace River area because there were no missionaries there. "The missionary comes in and is constantly telling Indians about their rights and making the Indians believe that they are better than white men."

Clifford was followed on the stand by Bishop Ridley, who related the various confrontations of the past three years in vivid detail. Ridley said he feared for his safety after the commissioners returned to Victoria. But John Tait, speaking on behalf of the Indians supporting Duncan, assured the commissioners that no harm would come to the bishop. "Nobody intends to touch him, but we know that he is on our property."

When Duncan was called on the 15th, he began by explaining why he acted as spokesman for the Indians on a number of issues. "The people concerned are the aborigines of the country whose language and surroundings present many and great difficulties to their being properly understood by the whites, and which render them more or less dependent upon their teachers as a medium of communication when they feel called upon to speak on matters of importance or when they feel their rights are being infringed." Duncan also described the events of recent years in graphic detail from his point of view. He was questioned more closely by the commissioners than Ridley and became embroiled in numerous disputes with Davie.

On the land issue, Duncan said attempts made in other parts of the province to consult the Indians had not been undertaken on the north coast, where reserve boundaries had been hastily drawn. "I think proper explanations should be given instead of bald announcements. This is not the right way to deal with the Indians." The natives were not "Fenians or boycotters." They wanted the help of the law in settling their grievances. In other parts of the world, Duncan said, it had been found unwise to leave land disputes to take care of themselves by presuming on the ignorance of the aborigines. "The sooner all rights, both of the government and the Indians, are fairly adjusted the better and safer for the peace of the country." He concluded: "The question of rights on land, both at Metlakatla and at Fort Simpson, is not, as some would suppose, the offspring of the rupture at Metlakatla, though that rupture has given a new impulse and vitality to the subject, arising in the question of the power of the Indians to eject from their lands what they feel is objectionable."

One of the most articulate native spokesmen was Robert Hewson. "For nineteen years Mr. Duncan was here by himself and things went well," Hewson told the commission. Now there were too many ministers and too many magistrates at Metlakatla, and the people were worse off. On the question of Mission Point being ceded to the C.M.S. at Duncan's request, Hewson said the Indians understood the two acres "were simply held in trust for the parties that were to teach us, and for them to live in." But now Bishop Ridley was attempting to secure control of the point even though the great majority of Indians did not recognize him as their teacher.

When Tomlinson took the stand he was subjected to a hostile cross-examination by Elliott and Davie. After he questioned the application of some clauses of the Indian Act, Tomlinson was told by the attorney-general that, like it or not, the Act was in force. It was not a question "for you or for the Indians to discuss whether the law be right or whether it be wrong." So much for the spirit of inquiry.

The hearings in Metlakatla concluded on November 22 when the commissioners returned to Victoria to draft their report. Presented to the government December 9, its recommendations were not surprising. The commissioners found the reserve set out for the Tsimshians "more than ample for Indian purposes." They joined the chorus against Lord Dufferin for raising the idea of Indian title during his visit in 1876. "Those remarks, which the Commissioners believe were wholly foreign to the mission of the Governor-General, have been seduously inculcated in the Indian mind by some of the missionaries, who appear to have been ignorant of the constitutional law upon the subject."

The commissioners said the fact the Metlakatla town council was not properly constituted under terms of the Indian Act, was "fraught with danger to the peace and order of the North-West coast." The council, the report declared, acted "in disregard of the laws of the land, and thus set an evil example to neighboring Indians." Since the Metlakatla council had been the only such body in the province for more than 20 years, long before there was an Indian Act, the criticism seemed gratuitous. But it reflected the bias of the commissioners, who wanted to maintain the status quo by keeping the Indians and their missionary supporters quiet. To this end they recommended that the survey of Mission Point go ahead, supported by force if necessary, to convince the Indians of the province's resolve to assert its right to the land in the name of the Queen. The report also urged that management of Indian affairs be transferred from the dominion to the British Columbia government. Ottawa, of course, should give Victoria the money to carry out its new responsibility for the Indians. The commission made it abundantly clear that Duncan and the Indians should not expect support from the government of British Columbia. Their only hope rested in Ottawa, and it was there they turned now.

Chapter 15

The Final Break

OMENS FOR SUCCESS were scarcely more evident in Ottawa than they had been in Victoria. Prime Minister John A. Macdonald, who was also Superintendent-General of Indian Affairs, had little interest in Indian matters. Ottawa had hoped to bring Metlakatla under the terms of its 1876 Indian Act, which would make the powers of the town council less sweeping. But Duncan insisted the Indians were sufficiently advanced to be excluded from the Act, which he told Ottawa was drawn up for less civilized natives living in primitive conditions. When the dominion government appointed a former H.B.C. man, Joseph W. Mackay, as Indian Agent for northern B.C., Duncan and the Metlakatlans refused to accept his authority. As a result, the government was forced to appoint ex-premier Elliott in his place.

Duncan's arguments must have made some impression, however, because in 1883 Parliament passed the Indian Advancement Act. A copy was forwarded to Duncan by Lawrence Vankoughnet, the Deputy Superintendent of Indian Affairs and the man who ran the Department. Vankoughnet said the new Act would help the Indians attain a status they couldn't achieve under the old laws of the country. It was especially adapted to the needs of Metlakatla, and had been approved by Senator Macdonald. Under the Act the Indian council would be given wide powers for managing the band's local affairs. It would have virtually the same powers as the councils of white communities, except of course the Indians still could not own land. The deputy superintendent wrote a warm letter, sympathetic to Duncan's work and asking his co-operation in persuading the Indians to accept the Act. Duncan was invited to suggest possible amendments.

Duncan replied coldly to Vankoughnet in a letter written on Christmas Day, 1884. He said any confidence the Indians might have had in the dominion government had been shaken by the recent "strange inconsistencies and unwise proceedings" of Dr. Powell in support of Bishop Ridley. "It is to be hoped that wiser counsel will soon prevail or else I fear the real trouble with the Indians will take the place of the imaginery ones which of late have been permitted to engage so much serious attention. If a little honesty and common sense had been employed instead of deceit and bluster there would have been no cause for alarm to anybody..."

Duncan's negative response disappointed Senator Macdonald, who said Vankoughnet was friendly to him and Metlakatla. "I do hope that you will not stand aloof." If men like Duncan who knew the Indians would not co-operate, then the government's laws could not be enforced. Macdonald said the Metlakatla town council should be reconstituted to conform to the new Act, which applied to the village whether the people liked it or not.

But Duncan was not inclined to compromise at this stage. He told the senator the council had "unfortunately learned its business too soon and without the aid of the Indian agent or the Indian Act. Had the Indians but remained 25 years longer in barbarism to suit the convenience of the Indian Department, they would now, we are asked to believe, be blessed with a legitimate council in place of our illegitimate one, and be partaking of the benefits pertaining to the Indian Agency." Noting that Powell had accused the council of being a band of "lawless ruffians," Duncan asked why, if that was the case, they had not been charged and put in jail. "Indian Agents are noted for being—generally speaking—a selfish and useless set and not over-honest," he added. "It is to be hoped the day is not far distant when the title and office disappears. That day will be a blessing to the Indians and a benefit to civilization."

Edward Cridge also tried to persuade Duncan to work with the dominion government. Because the provincial cabinet, which Cridge said included a number of bitter foes of Metlakatla, intended to turn over the whole dispute to Ottawa, the dominion government should be pressed in an attempt to shame it into action. Cridge said Premier William Smithe and Attorney-General M. T. Drake favoured a motion recommending to Ottawa that Duncan be removed from Metlakatla, but they did not have enough votes in the legislature to get it passed. "They are a mean pair," Cridge added.

In a "last resort to obtain justice," Duncan wrote Sir John Macdonald. He did not plead. A letter signed by the Metlakatlans said, "We beg to assure you we have real grievances to lay before you and feel prompted now to appeal to your judgement, wisdom and sympathy." In Duncan's unmistakable language, the natives declared they were losing confidence in the country's political leaders. "Where our interests as Indians are in conflict with the interests of any party of whites we have but little reason to hope for impartial treatment at the hand of the present persons in power... and all the kind words and promises which have been lavished upon us in the name of the Queen have proven to be but empty sounds." The Indians were changed from what they were 25 years before, but the Indian agency remained the same. The Act was, in fact, merely a "plausible contrivance for passing the money voted yearly by the Government for the Indian Department into the pockets of white men." The Indians of Victoria "right under the eyes of the Superintendent of Indian Affairs" were in a more wretched state than they were a quarter of a century before. The occupancy and use of land at Metlakatla had always been communal and the village was a success because of the controls that had been agreed upon. No one could settle there without the assent of the community. But now the unity which had encouraged peace and civil order had been broken.

At the same time Duncan was writing to Sir John, David Leask approached Provincial Secretary John Robson, considered the B.C. political leader most sympathetic to Metlakatla and the Indian cause. Leask said the natives were being deprived of rights to the land even though their ancestors occupied it long before the white men arrived. Now they were seeking a peaceful settlement. "We do not wish to depose the whiteman nor to live at enmity with him. We wish for peace and to be able to act as law-abiding people." Leask said Reserves Commissioner Peter O'Reilly had not explained to the Indians what hunting and fishing rights they would be asked to give up if they agreed to the reserves he had laid out. For that reason, they had never been accepted.

In June, Duncan sent another letter to the prime minister. The situation had become even more serious since his first letter, he wrote on his new typewriter. If Ottawa followed the same "arbitrary and menacing" policy as the province, "then I fear an implacable hatred of the whites and utter disloyalty to the Queen will be the sad result." Duncan said B.C. had been about to turn the disputed two acres of Mission Point over to Bishop Ridley, but backed off when threatened with legal action. Duncan admitted he had persuaded Governor James Douglas to set aside the point for the

176

C.M.S., but only in trust, which the Society had now abrogated by going against the wishes of the majority of Indians. The people were also insisting, he said, that they had not been a party to the 1864 agreement. The provincial government was offering to give the two acres to the majority if asked by Ottawa. "To this concession however the Indians demur. They want the two acres not as a gift but as a right, and as such they will only accept it." Court action was necessary because if the seizure by the province of the two acres was not ruled illegal, the Indians would know their position in the country was that of "mere slaves or paupers."

Earlier in 1885 Senator Macdonald had urged Duncan to go to Ottawa to see the prime minister. He should then proceed to England, Macdonald said, to present his case to the Society, which was trying to portray him as an outcast. Duncan agreed to set out on the long journey. The cannery was not operating that summer and he knew he could leave the other industries and village affairs in the hands of Tomlinson and Leask.

He arrived in Ottawa with two natives at the beginning of July, but Sir John kept the delegation cooling its heels for more than three weeks. In the meantime, Duncan presented Vankoughnet with a list of detailed proposals for dealing with the north coast Indians. Above all, he said, the 36 tribes of Tsimshians and Haidas, now comprising just 7,000 people following the epidemics of small-pox and other diseases, needed "careful and sympathetic management of their affairs." They should have a superintendent living among them and as much land as deemed necessary for their welfare set aside as "special property." The federal government should subsidize each community with a $2 per person annual grant until they had attained full citizenship.

Duncan described the provincial grant of 10 acres per family as "miserable." He noted that Ottawa had obtained reasonably sized reserves elsewhere by overriding the terms of union against stiff provincial opposition. When he asked the province to reimburse the natives for hunting lands seized by miners along the Skeena, Duncan said, he was told the loss of game would be "more than compensated for by the opportunities afforded by the presence of a mining population for the Indians to earn money." It should be evident to the national government that the province would grant nothing to the Indians unless compelled, "nor do they fear to provoke hostilities so long as the Dominion Government is between them and the Indians."

On Saturday, July 25, Vankoughnet sent Duncan a note informing him Macdonald had agreed to see him at his home on Monday morning. "He says nothing about the Indians," Vankoughnet added, "so that I suppose they had better not come." Duncan did not protest. The meeting lasted three hours. Macdonald had seemed prejudiced at first against their position, Duncan wrote Tomlinson, but appeared to be persuaded by his arguments. The prime minister was annoyed at Victoria's attempt to unload the problem on him, and agreed the land question must be settled by law before Ottawa could act. Sir John also said he would ask the C.M.S. to withdraw from Metlakatla.

Satisfied with what he considered a successful meeting, Duncan travelled on to London, where he proceeded to play a cat-and-mouse game with the C.M.S. Arriving September 7, he wrote a number of letters to the Society but avoided a meeting, despite an invitation from the committee. Duncan seemed to be waiting for Sir John to present a withdrawal ultimatum to the Society which would result in a clear-cut victory. His letters attacked the Society's support of Ridley and defended his own actions. His attempt to play a strong hand was based partly on his mistaken trust in Macdonald's promises. The prime minister had invited him to his hotel in London where he reiterated the pledges made in Ottawa and offered to appoint him Government Agent for all the north-coast tribes, independent of the Indian Agent in Victoria. Macdonald later claimed he had merely offered Duncan the job of Indian Agent for Metlakatla, which had been declined.

"Though the lines on which I have worked may not be in strict accordance with Church of England ritual," Duncan wrote the Society, "yet they have been of an essentially Christian character and such as have been approved and even eulogized by the Society for many years." His departures from Church ritual were not mere caprice, but an informed adaptation to the Indian mind. "My experience has led me to recognize the necessity for a missionary being everything to the poor people for whom he labours in the Gospel. And if he would have his work prosper he must aim at doing good to the bodies as well as the souls of his people—and concerning himself with whatever concerns them." Markets must be opened to the Indians, for what they could be taught to produce. In areas of Canada ruled by the Hudson's Bay Company, which saw to it that teaching the natives was limited to the gospel, the natives remained as poor as they had been 50 years before.

The successful result of his policy was the only justification needed, Duncan said, and he did not intend "to change my plans at the dictation of those who were devoid of such experience." The Society should abandon the Tsimshians altogether and move to a more needy and congenial location. Perhaps the government would grant a special reserve for any natives who wanted to leave Metlakatla and stay with the C.M.S. Duncan said it was the Society's "mistaken confidence in its agents and its ignorance of the essential character and conditions of the community which provoked this ignoble conflict and is alone responsible for its continuance."

Sir John did meet the committee, but the result was not what Duncan had expected. The prime minister was a man of infinite political flexibility. He did not care much about the Indian land question or the tiresome Metlakatla squabble, being more concerned with the immediate problem of the Riel Rebellion. The long-term consequences of the B.C. coast Indian grievances did not loom large in his eyes. Besides, he had taken a personal dislike to the aggressive little missionary who peppered him with *his* problems.

"From my personal communication with Mr. Duncan," Sir John wrote Senator Macdonald some time later, "I have satisfied myself that he is an ambitious man, brooking no control, and refusing to obey the laws of the land." Like other Duncan critics, the prime minister said Duncan had done good work at first, but had become "so accustomed to unrestrained power that he lost his head altogether." It is significant that the change in attitude toward him came after Duncan began to place the blame on white society for the Indians' predicament.

It did not require much effort by the august Secretaries of Salisbury Square to persuade Macdonald to come over to their side. They needed only to remind him that the opposition of the rich and powerful Church of England could be much more damaging to him in the forthcoming Canadian general election than a remote rag-tag band of Indians and an isolated, unpopular missionary. Macdonald agreed on the spot that Mission Point did indeed belong to the C.M.S., despite his earlier contrary assurances to Duncan.

Word of Duncan's defeat reached him in roundabout fashion. First there was a note from Sir John in Ottawa to say Duncan's letter had reached him in London just as he was leaving for

179

Canada, so there had been no time to meet again. He hoped Duncan was able to reach a friendly compromise with the C.M.S. That was all. Duncan had been dumped.

Confirmation came a few weeks later in a letter from Metlakatla. Ridley had recently read a letter to his people, purportedly from the prime minister, declaring that Mission Point was theirs. Victory flags were hoisted over the bishop's house and his little group paraded through the village holding banners aloft while their cannon boomed in the background. It turned out the letter had been written to Ridley by his friend Christopher Fenn of the committee reporting what Macdonald had told it, but the gist was the same: Duncan had now lost to both the provincial and dominion governments. Ridley also spread a rumour calculated to dishearten the Metlakatlans that Duncan would not return from England. Now that Duncan was off the C.M.S. payroll, the bishop hinted, he was too poor to come back. That was at least a switch from the usual accusation that he had become rich at the Indians' expense.

The Indians assured Duncan in a letter, however, that they were holding firm in the face of the pressure to change sides. The C.M.S. spent a total of $30,000 maintaining Ridley's tiny mission for five years, compared to $15,000 it gave Duncan over a 20-year period. The Indians said the people brought in by Ridley to teach and preach—he now had a staff of eight—were "holding a lantern in one hand and a gun in the other."

In desperation, Duncan turned in London to the Aborigines Protection Society. That worthy group, with fewer and fewer calls upon its services, was willing to take up the cause of Indian land rights, but with little of its old fervour. Secretary F. W. Chesson wrote a mildly-worded protest to the C.M.S. and called on the Canadian High Commissioner in London, Sir Charles Tupper. The tepid A.P.S. efforts achieved little.

While in London, Duncan wrote a detailed history and defence of his Metlakatla policies which he intended to publish, but never did. He also kept in close touch with Tomlinson, paying attention to detail as usual while involved with larger concerns. He sold 8,000 cases of stockpiled salmon to a London firm and was concerned about the new canning season. "I would be very careful to get good solder," he advised Tomlinson, "that is the right proportion of lead to tin—half and half—or buy solder ready-made." And don't pile the cans too high, he added.

Duncan waited three months before making a quick trip to

Beverley and then only after being pressed by George Cussons on behalf of his mother. After returning to London he met with the C.M.S. for five hours rehashing old arguments. The only new development to emerge was the committee's disclosure that it was sending two senior Society members as a deputation to study the Metlakatla situation first-hand. Duncan welcomed the new inquiry, but made no effort to hurry back for its hearings.

General J. G. Touch and the Reverend W. R. Blackett— Admiral Prevost had been dropped—left Liverpool March 11 on the first leg of the journey to Metlakatla. Blackett was vicar of Holy Trinity Church in Nottingham, a former missionary who had headed a divinity school in Bengal; General Touch was a full-time member of the committee. They stopped in Ottawa but Macdonald was too incapacitated by drink or illness to see them. Vankoughnet provided letters of introduction to Trutch and Powell in Victoria, where they spent eight days before arriving in Metlakatla April 19. As Duncan had warned them, most of the Indians were away at the Nass oolichan fishery, but those remaining, from both factions, gave the visitors a warm welcome. In order to create an impression of impartiality, the deputies did not stay with the bishop, but accepted an invitation to occupy a vacated Indian home in Duncan territory.

After more natives had returned from the Nass, a meeting was called of 64 Duncan supporters on April 22, at which Touch and Blackett explained the purpose of their presence and outlined the background of the dispute from the Society's point of view. The committee hoped, they said, to find a compromise that would restore peace to the community. They regretted Duncan was not present but expected he would arrive soon.

After their opening speeches the deputies invited the Indians to question them. The natives asked instead for copies of the addresses and time to study them. Five days later Leask advised Touch and Blackett that the people had nothing further to say to them. "We do not think anything would be gained by going over everything, when we have already told the Society in our letters what our troubles are. We have not asked the Society to send you . . . we feel that the Society is not working for us any longer, but is opposing and hindering us, and we wish them to move off our land."

The two men had not travelled 7,000 miles to be dismissed so peremptorily. In a letter addressed to Leask they upheld the Society's right to the disputed two acres and told the Indians they were wrong in supposing they had any claim to Mission Point. Critical of Duncan's religious teaching, the deputies said the Indians had a right to receive "an unmutilated Christianity." Their letter also raised questions about Duncan's handling of mission funds, declaring that all donations and profits from the industries belonged to the Society under the terms of his employment.

If the deputies' object was to keep a dialogue open with Duncan's supporters, they more than succeeded. The letter was read to a second meeting on the 30th at which the Indians again remained silent but Tomlinson angrily accused the two men of slandering Duncan by implying he was "a liar and a thief." They denied any such imputation and offered to withdraw their remarks, admitting the committee had never asked at any time to inspect Duncan's private account books. "We have no suspicion whatever that Mr. Duncan misused or in any way misapplied the funds entrusted to his care. On the contrary we believe that he used them strictly and wisely for your benefit, and in a manner probably which the Society would heartily approve."

Leask sent off another letter steeped in an eloquent bitterness that hinted of Tomlinson's helping hand. It accused the Society of being "the champion of disunion, civil and religious." The people had moved to Metlakatla to achieve unity, the letter said, and for unity they were prepared to contend to the last. Leask said the Society professed to care for the Indians, but had shown its interest "by bringing ships-of-war and government officials to overawe us; by dragging us before courts and magistrates; by fining and imprisoning some of us; by upholding and supporting everything they have seen to be objectionable to us, and by refusing to do any one thing we asked for. We do not call this love and care, but persecution."

The deputies stayed six weeks in Metlakatla. Duncan returned on May 10, three weeks after their arrival. He kept them waiting another 10 days before consenting to an interview and was coolly courteous during the six-hour session.

In their report to the Society, Touch and Blackett regretted that Duncan's attitude offered "no ground of hope of any arrangement with him." Their report was critical of almost all facets of Duncan's program for Metlakatla. His emphasis on secular work had resulted in a sacrifice of spiritual life. The "Christian village" concept had proved a failure in India because the inhabitants had become too dependent on their leaders, as was now evident in Metlakatla. In all important matters what was ostensibly done by the Indians was actually the work of Duncan or Tomlinson. "The Indians are but children, and quite incapable of acting in any important matter for themselves." Echoing Ridley, the deputies claimed Duncan's hold on the majority depended on terrorism.

Tomlinson was accused of writing the Indians' letters to the deputies, although Leask had proven on more than one occasion his ability to express himself clearly and pungently. He would have had Tomlinson's help with the letters, but the deputies were mistaken in supposing Leask and the others were just puppets.

According to Touch and Blackett, the Society was the only defender of religious liberty in Metlakatla. They praised Ridley's "unwearied zeal and courage" and contrasted the gentlemanly air of the bishop's supporters to the roughness of the Duncan faction. There was also a grave misreading of the natives' views on ancestral rights. "It did not appear to us," the deputies told Prime Minister Macdonald on their way home, "the Indians themselves were much moved by the land question."

Sir John was planning to visit Victoria in August and Senator Macdonald told Duncan he should come down to see the prime minister—"not that the mission has anything to expect from him but to give him a piece of your mind as you did before." The senator dismissed Touch and Blackett as "miserable men" who had gone to Metlakatla full of prejudice, talked against Duncan before they went, and on their way back "blazed abroad their opinions before reporting to the Society."

The two Macdonalds met in Victoria during the prime minister's stay and the senator came away more bitter than ever. "I am afraid he has very little heart in Indian work," he wrote Duncan. "He plays the game of procrastination too much." It would be wiser and cheaper in the long run for the government to deal promptly and liberally with the Indian demands rather than provoke a quarrel. But it was clear that no lead would come from Ottawa voluntarily. "Everything must be wrung out of them with difficulty." Macdonald also noted that Sir John had recently sold one of the Songhees Indian reserves adjacent to Victoria to coal and railway tycoon James Dunsmuir for $60,000. The Indians had not been consulted, the questionable transaction was never explained to them, nor were they asked where they wanted a new reserve. When Macdonald had asked Sir John whether he had met the

Indians before the sale, the prime minister had replied, "No, I don't want to see them."

In August a court case was held in Victoria which was to have far-reaching effects on Metlakatla and Indian land claims in general. Five Metlakatlans appeared before Chief Justice Begbie on charges of trespass resulting from the construction of a building on Mission Point by Duncan's supporters, who wanted to force a test case on ownership of the disputed two acres, since both governments had evaded making a decision.

Begbie ruled the Indians had no rights to the land "except as the grace and intelligent benevolence of the Crown may allow, and has always allowed." In another case in 1885 dealing with a coastal reserve, Begbie had speciously denied the Indians' claim because of what he said was their innate superiority over natives in other parts of the country. "In the course of a generation our Indians have acquired habits of life and . . . thought exactly the reverse of what is found east of the Rocky Mountains." In the East they were all "fed by the daily eleemosynary daily bounty of the state," but in British Columbia every Indian was self-supporting. "Clearly, a code of laws which may fit a mass of state-fed hereditary keepers educated with habitual idleness is not necessarily adapted for a race of laborious independent workers." The politicians could not have asked for more—legal rationalization and justification for the province's niggardly treatment of the Indians.

In the fall the provincial government sent surveyor C. P. Tuck to lay out the reserve boundaries as well as those of Mission Point. Tuck was continually harassed by Duncan's supporters, who pulled up stakes and stood on the chains, making it impossible to carry out his assignment. Frustrated, he called for a man-of-war to provide protection. When H.M.S. *Cormorant* arrived, the captain was presented with a petition from the Indians asking him to protect *their* interests. He was sorry, the captain said, but he was there only to help the surveyor, and "any attempt to impede this work will after this warning become a serious offence." When the Indians continued pulling up stakes, seven were arrested.

Duncan had left for Victoria before their trial was held, but Tomlinson, who was scathing about the proceedings, kept him informed. The cases were deliberately called out of sequence, he said, so that the Indians could not properly prepare their defence. Witnesses were refused permission to speak in their own language despite the fact most did not have sufficient command of English for their testimony. The natives were browbeaten by the magistrate, who held sittings until midnight, called white witnesses to tell of the bad things they had heard about Metlakatla, and generally supported the prosecution.

The people had stayed calm despite great provocation, Tomlinson reported. The affair had brought them closer together. "Things are rapidly changing for the better here among these people. The wretched farce of justice which we have just witnessed has done more to consolidate and unite the people and in determining them in not putting themselves under the thumb of any mere government department than anything that had happened before . . . we have nothing to hope for from either government so long as the present policy is maintained but this should not dishearten us." Other possibilities were in the wind.

Duncan, meanwhile, penned a sharp attack on Powell's annual report, which he said "sneered" at missionaries. He also disclosed that Powell, who had echoed Ridley's accusation of Senator Macdonald profiteering at Metlakatla's expense, had himself attempted to do just that. When the government turned down an application for an industrial loan, Duncan said, Powell had offered to put up the money personally. "That loan would have been accepted if the missionary could have seen his way to ensure the high rate of interest which the Superintendent expected to receive." Duncan accused Powell of "working side by side with land-grabbers and ecclesiastics to serve his own political ends."

As the year drew to a close, Tomlinson was active with his pen too. He wrote the C.M.S. *Intelligencer* refuting its account of the Touch-Blackett inquiry. Tomlinson said the Society would not admit its policies had changed over the years while Duncan had remained constant in his work on behalf of the Tsimshians. The Society had once been satisfied with a "union in spirit and doctrine," but was now demanding uniformity in ritual and church practice. Tomlinson also disputed the deputies' facts. They had reported the population of Metlakatla as less then 600, but Tomlinson said a recent head count had shown 854 members of Duncan's church and 94 with Bishop Ridley. His tally revealed the fact that more than 100 natives had left the community as a result of the schism.

At least one C.M.S. official recognized that land was the key to the dispute. Henry Morris wrote in the *Intelligencer* that if Duncan's objective was to hold power, that of the Indians was to hold land. "The land question is here, as it has been elsewhere, the secret of all the discontent, and Mr. Duncan has skilfully fed and worked upon the prejudices of the people."

If Duncan and Tomlinson scored more debating points in these final exchanges, they did not count for much. The struggle had been lost. Duncan admitted as much in a parting shot at Powell. "The Government of B.C. may decide they can trample with impunity on the rights of the Indian while he is ignorant and weak; but when the Indian feels himself to be a man it is not likely he will accept the doctrine that his foothold in the country, which his fathers have owned, depends upon the charity of Queen Victoria." Duncan decided to look elsewhere for relief.

Chapter 16

Move to Alaska

A WAY OUT OF THE IMPASSE had begun to take shape in Duncan's mind. Why not take all the people who would follow him and move across the water to Alaska? Duncan first raised the idea with Cridge in 1885, before mentioning it to Tomlinson and some of the leading natives. Cridge thought it was premature to be thinking of an exodus at that time. "Besides," he added, "the Americans have not been very noted for their consideration toward the aborigine."

Duncan said nothing about going to Alaska while his negotiations with the provincial and dominion governments and the C.M.S. dragged on. Even if he had been thinking about it at that time, he was astute enough to realize his opponents would welcome the idea and wish him godspeed. Sir John Macdonald, in fact, had observed that since the two factions appeared unable to live peacefully together, "it could scarcely be a subject for regret were one or other of the parties to remove elsewhere."

The fateful decision to approach the Americans for permission to emigrate was made in the fall of 1886 while Duncan was in Victoria. He had written Tomlinson advising him of Judge Begbie's verdict which supported Bishop Ridley and denied the Indian claim of aboriginal land rights. Tomlinson relayed the news to the natives without attempting to soothe their anger, and likely imparting some of his own. The council met hurriedly and sent three men, David Leask, Robert Hewson and Josiah Guthrie, to Victoria. When Duncan met the agitated natives on the crowded dock they were reluctant to tell him the purpose of their journey, but agreed to talk next day in the privacy of Senator Macdonald's home.

Because Premier William Smithe and Attorney-General Davie had been avoiding him, Duncan went that evening to the home of Hubert Robson, secretary to the premier, and almost pushed his way in. He refused to be seated and in a cold but dignified manner told of the arrival of the Indian delegation. It meant one of two things, Duncan said. Either they had decided to join with the up-river Indians to launch a war against the government on the land issue, or had opted for the peaceful solution of moving to Alaska.

Next day the natives told Duncan the council had decided upon Alaska, and that same evening he set out for Washington, D.C., bearing a letter signed by four of his prominent Victoria friends:

Victoria, B.C., November 16, 1886

TO THE LOVERS OF CIVIL AND RELIGIOUS LIBERTY IN AMERICA

The bearer, Mr. William Duncan, for thirty years a devoted missionary of religion and civilization, in North British America, and during the whole of that period well known to the undersigned, is on his way to Washington, deputed by the native Christian brethren of Metlakatla, to confer with the United States authorities, on matters affecting their interests and desires.

Like the Pilgrim Fathers of old, this afflicted but prospering and thrifty flock seek a refuge from grievous wrongs, and hope to find it under the American flag.

They prefer abandoning the home of their fathers, and the precious fruits of their industry, to submitting to the violent seizure of their land, and the intolerable stings of religious greed, and interference.

We therefore, most respectfully commend Mr. Duncan, and his mission, to such brothers and friends in our sister country—the land of the free—as may be disposed to use their influence, in aid of the oppressed.

(signed)

E. Cridge,
Bishop, R.E.C. Resident since 1854.

B. W. Pearse,
Formerly Surveyor General, Vancouver Island; also Chief Commissioner Lands and Works, British Columbia; also Resident Engineer, P. W. Department, Canada. Resident since 1851.

W. J. Macdonald,
Life Senator of the Dominion Parliament of Canada from British Columbia. Resident since 1850.

Turner, Beeton & Co.,
Merchants, British Columbia.

J. H. Turner,
Member Provincial Parliament, Victoria, B.C.

The first person Duncan met in the East was Henry Solomon Wellcome, who was just starting to write a book about Metlakatla and would become the most influential supporter of his work. At the age of 34 Wellcome was a wealthy businessman who had cultivated important people in government and the church. His was a classic success story of the booming late 1800's. From a storybook birth in 1853 in a log cabin on a small Midwest farm, the slender, dashing Wellcome had gone on to acquire riches and fame on both sides of the Atlantic.

Both his parents were deeply religious. His father Solomon was an Adventist minister as well as pioneer farmer in Minnesota.[22] Soon after the family's arrival the Sioux rebelled in 1862 against the wave of new settlers taking over their lands. Young Henry helped his uncle, a doctor, care for the wounded. Some 2,000 whites were killed before the Indians were crushed by the army and their chiefs hanged. "My hatred for red-skins was then so intensified by these horrors," Wellcome later wrote, "that I, in common with many, regarded them as so many reptiles, and their extermination but meet and just. However, on careful study of the cause of that war, and a retrospection of nearly all our Indian wars, I have found the Whites' injustice and outrages upon the Indians the primal cause."[23]

After graduating from the Philadelphia College of Pharmacy in 1874, Wellcome took a job as a travelling salesman for the New York drug firm of McKesson and Robbins. His trips peddling newly invented gelatine-coated medicine capsules took him as far afield as South America and the Pacific Northwest, where he first heard about Duncan and his work. He did not meet him, however, until 1885, when they were introduced in London. By that time Wellcome had formed the British pharmaceutical firm of Burroughs Wellcome & Co. with a former college friend from Philadelphia, Silas Burroughs. The company scored a coup by introducing to the British market the popular new pills developed in the U.S. Wellcome had a flair for salesmanship and made the company a household name by coining one of the best-known trademarks of the era, *Tabloid*. He assembled a Tabloid medicine chest for travellers which was presented with suitable fanfare to kings and sportsmen, explorers and presidents. The recipients included Henry Morton Stanley, renowned as the rescuer of David Livingstone in Africa, and Duncan.

---

[22] Turner, Helen. *Henry Wellcome: The Man, His Collection and His Legacy.* Heinemann, 1980.

[23] Wellcome, Henry. *The Story of Metlakahtla.* Saxon, 1887.

Wellcome drove himself at such a frantic pace expanding the new business that he was felled by exhaustion in 1886 and ordered to take an extended rest. He returned to the U.S., to the woods of Maine, where he camped, canoed, hunted and began writing *The Story of Metlakatla*. By the time Duncan arrived, Wellcome had left his wilderness retreat for the winter comfort of the exclusive Lotos Club on New York's Fifth Avenue. Soon he was again working at fever pitch, interviewing Duncan for the book, assuming management of a campaign to gain support in the East for the move to Alaska, and at the same time taking care of the U.S. interests of Burroughs Wellcome.

This fast moving world was new territory for Duncan, who was dependent on Wellcome's shrewd guidance. Stanley was in New York at the time and joined in the strategy planning for Duncan. The intrepid Welsh-born journalist had met Duncan previously in London and was an advocate of the Metlakatla system. In his book *Through The Dark Continent* Stanley had urged a similar approach in Africa. "It is strange how British philanthropists, clerical and lay, persist in the delusion that the Africans can be satisfied with spiritual improvement only. They should endeavour to impress themselves with the undeniable fact that man—white, yellow, red or black—has also material wants which crave to be understood and supplied... if the missionary can show the poor materialist that religion is allied with substantial benefits and improvements of his degraded condition, the task to which he is about to devote himself will be rendered comparatively easy... it is not the mere preacher that is wanted here... it is the practical Christian tutor who can teach people how to become Christians, cure their diseases, construct dwellings, understand and exemplify agriculture, and turn his hand to anything." Such a man should not be tied to any church or sect, Stanley added. Duncan could have been the prototype of his ideal missionary.

On December 10, 1886, Duncan made his first formal approach to the U.S. government. He told Commissioner of Indian Affairs J. D. Atkins the Tsimshians were a "patient and deserving people" who were being treated as a conquered race and had lost hope of gaining justice from Canadian governments or courts. They were begging for a place where they could live in freedom and peace and become full citizens. Atkins was unmoved. The Bureau of Indian Affairs had enough problems with its own natives and no desire to import more. Congress was opposed on the grounds that, despite

190

Duncan's assurances they would be self-supporting, the Metlakat-lans were likely to become a burden on the government in the future.

It became clear that public opinion would have to be marshalled behind Duncan and his persecuted natives if they were to gain admission to the U.S. No one was better equipped to direct this operation than Wellcome, a public relations wizard. He arranged for Duncan to make his first address in Washington to a joint meeting of the Board of Indian Commissioners, the Conference of Missionary Boards, and Indian Rights Associations.

Duncan was applauded when he declared the Indian "has all in him that is necessary to make him a president of the United States, and it may be that some day you will have a man of Indian blood the president of this great nation." The cheers were more enthusiastic, however, when Duncan attacked Canadian Indian affairs policy-makers. "They do not believe in helping the Indians, They believe in paying the Indians to keep quiet." That was music to the Americans, smarting over widespread criticism in England and Canada of *their* treatment of Indians.

His audience was not so pleased when Duncan went on to say there was no Indian problem, only a white problem. "The insatiable greed of the white man leads him to desire to obtain all that the Indian has, and if he cannot get it without law, he will have a law enacted which will enable him to get it."

Duncan's most formidable critic at the conference was Captain Richard H. Pratt, head of the Indian Training School in Carlisle, Pennsylvania. "The picture that Mr. Duncan has drawn is a very beautiful one," Pratt declared, "but I would like to ask him what would become of that community today, if the head were taken away?" Duncan replied that there were enough capable Indians to look after their own affairs without any assistance from him. The gruff-spoken Pratt was unconvinced, and the two men became bitter foes from that day.

Wellcome turned next to the churches, where invitations to speak from some of the most prestigious pulpits would allow Duncan to reach influential congregations and a wider public audience through the press. Phillips Brooks and Edward Everett Hale of Boston became ardent supporters, as did the noted orator and scandal-plagued Henry Ward Beecher of Plymouth Congregational Church in Brooklyn, where Duncan spoke for 90 minutes. Beecher was moved to start a fund-raising drive. The campaign generated considerable publicity. Pews were packed when Duncan spoke. The parishioners were curious to see and hear the dynamic little missionary from the distant North Pacific.

Wellcome formed a special committee of 25 prominent men to support Duncan's proposed move. The chairman was diplomat John W. Foster, a future secretary of state. Chief Justice Morrison R. Waite and two associate justices of the Supreme Court served as members, as well as four senators. Others included publisher Henry O. Houghton, who persuaded a number of businessmen to put up loans to help Duncan rebuild his industrial plants. Houghton described Duncan as "the most remarkable man in many ways I ever met. He has wonderful executive ability, great modesty and great self-reliance . . . his work is an object lesson for all parts of this country in the method of treating the Indians."

In March of 1887 Wellcome advised Duncan that the government and legal authorities he had been courting now seemed more kindly disposed toward the move. "The point of international courtesy seems to be strongly regarded and prevents the department from a full committal, but they verbally recommend that if you take your people over and then after selecting ground for a settlement fully notify the Interior Department—the fullest justice will be done." Wellcome stressed the delicacy of the matter and the reluctance of the government to extend official recognition until the Metlakatlans were on American soil.

The attorney-general said if the Indians came as individuals they would have fewer rights than white immigrants, because the provision for naturalization would not apply to them. The Homestead Law of 1875 for Indians who had abandoned the tribal system applied only to Indians born in the U.S. The President could not by law grant the Metlakatlans a permanent reservation; only Congress could provide "relief" for natives seeking asylum. Another concern was church affiliation. Duncan had been urged by a number of his new supporters to join one of the established churches, but Wellcome advised him to remain independent.

Wellcome also cautioned Duncan not to describe his people as "Indians," otherwise they would be placed under the restrictions of the various U.S. Indian Acts. The Interior Department did not regard the native peoples of Alaska as Indians, and Duncan should use such terms as aborigine, Tsimshian, native, or Metlakatlan. Wellcome complained to the New York *Herald* when it used the phrase "tribal exodus." The Metlakatlans had given up their tribal bonds, he told the editor.

The high point of Duncan's trip was a meeting with President Grover Cleveland. The President supported the move, but was concerned about taking any step which might be construed by Britain as an unfriendly act. The two countries were bickering over the boundary line between British Columbia and the Alaska Panhandle following American purchase of the territory from the Russians in 1867. Land tenure did not exist in Alaska, Cleveland said, so the Metlakatlans could not buy property. They could be granted squatter's rights in the same way as other Alaska settlers. The Metlakatlans had raised $1,300 among themselves during the winter toward the purchase of land, and Wellcome had pledged to put up more money for that purpose, but Duncan had little choice but to accept the compromise arrangement. The government had promised it would take steps to secure the rights of the Metlakatlans after they had moved.

Duncan sent a telegram to Metlakatla telling the people the way had been cleared for their move and they should look for a suitable site. He followed up the wire with a letter conveying the mix of warmth, paternalism and attention to detail that had been so effective in winning over the Tsimshians. "I am making new friends every day and many hearts are being moved in sympathy for your welfare," he told them. "The more I think about your moving into Alaska, the more clearly I see it is the right step for you to take ... the beginning of a new and brighter history for you and your children."

Duncan told the natives he was not begging for funds, but simply telling their story. "Then I leave it for God to touch the hearts of any whom he chooses to assist you." He urged them to write letters of gratitude to everyone making a donation. The money would be sent to a bank in Portland where it would be safe "until we ask for it." Duncan warned of hardships in the beginning. There would be no industries operating while he was away, so the people should take jobs in nearby canneries. He did not want them to go to Victoria or Washington Territory to pick hops because those places had too many temptations. Firewood should be cut for their own use and for sale, and it was important to put away plenty of dried salmon for the winter, when many of the men would be working on the new townsite.

"You would be astonished with what favour this proposed move to American soil is looked upon," Tomlinson wrote Duncan. "In fact things have as it were solidified since you left ... there is less excitement, more true union, a greater realization of the duty they owe themselves and their children." In a letter to Macdonald, Tomlinson said the recent court case was responsible for the community's new attitude. "The wretched farce of justice which we have just witnessed has done more to consolidate and unite the people . . . than anything that has happened before."

Tomlinson was worried about the Tsimshians left behind in B.C., a consideration which did not seem to concern Duncan. A large number of Metlakatlans were in Fort Simpson explaining the situation to the natives there, Tomlinson wrote. "The case of these villages ought not to be lost sight of. My mind is greatly exercised over this problem and as yet I see no satisfactory solution." There was none—traces of the bitterness over the split felt by those who stayed behind have remained to the present day.

Late in March of 1887, when the worst of the winter storms had abated, a party of five natives and Dr. Bluett set out by canoe up Chatham Sound to investigate a number of places under consideration for the new colony. They would have been familiar with the area from fur sealing expeditions and trading junkets made by the Metlakatlans up the coast as far north as Chilcat. Within two weeks they had agreed upon Annette Island, which had been first suggested by Sheldon Jackson. It was just 70 miles north of Metlakatla and 30 miles inside Alaskan waters. That was close enough to make feasible the task of moving hundreds of people and their possessions by small boats. The unoccupied island was 18 miles long and five to eight miles wide, with 10 salmon-spawning streams flowing down its slopes. A third of the island was considered suitable for farming after the thick growth of cedar, spruce and hemlock had been cleared.

The spot chosen for the settlement was a bay on the west side known as Port Chester, once the site of a Tlingit village. Few signs remained of its earlier history apart from a lone totem near the water's edge. The gently sloping beach was pebbled and sandy, ideal for pulling up canoes. The harbour was not as protected from the winds as desirable, but when a wharf was built large ships would be able to dock in all but the worst storms. There were a number of lakes in the mountains and from one flowed a stream with a steep 800-foot drop which could be utilized for power. Most important, the advance party was told by natives at nearby Tongass Narrows that the surrounding waters were dark with salmon every summer.

194

The setting was spectacular. "It is impossible to imagine a more lovely place," one visitor wrote. "Semi-circular in shape, it opens out through a number of small islands to the sea on the westward. On the east and north, wild rugged mountains come down to the water's edge and on the south a low, green shore, skirted by a gravel beach, winds in beautiful curves."

While Bishop Ridley attempted to persuade Duncan's natives to stay with him in B.C., John Tait and Edward Benson erected a temporary store at Port Chester. David Leask began putting up a salting house. "The idea of leaving him (Ridley) behind don't agree with him," Leask wrote Senator Macdonald. "His people are trying to make friends with our people, begging some of us not to go away. When His Lordship finds that such kindness has failed, he one day scold the people by saying that those who used the logs etc. for firewood will be sent to prison for three months."

Meanwhile, Duncan's campaign for public support in the U.S. was about to reach a climax in May with the publication of *The Story of Metlakatla*. Wellcome's book received an astonishing amount of attention. More than 160 newspapers and magazines took notice of it, in fulsome reviews, prominently displayed news stories, or editorials commenting on the plight of Duncan and his natives. Many likened the story to *Evangeline*, Longfellow's tearful saga of the Acadians who were driven out of Nova Scotia more than a century before and given refuge in the U.S. Others mentioned the Pilgrim Fathers as a parallel.

The New York *World* said Wellcome had written "one of the most thrilling stories in the history of civilization." Echoed the *Deseret News* of Salt Lake City: "The missionary work of Mr. Duncan is one of the most marvellous in its success that has been performed in modern times." The tale told by Wellcome aroused "indignation, sorrow and sympathy," said the New York *Star*. To the New York *Tribune*, "nothing stupider, nothing more dishonorable, nothing baser in the long list of outrages committed by the powerful of the earth against the weak can be cited than the story of Metlakatla." Both the dominion and provincial governments had treated the model settlement in an infamous manner, the *Tribune* said. "The State has upheld the Church and the Church has given its sanction to the State in a program of spoilation and tyrannical abuse and interference such as might well have justified an Indian war."

Some clear-eyed editors observed, however, that Duncan was

not proposing to take his charges to an Indian paradise. "It must be a dark exigency that brings the Indian to the United States Government for protection," said the *Alta Californian* of San Francisco, "as a tender regard for his rights has never been one of its conspicuous traits."

The explanation for the fame of Wellcome's book does not lie in its literary merit. In the Introduction, he wrote that in sticking to his objective he had been "compelled to subjugate literary effect too often to the recordance of heterogeneous facts." The book is weighted with such turgid writing, as well as Wellcome's ponderous theological theories and musings on the white man's burden. An obsessively reticent man about his own life, Wellcome saw no need to spice his book with personal details about Duncan. What the Americans saw in the book was simply a chance to twist the British lion's tail.

The howls from across the border confirmed their success. Wounded pride and defensiveness marked the reaction of the Canadian press, except for those newspapers eager to place the blame on Sir John Macdonald's Conservative government. The Toronto *Mail* said that to claim the Indians had been driven out of Canada was incorrect. "The Indians have their homes and a large tract of country besides," the editorial said. "But the Canadian Government refuses to acknowledge that they own the entire Province of British Columbia." The *Globe* said "a stupid crime has been committed at the expense of these Indians for no benefit to anybody, but simply to gratify the dominating spirit of an Anglican Bishop . . . henceforth Canada cannot pretend to have a Government which protects Indians from cruel injustice."

The bitterness was most evident in the columns of the Victoria newspapers. The general feeling of betrayal was expressed by an anonymous letter writer in the *Times*: "The wronged are not the Metlakatlans but the people . . . who subscribed annually, for more than twenty years, their money and their influence. Without any just or irremovable cause, this teacher goes . . . to a foreign country . . . and then drives these Indians (whom the British had paid him to civilize) there like a herd of cattle, as though they were *his* property, his goods and chattel, and not subjects of Her Majesty and residents of B.C." In an editorial, the *Times* claimed Turner and Macdonald were guilty of treason in urging the Americans to accept Duncan and the Indians. "You cannot, Mr. Turner, be loyal to Canada and to the United States," thundered the *Times*. "Choose your flag."

No one in Victoria was more indignant than Dr. Helmcken. Missionaries who have "such intimate relations" with the Indians, he wrote slyly, had a duty to disabuse them of the idea that government was stealing their lands. Dr. Powell wrote to a number of papers in the U.S. claiming that donors to Duncan's fund were "grossly misled." The area around Metlakatla had been kept in a constant state of fear and alarm by Duncan's antics, Powell said. "It is to be hoped that the prime author and misleader will be less treasonable to his new allegiance than he has been to the country which gave him birth."

Unaware of the war of words he had set off at home, and in which he would have been a zestful participant had he been there, Duncan wrapped up his affairs in Washington and prepared for a triumphant return to his people. There was one detail remaining to be settled, however—what should the new settlement be called? In gratitude to the President, Duncan wanted to name it Cleveland. (The city of Cleveland had been named after a surveyor.) Well-come objected. He knew that most of the wealthy businessmen he had recruited were Republicans, and Democrat Cleveland would not be in power forever. "I strongly urge that you call the new village 'New Metlakatla'," Wellcome wrote Duncan. Naming it after the President "would call up intense political party prejudice, which is nearly as bad as ecclesiastical prejudice." Duncan agreed. New Metlakatla it would be.

Duncan's long stay in the East wound up at a solemn ceremony in Philadelphia's Independence Hall at which Wellcome presented him with a large new 36-star American flag. The Stars and Stripes were unfurled under the Liberty Bell and spread symbolically over the table upon which the Declaration of Independence had been signed. After pledging his allegiance to the Constitution and declaring his intention to apply for citizenship, Duncan caught the train for Chicago, where he made a number of public appearances before boarding the trans-continental to San Francisco. There he was given free passage on the steamer to Portland, arriving in early July.

Weary and feeling ill from the strain of his activities in the unaccustomed heat and humidity of the East, Duncan nevertheless undertook a tour of salmon canneries along the Columbia River. He spent a few days studying techniques and equipment for a new plant in Alaska. He bought a portable steam sawmill, which he characteristically learned to assemble and operate so as to avoid the cost of hiring an engineer.

In the midst of this activity, Duncan received some startling news. He had intended that most of the people would remain in Metlakatla until the following year while a small group of men worked through the winter preparing the Port Chester site for building homes. But on July 14 a letter from Tomlinson reached him in Portland advising that all were determined to move in the fall, whatever difficulties they might face. Duncan immediately ordered 30 tons of supplies to take with him on the steamer. Most of the goods, along with the sawmill, were aboard the *Ancon* when she sailed from Portland July 29. The ship made a brief stopover at Victoria, giving Duncan an opportunity to visit his agent, settle some old business accounts and happily discover there was an $8,000 balance to apply to the work ahead.

The next stop was Port Townsend, Washington, where Duncan was joined by lawyer Thomas N. Strong of Portland, who was his new legal adviser and representative in Oregon. Strong and Portland banker W. S. Ladd, who also boarded the *Ancon*, had been rounding up Western supporters and investors while Duncan, Wellcome and Houghton worked in the East.

There was a letter from Wellcome waiting at Port Townsend, written aboard the Cunard liner *Etruria* bound for England. He told Duncan that before leaving New York he had made arrangements with the editor of the *World* to receive contributions for the New Metlakatla fund. Wellcome regretted being forced to return to London to deal with business matters that had accumulated in his long absence, but promised to "keep things stirred up with my pen."

In the telegraph office at Port Townsend, Duncan was introduced to Nathaniel H. R. Dawson, the federal Commissioner of Education, who had come from Washington to board the *Ancon* for a tour of school facilities in Alaska. As the steamer threaded its way up the Inside Passage, Dawson and Duncan discussed the education needs of the new colony. After passing by Metlakatla and Fort Simpson, the *Ancon* arrived off Port Chester in the early afternoon of Sunday, August 7, 1887. She was decked out in all the bunting and flags that Captain James Carroll could muster.

It was a warm, sunny day and the weather was matched by the greeting Duncan received from the 40 members of his advance party. Dawson later described the scene: "Old men and women, girls and boys, gathered around this good man and expressed with tears their intense joy and gladness. Two United States flags...

were raised upon an improvised staff, and the Indians and passengers assembled under their folds in the shade of the trees on the shelving shore."

Passengers and crew members of the *Ancon* who went ashore to join the celebration on the beach were surprised to find the Tsimshians neatly dressed for the occasion and making polite conversation. Three or four of the native women formed an impromptu welcoming group, shaking hands with all the visitors. Duncan spoke briefly in Tsimshian, then introduced Dawson, asking him to allay the fears of the Indians about their new ties with the U.S. Interpreted by Duncan, Dawson said that although land laws were not in force in Alaska, the Metlakatlans would be protected by the government in the possession of any lands on which they might settle. When the laws were extended to the territory they would be allowed to hold them.

Chief Daniel Neashkumackem responded to Dawson's speech on behalf of the Metlakatlans. "The God of Heaven is looking at our doings here today," the chief told Dawson. "You have stretched out your hands to the Tsimshians. Your act is a Christian act. We have long been knocking at the door of another government for justice, but the door has been closed to us. You have risen up and opened the door to us, and bid us welcome to this beautiful island, upon which we have taken refuge from our enemies, and where we have decided to build our homes. What can our hearts say to this, except that we are thankful and happy." The chief's address, delivered in the graceful musical tones of the Tsimshian tongue, was translated by Duncan.

After the speeches, the *Ancon* fired a salute from its single cannon and the natives sang *Rock of Ages* in their own language. A minister stepped out from among the tourists and gave a blessing and a prayer for the new settlement. Everyone joined in the singing of the hymn *Coronation*. The church bell which the Indians had brought over from Metlakatla was tolled, echoing from the mountains across the water. The passengers gave a rousing three cheers for the flag, and later joined the Indians in an evening prayer service on the beach in the glowing light of a spectacular northern sunset.

Chapter 17

Starting Over

Nstyle="small-caps">OT LONG AFTER THE DEPARTURE of the *Ancon*, a canoe left for old Metlakatla. Its paddlers carried the news of Duncan's arrival and told the people to begin the move to Alaska. As the canoe approached the beach, George Usher stood up in the bow to address the eager crowd lining the shore. "We are free," he shouted to the cheering Metlakatlans. "The flag of the United States has taken us into its folds." Usher extemporized a freedom song intoned in an inspiring Tsimshian chant.

So began one of the largest hegiras in Canadian history. The first flotilla of 50 canoes left almost at once. Over the next 10 days boats of every shape and size ferried the natives and their possessions across the 70-mile stretch of water, some of it open Pacific. Six separate fleets, each comprising from 30 to 70 craft, including canoes, fishboats, scows and rafts, made the voyage. They carried 800 men, women and children and assorted belongings. Two little steamboats were employed, including the *Princess Louise*, Duncan's cannery ship, and the *Glad Tidings*, chartered from the Methodists at Fort Simpson. Thomas Crosby was no doubt delighted to help his old nemesis leave their contested area. On one trip 60 canoes were roped together behind the *Glad Tidings*.

When all the people had been ferried across, the canoes and steamboats returned to pick up as much movable material as possible before winter set in. Household furniture, doors, windows and lumber from dismantled houses were piled aboard. Two convoys caught by storms sweeping through Dixon Entrance almost capsized before reaching sheltered water. The Tsimshian were expert seamen and despite overloading of their primitive craft, there were no serious mishaps during the entire operation. Duncan had considered using the *Ancon* to bring the people across, but the steamship company wanted $3 a head, which he considered excessive.

Duncan had been urged to reboard the *Ancon* on August 8 when she continued on to Sitka, the District capital, but decided he should be on hand for the arrival of the Metlakatlans. He asked Thomas Strong to represent him in talks with Governor Alfred Swineford and other Alaska officials, including the influential General Agent of Education, the Reverend Sheldon Jackson. As a goodwill gesture, Duncan sent some Indian carvings which Jackson had asked for at old Metlakatla during his earlier visits.

It was Jackson who had pressed Duncan to come immediately to Sitka, where he presided in the summer months in the manner of a latter-day Napoleon. The comparison, often made by his many critics, was inspired by Jackson's five-foot height and imperious manner. With his long black beard, however, the slender Jackson more resembled an Amish Toulouse-Lautrec than the French emperor. Bursting with ambition, brash talk and wild ideas, he had an enormous impact on Alaska in the chaotic period from 1880 to 1900.[24]

Jackson was an unlikely candidate for his self assumed role. Born to religious parents in New York, he graduated from Princeton Theological Seminary in 1858 and moved west. He was employed by the Presbyterian Board of Home Missions for the next 20 years teaching in Arizona and New Mexico, and served as a chaplain in the Civil War. In 1877 he made a trip to Alaska and found a raw, anarchic land waiting to challenge his boundless energies. Each year thereafter Jackson whisked around the territory in the summer and spent the winter lobbying in Washington and speaking on behalf of his adopted land. A spell-binding orator, he was a hit on the Eastern Seaboard lecture circuit where eager audiences devoured stories about the recently acquired frontier land. They were entranced by his highly-charged tales of native witchcraft and female slavery.

In fact, Jackson didn't need to embellish his stories. Alaska *was* an untamed land. Duncan at times seemed blissfully unaware that a mere 70-mile voyage had taken him from a peaceable kingdom to a lawless backwater. One national government official had this to say about Alaska in the 1880's: "There are in this country as God-abandoned, God-forsaken, desperate and rascally a set of wretches as can be found on earth. Their whole life is made up of fraud, deceit, lying and thieving."

[24] Hinckley, Ted C. *The Americanization of Alaska 1876-1897.* Pacific Books, 1972.

After buying the sprawling territory from the Russians for $7,200,000, the Americans were not quite sure what to do with it. The district was placed under military rule for the first 10 years. The soldiers had little to do but drink home-brew, brawl, and debauch the Indian women. When the troops were withdrawn in 1877 to put down an Indian uprising in Idaho, conditions worsened. The only federal official in Alaska was the collector of customs, who had no means of enforcing regulations. In one three-month period, 5,000 gallons of molasses were landed at Sitka to make hooch.

Conditions became so riotous in early 1879 that an alarmed group of Sitkans, fearing Indian violence, asked the British navy for protection. It was an unprecedented act in American history that paralleled the later intervention of the U.S. revenue cutter *Oliver Wolcott* at old Metlakatla. An appeal was sent on the mail steamer from a citizens' committee in Sitka, addressed to "the Captain of Anyone of Her Majesty's Ships at Esquimalt." Without waiting for higher authority, Captain H. Holmes A'Court of H.M.S. *Osprey* sailed at once. He arrived at Sitka on March 1 and remained for more than a month without incident until relieved by the U.S. warship *Alaska*.

Responsibility for controlling Alaska for the next five years was handed to the navy, which had no more success than the army. Since the land had not been surveyed, or provision made for the acquisition of property, the populace felt little sense of responsibility for preserving order. Nor were the politicians much help. As one historian put it, Alaska was "a political preserve for the payments of small debts owed by big politicians to little ones."

Much of the blame for the lack of effective civil government can be placed on the giant Alaska Commercial Company. Its stranglehold on the country was as tight as that of the Hudson's Bay Company to the south in earlier days. The A.C.C. simply wanted to be left alone to harvest fur seal pelts. In the 15 years after 1867 some 25 bills were introduced in Congress to provide for the proper administration of Alaska, but intense lobbying by the company prevented any of these reform measures reaching the floor for debate.

Like its Canadian counterpart, the A.C.C. was not noted for a tender regard toward the native peoples. In his final report as governor in 1889, Swineford said the company had "reduced the native population to a condition of helpless dependence, if not one of absolute and abject slavery . . . its insatiable greed is such that it

202

is not content with robbing the poor native in the price it sets upon the product of his dangerous toil, but it robs him also in the exorbitant prices it exacts from the goods given in exchange."

This was the moral vacuum Sheldon Jackson moved to fill. He had been impressed by Duncan's methods at old Metlakatla, where he had observed the level of civilization and economic independence reached by the Tsimshians. Jackson lent his full support to the move and tried vainly to persuade Duncan to join the Presbyterians by holding out the promise of financial backing.

Swineford was sympathetic to the natives, but made little headway against the traders and opportunists who followed the gold seekers into the territory. This motley group saw no need to support native education or welfare. The Indians were looked on simply as cheap labour. As in British Columbia, the missionaries were left to educate the natives. Jackson wanted the churches to provide teachers and buildings while the government furnished school supplies and all or part of teachers' salaries. A poor administrator, he was too headstrong to maintain the delicate balance required for such an arrangement. To Jackson the line between church and state was almost invisible. The Presbyterians soon became dominant in the schools and in politics as the result of Jackson's appointments. He made many enemies.

The potential of New Metlakatla as a showcase for native education was apparent to Jackson. In a report to the Territorial Board of Education two months before the exodus, he said the new settlement would "make a centre around which the scattered populations can cluster and secure good school facilities." Commissioner Dawson had promised Duncan he would try to obtain financial aid for his school. After conferring with Jackson in Sitka, Dawson sent word to New Metlakatla that the Bureau of Education, a branch of the Interior Department, would pay the salary of a teacher for the 1887-88 school year.

At old Metlakatla, meanwhile, there had been no interference from Bishop Ridley and his few remaining supporters until Duncan sent off a party of 10 men in October to dismantle and remove the church. The council at first planned to send all the men of the settlement, but wisely decided such a step would be provocative. When the small work crew arrived and began taking out the church windows, pews, altar rails and shingles from the roof, Ridley sent his little steamer, the *Evangeline*, to Fort Simpson to fetch a constable and a magistrate. They arrived the next day and swore in all Ridley's supporters as special constables, who proceeded immediately to the church. When the demolition crew ignored an order to stop work, a scuffle broke out. It ended quickly when Duncan's men decided to return home after lodging a formal protest with Magistrate S. Y. Wootton over the interference. Once again Ridley claimed he had narrowly escaped death in the brief altercation, but nobody took him seriously.

Before departing their old village, Duncan's party locked up the church windows in the main cannery shed with the idea of retrieving them later. But some of Ridley's men broke in through a skylight a few days afterward and returned the windows to the church. Wootton issued a proclamation that in future no one would be allowed to remove doors, windows, or any part of their houses, including plants and shrubs in the gardens. When challenged on what authority he was acting, the magistrate said the dominion government had ordered him to prevent further removal of property.

Duncan was furious. He sent off a heated letter to Wootton, demanding to know what the natives would be allowed to remove and what they were supposed to leave behind. The Metlakatlans were angered by the "malicious spirit" which still existed against them in B.C., Duncan said. He signed the letter over his new title of Justice of the Peace, although it had no relevance in this instance. The position carried little real authority in Alaska, although Duncan tried to make full use of it on his island.

Duncan was cooled down by some sage advice from Thomas Strong, who had returned to Portland. Strong said the church materials were not worth the risk involved in possible criminal proceedings, or the loss of the moral stature they had gained in the U.S. through their patient endurance of persecution in Canada. It would be better to claim for damages from the dominion or provincial governments. "However unjust it may be, the Indians must keep within the law. Their most cunning enemy could not devise a better scheme to harm them than to provoke them to violence."

Some cannery equipment was recovered the following spring, but the sawmill machinery which Duncan was going to give Tomlinson to take up the Skeena was not released. It is assumed that pressure from Thomas Crosby and the Methodists, who did not want Tomlinson in what they regarded as their territory at Skeena Forks, was likely a factor in the arbitrary decision. Tomlinson had been urged by Duncan and Cridge to join the exodus to Alaska, but felt an obligation to his own small band of converts. He had scraped together $500 and with the help of his growing family, hoped to "find enough to cover and feed ourselves and at the same time preach and teach the word of life."

Tomlinson possessed a rare humility among the coast missionaries, whose egos often were inflated by their power over the Indians. He could be a more stubborn battler than Duncan when convinced the cause was right, but his self-honesty never deserted him. "You know well that I have not the ability for starting or managing larger matters," he told Duncan. Though working apart, they would not be separated in plans or principles, he said. Writing to Duncan in the U.S. before the move, Tomlinson said he had not yet advised the Metlakatlans of his plans, "but when you come back I will be forgotten in their joy in having you again among them and I can quickly slip away up the river and not be missed."

As winter approached at New Metlakatla, the natives worked feverishly to clear the land, build shelters and stock up on food and firewood. There was no time to erect permanent dwellings, and crude huts were strung along more than a mile of beachfront. After the new sawmill was assembled boards were cut for the first permanent building—a 90 by 34 frame structure which would serve initially as a church and school and later become part of the cannery. The work was directed by Duncan in conjunction with a new council elected at a mass meeting in late August after everybody had arrived. John Tait was chairman and David Leask secretary.

By early October the supplies brought on the first trip of the *Ancon* had been consumed and the community was short of food. Duncan sent orders to Portland for three tons of potatoes, a ton of apples, 50 boxes of pilot bread, three kegs of butter, 400 bags of flour, five chests of tea, 10 barrels of sugar, some candles and coal oil. For the land-clearing work he ordered 12 crosscut saws, 24 axe handles and a stump-puller. The few frills in the order included candies, 12 black silk handkerchiefs—and 12 umbrellas for the elderly to fend off the incessant rain.

Duncan was a meticulous and niggardly storekeeper. His suppliers soon learned they would be called to account for the least mistake. After one shipment arrived he complained of leaking coal oil tins, broken castor oil bottles and chocolate bars missing from opened cartons. There was no need to ship shoes in space-consuming boxes, he wrote. "We do not care for that sort of grandeur up here." And the half-dozen silk hair ribbons should have been wider. "We have so little taste in our customers we have to be very careful in buying goods lest we accumulate unsuitable stock." The Indians were not yet adventurous in their new role as consumers.

Maintaining morale was one of Duncan's most difficult tasks. The natives were nervous about the ramifications of the step they had taken. They feared they would be forbidden to fish in Canadian waters and discouraged by tariffs from trading in Victoria, still their most accessible market. They were lonely and frightened, cut off from families and friends, unsure of the future. The weather was colder and wetter, with heavier snowfalls than old Metlakatla. Family accounts passed down from that first bleak winter tell of people sobbing in their ramshackle huts in the damp gloom of evening.

For the first time since his arrival among the Tsimshians, there was no mention in Duncan's letters of Christmas or New Year's festivities. Food supplies were limited to the basics. The only place available for meetings and church services was the drafty, unheated workshop. Everyone was busy, but the work of establishing the new community proceeded slowly under difficult conditions. Some families desperate for money to buy food and clothing left for other nearby Alaska canneries and sawmills to find temporary jobs.

Duncan had hoped to start school classes in the fall, but it was mid-January before they began in an unheated building. Duncan made a virtue of that, however, telling Commissioner Dawson that students in heated classrooms caught more colds. There were 140 pupils under the age of 12, and Duncan planned to build a combination day and boarding school for another 35 boys and girls between 12 and 14. He wanted the government to fund the boarding school, while the community took responsibility for the younger children. Eventually he hoped to have an industrial training school, but in the meantime did not know what to do with 30 teen-aged boys. Dawson and Jackson had urged that they be sent to the residential Sitka Industrial School founded by Jackson.

That prospect was not pleasing to Duncan. "By leaving us there is a fear they might be so much puffed up by their superior advantages as to prove worse than useless to their people and home." He was worried about losing his tight control over the young people, but there were other reasons for his concern. The record of

Indian boarding schools in the U.S. was not good. The students lost a means of subsistence in the neglect of native arts and handicrafts, and their education made them unfitted for the environment to which they returned. There were few opportunities for employment in their newly acquired skills.

Jackson was persistent. He arrived in Metlakatla April 23 and stayed a week before persuading Duncan to let him take 24 boys to Sitka. He picked up another eight at points along the way where they were camped with their families. For most of the parents it was the first time they had been separated from their children, and there were tearful good-byes on the shore. Edward Mather, gun-smith, jeweller, blacksmith and one of Duncan's leading converts, wrote to Thomas Strong about the departure of his two sons for Sitka. "Their parents are sorrow but they wish to educate them . . . so all the parents try to do what they can for them."

The boys made a striking impression on their arrival. They marched off the ship in single file, a trumpeter in the lead, swinging their bags over their shoulders. Neatly dressed and groomed, they paraded in step through town to the school. The Sitkans had never seen such wholesome, disciplined young natives.

Jackson may have been proud of his new charges, but the boys were not equally impressed with his school. One said the level of Jackson's 6th grade was not up to Duncan's 4th grade. When Duncan visited Sitka in the fall the boys complained they were not receiving industrial training, sanitary conditions were poor, and they didn't like the food. Duncan took two boys back with him who were suffering from pneumonia. During his school inspection he found 12 boys learning to make leather shoes, which he considered a waste of time since most natives were switching to rubber boots.

In his new capacity as adviser to the Territorial School Board, Duncan visited government-funded schools at Juneau, Douglas and Haines. He found the number of children attending classes small and the calibre of the teachers disappointing, a common complaint among parents in Alaska. It was not easy to attract good teachers to the area, or to keep them. Salaries were low, the physical and psychological risks high. Job-hunters in Alaska were often dreamers, failures or misfits from "down below" hoping to start a new life in a faraway place. Among the teachers were many women hunting husbands in a land where the ratio of the sexes was 10 to 1 in their favour. The turnover rate was high. Most lacked the mental toughness required to meet the demands made on them to be sanitation officer, medical adviser, judge, social worker and reindeer manager in addition to teacher.

Domesticated reindeer herds supplying food, clothing and sled power were part of Jackson's grandiose vision for Alaska. He persuaded the government to spend more than $200,000 on the ill-fated project, money which would have been better spent on education. It was another case of a well-meaning churchman misjudging the natives' willingness to give up the freedom of hunting and fishing to become herdsmen. Some of the reindeer purchased by the government from Lapland and Russia were sent to Metlakatla, but in one of the many blunders associated with the project their horns had been cut off for easier shipment, making them easy prey for the island's wolves.

A number of education issues were debated at the Board meeting in Sitka and Duncan found himself in the minority along with Jackson and Judge James Sheakley of Wrangell, another Presbyterian and future governor. The Board decided to ban corporal punishment in the schools despite protests by the Christian trio. New rules issued by the Bureau of Education were rigid enough to prevent "excessive punishment," Jackson insisted. The Board also acted against the wishes of the three men in banning religious observances in schools where the parents were not all of the same denomination. Only a reading of the Lord's Prayer would be allowed. Bible readings must be unaccompanied by comment or interpretation.

In making its rulings, the Board was attempting to meet the protests of the Russian Orthodox Church schools and the "creoles" against the spreading Protestant influence. (In Alaska parlance of the day, creoles were the offspring of Russian fathers and native women.) Although he was against sectarianism in the schools, Duncan protested that "of all places in the world, Alaska surely needs the Bible." He also observed that it seemed "strangely inconsistent that the Russian Church authorities in pleading for religious toleration in America demand suppression of the Scripture, while in Russia the same authorities suppress the Bible for the opposite reason."

Duncan was also concerned about textbooks. "I attribute in great measure the tardy progress of our people in learning the English tongue to the miserable school books we had to use in B.C.," he told Dawson. "The book that is needed should be adapted for teaching language and should contain nothing but sound sense, and be an epitome of useful information on all subjects in which the Indians especially need enlightenment, and in which they are interested." Typical of the attitude he was up against was that of William T. Harris, who succeeded Dawson as commissioner of education in 1889. Harris urged Bureau teachers in Alaska to use books which "portray in the most powerful form the ideas and convictions of the people of England and the United States." The works of Shakespeare, Dickens and Walter Scott could provide "exactly the material to inspire the teacher and to arouse and kindle the sluggish minds of the natives of Alaska with sentiments and motives of action which lead our civilization."

Duncan was not alone in calling for change. Governor Swineford put the blame squarely on Jackson for the low standard of education in the territory. In a letter to Dawson before leaving office, Swineford declared: "I consider the condition of educational affairs a disgrace to the Department . . . it is about time that someone should be appointed who would regard the place as something else than one especially designed to enable him to make an annual summer pleasure trip to Alaska." The schools were being left too much to themselves, with no one in charge to compel attendance or control teachers. Although an admirer of Duncan, Swineford said he did not believe the duties of teacher and missionary should be combined.

Duncan turned increasingly against Jackson as more ailing youths returned from Sitka. In less than a year eight had been forced to leave. Duncan said the others were strong when they left home but now all were unhealthy. He was convinced there were some "radical defects" in the school. In September he began construction of a boys' industrial school in Metlakatla with a floor space of 4,000 square feet. Duncan proposed to teach the boys carpentering, gardening, coopering, printing, making furniture and sash, building boats and canoes, blacksmith and tinsmith work, and Indian carving in wood and metal. Industries would be introduced in the community year by year to provide employment when the boys left school. "I do not despair of seeing farming and gardening fairly remunerative industries for the people as soon as they can start the work," he told Dawson. His old dream died hard.

Although Duncan and Swineford moved closer together in their common dislike of Jackson, the governor lost esteem among the Metlakatlans by failing to keep a number of promises made on their arrival in Alaska. One was citizenship. At the time of the exodus Swineford told Duncan: "I am inclined to regard them in the light of citizens 'to the manor born'. If I find the law does not bear me out, I shall, with your concurrence, take such steps as may be necessary to make them full citizens."

The governor soon found, however, that U.S. law made no provision for Indians to become citizens. As in Canada, they were regarded as wards of the state. Duncan argued in vain, as he had in B.C., that the laws had been enacted to deal with "uncivilized Indians" and the Metlakatlans should enjoy the same privileges as whites. Swineford also failed to persuade Congress to enact legislation enabling the natives to secure title to the land they had occupied.

Another promise made by Swineford was to have the Metlakatlans form a special military company. Duncan and the natives were delighted. "If you can provide them arms and a uniform," Duncan wrote the governor, "I will undertake to enrol a goodly number and feel sure the discipline will be salutary for the men." Once again their hopes were dashed when an embarrassed Swineford discovered Indians could not be given any military status because they were not citizens.

Despite these setbacks, the natives under Duncan's tutelage had developed intensely patriotic feelings toward their new homeland. The first July Fourth celebration in Metlakatla in 1888 was a gala affair. Duncan described the day in a letter to Dawson. "In holiday attire they gathered round the flagstaff in the morning. The flag was hoisted and saluted with a small cannon. The brass band played appropriate airs. Children, each with a flag in hand, marched and sang school songs. Canoe races and other games followed . . . seven stirring speeches were made honouring the day."

A month later, on August 7, a high-spirited celebration was staged by the Metlakatla youths remaining at the residential school in Sitka. They were observing the first "Founders' Day," an anniversary of Duncan's arrival on Annette Island that has been marked in some fashion each year since. The boys put up a wreath with a big eagle figure and a scroll inscribed: "The British lion always told us he was our friend, but we found him a gay deceiver. Every year he brought up his gun-boats and pointed his guns to blow down our village. Now we have found out who our true friend is. It is the king of birds. He has a sharp eye for our worth, and now we bid the British lion farewell." For better or worse, they had committed their future to the United States.

The town was plunged into gloom that summer when word arrived that a landslide at the North Pacific Cannery on the Skeena had engulfed a number of cottages and killed eight Metlakatlan women and children. The natives had taken jobs at the cannery at the urging of the cannery company, whose biggest concern about the exodus was the loss of skilled workers and fishermen. The Vancouver *World* editorialized that "many of our businessmen have suffered large financial loss by the withdrawal of the Indians, and they will gladly welcome them there again." The *World* commended the dominion government for its half-hearted attempt to induce the Metlakatlans to return by not closing off their fishing and working privileges in B.C. Some of the Indians were not so accommodating, however. They brought oolichan grease and dried fish to trade at New Metlakatla, but would not allow any of the deserters to return to the Nass each spring to obtain their own supplies.

Bishop Ridley claimed Metlakatlans who returned to work in B.C. told him they regarded the exodus as a "blunder." Large numbers were taking up permanent residence in the province again, he said. In fact, less than 40 failed to return to Alaska after the canning season. The population of New Metlakatla actually increased when 60 Tlingits from surrounding villages moved in. Duncan said more would have come but for the strict rules against liquor and gambling. Others were kept away by "bad advice given them by white men interested in keeping them from us."

Indian Agent Charles Todd at old Metlakatla warned Duncan that if any of his Indians returned for any other reason than to resume residence, they would be treated as trespassers. When Duncan asked Strong what he should do about the ultimatum, the lawyer replied: "The Indian agent as I expected takes the ground that your people had no proprietory rights to their homes. That the old Metlakatla was in fact a sort of poor house or pauper farm, where the Colony saw fit to keep its wards." Strong said the U.S. government could not deal with property rights in a foreign country and Duncan's only recourse was to the B.C. legislature.

Duncan bypassed Victoria, however, to appeal directly to Ottawa for compensation. He estimated property worth $80,000 had been left behind, not including public works such as roads and the sea-wall. Some 80,000 feet of lumber had been seized with the sawmill and 40,000 bricks. The government was unsympathetic, claiming that much of the property had been "wantonly destroyed" by the departing Indians. It also repudiated a rental agreement made by Todd with Tomlinson for the use of Duncan's cottage.

Meanwhile, a commission set up in B.C. in 1887 to investigate Indian affairs on the north coast and hear grievances over their loss of ancestral lands issued its final report. It described what was left of old Metlakatla. "The aspect of the once flourishing Indian village . . . was dreary in the extreme. On viewing the large number of empty houses, stripped of windows and other movable parts, the ruins of buildings levelled to the ground by former occupants, the deserted streets, the wrecked condition of the church and sawmill, and the desolate appearance of the whole settlement, the Commissioners were impressed with the stern reality of the deplorable disaffection which had culminated in the voluntary exile of so large a majority of the villagers, and the abandonment of their comfortable homes, old-time hunting grounds and associations."[25]

There were about 100 natives remaining at the old village, but its vitality had been drained. The commissioners also found the Fort Simpson Indians demoralized by the events at Metlakatla. Disaffection was general among the Tsimshians along the Skeena. The commission blamed their alienation on the missionaries rather than the government's denial of land rights.

[25] *Papers Relating to the Commission Appointed to Enquire into the Condition of the Indians of the North-West Coast.* B.C. Government Printing Office, 1888. P.A.B.C.

Chapter 18

Money Troubles

DISAGREEMENT OVER WHAT DUNCAN PROMISED the Tsimshians and what he actually delivered has divided Metlakatla, Alaska, since its inception. The manner in which Duncan proceeded to set up the community's finances and industries shows clearly that he intended to involve the natives even less than he had in B.C. As a U.S. fisheries officer said in a 1900 report: "The common impression is that Metlakatla is a communal organization, with everything in common among its inhabitants. Such is not the fact. The Metlakatla Industrial Company is the principal business concern, owning the cannery and sawmill. The corporation is owned almost entirely by Mr. Duncan."

Duncan employed curious bookkeeping methods. His private and business accounts often overlapped, making it difficult to trace the source of funds and how they were spent. In a letter to his agent in Portland, William Wadhams, Duncan said he hoped to keep the business accounts "as free as possible" from the charitable donations. Later, when he was overdrawn at his Portland bank, he authorized W. J. Macdonald in Victoria to forward $5,000 out of his personal account to Wadhams.

Years later, Henry Wellcome attempted to defend such financial juggling. He said during 60 years among the Indians Duncan had received contributions from various sources intended as gifts to assist him in the mission work. These monies were to be used at his discretion, Wellcome said. But Duncan was his own accountant throughout his missionary career, and often succumbed to the shortcuts which that arrangement allows. The fact he had trained as a bookkeeper with Cussons and was adept with figures did not eliminate the need for an outside audit. In B.C. his accounts had been submitted to the C.M.S., but in Alaska Duncan was on his own.

Wellcome, who became a lone wolf financier himself after

buying out his partner Silas Burroughs, approved of Duncan's methods. When a stock company was proposed for the New Metlakatla business enterprises, Wellcome urged caution. "The less outside dictation you have the better, and you will need to guard against entering into arrangements that may not prove agreeable after a time and which you may find it difficult to throw off." In Duncan's situation, this was not good advice.

Wellcome told Duncan in the fall of 1887 that raising money for New Metlakatla was their most important task. He promised to do all he could to assist. "I contributed my mite $200 before sailing," he wrote in disclosing that six leading businessmen had agreed to act as a fund-raising committee. Industrialist Andrew G. Agnew had been placed in charge, but Wellcome was not satisfied with his efforts. Most of the early charitable subscriptions had come from the Quakers in England, led by Alfred Fryer and his daughter. They wrote articles about Duncan's work for a number of journals that raised several hundred dollars, and donated $350 themselves.

In the U.S., Henry Houghton worked in the East and Thomas Strong in the West to raise an industrial loan fund. Duncan estimated the cost of moving and re-establishing his businesses at $50,000. He tried to borrow that amount from the banks in Portland but was turned down because he owned no property to put up as collateral. Expenditures incurred during the move had reduced Duncan's assets. He had $8,000 deposited in a Victoria bank, store goods valued at $2,500, and the cannery building worth an estimated $8,000. "In all sincerity I would announce that if anyone will come and occupy the place I fill in business matters and work upon these lines," he wrote Strong in December of 1887, "I will most gladly resign all business affairs of the settlement into their hands." It was a proposition he had advanced before in B.C. and would again in Alaska, but which was never acted upon. No one could have worked under his controlling thumb, and he knew the businesses were the key to his work. They generated jobs for the natives and the revenue the mission needed to sustain itself.

It seemed a joint stock company was the only answer, whatever Wellcome thought of its drawbacks. Houghton, Strong and banker Ladd proposed that $25,000 be raised by issuing shares of $10 each. They had rounded up eight investors who would put up a total of $11,000, with the rest to come from Duncan and any Indians who had cash to spare. But only six were able or willing to buy a total of 300 shares. Duncan took the remaining 1,100 by turning over the cannery building and $3,000 of his private funds.

Houghton said the money subscribed by the U.S. businessmen should be regarded as a loan to help re-establish the industries. If the enterprises were successful the investors would accept the return of their money. If there was no profit they expected nothing. They had not invested with the idea of making money, but simply wanted to help Duncan in his work. This proposal was turned down by Duncan, however, on the spurious grounds that the heirs and successors of the investors might demand that the loans be repaid at an inconvenient time. Duncan insisted on setting up a registered company with bona fide shareholders. After considerable delay, the Metlakatla Industrial Company was established.

There was also the so-called "Benevolent Fund" launched by Henry Ward Beecher at Wellcome's prompting, which now totalled $7,000. Duncan exercised sole control over this money and refused to budge from his long-held policy that the Indians should not be given grants or even interest-free loans, despite the donors' intentions. When someone sent $20 to start a revolving loan fund for the natives, to be repaid and loaned again, Duncan rejected the idea out of hand. It would be harmful, he claimed, to the sense of self-reliance he was trying to instil if the Indians were given loans for their personal use. Duncan said the truly poor were the aged, the sick and the indolent, and gifts or grants were of no use to them.

Duncan's stated goal was to elevate the Indians to financial independence within the white man's economy, but that proved difficult to achieve. Jobs must be created for them at Metlakatla, he often said, because working away from the controls of the community was harmful to their moral and social development. Few jobs appeared, however, and despite his virtuous justifications, the natives did not always appreciate that the rigid standards of self-reliance he imposed were in their best interest. At times they suspected Duncan of turning the doctrine to his own advantage. They complained that during the exodus Duncan received donations of clothing and food which had not been distributed. Some of the natives were also concerned about the status of the cannery building, which they had built for public use but which was taken over by Duncan as his private property. If Duncan was aware of the incipient rebellion, he ignored it.

Duncan was in Portland on business when Tomlinson visited in August of 1890 and the natives felt free to talk about their misgivings to their trusted friend. But Tomlinson did not suspect that anything had gone awry in Duncan's work, and his loyalty to his longtime ally did not waver. He wrote Duncan after his return to the Skeena that "it was truly painful to see the utter lack of thankfulness . . . and their apparent forgetfulness of the advantages they had received from your care and training. I can understand the keen sense of disappointment you must feel in the case of many of whom you had hoped better things."

Tomlinson was concerned, however, that the aging Duncan was not preparing the natives to take over his work in the future. Instead, he was shouldering more jobs himself. Duncan regularly worked from 7 a.m. to 11 p.m. When the cannery was running he started work at 4:30 a.m. every day but Sunday, and often worked on his accounts until past midnight. Wadhams told Duncan he was trying to do too much and should supervise and direct instead of doing manual labour himself. "Your eyes are worth more than your hands."

The investors were also growing restive. They complained that Duncan, whose timetable no longer allowed for regular letter-writing, was not keeping them informed of the company's affairs. "We have entire confidence in Mr. Duncan's management and business-like methods," Houghton told Strong, "but we do think that a statement to the directors once in three months, in addition to the yearly report, would not be a great burden to him." Houghton wanted the treasurer, a post which Duncan had appropriated himself, to be elected from the board of directors. The investors may not have been concerned about profits, but they did want the company run in a business-like way.

In Strong's eyes, the Eastern investors were questioning Duncan's character. "I have enquired concerning him from here to Chilcat," he wrote defensively to Andrew Agnew, "and I have not heard or seen anything that shakes the belief that he is an honest Christian man with rare business capacity and common sense and with an especial fitness for an entire self-dedication to his life's work. He is loved and respected by the Indians, who would be the very first to detect any selfish or moral taint." Nevertheless, some of the Indians were having doubts, and the very fact that Strong felt compelled to make a ringing testimonial to Duncan's honesty indicated that all was not well.

Others fed the rumour that Duncan had collected a large sum of money from donors in the U.S. which he was not sharing with the Indians. W. H. Woodcock, a former Skeena River trader living in Wrangell, denounced Duncan and the move to Annette Island in a letter to the Portland *Oregonian* in early 1888. "I hear that he collected in the East over $100,000 and that subscriptions are still pouring in," Woodcock wrote. It was wrong to turn the island, which Woodcock said was worth $100,000, over to Duncan and the natives for nothing. Although recently unoccupied, the island had always belonged to the Tlingits of Tongass and Cape Fox, Woodcock said, and these tribes neither wanted nor needed government assistance. "For a tribe of foreign Indians to come in and want a reservation is, to say the least, impudent in the extreme." There is no evidence, however, that Duncan was given anything close to the $100,000 mentioned by Woodcock, or even the $50,000 amount bandied about by some of the natives. The latter figure was what Duncan said he *needed* to re-establish in Alaska, not what he received.

The cannery began limited operations in the summer of 1890, turning out just 420 cases of one-pound tins. Duncan blamed the delay on the native builders leaving to earn money elsewhere for their new homes. He conceded, however, that the accountancy chores he had assumed were taking time away from his managerial duties. The Eastern shareholders had reluctantly agreed that he should continue as both manager and treasurer of the Metlakatla Industrial Company, and Duncan boasted he was saving $6,000 a year for the firm by not hiring a bookkeeper. The sawmill was the principal source of revenue, shipping lumber and packing cases to the cannery at nearby Loring. Trapping was also good in the area and early in 1888 Duncan sent 1,200 pelts to San Francisco.

When the cannery went into full production in 1891, some 120 natives were employed. They turned out 6,000 cases of salmon in 1891 and 11,000 cases in 1892. In the fall of that year Duncan issued his first dividend cheques of 15 per cent, an extravagant amount that was obviously intended to impress the shareholders. One of them, Moses Pierce, of Norwich, Connecticut, objected. Duncan should pay a maximum of 10 per cent, Pierce said, until the company had accumulated a surplus fund for capital expansion and to cover unforeseen losses.

In a letter accompanying the dividend cheques, Duncan proposed that the capital stock of the M.I.C. be increased to $50,000 in order to take in the store and sawmill, as well as enable him to put in electricity for the town and industries. Houghton was reluctant. Providing electric lighting for the village would be a "luxury," he said. Many established communities in the East still didn't have it.

He favoured borrowing money instead of issuing more shares, and Duncan agreed to try to raise $5,000 among the Indians.

The store was not as profitable as the cannery, but Strong said the prices of food, clothing and hardware should not be raised to increase revenue. Duncan's store fixed prices all along the coast, he said, making him the enemy of all the other traders in Alaska. "An Indian family will just as readily go 200 or 300 miles shopping as ours will go downtown. They love to wander and barter and buy and sell and time is no object to them." Metlakatlans working outside the village brought their wages back to spend in the store because the prices were fair.

The decision to expand the holdings of M.I.C. was held in abeyance, but the natives, who were critical when Duncan failed to provide jobs for those who wanted to stay on the island year-round, now began agitating for funds to start their own businesses.

The island's natural resources, not yet ceded to the Metlakatlans, were being eyed by whites. Fishermen from outside were already threatening the natives' livelihood by placing their nets across the mouths of the island's salmon streams. Duncan urged the government to impose conservation measures because the people needed the salmon for the cannery and their own food supply. He proposed that each stream be monitored and its salmon yield ascertained in order to determine the extent of fishing that could be allowed. Where it was necessary to limit fishing, the fishermen should be licenced. Preference should be given to the natives, Duncan said, because they outnumbered whites in the District by 100 to one and were dependent on the salmon for their own food supply. Because of this dependence they were more likely to be conservation-minded than cannery employees brought in from the south, he argued.

Prospectors began hunting for minerals soon after the Tsimshians' arrival. Duncan protested that although gold had been found on other nearby islands, the whites did not attempt to develop these deposits because they coveted Annette and hoped to sell claims on it. But after combing the island for minerals for two years without success, the prospectors left.

The first contract undertaken by the natives on their own was to supply custom-made wooden bedsteads and bureaus to a Portland furniture dealer. Duncan said he would order windows and doors for the new school from the natives' carpentry shop, "if we can agree on terms." He would drive as hard a bargain with them as he would with any other firm.

218

Duncan sent one of the natives to Portland to learn typesetting and the operation of a press, then bought equipment to put out a community newsletter. The first issue of *The Metlakatlan* appeared in November of 1888. Duncan supplied news of village developments and an accounting of sorts of the various public donations which continued to arrive.

When the steamer *Elder* called at Metlakatla, passengers came ashore to inspect the budding settlement and contributed $60. It was the first of many donations to come from tourist ships over the next decade, before they began to bypass Metlakatla for the new and fast-growing community of Ketchikan.

Duncan firmly resisted suggestions that he actively solicit funds by issuing promotional pamphlets on Metlakatla. "It is ours to do the work and leave God to provide the means." He was not willing to leave everything in God's hands, however. The collection of bad debts was a task he pursued himself with relentless zeal. In May of 1891, more than a decade after his former Victoria agent, Englehardt, had declared bankruptcy, Duncan wrote asking him to pay up the $3,833 he was owed. "Through my leniency," he said, "you have allowed yourself to become indifferent to your obligation ... depend upon it, there remains a bitter experience before you which my leniency will not avert." It was the ultimate threat from a man of the cloth—pay up, or you're going to hell.

In a letter to Agnew, Duncan gave a brief but encouraging progress summary on the community. He reported the cannery and sawmill bustling, houses and boats under construction, rock quarried for a breakwater and wharf, dogfish oil lubricants exported, and the vegetable gardens flourishing. A three-quarter mile road had been built to the site of the new church. For such public works the men put up $3 each in cash or labour, which Duncan matched from the Benevolent Fund. Friends in Portland had collected $340 for the purchase of new band instruments and Christmas was once again a festive occasion. The young people decorated the roads with arches of evergreens and banners, and sang carols around the village.

A new governor, Lyman E. Knapp, had been appointed to succeed Swineford, and his visit to Metlakatla in the summer of 1890 gave Duncan an opportunity to outline his plans for the community and ask for help from the government. The townsite had now been laid out, with 140 lots, each 80 by 90 feet, allotted to families. Ten-foot wide lanes separated the blocks, and houses were to be built on alternate corners of the lots so that each would have an unobstructed view of the beach and harbour. There was to be a mile-long main street running parallel to the shore but set back so the beachfront would be a public levee. The best land was reserved for the school, church and public hall. Duncan wanted to allot 20 acres outside the town for every resident who would agree to improve the property. He told Knapp the settlement required a minimum of 5,000 acres, and the rest of the island should be reserved for the Metlakatlans as a source of timber and firewood and to prevent the establishment of another community.

The new community was set up much like the original in B.C., with a slightly altered set of regulations. New residents were required to declare they would: 1. Observe the Sabbath; 2. Be loyal to the U.S.; 3. Vote in community elections; 4. Support the schools; 5. Abjure liquor, gambling and heathen customs; 6. Be sanitary; 7. Utilize the land; 8. Don't give or sell land to outsiders.

Able-bodied men were taxed $3 a year or three days' labour on public projects. All the men were organized in groups as before. "In one capacity or another," Duncan wrote, "every man in the village has the means to be useful to the community." There were 25 council members, 20 church elders and 24 constables, as well as a fire brigade, military training brigade, and 20-member brass band.

In March 1891, Annette Island was formally reserved by Congress for the Metlakatlans. A special Indian reserve was created which was separate from the general reservation system and could be revoked by Congress. A single paragraph in an omnibus bill states: "Until otherwise provided by law the body of lands known as Annette Islands, situated in Alexander Archipelago in southeastern Alaska on the north side of Dixon's Entrance, is set apart as a reservation for the use of the Metlakatla Indians, and those people known as Metlakatlans who, on March 3, 1891, had recently emigrated from British Columbia to Alaska, and such other Alaskan natives as may join them, to be held and used by them in common, under such rules and regulations, and subject to such restrictions, as may be prescribed from time to time by the Secretary of the Interior."

That statute is still in effect today, but two of its clauses proved a source of trouble to the community for many years. The phrase "... and those people known as Metlakatlans" was not included in the original version of the bill. It was inserted by amendment after Duncan's supporters lobbied to ensure that he personally was

220

included. And the power given to the Interior Secretary to intervene in the community's affairs was the cause of much future
controversy.

Chapter 19

A Young Rebel

AFTER THEIR MARRIAGE, Samuel and Catherine Marsden had remained close to Duncan. The couple took turns preparing meals for him, and their son Edward, a bright little boy born May 19, 1869, spent many hours at Duncan's knee learning to read and play music. Samuel hoped his son would enter the ministry.

When Samuel died in 1878, Catherine wrote Duncan: "I have write this letter to you sir to tell you what my husband said about me and the children. I wish you could help me a little and teach them as their father was very anxious about them; he did not wish them to grow up and be worthless children but to grow up a very good children." Catherine moved with her brood to the home of another widow with four children, Catherine Ryan, but continued Duncan's housekeeping chores.

Duncan's supporters later emphasized how much he had done for the Marsdens, but Edward remembered it differently. After breaking with the C.M.S. in 1882, Duncan had virtually been taken in by the Marsden family, Edward said. "My mother looked after him for many years." Edward also complained that when he was 15 he worked for Duncan for an entire summer and received only $3, a pair of worn corduroy pants and a sack of potatoes. "At 18 I built his fire, blacked his shoes and ran for his water."[26]

Whatever the circumstances of the relationship, Duncan was undeniably fond of both mother and son. He taught Edward to play the organ so skilfully that he performed at church services by the time he was 14. Duncan also gave the boy work in the office and store to learn about business. Edward made such a favourable impression on a visitor from Victoria in 1883 that he was offered a chance to attend school there, with the guarantee of a job to pay for

[26] Beattie, W. G. *Marsden of Alaska*. Vantage Press, 1955.

his board and lodging. Duncan was opposed, however, and he and Catherine refused to let him go.

At the time of the exodus in 1887, Edward was working as an engineer on the Metlakatla cannery vessel *Princess Louise* and was a member of the second party to land on Annette Island in May. He made numerous trips back and forth that summer carrying people, lumber and supplies. He worked on the site for the new sawmill and was a member of the advance party on the shore August 7 when Duncan arrived aboard the *Ancon*. The 18-year-old youth was standing beside N. H. R. Dawson after the education commissioner had addressed the crowd. Dawson asked him in English if he had been to school and whether he could read and write. Edward answered "yes" to both questions. Dawson then gave the boy his card and asked him to copy his name, title and address. Again Edward eagerly complied. "Mr. Duncan!" Dawson exclaimed. "Why this is wonderful. We must help you."

When Marsden told Dawson he wanted to go to the Eastern U.S. to complete his education, the commissioner promised to help. A month later he wrote Duncan asking whether "my young friend" still wished to go away to school. "Tell him that I have not forgotten my promise, that I have made mention of his case to both the Secretary of the Interior and to the Commissioner of Indian Affairs." Duncan should have been pleased by the attention paid to one of his proteges, but was non-committal in his reply to Dawson. He was rigidly opposed to the youths of Metlakatla leaving the community for outside boarding schools.

Edward was kept busy that fall building a home for his mother and sisters and stripping the dilapidated *Princess Louise* to recover her steam boiler to power the sawmill. He worked in the store during the winter and dreamed of getting away to school. Frustrated by Duncan's lack of encouragement, he wrote Sheldon Jackson in the spring that he was anxious to further his education. His letter prompted Jackson's visit to Metlakatla and Edward, with the reluctant permission of Duncan and his mother, was among the first party of boys sent to the industrial school at Sitka.

Marsden was the top student and a leader. After winning a gold piece for the highest marks in both vocational and academic courses, he wrote proudly to Duncan: "All the ladies and gentlemen in the town are very pleased to see how we are getting on very well, careful, doing our work with our will, and obedient boys. They asked us where we were taught to do such things and how to play on different musical instruments. We told them we have been taught by you." When he was pressed to join the Presbyterian Church, Edward asked Duncan for advice. He was told to wait until he was better able to judge which denomination would be best for himself and his people.

Edward's letters were not unlike Duncan's journal entries when he was a student at about the same age. "I thank you, dear sir, that you trained me before I came here. I was thinking that if you did not mind my faults some years ago, and that if your hand was not on me, I would grow up and be a vain and useless foolish man."

Despite his expressions of gratitude and loyalty to Duncan, Marsden was falling more under Jackson's influence. Jackson made him a school prefect and then "assistant superintendent" in 1889. Although he had not joined the Presbyterians, Edward preached in the Presbyterian Church on Sundays to the Sitka Indians. He addressed them in English which was translated into Tlingit.

One of the Metlakatla boys urged him to lead a group in planning a new village where the young Tsimshians would be freed from the old ways of their fathers, which they feared would hold them back in the new world they were about to enter. Marsden was sympathetic, but determined to get more schooling. That opportunity came when Jackson offered to send him for four years to Marietta College in Ohio, where he would have a job to help pay his tuition fees. In recommending Marsden to the college, Jackson said he was the most advanced and promising student at the Sitka school, adding that "he has more egotism than any person I ever met." In Jackson's eyes, that was no handicap.

When Duncan said his mother needed him at home, Marsden anguished over what he should do. He turned for help to David Leask, who was now a Church Elder, secretary of the Council, store bookkeeper and Sunday school teacher. Leask told him there would be a need for educated Indian leaders in the future, and assured him his mother agreed, despite what Duncan had written. Edward decided to accept Jackson's offer. "I made up my mind to go as far as I could go," he said years later, "when Mr. Duncan thought it was enough, and he and I misunderstood each other right there." Marsden said his differences with Duncan had arisen over education. "Perhaps I was more ambitious than he had planned for me to be. And perhaps I overstepped his idea of an Indian education."

Duncan happened to be on the boat to Seattle when Edward was starting out for Ohio. They chatted amicably on the way south and parted cordially. A few months later Marsden wrote Duncan that he intended to return to Metlakatla after graduating to help him in his work. But Marsden soon after joined the Presbyterian Church and the breach between them widened.

Duncan tried to get Edward back. At his urging, Catherine wrote asking her son to come home. The young man was upset by his mother's pleadings but stayed put. Duncan sent $40 in the fall so Marsden could buy a typewriter, and added some fatherly advice. "In your studies take care not to overwork yourself or try to grasp too much...I have seen students who tried to learn everything, taxing their brains so much they broke down and proved of no use to the world." The real reason for his concern, however, was that Marsden was taking courses in the sciences, history, philosophy and theology, which Duncan considered too ambitious a program for a native. He could not accept that Edward might want to work as hard as he himself had done at Highbury.

On the morning of February 7, 1893, fire broke out in Metlakatla. The weather was cold and the ground dry when a spark from a stovepipe set fire to an unoccupied house. The flames were fanned by a strong east wind and within 90 minutes 28 houses had been destroyed. Many families were away hunting and trapping and little was saved from the burning homes. Duncan made an exception on this occasion and begged for aid outside the community. "I cannot resist their earnest appeal to me, to let their friends know of the great loss." The people collected $1,500 among themselves and Duncan contributed $500 out of his own pocket. Another $3,000 in goods and cash was received from outside, including a $500 donation from Wellcome.

Marsden and others later charged that instead of being distributed among the villagers, donated clothing and bolts of cotton were left to rot in a room off the boarding school. Duncan maintained it was the council that decided it would be unwise to distribute the clothing directly to the victims because of the likelihood of creating jealousies if someone received a more attractive garment than another. According to him, the clothing was placed on sale at his store and the independent stores which some of the Indians had opened, and the proceeds went into a cash fund divided among the fire victims. Whatever the facts, it is not surprising the natives felt suspicious about the method of distribution. Duncan did not believe the Indians could sort the matter out for themselves.

Marsden, meanwhile, kept doggedly at his studies. In the fall he asked Duncan for a $60 loan and a share of the government school grants received by the village. Duncan replied that Catherine had forbidden him to send any more money which would prolong her son's stay at Marietta. She thought he appeared exhausted in a recent photograph. He asked Marsden to come home at the end of the term, enclosing $20 from himself and $20 from Catherine. Duncan refused to send any money from the school fund. Edward thanked him, but insisted his mother be given her $20 back because she could not afford it.

Jackson urged Marsden to enrol for three more years in a theological seminary after he completed his four years at Marietta. "I notice what you say with regard to Mr. Duncan's increasing age and work," Jackson wrote, "but he is still strong and will probably live at least 10 or 15 years longer, and can get along better without you now than he can when he is several years older. You could go back and help him a year from now, but unless you take a full and liberal education, you can never expect to take his place when he dies and make a success of it."

Marsden agreed to enrol at Lane Theological Seminary in Cincinnati to become an ordained minister. He planned to take some law courses at the same time, but kept his plans secret for a while, telling only Leask. Finally writing Duncan in January, 1895, Marsden asked for a $50 loan for books and made another bid for his support. "I do realize that you are very busy, but a word from you occasionally will do me much good. You know me very well, and if anyone that will be faithful to you in your closing years, it is the writer, who has always respected and praised your name and good work."

Duncan replied that if Edward was determined to spend three more years studying it should be in medicine, which was more useful in missionary work than theology and law. "I think any well educated man should be able to read up as much law as he would require in a settlement like ours without having the assistance of lawyers." Duncan was unable or unwilling to see beyond the present level of the community. "If your aim is to be a missionary of the gospel to your own kith and kin, I can see no good in your studying abstruse theological questions which may only, after all, unhinge your mind and impede your usefulness." Duncan held out no prospect of a future for Marsden at Metlakatla, but "if you write to tell me you are willing to study for a doctor instead of wasting your time on law and theology, I will be willing to help you financially all I can."

That was the last straw. "Heretofore," Edward replied," I have never minded your constant disapproval and opposition in my pursuit of learning; I have been very faithful to you in spite of your seeming distrust in me and my work; but now, since my patience can no longer hold out, I think it is wise for me to say something about it. If I indulge in the idea that learning and spread of knowledge among the Indian race are the means by which that long down-trodden race can be lifted up and made to stand on an equality with any other enlightened and Christian race, I am not mistaken . . . we have learned many lessons from the late 'Century of Dishonour' and we had better be wise."

Marsden said he could not afford to take medical training because Duncan had given him nothing but loans. He did not understand why Duncan advised him against studying law, unless it was from "a fear of being compelled to respect true justice in your relation as an employer with my people." Except for one or two, the people of Metlakatla were still illiterate. Then Marsden asked pointedly: "What accounts for the frequent violation of the 7th commandment among your followers?"

Strong said the Eastern friends of the mission were so surprised to see an Indian accomplish anything, they were likely to magnify Marsden's modest attainments. "They have undoubtedly petted and flattered young Marsden until he thinks that he amounts to something more than the ordinary man, even the Anglo-Saxon race, and this I fear will be the result of an education in the East of any of our native Indians." Strong added prophetically that "a new generation will be growing up from now on who will have no personal remembrance of the hardships of the past and from this class we must expect trouble." Marsden's harsh letter typified "the tendency that I fear will within 10 years after your control is ceased very likely wreck the city of Metlakatla." Duncan agreed it would be difficult to guard his work against such "upstarts" as Marsden.

Strong then touched on the crux of the problem. Metlakatla was too dependent on Duncan. He urged him to pick an understudy and take 10 years to train him, giving up more duties and responsibilities each year. Strong was clearly thinking of a white successor to Duncan and it seems never to have occurred to either man to consider Marsden as a potential candidate. Some years later a report prepared by Duncan's white supporters declared that if

Marsden had "possessed character and the true missionary spirit" Duncan would have trained him for the position he coveted.[27]

Relations between Jackson and Duncan, never cordial, became more strained. Despite his excesses, Jackson seemed genuinely to believe that the most accomplished Indians could and should become leaders among their people. Duncan, while paying lip service to the ideal, did not. Jackson wrote to General Pratt of the Carlisle Indian school: "Every suitable young person that you take from Metlakatla is a great gain to humanity; those people should have a chance—they are worthy of it. And now that it is evident that Mr. Duncan does not intend giving them a chance, those of us who know the situation are in duty bound to try and help them."

David Leask and a few other natives became increasingly restive under Duncan's leadership and made known to Marsden their suspicions about his financial dealings. Leask had also seen a copy of Marsden's letter to Duncan, and he applauded the young man's stand. "No doubt Mr. Duncan has meant for your own benefit and good according to his view. But it should be remembered our generation is a growing one. My experience with man, brother, has taught me a lesson not to mind what people think of me, but the work we have in our hands speaks for us." Leask said he intended to apply for U.S. citizenship papers so he could leave Metlakatla and acquire land elsewhere in Alaska.

Marsden had been granted citizenship in May 1894, a year before Duncan. On applying, Marsden was asked whether he was an Indian and declared that he was an alien born under the British flag but was not a citizen of the British government. He had taken an oath to the Constitution when he arrived in 1887 and there were no legal objections to his application, even though he was only 18 at the time. Marsden's friends wanted to know how they could become citizens. He said he would help them, but made it clear he was not yet prepared to lead an insurrection against Duncan. He urged Leask to remain in Metlakatla, and gave the same advice to Alfred Atkinson when he complained that Duncan boasted of making big profits while paying lower wages than other canneries. Atkinson was also dissatisfied that there was still no school for the older boys and girls, and that Duncan refused to ask the government to provide one.

[27] *Matthews Report*, published by the U.S. Senate Subcommittee on Indian Affairs in *Survey of the Condition of the Indians in the United States, 74th Congress, 2nd Session.* U.S. Government Printing Office, 1939.

Marsden told Atkinson he should be patient and maintain "propriety and goodwill" toward Duncan. "Although he has not given you just the things you wanted in various departments of this life, yet we cannot doubt the good he has accomplished among the Tsimshian people. To oppose him or in any way to trouble him in his attempts to do good, is to do him injury and injustice."

Marsden had become a minor celebrity in the East, receiving many invitations to speak to churches and other groups. He was not imposing, a short, flat-featured and less handsome figure than most Tsimshian men. But his voice was strong and hair "as black as a raven's wing" made him an exotic figure in Ohio. He took an interest in politics and worked on the successful presidential campaign of William McKinley in 1896. After McKinley's election, Marsden wrote the President at Jackson's prodding supporting the appointment of John G. Brady as governor of Alaska. Brady was a former Presbyterian missionary and ally of Jackson who had gone into business in Sitka. Marsden also wrote McKinley later urging him to veto a bill in Congress which would have restored Annette Island to the public domain.

In April of 1897 Marsden became the first Indian in North America granted a licence to preach. A year later he graduated from Lane Seminary and was ordained. Before graduating, Marsden had written Jackson asking if he could now expect to be appointed by the government to take over the educational affairs of Metlakatla. Jackson replied that Duncan would object, "and our funds are too precious to put a school anywhere which would bring a quarrel on our hands." When Jackson had tried to place a government teacher in Metlakatla in 1895 Duncan said if that was the only way the community could get school aid then it would manage on its own. And it did—no government school funds were accepted in Metlakatla for the next 20 years.

Jackson told Marsden the Presbyterians would appoint him missionary to the Indians at Saxman, a small native community across the channel from the north end of Annette Island and adjacent to Ketchikan. Soon after Duncan had arrived in Alaska, Jackson asked his approval to set up a Presbyterian mission on Annette Island for the Tlingits. Duncan refused, so Jackson later persuaded the Indians at Cape Fox and Tongass Narrows to move to Saxman, leaving their homes behind as the Tsimshians had done at old Metlakatla. He promised them land and a similar industrial mission. To Duncan's annoyance, Governor Brady helped facilitate the move. About 60 Tongass natives were already settled in Metlakatla and more had been expected before Jackson intervened. There were only a dozen or so white men in Ketchikan at that time, but Duncan said Saxman would prove a singularly unsuitable site for an Indian settlement as Ketchikan expanded. Their move would end in the "demoralization and ruin" of the Tlingits, he said.

Jackson told Marsden that if he built up a good school at Saxman the Metlakatlans would send their children there to be educated. He urged him to set up a council of natives and system of government similar to that at Metlakatla, with himself at the head. "If you have headquarters at Saxman you will be near enough to keep in touch and sympathy with your people, and then when Mr. Duncan dies I have no doubt that they will turn to you as their leader and unanimously elect you to take Mr. Duncan's place."

Marsden was not keen about the appointment. He told Jackson he would rather teach at the Sitka school, but reluctantly set out for Saxman in the summer of 1898. When he spent a few weeks in Metlakatla, repairing his mother's house, Duncan studiously ignored him. On September 1 Marsden crossed to Saxman, where he could look over at the domain of his one-time patron and contemplate the future. Another struggle for control of Metlakatla had begun.

Chapter 20

The Mailbag

KEEPING UP WITH HIS CORRESPONDENCE was a continuing struggle for Duncan. He spent one or two hours a day at it and was always behind. The volume of business letters alone was overwhelming. There were orders for food, clothing and hardware for his general store, parts for the sawmill and cannery, fishing gear, tin-plate and solder for making cans, as well as a running correspondence with his agents on disposal of the salmon pack. A stream of letters flowed between Duncan and Thomas Strong on business and community affairs. Duncan told Strong that outside supporters of the mission "have good reason for complaining that I write too little, but you have reason to complain that I write you too much."

Every two weeks the steamer would drop off a mail-bag bulging with letters from well-wishers and admirers, job-hunters, donors, old friends in Victoria and England, recipients of the many gifts Duncan bestowed, school children wanting help for their essays on Indians, as well as the simply curious who had read about Metlakatla and wanted more information on the man and his work. Some assumed he was an authority on all things Alaskan, asking where was the best spot to hunt, catch fish or buy Indian relics. To the latter, except for friends for whom he would commission the Indians to turn out carvings, Duncan always replied that Metlakatla was a poor place to acquire "curios" because the crafts were dying out among the people and the few available objects were taken by shipboard tourists.

Some letter writers wanted work. A disenchanted Klondike gold hunter asked for money or a job, saying the gold rush was "a gigantic fraud and scheme of the big companies doing business in there and the newspapers of the coast towns to prosper themselves."

Duncan did not offer encouragement to those who wanted to become missionaries in Alaska as he had done. "As health is a matter of very great importance to a missionary," he wrote one inquisitor, "I would strongly advise you not to undertake to come out to Alaska unless you have a robust constitution."

Duncan seldom engaged in gossip himself, but never objected to receiving it from others. The insular little city of Victoria was a constant source of titbits on liaisons, scandals and business failures. The Macdonalds, husband William, and wife Kate, were inveterate tattlers who provided Duncan with a stream of items for his amusement or indignation. Smug and cosy in their gracious mansion "Armadale," with all the children doing the right things, they took satisfaction from the misfortunes of others. Wasn't it too bad about poor Richard Cridge, but have you heard the latest? Richard was the ne'er-do-well son of the Cridge family, and the Macdonalds made sure Duncan didn't miss a step on his staggering path to destruction.

There were other victims of the Macdonalds' busy pens. "What a time-serving old weathercock Sir J. (Macdonald) is," Kate declared. "I perfectly loathe and despise such a man to be at the head of affairs." Her husband wrote with righteous scorn of the recent "miserable marriage" made by Harry Helmcken, brother of Dr. J. S. Helmcken. "He has taken for his wife a woman who was divorced by her former husband and has since been living, it is said by San Francisco people, on the down grade with no brake on. They live in Sir James Douglas' home to the disgust of Martha and others. I cannot imagine what possessed Harry to be so infatuated. She is very common looking, fearfully painted and made up and has two grown up daughters, one twenty years old. Harry is our Bishop's church warden so it is an unpleasant complication for everyone concerned."

And then there was the disgrace of Edmund Verney, member of a prominent British family and former captain of the Royal Navy gunboat *Grappler* on the coast. Verney was sentenced to a year in jail for "luring French girls to Paris for governesses, etc. and then using them for immoral purposes." It was later learned that he did not seek out the girls for himself, but for the amusement of his master, King Edward VII. In the best British tradition, Verney protected the King and went silently to prison.

Money was a constant concern of the Macdonalds. Kate expressed concern about the homeless victims of the fire in Metlakatla and hoped to gather a few dollars for them, but said the call came at "an inopportune moment" because the economy was depressed and the family heavily in debt. The senator complained

232

that taxes had increased "to an almost unbearable extent" because Victoria was spreading out into adjacent rural areas. He had to pay $1,500 on Armadale last year, and "all the money is being swallowed up by sewerage works." And the senator wrote from Ottawa on the financial scandals in which political favourites "are getting the pick of the land at low prices—insurance companies are lending money to their friends, putting the profits into the pockets of friends instead of that of shareholders." Macdonald added that English syndicates had been buying up canneries on the Skeena and Fraser rivers, and English capitalists were taking over breweries and other industries in the U.S. "There is so much money in England that they do not know what to do with it."

Daughter Edythe, who married a British Navy admiral with the propitious name of Fleet, was a true Macdonald. "You will be sorry to hear that both Bishop Alford's grand-children have married Catholics," she told Duncan. "The girl turned R.C. too and no doubt the boy will too. He is in Italy and has married an Italian—it is very sad and strange. I am afraid their mother was not careful about their religious welfare."

Edward Cridge's letters often had a whining tone: "Pray for us. We much need it in the work. The devil is very busy. What an engine driver he is!"

Robert Tomlinson kept in touch from the Skeena, thanking Duncan for his "kind and liberal assistance" in sending money to his little mission. He reported that Collison had not been happy since the break. "I don't believe he has ever felt himself a free man since you left the CMS." Tomlinson added warmly that neither he nor Collison "have ever felt we had a *brother* missionary since."

Hamilton Moffatt, who left the H.B.C. to join the Indian Affairs Department in Victoria, was pleased at the prospect of his upcoming transfer to Kamloops. The population of Victoria "seems to be made up of thieves, gamblers and loafers," he told Duncan. "It is without the least exception the very *worst* place I was ever in. The whites here require more civilizing than the Indians of the north."

Duncan's correspondents on the U.S. Eastern Seaboard had difficulty visualizing what life was like in Metlakatla. Company shareholder Fred D. Allen of Boston wrote: "Your people are becoming civilized and perhaps it might be well for you to sleep on bedsteads and on mattresses, between cotton sheets and under common bed blankets and quilts. Don't you use cotton cloth for shirts and underwear and sheets to sleep under?" A Boston merchant who promised to fill his order as soon as possible asked, "As to blankets for your people, we suppose you want the regular 'Indian Blanket'... are they used as a garment or for beds to sleep under?"

Duncan attempted to answer all the letters, even the most trivial. During the canning season he wrote only business letters, catching up with the others on winter evenings. Despite numerous requests, he refused to provide any information on himself. Strong sent him a form to fill out that could be provided by his Portland office to reporters, writers and supporters eager to know more about this man devoting his life to the Indians. Duncan tersely filled out most of the form, but left blank the spaces for his birthplace and the names of his mother and father. Strong chided him for his secretiveness. "We men and women are sad gossips," Strong said, "but the fact still remains that the most interesting study to men and women is the study of the lives of men and women."

Duncan was warm and genial in his letters to mission supporters. He invited Chicago tycoon and Metlakatla investor J. K. Armsby to visit the settlement with his wife to recover his health in the "pure and temperate climate we enjoy in summer." He added: "We have no street-car racket—no roaring steam pipes—no clouds of dust or smoke and better still no daily mail or telegrams to distract... we are indeed alone with nature in all its primeval beauty—added to a little of the hum of home and quiet industry."

On occasion, he was ready to offer personal advice, even when unsolicited. Such was the case with Lieutenant "Willie" Macdonald of the Royal Navy, son of William and Kate, who had announced his intention of marrying a Catholic, despite the family's scorn for that denomination. No doubt she was a well-bred Catholic girl. "Now, dear friend," Duncan wrote, "I should shrink from further advising you on the step you contemplate taking did I not firmly believe that your marriage with a Roman Catholic lady, if consummated, will prove a life-long sorrow to you and to others who love you and therefore permit me again lovingly to urge you to make the matter the subject of earnest prayer and I believe you will be guided and kept from taking the fatal step." After subjecting Willie to some murky theological ramblings, Duncan concluded his 7-page letter bluntly: "Take my advice—keep away from Rome and from everything that belongs to it."

234

He was also an early conservationist. "It is a pity the Government do not see the necessity of taking hold of the salmon streams before they are denuded of salmon life," Duncan told Thomas Strong. "I feel they will bestir themselves when it is too late. Our natives are a good deal alarmed over the food supply prospects—fearing they will be by and by left without daily bread, salmon being their staple food. As the laws stand and the country is governed—anyone can it seems come and invade others' rights without let or hindrance."

But the preservation of morality, particularly in Metlakatla, was Duncan's greatest concern. For example, he asked government attorney Charles Ingersoll in Ketchikan to deal with "a young scamp" caught climbing in the bedroom window of a girl whose father was away from Metlakatla fishing. The grandmother heard the boy enter the house and he was caught by the girl's uncle. Duncan sent a constable to arrest him but he no longer had the powers of a magistrate to deal with the case as he did in British Columbia. "I fear if nothing is done to vindicate the honour and purity of home life . . . the evil will grow and someone will be likely in such a case to avenge his own wrong and blood may be shed."

In another case of youthful indiscretion, Duncan reported to Judge E. S. Stackpole of Ketchikan that a girl in the village had been made pregnant by a young man who had refused to marry her. "Though it was evident from the testimony given me that both the parties were in love with each other for some long time . . . I hope you'll uphold the law and lay a charge . . . and thus help us to put down such immorality."

In a similar vein, Duncan asked Governor Brady whether the Metlakatla Council had the power to eject undesirables from the settlement. "Some of our young men who are now coming in contact with a certain class of whites are being inoculated with ideas which disdain self-restraint and parental authority." He had in mind two young men who had married girls without the consent of their parents, "in utter defiance of strict Indian law regarding consanguinity." From time immemorial the Indians of North and South America had been forbidden to marry members of the same crest, he said, and the ban "has been beneficial both physically and morally to the race." The government should not interfere with the custom, which was "still deeply reverenced." Duncan was obviously selective about which ancient customs he believed should be preserved, and was no doubt influenced in this case by the fact that both marriages he described were performed by the Reverend Edward Marsden.

If these three letters displayed Duncan's intemperate side, another showed his compassion and skill as a marriage counsellor. It was written to a Metlakatla man living in Ketchikan. "Since you were here and told me of your wife's conduct I have received a letter from her telling me of your conduct to her. Now let me write to you, as a friend, as I have also written to her. Do not think that I believe her more than I believe you, or that while I would help her I frown on you. No indeed. I am very sorry for you both and heartily do I wish I might persuade you to forgive each other and live together as Christians during the few days you have on earth."

Duncan managed to keep liquor and its troubles away from Metlakatla for many years. But as he reported to U.S. commissioner D. W. Figgins in Ketchikan, December 26, 1900, was a black day in the community's history. "I am sorry to inform you that an Indian young man was found drunk on the street here last night, the first case of drunkenness I have ever seen at Metlakatla." The man was in custody and Duncan hoped an example would be made of him so there would be no repetition. But there was worse to come. He wrote again the next day to say he had discovered there were two young men involved. One of the natives had found them wandering drunkenly around the houses and guided them away along a road which happened to lead to the church. "Whereupon one of the young men vomited on the steps of the church and then staggered off." The other lay in front of the church door, where he was seen by Josiah Burton, who was lighting the church for the Boxing Day service. "Alarmed at seeing the drunken man on the way of the people who would be soon entering the church, he came running to me." Duncan called a constable to arrest him. It was unclear where the pair got the liquor. "It was reported they had cider—but several who smelt the odour of the vomit on the church steps state the liquor was some alcoholic drink."

His letters from Alaska also confirmed his persistent refusal to entrust the natives to assume business responsibilities on their own. To a Seattle bank which sought his approval on an application for a loan by some Metlakatlans planning to build a sawmill on neighbouring Gravina Island, he replied: "I believe they are honest men yet I have reason to fear they are too ambitious and visionary in business affairs. Their prospects of success are not by any means so bright as they anticipate. There are already six sawmills around

236

here and a sparse population. They are behind in their payments and can't pay workmen's wages as they ought. I have reason to believe that Edward Marsden—the secretary of their company—is urging them on . . . far beyond their means. And worse than that I find the Indians are very reckless in their use of borrowed money."

Duncan gave the same advice to the Lévi-Strauss Company in San Francisco in a letter in which he enclosed a cheque extracted from native storekeeper John Tait. "I would advise you to be careful in your business with these people. They persist in loaning goods to their customers—though they know how difficult it is to collect that money when they want it."

Neither did he want the natives to become involved in politics. To an invitation to send some native delegates to a political convention in Juneau, Duncan replied: "I do not consider our community of natives, not yet naturalized citizens, are fitted to take any part in the political affairs of Alaska. For lack of knowledge and experience in such matters as will be discussed . . . our people's vote on any question would not be given with any intelligence and therefore had better not be given at all. For the present we are willing to leave all government questions of the District to the wisdom of its citizens."

Although he had cut himself off from almost all his old English associations, Duncan was nostalgic about some events. In a letter dated "8:30 p.m., December 21, 1896," he wrote Bishop Alford: "This very hour, forty years ago, you and I started from Paddington Station, London, en route for Plymouth. How often during these eventful years have I thought of your kindness in accompanying me on that first stage of my journey to this country."

And he wrote a gracious reply to Henry Wellcome on receiving an invitation to his wedding in 1901. "The Star Spangled Banner which you kindly donated to our native community in 1887 was waving over our town hall in honour of the Fourth of July when the announcement of your approaching marriage reached me. It was very kind of you to give my name to Dr. and Mrs. Barnardo as one of your friends and I have to thank them for honouring me." Duncan offered a prayer for the marriage, but it would take more than his blessing to bring wedded bliss to the 48-year-old Wellcome and 21-year-old Syrie Barnardo, glamorous dark-haired daughter of the renowned benefactor of London's slum children.

Chapter 21

Juggling the Books

DUNCAN'S WORKLOAD became even more demanding in 1894 when Dr. Bluett left him after 12 years' faithful service as unpaid physician and teaching assistant. Bluett was an unassuming man who worked comfortably with Duncan. But like Doolan, he was discouraged at his inability to master the Tsimshian language. He also admitted a crisis of conscience that would not have endeared him to Henry Wellcome: "I have lost faith to such an extent in the efficacy of drugs to cure disease that I feel more and more strongly day by day I am occupying a false position."

The previous year when Duncan had let it be known he was looking for someone to take an interest in the mission and possibly take over from him in the future, he had received an application from Dr. Henry J. Minthorn of Salem, Oregon. Minthorn had practised medicine for six years before joining the Bureau of Indian Affairs. Later he became superintendent of the Pacific Academy educational institute at Newburg, Oregon, and was now involved in the fruit business. He was a Quaker minister and told Duncan that at the age of 47 he could work for the rest of his life with little or no income. Despite that inducement, Duncan turned Minthorn down. He said he wanted a younger man.

Duncan told Strong the colleague he was looking for should be under 40, married, belong to no established church, and prepared to work as teacher, mechanic, bookkeeper and manager of the native workmen. His wife would be the school matron. For these services the couple would be paid $1,000 a year. "The man who wishes to do God's work in the world for its own sake has few questions to ask about his own trimmings," Duncan said in defence of the meagre pay. He soon gave up his half-hearted attempt to find a successor, however, and after Bluett left advertised for a doctor only.

Minthorn sent another application. He was now in charge of a sanitorium in Muscatine, Iowa, after taking some post-graduate courses in a Chicago medical college. His wife was a church worker, and the couple had two daughters, aged 8 and 13. Minthorn did not mention that he was the uncle and foster-father of a promising young mining engineer named Herbert Hoover. The future President had been adopted by the Minthorns as a young child when both his parents died.

Duncan asked his terms. Whatever the last man got, Minthorn replied. Climate was clearly not a priority because Minthorn said he had received an offer to do mission work in Jamaica but would rather go to Alaska. Duncan asked him to come as soon as possible. Bluett's independent means had enabled him to work without salary and assume all the costs of his practice, including his own house, but Duncan said he was willing to pay Minthorn $1,000 a year and provide a house for his family.

Minthorn accepted and began a 40-year, off-and-on association between his family and Metlakatla. He sent along a package of seeds with a request that Duncan get someone to plant a flower garden to be ready for his children when they arrived. He also intended to keep a cow and wanted to know if there was any hay on the island.

Minthorn's arrival solved one problem, but there were many others demanding Duncan's attention. The school was suffering from neglect as a result of his preoccupation with business matters. The situation worsened in 1894 when the principal of the Sitka school notified Duncan that because of financial difficulties all students who were not on special scholarships or could not pay for their board and lodging would be sent home. Duncan turned down Jackson's offer to put him on the government payroll by appointing him as a Bureau of Education teacher.

He wanted government help, but only on his terms, which included a guarantee there would be Bible instruction. He found it difficult to get teachers who could meet his rigid criteria and were willing to work for a small salary. After going through a succession of unsatisfactory candidates, Duncan decided to muddle through by taking some classes himself and using native assistants for the primary grades.

Although he was critical of the teachers, Duncan said they could not be blamed for all the faults of the Alaska education system. In 1901 he proposed to Commissioner William T. Harris that teachers learn the native tongue and instruct in it; students be taught in their own towns, with parents participating; Indian villages be isolated from white settlements; native police be appointed to enforce the law; and girls not be allowed to leave training school until the day they married with their parents' consent.

Harris was not the only government official to receive advice from Metlakatla that year. Duncan also wrote a long letter to Senator J. H. Gallinger, which was referred to the Senate Committee on Indian Affairs and printed in the Congressional Record. In it, Duncan noted that one policy under consideration for Alaska's natives was abrupt assimilation. Let them sink or swim in competition with whites. Government would provide only some extra schooling to allow the natives to catch up in education, while granting citizenship and the privilege of acquiring land on the same basis as whites. Such a policy had a semblance of fairness about it, Duncan said, "but when we contrast the condition of the two peoples—whites with centuries of experience behind them, and Indians still as children taking their first lessons in civilized life—then the seeming fairness of this proposition vanishes." Duncan proposed giving the natives a protected status, with reserve sites chosen by them at least five miles from a white settlement. Each reserve would have its own school, with "a practical Christian teacher" who would also be a magistrate.

He advanced these ideas again two years later in a letter to the Director of Indian Affairs in Washington, J. Forrest Witten. He was beginning to feel concern for the future of Metlakatla itself, Duncan told Witten. The actions of Jackson and Marsden had resulted in feelings of "distrust, discontent and insubordination." Village rules were being neglected. But providing more jobs was still his prime objective. "These natives to a great extent are now loosened from their ancient moorings and in the absence of a definite government policy being initiated for their guidance and protection, they are drifting." Duncan condemned the reservation system and came out again in favour of "sanctuaries" which would not restrict the movements of the Indians. With its abundant natural resources, Alaska should have plenty of jobs for them. Despite the lack of evidence, he had not given up hope of finding gold on the island. His dream of mineral wealth was kept alive by the persistent attempts of whites to open up the island for mining.

The first serious campaigns against his domain were mounted in 1897 and 1898 when two bills were placed before Congress which

240

would have restricted the Metlakatlans to a small tract of land around the bay at Port Chester, leaving the rest of the island open to white prospectors and speculators. Duncan took the threat seriously enough to travel to Washington to fight the bills. He found some influential allies. W. H. Dall, the noted Alaskan explorer and writer who bestowed his wife Annette's name on Duncan's new island home, published a plea for Metlakatla in the *National Geographic*. He called on "friends of justice" to make themselves heard before it was too late to save the villagers' bid to determine their own destiny. A New York *Tribune* editorial headed "The Annette Island Grab" said the bills were "a menace to the civilization which has been established among these Indians by a faithful and devoted missionary in spite of great trials and discouragements." The bills were opposed by Interior Secretary Cornelius Bliss and died in committee.

Despite these diversions, Duncan pushed ahead during the 1890's with a number of projects for the community. The most ambitious was construction of a dam and water pipe from Chester Lake where its outlet tumbles over an 800-foot cliff into the bay. He had decided to undertake the work after fire gutted the second steam sawmill in 1892. As well as powering the sawmill and cannery machinery, the water was to be used to generate electricity. The pipeline would also supply water for drinking and fire-fighting. When Duncan found the hydro-electric plant would cost $6,000, he postponed that aspect of the development as well as the costly pipe network to deliver drinking water to individual homes. Instead, a single tap was placed near the store on the pipe from the sawmill to the cannery.

The cannery was enlarged in the spring of 1894 with the aid of a homemade steam pile driver. A metal lathe was purchased so machine-shop work could be done on the spot as needed. Duncan also attempted to build another brickyard and open up a slate quarry on nearby Prince of Wales Island, but both projects were abandoned as uneconomic.

A number of public buildings went up in the first decade, including a town hall that could seat 400, a guest house for visiting natives, and a six-cell log prison. Duncan reported to the Interior Secretary in 1898 that the jail was "very rarely" used, mostly for prisoners brought in from the surrounding area. The buildings reflected Duncan's quirky architectural tastes, but all had practical reasons for their strange shapes. The 12-gabled town hall proved easy to keep warm during the coldest winter weather.

The houses were more conventional in design but decidedly grand for an Indian village. Some had as many as 10 rooms. Most were freshly painted, neatly gabled with Victorian gingerbread and surrounded by picket fences. Many had flower gardens in the front yards and vegetables in the back. Despite its inner tensions, the town was beginning to take on a settled look. The Council borrowed $2,000 at 10 per cent interest from Duncan to build a network of 8-foot wide board sidewalks around every block. Members of the young men's athletic club cleared a park-playground area on a scenic point of land where Duncan later installed a 12-seated musical merry-go-round.

Despite his isolation, Duncan kept abreast of the latest scientific advances and whenever possible acquired them for Metlakatla. On one of his trips to the East he had met Thomas Edison and asked if he could have Edison's first instrument for recording voices and music. Edison said the original had too many faults, but presented him with the second machine. Later Duncan ordered a more advanced phonograph from Portland with some pre-recorded cylinders. He intended to preserve some of the Tsimshians' legends by having an old man speak into the machine, but had difficulty making his own transcriptions and eventually gave up on the project. Duncan, perhaps because of the other demands on his time, never succeeded in chronicling the Indians' history before his arrival, or for that matter, afterwards. His letters and daily journal, which was abandoned before he left B.C., leave only a fragmentary account of the two Metlakatlas.

For the first few years there was no real church in the village. During the first few months Duncan preached on the beach. In the winter he moved into a log building intended for industrial use. In the next few years church services were shifted first into the cannery and then the day school building. Work began on a new church in 1894. Money was raised as the $10,000 project went along. Duncan appealed for outside help again, and the natives contributed whatever they could manage. One winter they collected $324 at the Christmas Day church services and another $54 in cash and clothing on Boxing Day. The offerings ranged from five cents to $20, with many giving 25 cents each. The women collected money for carpeting the aisles and the men subscribed $500 for a pipe organ. In the final accounting, the natives contributed $1,800 and outsiders $2,500, while the remaining $6,000 came from the M.I.C. treasury.

The church was nearing completion in the fall of 1896 and Duncan hoped to consecrate it on December 22, the anniversary of the day he sailed from England 40 years before. But it was not ready, and the opening was delayed until the first Sunday of 1897. The structure seated 800, making it smaller than the great edifice at old Metlakatla but still the largest in Alaska. Its twin towers, one for a bell and other for a clock, were 70 feet high.

Four years later fire destroyed the church, school, mission house, cannery and a few houses in old Metlakatla. Duncan was unmoved by the disaster, commenting sourly that the flames had "only consumed stolen property." Government aid was quickly provided to help the natives rebuild their homes and the settlement shared a bonanza in 1906 when the Grand Trunk Pacific Railway paid the Department of Indian Affairs $90,000 for a portion of the Tsimshian reserve lands on Kaien and Digby Islands for the Prince Rupert terminus of the new railroad. Half this money was distributed at the time of the sale to all natives living in the village over 21, an amount of about $500 each. Most used it to build or buy new fishboats. Native children living at the time of the sale were given $200 when they reached 21. The other half of the railway money was placed in a fund for the Tsimshians, and as late as 1926 a large portion was still held by the department.

Fire was not the only hazard in the coastal villages. In the winter of 1900 six adults, five babies and three youths died in New Metlakatla from influenza and pneumonia. Many men lost their lives fishing for halibut in the open ocean and travel was dangerous even on the larger vessels. Duncan was aboard the steamer *Willapa* northbound from Seattle in March of 1897 when she struck a reef during a snowstorm at 2 a.m. near Bella Bella. No lives were lost but the ship was badly damaged before being freed and towed to Fort Simpson. Most of the freight was ruined.

Five months later the steamer *Mexico* hit a rock in the night near Annette Island and sank in 100 fathoms. All 140 aboard, mostly tourists, were rescued and taken to Metlakatla. Dr. Minthorn complained that the 35 women billeted in his house spent the time fighting over the limited supply of bedding. Duncan sent a bill to the steamship company for the cost of the survivors' upkeep.

In 1898 the Minthorns departed suddenly for Oregon. The man in charge of their farm had left without notice and they were forced to return to protect their investment. Minthorn was another Metlakatla worker discouraged by his failure to learn the native tongue, which made his medical practice more difficult. He also preferred rural life and was frustrated by the futility of trying to farm at Metlakatla. His cow had died because there was no pasture and his chickens floundered in the mud.

The only white helpers Duncan now had were the Wallaces, a Scottish couple Strong had recruited in Oregon in 1896. James Wallace worked as a general handyman and gardener around the mission, while his wife served as Duncan's housekeeper. They gave devoted service to a demanding and unappreciative employer. As Strong told one of the shareholders, "Mr. Duncan is not given to praising his subordinates . . . expecting more than he has a right to expect from the average assistant. He is so wrapped up in the work that he . . . sometimes lacks sympathy with people who know nothing of the Indians and have everything to learn, and new people in Alaska need sympathy." By 1900 the Wallaces returned to Oregon, too, but agreed to spend six months at Metlakatla each year during the canning season.

At first, Duncan and the natives paid little heed to the special Act of Congress in 1891 setting aside Annette Island for the colony. It was accepted without question as being in their best interests. With the memory of government double-dealing in British Columbia still rankling, it is surprising Duncan was not more on his guard. In the beginning he was too overcome by feelings of gratitude and patriotism towards his benefactors to question their deeds on his behalf. He paid little attention to the ramifications of the wording of the Act, especially its failure to deal with individual land holdings and citizenship.

The warnings came from outside, from people with less trust and more cynicism than Duncan in the continuing goodwill of governments. Houghton expressed concern to Strong in 1894 that the Metlakatlans did not have title to the island. If the colony prospered, or if minerals were discovered, then speculators were sure to move in. Strong told Duncan he should try to obtain separate title for individual holdings and avoid communal ownership except in the case of public buildings. Otherwise, he warned, "designing persons" like Marsden could, after Duncan was gone, break up Metlakatla with lawsuits claiming everything was community-owned. Strong was also pessimistic about the likelihood of citizenship being granted to the Metlakatlans. "In the light of past experience I do not think the American people will ever extend the right of suffrage to the Indian people as a whole."

244

The strongest warning came from an unexpected source. Not long after taking office in 1897, Governor Brady told a group of Metlakatlans visiting Sitka that their legal status in Alaska was perilous. Upset by this news, the natives returned home to tell the others their eyes had been opened by Brady and the people must take immediate steps to become free men. Brady did little in the ensuing months to calm their fears. In his 1899 annual report the governor described the 1891 Act as a "blunder" because it introduced the reservation system into Alaska, and wrote a letter to the Metlakatlans pointing out they were subject to the whims of the Secretary of the Interior. "If he sees fit to put an agent over you and confine you to the limits of Annette Island, he would have this law as authority for doing so," Brady told them.

Duncan chose to ignore the warning. Brady's statements, he said, insinuated underhandedness by the government, and insincerity or ignorance on the part of the outside supporters of Metlakatla. Why should the natives assume some future Secretary would use the Act to their detriment? "All they need to do is to live properly and thus prove themselves to be worthy of his confidence and then face the future without any fear." It was true the Metlakatlans were living on a form of reserve, Duncan said, but they did not come under the regulations of the reservation system.

Most of the Indians were not ready for citizenship, Duncan told Brady. They saw only the benefits and status which citizenship conferred, without recognizing the duties and responsibilities. "The standpoint from which the natives view the question is not the same from which you and I view it." The fact that some of the natives had asked the government to establish a residential industrial training school at Metlakatla showed they were willing to be treated as paupers or wards of the government. "They are still children in many aspects and need the same watchful care, guidance and discipline."

Brady suggested that 160 acres of land be deeded to each native on the island to avoid the "odium" of a reserve, but this proposal was also rejected by Duncan. The Indians might think it would be a "grand thing" to own 160 acres, he said, but the land would be of no real benefit to them. "The natives are not farmers nor ever will be in Alaska," he said in final recognition of the obvious. The island was not suitable for agriculture and the Indians had neither the will nor the means for clearing the forest. They wouldn't pay tax for land they couldn't use and it would soon pass into the hands of others. Duncan told the governor he favoured community ownership rather than individual title to the land. That conclusion was clearly influenced by concern over his ability to control rebellious elements in the town in the future.

The feud between Brady and Duncan, which carried on for six years, resulted partly from opposing loyalties. Duncan felt beholden to the national government which had granted him asylum. He kept aloof from Alaska politics. Brady, on the other hand, like all the Alaska governors of the period, was engaged in a running battle with Washington over the District's rights, representation and legal status. The differences between the two men were exacerbated by the Brady-Jackson credo that what was good for the Presbyterians was good for Alaska.

The days of power for both Jackson and Brady were numbered, however. The chorus of opposition to Jackson's education policies had been rising in volume. In 1899 a Grand Jury in Juneau concluded that a large part of the Bureau of Education's budget had been "frittered away in payment of expenses of wholly useless summer jaunts of (Jackson) to remote parts of the territory, and in the establishment of schools where none were needed." These views were echoed by the *Mining Journal* of Ketchikan, edited by former governor Alfred Swineford, which said not one native graduated from the Sitka Industrial School was practising a trade learned there. The paper also scoffed at a map prepared for Jackson's reindeer program which showed Saxman as one of the larger towns of Southeastern Alaska, although it consisted of only a half-dozen native families. Metlakatla, "by far the most successful mission in Alaska," was designated merely as a post office.

In 1905 President Theodore Roosevelt ordered the Interior Department to carry out an investigation of Jackson's activities. The inquiry was conducted by a special agent of the department, Frank Churchill, who concluded that the favouritism prevailing under Jackson had led to laxity and extravagance in the Alaska school system. A shake-up was ordered in the Bureau of Education and Jackson was forced to resign. The Bureau would now be responsible for native education only, with schooling for whites and mixed-bloods placed under the governor.

Brady soon followed Jackson out the door as a result of his close connection to speculators and promoters in the District. Another victim of Roosevelt's purge was Pratt, ousted as head of the Indian school at Carlisle. Few mourned his departure. A St. Louis newspaper called Pratt an "honest lunatic."

Roosevelt was sympathetic to Duncan and the Metlakatlans, declaring in his Annual Message to Congress they were "hard-working, decent living Indians... these particular Indians are civilized."

Although Roosevelt's house-cleaning brought more democracy to Alaska's political and education systems, it did little to resolve the problems pressing in on the District in general, and William Duncan in particular. One of the biggest threats was posed by the new California-based syndicates set up to exploit the rich Alaska salmon runs. The fur seal had been slaughtered to the edge of extinction and salmon would be next if the companies were left uncontrolled.

When Brady claimed that only five per cent of the Metlakatlans were employed on Annette Island, Duncan retorted the figure was closer to 25 per cent and would be greater except for the syndicates. Pressure was applied by the big firms on the Tlingit fishermen not to sell their catch to the Metlakatla cannery. Duncan admitted that many Tsimshian fishermen returned each year to the Skeena, where the canneries offered higher prices, making him dependent on the Tlingits. So many of his people left one summer that Duncan tried to recruit Chinese workers in Seattle, but was unsuccessful. The cannery limped along short-handed until the families returned from B.C.

There was also the matter of the people wanting to start their own businesses. Although that was what Duncan supposedly encouraged, he had mixed feelings about such enterprises. He had little faith in their ability to succeed, resented losing funds that might otherwise be invested in his company, and feared the loss of control that might follow their increased independence.

These problems started him thinking about the future of the M.I.C. As early as 1893 he told Strong he would rather not raise money outside the community to support the company's expansion. He wanted the natives to buy up shares of the outside investors so the company could come under their control "in time." There were flaws in his plan, however. They became more apparent as his correspondence with Strong on the company's future continued over the next decade. Duncan knew the Indians did not have the money to buy many shares. Since he would remain the manager of all the operations, there was little chance he would risk his capital investment by turning shares over to the natives, let alone surrender authority to them. In 1896 Duncan reported that of the

247

outstanding shares he owned close to $40,000, outsiders $11,000 and the natives less than $2,000.

In 1897 Strong asked the outside shareholders to give up their stock so that it could be sold to the Indians at par. Only one objected that the company should retain experienced businessmen to act as advisers, but he reluctantly turned over his shares. Strong admitted it was "unbusinesslike" to be buying out the shares with the company's own money, but defended the step as being in the best interests of Duncan's work. He did tell Duncan, however, that it was "almost a sin" to be sending so much money out to shareholders who did not want it. In buying back the shares Duncan repaid them more handsomely than any had expected.

Just three months later Duncan told Strong that six native shareholders had decided to sell out too, leaving only seven with small holdings. He was admitting, in effect, that his intention all along had been to exclude native shareholders as well as outsiders so that he could become the sole proprietor.

Duncan was not motivated by greed or a desire to amass a fortune for his own use. He intended leaving behind whatever he had earned for the benefit of the Metlakatlans, honestly believing he was acting in the natives' best interests in managing affairs as he did. But Duncan's failure to train them to take over after his death created suspicion about his motives. How could they be sure he was going to will his money to them? In his desire to make the amount as large as possible, Duncan decided he must run everything himself. He had little faith in the Indians' business abilities. The Tsimshians had been astute traders before his arrival on the coast, but their exposure to the intricate white economy was limited.

In 1904 Duncan decided to buy out the last seven natives, who between them owned $1,900 in shares. They had gone three years without a dividend payment. Duncan claimed the cannery was barely breaking even and he needed the profits from the store and sawmill to pay for the new electrical plant. Strong chided him for his penny-pinching and urged that the dividends be paid, even if the company had to overdraw its account. Duncan refused. Paying dividends to the Indians was anathema to him.

Strong lost patience when Duncan broke with the banking firm of Ladd and Tilton in Portland and switched his accounts to Seattle. That meant dissolving the company in Oregon, where it was registered, and putting legal title in Duncan's name. When Duncan died, Strong warned, the whole operation would come to a halt

248

and become the prey of lawyers. He urged him to reincorporate in Seattle with Seattle directors, despite the additional cost. "The question of expense is hardly worth considering in the matter. You have had your outside affairs and corporate interests carried on at a cost that seems ridiculously small compared to what ordinary commercial companies have to pay." Strong said he had handled the company's business in Portland for 12 years without pay before recently starting to take out $50 a month. He also reminded Duncan that Ladd and Tilton had been more liberal with the M.I.C. than with other businesses, particularly when Duncan refused to sell his salmon pack in advance for fear of losing the best price and was short of cash while it languished in warehouses.

At other times, Duncan juggled his account books in order to use his private cash to avoid paying interest on bank advances, a practice which Strong strenuously opposed. "If you could but think of the company being as it is an entirely separate individual from yourself, you could then see what bad business it is for one individual to have his business carried on as you are now carrying on the M.I.C. affairs."

Duncan even objected to paying fire insurance premiums. Since he now had accumulated considerable surplus capital, he decided to set aside a fund to provide his own insurance. At least one native, Ed Benson, objected to the break-up of the company and was reluctant to return his 40 shares. Duncan told him taxes were so high in Oregon the M.I.C. would be better off as an unincorporated company. He persuaded him to sell by promising the company would carry on as it had in the past. When Benson pressed for a share of the fire insurance fund, Duncan brushed him off by saying everything was going to be turned over to the natives in time anyway.

Strong proceeded to dissolve the company, "very sorrowfully and with a very clear apprehension that it will work disaster to your work after you have gone." With a sense of sadness mixed with relief, Strong cut himself off from the day-to-day affairs of the community. "Let me hear from you once in a while in a friendly way so that I can tell how matters are going," he wrote. Except for a few faithful native supporters, Duncan was now isolated.

Chapter 22

Wheeler Dealer

IN THE SUMMER OF 1903 Minneapolis lawyer John W. Arctander travelled the Alaska coast on a tourist ship taking photographs for a lantern slide show. The steamer didn't stop at Metlakatla, but Arctander heard about the village and its founder. He wrote Duncan in September for information to include in his narrative for the slides. It was the start of an unlikely association.

He was born Johan Ludwig Wilhelm August Arctander in Stockholm in 1849, emigrating to the United States in 1870 after graduating from the Royal University of Norway. Along the way he jettisoned two of his names and anglicized another. Arctander studied law in Chicago, and after being admitted to the bar moved to Willmar, Minnesota, where he practised for 10 years. He soon earned a reputation for making money easily and spending it quickly. In 1879 the Minnesota Supreme Court suspended him for six months for falsifying dates on documents.

Arctander moved on to Minneapolis where he was said to have undergone a religious transformation. He built up a large practice, winning so many suits for injury against the city's Rapid Transit Company that the firm hired him as its own solicitor to defend damage actions. Arctander also wrote magazine articles on a variety of subjects, made numerous speeches around the city, and became involved in some questionable stock-promotion deals. With his fine-featured good looks and glib, confident manner, he found it easy to captivate audiences. Gossip had it that he was a "brute" to his wives, three in all, and was an aggressive womanizer. But his real passion was making money.

When his hectic lifestyle began to affect his mental and physical health, Arctander took time out for the relaxing summer cruise to Alaska. He was soon rejuvenated by what he found—a land of opportunity for a man with his particular talents. He wrote Duncan again in the winter and cajoled an invitation to spend the following

250

summer in Metlakatla. "It was then I conceived the idea of becoming the historian of this interesting little nation, and the biographer of their wonderful leader." Arctander spent the next five summers in Metlakatla, making notes for his book and doing chores for Duncan.

All went smoothly at first. In the winter months Arctander fired off a barrage of letters to Duncan brimming with ideas on how to make the Metlakatla enterprises more profitable. Instead of salmon offal being dumped from the cannery into the sea, he suggested a reduction plant be installed to produce fertilizer. Duncan promised to study the idea. Arctander had also observed an outcropping of serpentine stone on the island and proposed a quarry. But later examination of the deposit found it was not serpentine at all and was unsuitable for building. Duncan did accept Arctander's offer to go to Washington to lobby against further attempts in Congress to open up the Island, however, as well as press for citizenship for the natives.

Arctander said he would be studying medicine during the winter months and intended to help in the school next year. Furthermore, he had decided to raise a $50,000 fund to be presented to Duncan in 1908 to mark the 50th anniversary of his first preaching to the Tsimshians. It would be up to Duncan to invest the money as he saw fit to further the work of the mission. Arctander also drew up a new will for Duncan, with himself as one of the executors. All the while, he carefully courted Duncan's friends. On his way home to Minneapolis one fall, Arctander stopped off in Victoria to present his slide show, which had been promoted by Edward Cridge at Duncan's request.

As Duncan became more sceptical about Arctander's schemes, a note of caution began to appear in his replies. When Arctander said he was trying to recruit a teacher and a doctor for Metlakatla, he was told to hold off because money was tight. After speaking to a convention of Minnesota grocers extolling Metlakatla canned salmon, Arctander claimed to have sold a railway carload on the spot and told Duncan he could easily pick up more orders. A Benedictine monastery had expressed interest in buying 600 cases, he said. But Duncan turned down Arctander's "kind offer" to sell the salmon without charge. He also told him there was no need to press for extension of the Homestead Act to the island as the Metlakatlans did not require large land holdings. When Arctander offered to assemble a library for the community, Duncan said only texts in the simplest English would be suitable. He hoped to start night school classes soon to improve the natives' reading comprehension, Duncan said, but few potential students were left in the village. They had gone elsewhere for jobs. The population was dropping.

Despite these rebuffs, the smooth-tongued lawyer held Duncan under his spell. In February of 1906 Arctander told Duncan that his wife had volunteered to be his housekeeper in the summer while the Wallaces were visiting Scotland. She would learn from Mrs. Wallace what Duncan liked to eat and would, of course, work without pay. "We both agree upon the fact that we know no greater man in the world than yourself." Arctander had previously odered some furs to make a boa and muff for his wife and Duncan shipped 10 prime mink skins in March, with a promise that 15 more would follow for his daughter. Duncan offered to give him the furs but Arctander insisted on paying.

Not everyone in Metlakatla was smitten. Thomas Hanbury wondered what a smart lawyer like Arctander was doing there and told him he must have come "for some kind of mischief." Hanbury noted that Arctander had given flags to the children and ribbons and candy to the women, while asking the natives if they knew where gold could be found on the island. Duncan should have chased him out of town, Hanbury told Arctander bluntly.

Arctander continued visiting Metlakatla each summer. At times his behaviour seemed erratic, Duncan noted, but gave no cause for suspicion. He was alarmed when Arctander left suddenly one summer, but was satisfied when Arctander later explained he had gone to Nome to look for gold. Duncan expressed concern about his health in the fall of 1907 and suggested he was working too hard. But Arctander completed his book in the summer of 1908 and on his return to Minneapolis that fall told Duncan his health was good and he owed it all "to the wonderful Metlakatla air." Then he let Duncan in on what had been occupying his time in addition to the book.

Arctander had been thinking about how to raise the $50,000 fund he had proposed. At first he considered adding a chapter to his book in which he would make an appeal to readers for donations. Then he thought he would ask President Roosevelt, U.S. railroad tycoon James J. Hill, Bishop Cridge, and Senator Macdonald to act as a committee to receive subscriptions and invest the money for Duncan. But he knew, said Arctander, that Duncan was opposed to public appeals. "Then it seems that the Lord himself pointed to a way out."

The direction the Lord indicated was toward the Colorado River, where Arctander happened to have a gold dredging operation. He was confident it would make him a rich man, and now he was offering to cut Duncan in on the bonanza. "I am now getting in, as a result of correspondence and circulars sent out to my people, over $2,000 a day, which they invest on the strength of my statement and my connection with the company." His people were Scandinavian farmers in Minnesota and Dakota, and a larger group of 10,000 "Christian Scandinavian businessmen and ministers" scattered across the U.S. who received Arctander's promotional brochures. The farmers attended a lecture on "How to Make Money," then were separated from their savings after the meeting in return for shares in his ventures.

Arctander's pitch to Duncan was more subtle and personal. He told him there was a vast difference between mining and dredging for gold. Mining was pure speculation but dredging was a sure thing because it was possible to predict exactly how much gold could be extracted each day. Not one gold dredging operation had ever failed, he claimed, when the necessary capital had been put in to secure a proper dredge. What Arctander neglected to say was that the two companies he had acquired had forfeited their charters in 1906 for failing to pay licence fees. A dredge and steamboat belonging to the companies had sunk when the river was in flood. A minor setback like that did not deter Arctander, however.

He assured Duncan the 20 miles of river rights acquired by his corporation contained untold riches. A "great British mining engineer" named McCray had looked at the property and confirmed the presence of gold, although later inquiries turned up no trace of a McCray. With the new dredge he proposed to buy, said Arctander, a million and a half dollars in gold would be taken out each year at a cost of only $60 a day. Just think of the profit when there are five such dredges in operation, he tantalized Duncan. As for the management, "everyone here who knows the directors at all will admit that a more prominent and respectable, honourable and Christian set of gentlemen never has started an undertaking of this kind."

Arctander had a special deal for Duncan. "I also want privately to tell you that I have succeeded in getting the Board to agree that pastors and missionaries should get a deduction of 20 per cent ... my proposition to you is this, authorize me to buy 25,000 shares for you. That will cost you 5,000 dollars, and send me a check for that amount ... I will not cash the check or buy the stock unless I know that everything will be and is alright." By putting in $5,000 Duncan would earn $50,000 within five years, "which could be invested in farm mortgages or other solid securities and bring you the income that you want for the mission." Arctander invited him to put up a second $5,000 and said he had written a dozen natives at Metlakatla offering them 200 shares each for $40.

"I wish you would kindly give this your earnest and prayerful attention," Arctander wrote, "and will let me know as soon as possible. I have prayed a good deal about it and I feel that the opportunity has now been offered me by the intervention of the Lord to benefit Metlakatla in a way that I had never dreamed of." In a postscript, Arctander added modestly that, "I think I have some executive ability ... I have always carried out very gloriously anything I have undertaken."

Duncan was gullible about some things, such as the curative powers claimed for the patent medicines of the day, but he was hard-headed when it came to business. He told Arctander that his letters had "caused quite a commotion in our little community." It was generous of Arctander to extend the offer, but the Indians were not yet mature enough to take part in such speculative ventures. It was better for them to work by the sweat of their brows. Duncan also politely but firmly rejected buying any stock for himself. "I am not sure that God would approve my putting money, which is devoted to his service, into any scheme which offers such great returns for but little done—I think those who earn the money by labour should have it."

Arctander made one more try. He wrote to say his own pastor, "who could not possibly stand the loss," had borrowed the money to buy $1,000 in shares, and that "my favourite brother, the Catholic priest" had been persuaded to buy a similar amount. But Duncan would not be budged. He ignored this letter and did not write Arctander again for seven months.

A week after sending his last letter seeking to dredge up Duncan's motherlode of cash, Arctander mailed galley proofs of the first 100 pages of his book, *The Apostle of Alaska*. He asked Duncan to correct "anything that is absolutely wrong. Not anything that you would like changed, because you must leave me to my individuality in that regard." Duncan did not acknowledge receiving the proofs for more than a year, apologizing that he had been too busy to look at them. He had just heard, however, that the book was already out and "errors have gone forth to the public which will be a cause of great pain to me." He had examined only the first 60 pages, "but the corrections I have made already filled 11 pages of foolscap closely written, besides some pencil corrections I have made on your sheets."

When Arctander replied indignantly, Duncan tried to reassure him he was not alleging intentional wrongdoing. "You acted you thought for the best, but nevertheless an evil has overtaken the work upon which you spent so much valuable time that painfully grieves me." Duncan said the errors resulted from undue haste to get the book out in time for the 1908 Alaska-Yukon Exposition in Seattle. He had thought the galley proofs were the actual book, which could not be published as long as they were in his hands, and delayed making corrections because his initial examination of the first 60 pages had shown there would be a lot of work involved. "Many statements in it are not true and many words quoted as my utterances are not authentic," Duncan wrote. In the Introduction, Arctander disclaimed any credit for the book, declaring that he was "merely a reporter, not an author" and the words belonged to Duncan.

"What should be done?" Duncan asked. "Financial loss should not concern us in a matter like this. *I would say by all means destroy this edition.* Duncan suggested that Arctander rewrite the book. He offered to bear any temporary financial loss. Native storekeeper Benjamin Haldane had received 300 copies of the book and Duncan said it would not be right "for me to permit him to sell the book here." He seized all of Haldane's copies, saying he would pay the publishers' $270 bill and was also prepared to buy up the remainder of the first edition if necessary.

The book was much in demand in Metlakatla, however, and Haldane got a new supply through Arctander which he sold from a booth on Church Road. Duncan complained bitterly that Haldane didn't have a peddler's licence. But his booth was on property belonging to Ed Verney, who took 12 copies himself from Haldane for resale.

Arctander pressed Duncan for immediate payment to him of the bill owing the publisher, Fleming H. Revell, for the books taken from Haldane. Duncan retorted that the bill allowed four months to pay and he had no intention of sending Arctander any money. He denounced Haldane's character and told Arctander he had made a mistake in picking him as his bookseller in Metlakatla and guaranteeing his advance payment. Haldane would have been in prison for selling liquor if it had not been for his leniency, Duncan claimed. An epistolary slanging match ensued. Arctander accused Duncan of being high-handed. He retorted that Arctander was underhanded. "Would you have me wink at the errors in the book?" Duncan asked. "If so you have mistaken me." Arctander had indeed.

Duncan paid the $270 to Revell in September, telling the publisher the book had "pained more than I can tell." He had not believed that Arctander would be so unscrupulous as to publish it before he had examined it. He complained that other publications were already picking up and spreading the book's errors.

Arctander wrote airily that Duncan could send his petty corrections for the Norwegian and Swedish editions of the book. "I appreciate Mr. Duncan your peculiarities and I have no desire to respond in kind to your treatment of me but feel very thoroughly inclined to humour you in what I even think is unreasonableness." Arctander said the affair was Duncan's fault because of his delay in sending the corrections. He claimed to have shown the manuscript to Tomlinson, who was satisfied with its accuracy. The 300 copies commandeered by Duncan lay around Metlakatla in boxes for years until Tomlinson's son, Robert Jr., decided in the 1930's the books would be good for the natives to read and began spreading them around the community.

In 1909 Arctander took up residence in Ketchikan, where he practised law and became involved in mining speculation. He picked up some legal work by persuading clients he could help them evade taxes. The Colorado dredging scheme had collapsed, with the investors losing everything, and Arctander could not return to Minnesota for fear of being charged with obtaining money by false pretences. Of his stay in Ketchikan, lawyer Charles E. Ingersoll later said, "he was clever and he was crooked, there was no doubt. All he wanted was the chance..."

After three years, Arctander moved to Seattle and started up another law practice. After the First World War he was disbarred for the second time in his chequered career for helping young Scandinavians who were not American citizens avoid military conscription. The Washington State Board of Law Examiners described Arctander's conduct as "unpatriotic, unethical and unprofessional." He died soon after in 1920 at the age of 71, leaving an estate of $1,100.

If the book had contained only a few errors, Arctander would have been justified in his complaint that Duncan's objections were trivial. But the accumulation of errors destroys the book's value as a reference or historical document. It is excessively laudatory of Duncan, barely mentioning, and then apologetically, his blemishes. But Duncan was not so vain as to ignore the book's faults. He was an obsessive stickler for accuracy, especially on the part of others. He questioned whether the title was justified in that he was not sent to Alaska, had spent only 21 years there, and had done little missionary work outside Metlakatla.

In 1909, for the first time since 1887, there was no correspondence between Duncan and Thomas Strong. Duncan could have used some of his old ally's advice in the face of mounting problems. Increasingly isolated and withdrawn from his outside friends, tired and preoccupied with business affairs, Duncan declined an invitation in the fall from Henry Wellcome to take a week's rest at his expense in California where he was holidaying with his wife.

Nearing 80, Duncan's weariness and the onslaught of ailments such as rheumatism, a hernia and painful corns made him increasingly aware of his age. "The duties of each day almost overwhelm me," he wrote in the midst of the canning season. "I cannot overtake my work as once I could." Admitting a rare bookkeeping error to Thomas Strong, Duncan said, "I find I am getting old and signs of age are not wanting—leading me to forget many little things in the daily routine of life and business." His position was akin to that of an aging businessman with a young family. Instead of slowing down, he strove to build up his bank account to provide security for them after he had gone. He neglected the role of a father and became an obsessive worker with little time for his progeny. In pursuit of profits to turn over to the Tsimshians, Duncan lost sight of his original goal—to make the natives self-sufficient in the white man's world.

The salmon-canning industry in southeastern Alaska at this time was a competitive but highly profitable business. The Alaska Packers Association was the dominant firm, with several canneries in the area, but there were also a number of independent operators like Duncan. His was one of the smallest plants, and the only one to employ Indians almost exclusively. In the others 80 per cent of the workers were Chinese brought up for the summer from Seattle or San Francisco. Indians did most of the fishing for all the canneries, however. There was intense competition on the fishing grounds and frequent skirmishes between fishermen for competing canneries. When the A.P.A. cannery at Loring announced it intended to double its annual pack to 60,000 cases, Duncan growled that they would have to "scour every stream within reach" to achieve their quota. "It is too bad to have such a greedy syndicate to fight, but I suppose we shall have to enter the conflict."

Duncan was genuinely concerned about the conservation of salmon stocks and made a number of suggestions on the subject. He proposed to Governor Sheakley that all salmon-spawning streams be declared government property and placed under the control of a fisheries officer. Duncan favoured hatcheries and curbs on the use of traps at stream-mouths. The efficient traps were made of mesh chicken wire suspended from a wooden log frame anchored off stream mouths or on the salmon routes along the shore. It was their introduction first at Loring which enabled the A.P.A. to set such a high quota there. Duncan complained that the few fisheries officers in Alaska favoured the syndicates.

Duncan realized he could not survive an economic war with the A.P.A. and must reach a *modus vivendi* with the other canners. He asked Loring manager J. R. Heckman to provide him with the prices to be paid for salmon there that season, so that "I may not inadvertently be led, by false report, to name any price for salmon beyond your figures." Duncan hoped their "harmonious relations of the past" would continue. He was referring to an informal agreement among the cannery operators fixing prices paid to independent fishermen for salmon or wages on contract boats. When the price for canned salmon dipped in 1902 Duncan had written to Heckman and the other operators proposing that wages and prices be frozen at the previous year's level. The existence of a combine among the canneries was not so surprising as the fact that Duncan would be a party to it, conniving to drive down the income of his own people. However, when Heckman invited Duncan in 1908 to join a formal cannery "compact," he declined on the grounds that his production was too small to be significant. He was, as usual, reluctant to be bound by the rules of others.

It was characteristic of Duncan to set himself apart from the other canners except to fix wages. A loner who preferred to do things his own way, he placed great emphasis on the quality of

Metlakatla canned salmon and criticized the product of others. He resisted the movement toward such automatic machinery as the Iron Chink, and boasted that because his tins were hand-filled he was able to ensure that no bad salmon found its way inside his label. "Speed and greed in packing salmon is playing havoc with the business," he told his agent in Seattle, Kelley-Clark, "sending food to the civilized world which the Indians would not eat—and is scarcely fit for dogs." The Chinese contract workers had no interest in maintaining quality, Duncan said. He thought he should get a higher price for his salmon, but that was becoming more difficult in the dawning age of mass marketing.

Eventually Duncan's reluctance to use his profits for capital improvements resulted in his plant becoming inefficient and uneconomic. He was still refusing to enter a sales agreement in advance of the season, and rather than pay the cost of warehouse storage in Seattle insisted on holding the unsold salmon in Metlakatla, making it impossible to fill orders promptly. Some of his salmon was sold in Australia and Japan, but most went to England, although he complained testing requirements were too severe there.

Duncan's parsimony worsened with age and he had many spats with suppliers and agents. Rather than pay a $7.25 weekly bank charge, he persuaded the steamer purser to bring him a packet of cash on each trip for his payroll.

He also had a dispute with the government over his alleged breach of the District's rudimentary forest regulations. The restrictions were regarded by many as a joke. In a land covered with forest, trees were regarded almost as an endangered species, while salmon and fur seals were harvested without regard to the future. The demands of the small population were minimal, but the law said timber could be cut for personal use only. It was an Alaska joke that to adhere strictly to the rules, a man would have to build his own coffin before he died. The Metlakatlans originally took the timber they required for building homes from their own island, but when the easy access shoreline trees were all cut they moved on to nearby islands. Duncan's sawmill at first cut lumber only for use in the village, but later built up a profitable business selling wooden cases to other canneries.

Eventually in 1905 the law caught up with him. Treasury Agent H. C. Love informed Duncan the Metlakatlans were guilty of trespass on restricted forest lands and were subject to a cutting fee.

Love's letter arrived at the height of the canning season and Duncan was struggling each night with a mountain of business correspondence. Arctander was helping him out at the time and wrote a reply to Love without bothering to check with Duncan. "My position is," he wrote over Duncan's signature, "that we are in the hands of the Government, whatever it desires of us, when it makes its demands known, we will comply with them." That sounded conciliatory, but Arctander was being sarcastic. He wrote more on the subject in his arrogant manner. Love was not amused, and his second letter, which matched Arctander's in churlishness, went so far as to cast doubt on Duncan's right to cut any trees on Annette Island.

At that point Duncan decided to take over the correspondence with more reasoned arguments than those put up by Arctander. Stopping him from logging on the island, he told Love, "would be like giving us a sheep but forbidding us to touch the wool that grows on its back." Perhaps the people should be living in mud huts, Duncan added bitterly. "The law in a newly settled region does not run on all fours," he lectured Love. "In the history of new provinces, especially such as are tardy in growth, it is seen that some laws are kept in abeyance till the conditions of the new country are ripe for their inception. Many restrictions of the law which are both necessary and salutary in old established places would prove arbitrary and obstructive if enforced in their entirety on the pioneers of a wild territory."

Duncan was not so tolerant in his insistence on strict enforcement of the liquor laws and most other regulations in Alaska. But when his business interests were involved, he had different standards. Duncan told Love the sawmill was just a small operation set up only to supply lumber to the Metlakatlans. In an earlier report to M.I.C. shareholders, however, he had boasted the mill was a highly profitable operation. Such duplicity seemed to come more easily to him now.

Chapter 23

A New Teacher

FOR MANY YEARS the administration of education in Alaska mirrored the chaotic state of government. The Bureau of Education had been created in 1867 within the Department of the Interior as a small agency responsible for assembling statistics on the condition of schools in the lower states and territories. Its scope was expanded in 1884 when the Secretary of the Interior was given control of all education in Alaska. It was not until the ouster of Sheldon Jackson as General Agent of Education in 1906 that Congress moved to separate the education of Eskimos and Indians from that of whites and mixed-bloods. Deprived of its influence and prestige, the Bureau sought ways to enhance its limited jurisdiction in the field of native schooling. It moved beyond its statutory authority into the areas of sanitation, medical care and welfare. The Bureau became more openly protective of the natives, assuming responsibility for easing the pressures on them arising from the collision of the two cultures.

To shield the natives from the economic aggressiveness of the whites, the Bureau started co-op stores in the larger villages where provisions could be bought at wholesale prices. It acquired a small steamer, the *Boxer*, to carry supplies to the smaller villages and transport furs and other saleable goods to Seattle. In the words of one historian, the Bureau's role involved "a degree of paternalism and control which was not healthy in the long run, but was probably necessary at first."[28]

Like Jackson before them, Bureau officials cast covetous eyes on Metlakatla as the most prominent and promising field of operation, even though other settlements were in greater need of their attention. While deeply troubled, Duncan's community was at least

---

[28] Smith, Glenn. *Education for the Natives of Alaska: The Work of the U.S. Bureau of Education, 1884-1931.* Journal of the West, July 1967.

functioning. But control of Metlakatla would give the Bureau the prestige it craved. And with the old man beginning to lose his influence over the natives, it made a tempting target.

As education went into a steady decline at Metlakatla, the natives became openly critical of Duncan's priorities. In 1904, with Marsden's prodding, they drew up the first of a number of petitions calling on the Bureau to set up a residential training school on the island. Duncan was bitterly opposed and the Bureau, fearing the strife that its presence would create, declined to intervene.

In the summer of 1908 Duncan hired Bertram G. Mitchell to teach in his school with the help of a native assistant. Mitchell's arrival in August marked a turning point in the affairs of Metlakatla. He had originally signed on with the Bureau, which paid his way to Alaska to teach in one of its outlying native schools. But he settled in Ketchikan, where he taught school for a while before taking a better-paying job as bookkeeper for the Ketchikan Power Company. Some claimed later that Mitchell had been persuaded by the embittered Arctander to go to Metlakatla to undermine Duncan's work. Arctander was said to have prepared the way by warning Duncan that if he didn't hire a qualified teacher the government would be sure to move in. But Mitchell insisted he went only after being approached by native spokesman Henry Ridley, who made "the most eloquent appeal that I ever heard." Ridley spoke passionately of the people's desire to see their children properly educated.

On his arrival in Metlakatla, Mitchell was shown a third petition to the Bureau drawn up by some of the natives, but he persuaded them to withhold it for a year to see what progress he could make in improving the school. Before going to Metlakatla he had investigated all the negative things he had heard about Duncan from former teachers. "The result of this research was to arouse in me a strong sympathy and regard for Mr. Duncan and an earnest determination to disprove all these stories that I had heard."

It didn't take Mitchell long, however, to discover he was up against an immovable force. To meet Duncan casually, he observed, was not to know him. Only his best side showed then. To discover the true situation, one had to listen to the native grievances. Mitchell soon became as discouraged as the teachers who had preceded him. But instead of giving up and leaving, he decided to write to Bureau officials describing the conditions he had found and urging them to step in.

262

Mitchell wrote first in April 1909, to A. N. Thompson, Superintendent of Schools for Southeastern Alaska in the reorganized Bureau hierarchy. "I dislike very much to say anything against Mr. Duncan for he has done a great and noble work," he told Thompson, "but it is my honest belief that he is rapidly undoing all his good work since he has become so childish." Mitchell confessed to feeling "underhanded" in working against Duncan and feared he would be fired when Duncan discovered what he was doing. But the government should not wait for Duncan's consent, he said, to put in a school. "Procrastination rules here," he concluded.

Mitchell amplified his grievances in a letter May 2 to Commissioner of Education Elmer E. Brown. "Mr. Duncan has been out of touch with men in affairs for so long that he in no way realizes what a change has taken place. No leeway nor initiative is allowed the teacher and what original ideas he may introduce are at the risk of losing his position." Mitchell said when he arrived Duncan had given him the names of the worst boys and girls. "I followed his instructions for a while and ruled the school with a stick in my hand. The result was that I had in front of me a set of the hardest faces that I have ever seen."

Mitchell then tried to inspire his students instead of beating them. When he caught a girl cheating he called the attention of her classmates to the offence, explaining why it was wrong, then kept her in after class. "Instead of whipping her as Mr. Duncan had suggested, I talked to her as I would to my own sister...I said scarcely two words before her face softened and she broke down crying. She follows me now like a pet animal and gives me scarce any trouble, though before I could do little with her." The boys were responding to the same kind of treatment, he said, but Duncan had called him to task a number of times for failing to enforce discipline.

Mitchell said Duncan told him there was no point in teaching literature to the native students. "What they must learn in school is order, punctuality and obedience," he quoted Duncan as saying. "They will pick up reading and writing later. Anyone can learn to write. Look at Abraham Lincoln." Mitchell claimed Duncan made fun of the education of those who had gone away to school and refused to hire them when they returned. He was acting and behaving like a tyrannical old father who could not accept the fact his "children" were passing him by in their schooling and ambitions.

Mitchell also wrote to one of the Bureau's Alaska officials, Harlan P. Updegraff, complaining about Duncan's tight grip on the community and his outdated ways. Mitchell said one of the natives had told him that if they did not get a government school soon, the people would move back to British Columbia. They had come to Alaska because they had not been allowed enough freedom and privileges, but after 21 years in New Metlakatla were worse off than before. Mitchell quoted one native as saying, "We are slaves here. We are getting poorer all the time and Mr. Duncan is getting richer. What is the matter with the government? Are they afraid of Mr. Duncan when they do not let us have a school just because he does not want it?" Another native told him that "Mr. Duncan is the law. This is not our village. It is Mr. Duncan's village."

Mitchell was not the only one in Metlakatla that year writing to the government about the state of education in the village. Benjamin Haldane, who had come over in the 1887 exodus, was one of the most remarkable natives on the island. He was the community's most accomplished musician, official photographer and operator of his own store. He was leader of both the band and the choir, played the pipe organ in church, and performed on the piano, cornet, trombone and violin. He could read music without the benefit of any formal training. Haldane told Commissioner Brown he had started school at age nine and at 15, "after going through and through the third reader," had been asked to leave when Duncan told him there was nothing more for him to learn. He picked up the rest of his knowledge on his own, Haldane said, and now he wanted something better for his children.

Duncan's bitterness deepened as he became aware of the extent of the opposition to his iron rule. According to Mitchell, Duncan told him that if a government school was established in Metlakatla he would "put on his hat and go with his money." When Ralph Smith asked Duncan what he was going to do with his money when he died, whether he intended leaving it for the Indians, the old man replied hotly. "No! The money is mine." Said Mitchell: "I feel sure it is all bluff but it scares the natives so that they will do anything for him then."

Duncan tried other means of intimidation to keep the natives in line. Mitchell said he talked continually of the wickedness of the young people. "He runs them down, breathes fire and brimstone at them from the pulpit but does not do one thing for them to show them the love of God. He told Mrs. Mitchell that the way he got men and women to what they are now was by flogging them . . . he does not realize that he has educated these people so that the flogging days are over with and that he must win these young people to God through love." Mitchell said it would be a mercy to Duncan and a blessing to the natives if his work were taken away from him, but he conceded that would not be right. "He is an old man and the work that he has done in the past is simply wonderful. He is entitled to end his life in a blaze of glory." But Duncan might live for many more years, Mitchell said, and should not be allowed to stand in the way of the young people being helped to gain an education.

Duncan's criticism was not confined to the young. The older men became impatient at his night classes when he scolded them on health care and sanitation. "So often he has gotten after them merely to show his authority," Mitchell wrote, "that they have come to feel that there is not much to anything he says." The adults gradually stopped coming to the evening classes. "It is pitiful to see how blind he is to it all," said Mitchell.

Mitchell pleaded with the Bureau to establish a school in Metlakatla, but Commissioner Brown was reluctant. He was well aware of Duncan's powerful outside supporters and the furore that would ensue if the government appeared to be muscling in on his domain. Brown told his staff he would not act until more sentiment had built up in the community for a government school. Procrastination ruled in Washington too.

Meanwhile, Mitchell complained that he and his wife and two small children were forced to live in a "shack" that did not keep out the winter winds. Duncan claimed Mitchell did not do enough work for his $800 a year salary and forced him to do menial jobs around the cannery in the summer for 10 hours a day, six days a week. "I would be willing to do that all the time if it helped the missionary part of the work," Mitchell wrote, "but it is merely saving a few dollars for the treasury."

When Mitchell realized he was not going to improve the school himself, he enlisted the help of the people in a campaign to convince the Bureau to move in. He recruited Haldane, Edmund Verney and Edward Mather to draw up a third petition. Duncan accused the three natives of "envy and self-pride" and said he would shame them before their people.

Marsden was shuttling back and forth between Saxman and Metlakatla and playing an active role in the campaign. He wrote a letter accompanying the third petition in May of 1909 in which he used his strongest language yet against Duncan. "We attribute the very high and unnecessary death rate, the intoxicating propensities, the ignorance and the very common and shameful prevalence of immorality even among the young boys and girls... to the stubborn efforts of Mr. Duncan at keeping them from going to school after the age of 14 years."

Mitchell also solicited the aid of a Bureau medical inspector, Harry Carlos De Vighne, a much-travelled doctor with a colourful past. De Vighne was a rakish, worldly man with little appreciation for the work of the narrow-minded missionaries he encountered in his rounds. He sympathized with Mitchell's complaints even though he considered the health and sanitation practices in Metlakatla far superior to the other native villages in his jurisdiction. He agreed to deliver the petition to Bureau officials on his annual trip to Washington.

Duncan's defenders later branded Mitchell a "spy" for the Bureau and attacked De Vighne's character. They said the doctor had been charged with two offences in Alaska, selling whisky to natives and performing an abortion on an Indian girl, but neglected to mention he had been acquitted on both counts. De Vighne later wrote a frank, engaging account of his experiences in Alaska which tends to confirm he was innocent of the charges.[29] He took a firm stand against abortion, and after leaving the Bureau to go into private practice delivered a total of 3,000 babies in the District. De Vighne became a well-respected figure who was considered sympathetic to the plight of the natives.

When Updegraff made the contents of the petition known to him, Duncan was unmoved. He insisted school and church work were inseparably linked in Metlakatla, and as "the good works which have followed our plans are apparent... it would ill become me to alter fifty years of trial to sanction any change." Duncan informed Updegraff that his school would reopen in September with Mitchell and a native assistant. Also helping, he said, would be Robert Tomlinson and his son Robert Jr. In answer to Duncan's pleas that he needed a medical worker following the departure of Minthorn, Tomlinson had reluctantly agreed the previous year to come to Metlakatla.

[29] De Vighne, Harry Carlos. *The Time of My Life: A Frontier Doctor in Alaska*. Lippincott, 1942.

But Mitchell did not intend to stay. As early as the previous spring he had asked Updegraff for a Bureau teaching job in some other community. He was recommended for the native school at Haines, but didn't get the job. As far as the hard-headed Bureau officials were concerned, Mitchell's usefulness in gaining a foothold for them in Metlakatla was finished, and they weren't inclined to reward his efforts. He left during the fall to work as a bookkeeper for the YMCA in Portland.

As the campaign for government intervention went ahead without Mitchell, Marsden became more active. With the help of his mother and brother-in-law he had bought a 36-foot steam boat, the *Marietta*, to travel around the area. Not long after, he married a Tlingit interpreter employed on the vessel, Mrs. Lucy Harrah. Born Lucy Kinninook, she was the daughter of a Tlingit chief and was educated at the Thomas Crosby Methodist School in Port Simpson. Duncan was asked by Marsden to marry them after her divorce came through, but he refused because she was a "too-much married woman" who had lived with two Indian husbands and had been legally married twice at Sitka to white men.

In 1903 Marsden had hired Dr. John L. Myers of Kansas City to practise at Saxman. Myers and his wife did not stay long. They found the town almost abandoned. The few families with homes there were away fishing most of the year. The houses were half-finished or unpainted and the settlement was not at all as Marsden had pictured it. The Saxman school was described by the district superintendent in 1908 as filthy. It had scratched old desks, "walls black with smoke, woodshed falling down, walks rotted away, chimney cracked, everything in need of paint." Attendance was irregular because the parents were either absent or indifferent. At one point two Marsden children were the only pupils. Myers resigned and moved to Ketchikan, where he established a clinic with his two brothers.

Ketchikan was soon divided by pro- and anti-Duncan forces. One of the leaders of the group joining forces with Bureau agents trying to dislodge Duncan was Arctander. In 1910 he wrote to William Lopp, the Bureau's Alaska superintendent based in Seattle, asking for a meeting to disclose "some facts which have come under my personal observation as to the deplorable education conditions at Metlakatla." Lopp had gone to Cape Prince of Wales on Bering Straits as a missionary in 1890 and had advanced in the Bureau as a protege of Sheldon Jackson.

Arctander and the agents concocted a bizarre code to disguise what they were up to. The cooked-up words included "ultd" for Arctander, "gimtumf" for Duncan, "monoting" for money. "Whistle" was Duncan's will, and "infesting" was used at random to scramble the message. A typical coded telegram from Lopp to Bureau agent Fred Waldron in Ketchikan read: "Ask infesting ultd if infesting gimtumf monoting was provided for in revoked whistle." ("Ask Arctander if all Duncan's cash was provided for in revoked will.")

At the urging of Marsden and Arctander, a delegation of Metlakatla natives headed by Benjamin Haldane as secretary of the Town Council went to Seattle in 1910 to press their case with Lopp for a government boarding school. Lopp told the Metlakat-lans that if they would "go back and extinguish the Duncan Mission and all its work, we will be able to help you, and your people will be able to get all you want." According to Haldane, Lopp spoke to him privately, "and asked me to gather up material and publish in various papers all we could against Mr. Duncan to show that Mr. Duncan's mission was a drawback and prevented the advancement of the people." Haldane refused.

Lopp did not intend, however, to be held back by the natives' reluctance to turn on their old teacher. After visiting Metlakatla late in 1910, he wrote to Commissioner Brown recommending a government school be built in the summer and that the Interior Department send a special agent to the village to "investigate the needs of the people, ownership and management of the present industrial plant, and possible plans for its continuation and exten-sion after Mr. Duncan's retirement or death." Lopp maintained the Bureau was justified in going beyond its powers in conducting such an inquiry because Duncan occupied Annette Island through the sufferance of the secretary of the interior.

Lopp met Duncan at Metlakatla and told Brown he had been subjected to a two-hour harangue condemning government schools and abusing the natives. "He compared them to children whose babblings were of no more consequence than the droves of ravens which hover about the village." A public meeting was held at which the natives related their grievances in a manner which Lopp described as "eloquent, logical and to the point." The most emotional moment came during the closing speech of elder Sidney Campbell, who said the situation in Metlakatla recalled a tradi-tional Tsimshian dirge sung on occasions of great distress when their chief was dead and they were asking other chiefs for help. Campbell's singing was "weird, plaintive, and mournful," said Lopp.

Lopp concluded his report to the Commissioner by declaring that Duncan "no longer has the love and respect of his people. The power he now exerts over them is due solely to his store, mill and cannery." Brown approved the report and passed it along to Interior Secretary R. A. Ballinger. Lopp had urged haste because of his fear that Duncan might go to Washington to wage a fight against government intervention. On February 1, 1910, Ballinger wrote the Town Council that a public school would be established during the year and that a special Department agent, Major W. R. Logan, was coming to interview the natives.

Logan arrived in Metlakatla aboard Marsden's launch. He declined Duncan's invitation to stay with him and boarded instead with Haldane. A meeting was called at the home of one of the dissidents, Marsden ally Alfred Atkinson, to which Duncan was not invited. About 50 of the community's 650 people attended. The discussion was in Tsimshian, with Marsden interpreting for Logan. Some of the natives complained later Marsden had changed the meanings of Logan's questions and caused their answers to be misinterpreted.

Duncan wrote Logan a letter welcoming his investigation, which he hoped would "shed some cheering light on this perplexing question." Duncan offered to surrender to the government control of some of the industries, since the natives were unable to take over themselves. But it must do so "on the same lines and for the same purposes for which they were established, namely to bear the expenses of church, school, medical work and village improvements."

Haldane and Campbell told Logan that Duncan had threatened to dismantle the cannery machinery and take it away if the natives continued their efforts to get a government school. When they talked of going to British Columbia, Duncan promised that if they stayed he would divide a percentage of the profits of the canning season proportionate to their wages. That had been in 1908 and it was not until three years later that each man received a $10 bonus and each women $5.

In his report to the Secretary of the Interior, Logan blamed Duncan's action in taking over sole control of the Metlakatla Industrial Company for creating much of the discontent among the natives. They felt he had deceived them. Logan also said the industries had potential that was not being realized. The cannery could easily be enlarged and the sawmill would employ five times as many men if run at capacity. The population had dropped from 1,000 to 650 because of the lack of jobs. Logan noted that during canning season Duncan paid the workers in coupons redeemable only at his store, which hurt the business of the native stores.

Logan wound up his report with some damning personal criticism of Duncan, who he described as a "martinet" unwilling to accept any questioning of his policies. Duncan was a great organizer who had done a lot for the people, but at the same time had been "vacillating" in his business dealings with the Indians. "To me it seems as if that, at one moment the grasping money loving nature of the man predominates, and, at the next moment the love for his fellow man, his religion and his love of God, holds sway, and in the latter moments he is generous and really tries to do great things for the people under his care. But unfortunately, it seems that at other times the love of filthy lucre, and the love of power, dominates." Logan conceded that the natives had thrived under Duncan's autocratic rule. "I consider that they are the most advanced and progressive Indians that I have ever met."

Shortly after receiving Logan's report, Ballinger was forced to resign as interior secretary over yet another scandal in the management of Alaska affairs. He was succeeded by Walter L. Fisher, who on April 24 rescinded the order to establish a Bureau school in Metlakatla. Fisher shelved the Lopp and Logan reports and denied requests from both Duncan and the natives for copies.

After telling Logan he was prepared to turn over his businesses to the government, Duncan went to Portland to consult Thomas Strong. Subsequently, Strong wrote Logan to confirm that Duncan "has made up his mind definitely that the burden is becoming too great for him to bear and the U.S. Government is the only reasonable and available agency to continue the work." After 54 years of unremitting labour, Strong said, Duncan needed a vacation. The only conditions were that the industries be used as in the past to support the advancement of the Indians and the mission remain non-denominational. Strong was confident Duncan could reach an understanding with the government on schooling, but urged that the negotiations be carried out as delicately as possible. "It is naturally a somewhat difficult thing for a man of Mr. Duncan's age and who has been for over half a century building up so magnificent a work as he has, to give it up at once into alien hands."

Too difficult, as it turned out. Stung by the criticisms in the Logan report, which he had eventually obtained, Duncan suddenly withdrew his offer in March of 1912 and put forward another, less workable, plan to Governor Walter Clark. Duncan argued that the industrial and religious work of the mission were inseparable and the government was obviously unable to become involved with the church. He proposed the businesses be turned over to an incorporated company comprising all the natives, among whom the shares would be equally divided. They would select a board from the best-qualified people to manage the work. Profits would go to the natives in addition to their wages. For the maintenance of the church, medical work and school teaching, Duncan proposed to lend $40,000 to the company at a fixed rate of interest. But when the governor invited him to come to Juneau to discuss the matter, Duncan brought into question the sincerity of his new proposal by declaring his health was poor and he was too busy. Sure enough, he later withdrew the second offer.

Strong was concerned about the turn of events. He had told Duncan there were two choices—place the mission in the hands of the government or invite a denominational church to take it over. Strong favoured the first option. After a visit to Metlakatla that summer, he wrote Henry Wellcome that Duncan was "as interesting and as devoted to his work as ever, but it was inexpressibly pitiful to see this noble missionary enterprise headed for and apparently going with such speed on the reefs that encompass it." The cannery was virtually shut down, while others in the area thrived.

When Governor Clark visited that summer, Duncan ignored his questions and instead attacked Logan in bitter terms. He blamed Logan's attitude on the fact he was a Roman Catholic. Clark concluded there could be no solution to Metlakatla's problems while Duncan was alive. He may have been old and his mind deteriorating, the governor said, but Duncan was still shrewd and able enough to mount a bitter fight to preserve his work.

Chapter 24

Loss of a Friend

THE TOMLINSONS, FATHER AND SON, had come from the Skeena to help Duncan. They were aware of the problems at Metlakatla but had been keeping silent. "I was impressed by the loyalty, intelligence and good judgement of the members of this family," Governor Clark told Interior Secretary Fisher. Clark suggested Robert Jr. might be Duncan's successor, but quoted his father as saying, "Mr. Duncan has known Robert ever since he was a boy at Old Metlakatla, but doesn't realize that he has grown up." There was also the fact that Edward Marsden, in anticipation of a possible transfer of power, had persuaded the Town Council in 1911 to pass a resolution that no white man be allowed to take Duncan's place.

Duncan's erratic behaviour and the disintegration of Metlakatla eventually became too much for Tomlinson to bear. In a letter dated July 8, 1912, after 45 years of loyal service, he reluctantly told Duncan of his concerns. He had first realized all was not well when he arrived in 1908. "When you asked me to join you I willingly consented in the hope that I might be able to help you in bearing a burden that was too heavy for you . . . it was not until we were settled here for some time, and I had an opportunity to look into matters, that the causes for decadence of the place became apparent."

Tomlinson said the most serious mistakes were the disbanding of the M.I.C. without consulting the native shareholders, Duncan's failure to involve the Elders or Town Council in decisions affecting the community, and his refusal to provide adequate schooling. "If these matters had been mended in any way, no matter how it differed from the way I had suggested, I would have been satisfied; but nothing has been done to improve them . . . you have endeavoured to undertake the teaching of the school yourself and, though you are a born teacher, your age and other responsibilities render that a simple impossibility." Tomlinson said Duncan's failure to realize the need for change made improvements in the situation impossible. Although it was painful to consider, it might be best for Tomlinson to withdraw, "and leave the matters in your hands until the breakup comes." There had never been differences between them before, "but unless there can be true brotherly feeling between us, and united action in matters respecting the interests of the place, it will be better for me to leave."

Of all the protests that had reached Duncan in the past few years, this was the one that should have caused him to take stock of his position. He had recognized Tomlinson's strengths from the beginning; he was the only man in whom Duncan had complete confidence. His criticisms now were reasoned and well-intentioned. It should not have been too late, but Duncan had passed the point of reasonableness.

Tomlinson soon gave up any hope that Duncan would make a courteous, thoughtful reply. When after a few days there had been no response, he sent a second letter formally declaring his intention to leave Metlakatla with his son. Duncan's only reaction to this was to stop Tomlinson from conducting his regular Sunday evening service. After a heated confrontation in which Tomlinson's Irish temper flared, he wrote a third letter July 17 in which he declared that Duncan's actions led him to believe that after his departure attempts would be made to misrepresent the cause of his leaving. After repeating his reasons for going, Tomlinson referred to their recent heated meeting. "It was my plain duty notwithstanding that you are older and wiser than I, to withstand you to the face, for you are to be blamed. I spoke warmly, yes, vehemently—not from anger but from grief and pain. If in my manner of speech I seemed to transgress the bounds of respect due to you, I am only too willing to apologize and ask your forgiveness; but this in no way detracts from my protest; and once again I earnestly entreat, and affectionately urge you to clear yourself by taking such action as will remove the appearance of evil."

Two weeks later, after Tomlinson had returned in sadness to his new Skeena outpost of Minskinisht, the Metlakatla Council wrote him an appreciative letter expressing the natives' support for the stand he had taken. "We urge you to be not dismayed to share with our hardships. We have missed you very much."

There was another letter, not so supportive, from Cridge, taking Tomlinson to task for not sticking by his old ally. Cridge urged him to withdraw his resignation. Tomlinson replied respectfully that he could not go back unless Duncan changed his ways. This elicited a cranky response from the aged Cridge, who sought to defend Duncan's financial manoeuvring on the shaky grounds that he had tested the natives' business abilities and found them wanting.

To his credit, however, Cridge also urged Duncan to consult the Elders and turn over the money he had banked for the church into their hands. "Circumstances have made you almost despotic," he wrote in an unprecedented rebuke to his longtime friend. In his reply, Duncan ignored the reprimand and airily dismissed the Tomlinsons' departure as "no calamity to the mission. I have often felt they were not the men for the work here."

The following year Duncan received a letter from Alice Tomlinson at Minskinisht informing him that her husband had died after a three-day illness. The cause of death was hardening of the arteries around the heart. He was 71. Mrs. Tomlinson said four of their six children were with her and she expressed "kind regards from us all." Cridge also died in 1913. "There was no one whom he felt more at heart with than you," wrote Cridge's daughter Maude. She complained of being sick and lonely and thanked Duncan for his generous offer to pay the salary of a live-in companion, which would allow her to stay on in the family home.

Later Wellcome and other Duncan supporters tried desperately to discredit Tomlinson and play down the impact of his final letters to Duncan, fully aware how damning they appeared in the record of Metlakatla. They seized on the fact that Tomlinson had a row with cannery foreman Ed Benson and failed to persuade Duncan to fire him. Benson was well known for favouring his friends and relatives in hiring for the cannery and it was said that Tomlinson wanted Robert Jr. to have the manager's job. A number of the natives supported him. Wellcome said Tomlinson had been a steady figure in the old days, but ill health had made him "nervous and excitable." There is no evidence, however, either in his behaviour or coolly rational letters, that Tomlinson was not in full command of his faculties. He remained strong-willed and high-principled to the end.

The winter of 1912-13 was a bleak time in Metlakatla. The Bureau of Education agents were frustrated at coming so close to gaining a foothold on the island before being called back by Interior Secretary Fisher. The natives were edgy and belligerent as they had been during the last years in British Columbia. Duncan wound down the cannery operation in the summer of 1912 and

274

there were few jobs to be had. In an effort to pacify the people and provide them with work and money, Duncan offered to put up $10,000 for land clearing on a new road and some 10-acre plots for cultivation. The villagers agreed at first, but then a petition was organized to block the project. When Duncan died, some said, it would be on record what he spent on these improvements and somebody taking his place might then claim the land, houses and sidewalks. They remembered being given nails and window sash by Duncan in old Metlakatla, then told later the houses they had built did not belong to them. "So the best thing is to ... do our own scratching, make our own homes, and we will own them."

Thomas Hanbury told Wellcome later the people felt Duncan had been making many promises to them which had not been fulfilled, so why should they accept this one? Duncan had forfeited their trust. When the natives asked to run the cannery themselves because Duncan was allowing it to disintegrate, he had agreed, knowing they didn't have the money to do it. Hanbury asked why Duncan didn't start a business to provide work for the people. They did not intend to lend him money, Hanbury said, but turned it over with the expectation they would own the cannery. "When his business grew and he had money in the bank he returned our money and what do we get? Instead of $75,000 profit we get nothing."

At times Duncan seemed more concerned about the crumbling morality of the town than the insurrection led by Marsden and the Bureau agents. The village was without a constable, and in January 1913, he complained to U.S. Attorney John Rustgard in Juneau that "the youths of our community are taking advantage of the irregular state of things." Flouting parental authority, they were "guilty of parading our streets in midnight hours." A native store was burglarized and there had been a theft at the post office. The crimes were abetted by a lack of lighting. Duncan wrote to a Seattle firm that had supplied street lamps in 1908 to complain that they were still not functioning properly.

The discontent was not confined to Metlakatla. Bureau teacher Charlotte Doren wrote from Saxman to Superintendent Lopp at the end of February 1913, that "this year has been in many ways one I want to forget. Please don't ask me to reconsider Saxman. I can't. Courage fails. It is not that I am so physically tired, as tired in spirit ... the winter ... has been terrible. Death feasts and pot-latches and witchcraft, long days and nights of drinking and carousing—a totally demoralized village." Marsden had not been in the village for a year, Doren said.

District Superintendent William G. Beattie, another Jackson Presbyterian, admitted to Lopp that Saxman was a lost cause. "There seems little excuse for the existence of the town," he wrote. It was little more than a winter camp with more sickness per capita than any other village in the area.

But Marsden had his mind on other things than improving the lot of Saxman. He wrote the Presbyterian Board of Home Missions that "in the opinion of those intimate with Mr. Duncan and his work, the time is fast approaching when I shall be wanted as a minister of the Gospel over there." Marsden said there was not enough work for him at Saxman and he was anxious to preach to his own people. "Metlakatla has plenty of work for me and I am praying that God may soon lead me there to help my poor people."

When the government tried to collect the poll tax that summer from males between the ages of 20 and 50, there were only four. All the others had gone to find jobs. The cannery and sawmill were both shut down. When the people started drifting back in the fall, Duncan reopened the school, but few pupils showed up.

It was a situation made for Edward Marsden, who wrote Lopp cockily in September: "I fear Duncan not a single bit. I have clashed with him many times now to conclude that of all human beings he is foxy, dishonest, tyrannical, and a hopelessly bigoted teacher. He looks after William Duncan's affairs very carefully but is unmercifully sacrificing the welfare of my own people." Marsden said some of the natives had collected $250 among themselves with the intention of hiring their own teacher.

Two senior government officials who visited Metlakatla in late summer to assess the situation both recommended the government proceed with its plan to build the school which Interior Secretary Fisher had vetoed. The new Commissioner of Education, Philander Priestly Claxton, said the village had prospered initially but as the natives came in closer contact with neighbouring settlements the more intelligent and progressive of them wanted better education facilities than Duncan was providing. The new governor of Alaska, J. F. A. Strong, said after his visit that a spirit of unrest was clearly evident and he concurred with Claxton's assessment. In addition to a school, the governor said, the natives were pressing for individual land ownership so they could obtain citizenship. Some of them aspired to become business and professional men, he added.

Differences between Duncan and the Indians were "irreconcilable," the governor concluded. "He looks upon them as children who yet require his tutelage. They look upon themselves as having outgrown it." Strong hoped Duncan could be "induced by moral persuasion" to leave the island, but admitted there was little hope of that. The best solution seemed to be to put in a government school with a good teacher, leaving Duncan to devote his time to religious training and the industries.

Backed by these findings, the new secretary of the interior, Franklin K. Lane, decided to act. He ordered Claxton to proceed with the new school. The commissioner told Duncan on November 5 that in taking this step the government acknowledged the work he had done for the Metlakatlans. "I believe these people also fully appreciate what you have done for them and will long remember affectionately you and your work. I sincerely hope that in taking up this work for the education of the Indians of this village, we shall have your very hearty co-operation."

It was a vain hope. Two days after the school opened in November on the second floor of a building rented from a native, with equipment brought over from Saxman, Duncan saw teacher Charles Jones carrying water from the public tap. He promptly closed the pipe. Duncan maintained the water was turned off every winter to avoid a freeze-up, but some weeks elapsed before he ordered the pipeline closed from Chester Lake to the sawmill. He had acted out of spite.

Later that month Marsden moved with his family to Metlakatla. The Bureau suggested closing the Saxman school, but he protested this would make his motives too apparent. Keep the Saxman school open with a second-rate teacher if necessary, he said. "Any ordinary good girl teacher" would do. On November 20 Marsden wrote to the Presbyterian Board. He said Dr. Hall Young, the church's senior missionary in Alaska and a noted explorer and writer, had warned him to proceed slowly so as to avoid offending Duncan or the Episcopalians, who were beginning to expand their operations in the District. "This is very well," Marsden complained, "but I believe that we have been going a bit too slow all these years. We are somewhat responsible for the sad conditions of many of my people at Metlakatla." The pointed reference to "my people" was no doubt calculated to emphasize the racial nature of the growing schism.

In the year-end elections anti-Duncan candidates won majorities on Town Council and the Church Board of Elders. Duncan protested the vote had been manipulated by Bureau agents and their native confederates and refused to preside at the traditional New Year's Day ceremonies. He also complained the installation was being held in a room used as a dance hall, instead of in his cottage or the church as in the past. Duncan attempted to lay the blame on a small cabal of conspirators seeking to overthrow the mission. The election result made it clear, however, that a majority of the people now were in favour of change.

The Bureau estimated that as many as 80 per cent of the Metlakatlans were opposed to Duncan at this time, but that figure was probably high. Many of the natives had mixed feelings toward their mentor. While some complained about the lower wages paid by Duncan, others recognized that the deductions he made came back to them through maintenance of the church and school and medical services. "Although the impression is that the outside people pay more," said Casper Mather in 1913, "the people that stay here think that they receive more here than elsewhere. I do, for one."

Duncan complained his school had never been inspected by anyone from the Bureau and its decision to intervene was based on hearsay evidence of the dissidents. He told Claxton he would give his version of the dispute to any investigator the commissioner cared to send. He also suggested that Jones be transferred to his school and paid out of mission funds. "After having given 57 years of my life to the Mission work here it is scarcely reasonable to suppose I can quietly acquiesce in a change which forebodes evil to it."

Duncan summoned Jones and launched a tirade against the men he accused of being leaders in the campaign for the government school. Jones quoted Duncan as saying that if the government persisted, he would "unveil all the black deeds of all those men to their shame and to the community's sorrow." Duncan named the principal offenders as Mark Hamilton, Edmund Verney, Edward Marsden, Adolphus Calvert, Benjamin Haldane, John Tait and Sidney Campbell. Jones told Lopp that Duncan said things about the seven that he could not include in his letter. Although Duncan referred to Jones as a "devil," the teacher maintained respect for his aged adversary. Duncan was a forceful speaker, he said, who must have been a "giant" in his prime. "It is little wonder that before long the simple minds of these savages were entranced and held spellbound by the powerful little missionary."

In the pulpit Duncan harangued his congregation. "I pity you for you don't know what you are doing. The more you go against me, the more you fight God. Where is there any minister in all Alaska that can do such a great work for the Indians as I have done? You will not find a single one. You are now doing some things against me... you have elected some men to be Elders of this Church against my wishes... you are a people of drunkards... I warn you of our coming destruction." According to Marsden, Duncan's language was so violent the congregation was "utterly disgusted."

In mid-February Duncan locked the gate to the wharf and forbid the natives to land their boats there. He had threatened to cut the ropes on boats tied up to the dock, but cannery manager Ed Benson refused to carry out his order. Villagers who continued to moor their vessels at the wharf jetty were forced to ferry goods ashore by skiff because of the locked gate, which Duncan opened only for the mail steamer and tourist ships. He also ignored a request from Governor Strong that the water main be reopened.

The government looked for ways to bring Duncan to heel. The attorney-general claimed that since neither Duncan nor the Indians had secured title to land on Annette Island, he could be removed at any time. "But in view of his long service among these people and his efforts on their behalf, that course is unthinkable." A memo was prepared within the Department of the Interior for Secretary Lane which in referring to the 1891 Act of Congress deleted the amended phrase, "and those people known as Metlakatlans." The purpose was to make it appear that Duncan was not included as a beneficiary under the Act. Only the Indians had the right to occupy the island and all others except government employees were there by sufferance, Lane was told.

Armed with that erroneous advice, Lane sent a telegram to Duncan ordering him to restore water service. There was a menace to public health created by the enforced use of little streams running through the village, the secretary said. Duncan, who in his prime had battled the British Columbia and Canadian governments to a stalemate, was not easily intimidated. He told Lane there was no "water service" to restore. The water line was simply to supply the cannery and sawmill and for fire protection. A tap had been installed at the reservoir tank as a "convenience" for 20 families living adjacent to the cannery.

Duncan said before the Chester Lake dam was built one of the streams carried enough water to supply both the sawmill and the cannery. He mocked Jones' complaint about the difficulty of fetching water. "I walked his distance (at my age of 82) and took four minutes to the stream and three minutes to the tap." The extra two minutes a day seemed a "ludicrously small trouble for the rectification of which the attention of the U.S. Secretary of the Interior must needs be invoked."

Jones was persistent. He filed an official complaint with the Bureau that his family had to drink marshy surface water from a little pool near the church. "Out of this little hole in the moss practically the whole community dips its drinking water. A splendid way to disseminate disease germs." When a government sanitation officer checked 150 homes during April, however, she found only two per cent of the population ailing with minor complaints and no cases of dysentery or other illnesses that could be attributed to impure water. Nevertheless, Secretary Lane officially authorized the Bureau agents on June 19 to seize and reopen the pipeline. He wired Beattie, who was now on the scene directing Bureau activities, to advise Duncan it would be futile to oppose the government.

With the pipeline dispute out of the way, Jones, Beattie and Lopp launched an all-out campaign to get Duncan off the island. During the last week of June, Beattie sent off 15 derogatory letters and telegrams to Lane. On June 25 he told Lopp there was "a preponderance of evidence that will show either that Mr. Duncan is suffering from a form of dementia, or else that he has been crooked." Beattie also claimed the Indians had warned that Duncan intended to shoot him. In his annual report dated July 1, Jones enumerated a long list of sins and crimes alleged against Duncan dating from the early days in B.C. The next day a native petition, in Marsden's handwriting, was sent to Washington calling for "the enforced and immediate retirement (of Duncan) with what private property that legally belongs to himself, since within recent years he has only practised in our midst the arts of a shrewd, merciless trader and money tyrant, and has altogether forfeited his rights with us as a teacher of Christian righteousness and morality."

The drive to oust Duncan was so intense many natives grew apprehensive. The older ones saw the same heavy hand of government that had cracked down on them in Canada, and feared their homes and property might be appropriated again. Others were confused and alarmed by Duncan's defiance of the government. It was in sharp conflict with his earlier efforts to instil feelings of patriotism and obedience to the laws of their new homeland.

This state of unease among the Indians resulted in a new note of caution in Bureau correspondence. Jones warned that Duncan had many friends and "any action taken against him must be bulwarked with all manner of precaution." He further suggested that "in order to forestall the bad effects of a sentimental reflex on the part of the natives in case the Government deems it obligatory to forcibly remove him . . . it would be advisable to get the sentiment of a large majority of the natives in writing and the complaints and testimony of the older natives ought to be taken in the form of depositions before sickness or death disables them to furnish this valuable evidence." Duncan should be closely questioned and his account books inspected.

Lopp recommended that Jones leave before summer so Duncan could not tell tourists that trouble was being caused by someone forced upon him by the government. He also proposed that a Metlakatlan be placed in charge of the pipeline so that Duncan would be placed in the position of fighting his own people. The Bureau people were also annoyed by Marsden's overeagerness to replace Duncan. Claxton warned Beattie that Marsden might try to create discontent. "I wish you would see Marsden, talk with him, and explain to him carefully the importance of not appearing to desire leadership. Having undertaken this work we must proceed very carefully and firmly and build very solidly."

The plotters were aware Duncan might be around for a long time. Dr. William Pallister told Beattie he could see no reason why Duncan should not live another 15 or 20 years. Pallister was a Seattle physician who had recently failed a medical re-examination but was hired by the Bureau to test the eyesight of native children in Alaska. On the basis of a few conversations he concluded that Duncan was suffering from a psychopathic condition. He passed this opinion along to Beattie, who used it to bolster his verdict that Duncan was "demented."

The Bureau officials moved ahead with their plans to construct a permanent school by appropriating an eight-acre plot in the mission grounds. They seized land containing the old town hall, Duncan's first school building and an abandoned dormitory. It was considerably more property than required and the choice of site for the new school directly in front of the present mission school seemed deliberately provocative. Dr. Minthorn, who was now back helping Duncan, protested to no avail that there were at least two better locations in the village available to the government. When construction began, the Bureau used imported white labour exclusively, although there were several skilled carpenters among the natives.

After unsuccessfully attempting to lure uncommitted natives to his side by giving away sacks of flour and small amounts of cash to his loyalists, Duncan made one last effort to buy their support. Excluding his known foes, he called half the male inhabitants of the town into his office, one by one, and offered to divide his money among them if they renounced the government school. Each would receive a legal certificate for the specific amount coming to him. "If one hundred men agree to what I have told you they will have $500 each and if 50 men agree . . . I will give them $1,000 each." Duncan then called a public meeting where they could vote on the offer. Sixty-three men showed up. Two men stood up and warned the others not to accept Duncan's proposal because he had always deceived them in the past. When the vote came, 31 were in favour and 31 against. It was up to chairman Andrew Usher to cast the deciding ballot, but he astutely adjourned the meeting and ducked out. Duncan's offer, born of desperation, was abandoned.

The only reprieve for Duncan occurred when the Bureau became distracted by its own troubles. Dr. Hall Young set off a storm when he accused Lopp of taking "insulting familiarities" with women teachers in the government service. His charge was based on a complaint by Mary Gibson that Lopp had fired her after she refused an invitation to take a week's trip to an isolated native settlement with him. Mrs. Gibson said she had "slapped his hands away from my breast pin when he grabbed at it and asked, 'what kind of a pin is that you have got there?'" Lopp and his Bureau colleagues were not noted for sophistication or originality.

The antics of Lopp and the Bureau's District Superintendent Fred Waldron became the talk of Southeastern Alaska. Waldron warned the women under his jurisdiction that Lopp had told him if he didn't like a teacher she should be told to pack her bags. Complaisant teachers were rewarded with higher salaries for their favours. Rebels like Mrs. Gibson were refused funds to repair living quarters. Lopp, who had a wife and seven children, was later cleared by an internal departmental investigation because of a lack of evidence. After one of the women complainants recanted her testimony, Judge James Wickersham told Mrs. Gibson he believed

282

the woman had told the truth the first time, "but in the meantime the situation had changed so that she could not afford to expose her frailties to the public." Mrs. Gibson bravely carried on an unsuccessful campaign to have Lopp ousted.

It had not been a good year for the Bureau. Six of its native schools were closed down because of a lack of attendance and cutbacks in funds. Between 1912 and 1915 a total of 14 native schools shut their doors. Some had been in operation for as long as 16 years, but their standards had steadily declined. The question was asked by some why, with so many other places in desperate need of education facilities, scarce funds were being spent in Metlakatla, where rudimentary schooling already existed.

Chapter 25

Courtroom Battles

O N JANUARY 7, 1915, Duncan was arrested. He was charged with threatening to shoot teacher Charles Jones.

Jones had gone to the warehouse with a few natives to demand some iron water pipe. Bureau officials had tried to keep the pipeline running during the winter but it had frozen and burst. Duncan blocked their way, insisting the pipe was his private property. There were shouts and threats. "Mr. Jones was acting pretty wild," Thomas Hanbury declared in a sworn affidavit. "He was very rough and shouted loud threats that he would take the pipes... Mr. Duncan kept quiet and just walked up and down in front of his pipes." Duncan warned Jones not to get the natives excited. Hanbury, who had been working on the beach near the warehouse when the fracas began, stepped in and told Jones and the others to back off. Jones threatened to get a marshal to arrest both Duncan and Hanbury, then left. "Afterwards I heard Mr. Jones say that Mr. Duncan threatened to draw a gun but there was no such thing," said Hanbury.

Jones told Beattie that Duncan had threatened to shoot him or anyone else who attempted to take the pipe. Beattie sent a report on the incident to Commissioner Claxton. "Mr. Jones endeavoured to get Mr. Duncan to retract his statement that he would shoot any one, but Mr. Duncan in a rage declared that he would not. Robert Hewson, one of the oldest men in the village, who has stood by Mr. Duncan all the time, then said: 'I'll shoot too; I get my gun,' and hurried away to the house, returning presently with a heavy coat and a bulging pocket." Beattie admitted the only gun actually seen that day was brandished by one of the natives siding with Jones.

Jones went to Ketchikan, where he swore out warrants against Duncan and Hewson. Their hearing was fixed for 10 o'clock the next morning before Judge E. S. Stackpole. Duncan and Hewson were taken into custody by a deputy marshal and escorted to court to answer the charge. The hearing was postponed 24 hours and the defendants released on their own recognizance. The case was put off each day until January 16 when the prosecuting attorney, after interviewing witnesses subpoened by the government, asked for dismissal of the case. Judge Stackpole agreed.

It was obvious the 82-year-old Duncan was neither armed nor intended doing physical harm to anyone, despite his angry threats. Beattie admitted as much to Claxton. "I questioned Jones and the natives as closely as possible. They convinced me that there was a danger of bloodshed at Metlakatla. They did not convince me that Duncan was likely to do any shooting himself." Beattie also admitted Hewson's name had been added by Jones so the charges would not appear to be a spiteful attack on Duncan.

As a postscript to the unhappy affair, the Reverend H. W. Michener, pastor of the Methodist Episcopal Church in Ketchikan, who attended the court hearing, swore an affidavit declaring he heard Jones say in exasperation to Duncan, "Well, you've been their leader all these years, but I am now."

History was repeating itself. Metlakatla was divided into two camps, but this time Duncan was in the minority. Jones told Claxton he now had only about 50 followers, mostly old men and women.

Far from being chastened by their courtroom failure, the Bureau agents and Marsden-led native dissidents stepped up their campaign. Another of the "native petitions," containing more of Marsden's abusive language, informed Duncan he was being removed from the church leadership. Scrawled on the back by Mayor Andrew Usher were the words, "This is the paper that has been mentioned to you that Edward Marsden has been trying to force the people to sign." Duncan ignored the notice.

The independent native businessmen, with the apparent sanction of the Bureau, began to assert themselves more forcefully. Roderick Davis, presuming to speak for the Metlakatlans, sent Secretary Lane a strongly worded appeal to have Duncan removed from the island "out of our way."

Davis and his partner Charles Brendible had a special reason for wanting Duncan removed. Although the use of fish traps had always been banned at Annette Island stream mouths, the Town Council now granted permits to both men to install traps for a mere $25 licence fee. Davis paid with a promissory note, which was accepted after prolonged debate. Some councillors remembered he had previously borrowed from a bank to buy machinery for a sawmill, then reneged on the loan and left Duncan, the guarantor, to make it good. Further privileges and favours flowed to Davis from an accommodating majority on the council, including the right to cut pilings from reserve timber.

The Bureau was now guiding the council's affairs, including the fishery. Thomas Hanbury objected. "What does the Bureau of Education know about fish? The Bureau of Education don't know the difference between a bulldog fish and a squirrel or a frog. They couldn't tell the difference if I brought in a trout or a 'humpy'... there's no use for the Bureau of Education to go into it; it is their business to educate the people, but not to educate the fishes."

On February 3 Secretary Lane advised Duncan his Department had drawn up a number of regulations for the future administration of Metlakatla. Duncan's control over education and the council was ended. Power would now rest with an "executive committee" made up of the mayor, secretary treasurer and senior government agent. The agent would have a seat on the council but no vote. The commissioner of education, on the advice of the agent, could veto any ordinance passed by council. The agent was now in effect assuming Duncan's role, but with more clout behind him. Neither had faith in the Indians' ability to manage their own affairs.

The next skirmish in the ongoing struggle took place in the press and the courts. Mark Hamilton, one of the more enterprising and aggressive of the Metlakatlans, had been instrumental in starting up the native-owned and operated sawmill on Gravina Island just a few miles north of Annette Island. He submitted an article summarizing the natives' grievances to the Ketchikan *Progressive*. Hamilton alleged that churches in the U.S. had contributed $50,000 to Duncan in 1887 to establish a new village for the natives and to carry on the work begun at old Metlakatla. "This money was never used for either houses or food. This is the origin of the trouble at the mission. The cannery, sawmill and the waterworks was the result of the natives' labour together with $25,000 that was donated by the U.S. missions... it is the claim of the natives that the property is their own from the fact that they contributed their labour and that the money was given for their benefit." Hamilton said Duncan was opposed to the education of the natives.

The charges were not new but the facts were even more garbled than in Marsden's earlier allegations. Duncan decided to sue for libel. This was the first time such accusations had appeared in print, close to home in a town where the newspaper previously owned by ex-governor Swineford had once been so supportive.

Duncan and Hamilton had been feuding for some time, but it had not always been so. Hamilton was employed as a young man by Duncan to manage the sawmill in B.C., and was given the same position after the move to Alaska. In 1906 Duncan supported Hamilton's application for a licence to operate a small steamer, declaring that he was "very successful in his work, very sober, steady and intelligent...he has proved himself one of the most progressive natives in the country." But two fires which destroyed Duncan's sawmills while they were under Hamilton's management soured relations between them. Duncan accused Hamilton of being careless in wrapping inflammable sacking around the steam pipes and withheld some of his salary.

It was then that Hamilton left Metlakatla and persuaded a number of natives to invest in the Gravina mill. According to Duncan, the mill lost money because of mismanagement, and when it burned down carrying a heavy mortgage and no insurance, the investors lost everything. A number of natives in Metlakatla owed the mill money for lumber purchases when it was gutted, and Hamilton persuaded Duncan to help him collect by telling him he would use the money to reimburse the investors. But Duncan claimed Hamilton kept the money for his own use. When Duncan discovered Hamilton owed money to William Wadhams in Portland, he urged the agent to sue. "I find he is so unreliable that he deserves to be punished."

So there were some old scores to be settled in Hamilton's articles and Duncan's retaliatory lawsuit. Publisher J. E. Rivard of the *Progressive* was caught in the middle. He and Hamilton were charged with criminal libel and taken before a U.S. Commissioner. During the trial Duncan testified that he received only $11,000 in "borrowed" money in 1887, not $75,000 in donations as claimed by Hamilton. He also claimed he was not opposed to a residential school, only a government day school that would rival his own.

Dr. Ben Myers attended the court hearing and reported to Henry Wellcome that he had been amazed at Duncan's "alertness of mind, quickness of thought and accuracy of memory as he replied to the questions." The transcript shows, however, that Duncan was frequently confused and contradictory on the stand. His denials of Hamilton's allegations were couched in such terms as "utterly false . . . a malicious falsehood . . . it is a black lie. A black lie sir, as black a lie as ever the devil invented." Duncan said he did not know Hamilton's intention in writing the article, but it had led the Indians "to believe I am a rascal and a thief, when I have given my life to work amongst them and they have turned against me."

After Duncan's testimony, Rivard agreed to retract the Hamilton article and run Duncan's denial. The prosecution was dropped, but the *Progressive* got some revenge in succeeding weeks by running a number of articles by Marsden going over much the same ground as Hamilton. Marsden wrote that in the beginning the people had accepted Duncan's business activities because he was an independent unordained preacher, but now they claimed certain advisory and financial rights in his enterprises. They had risked their lives in 1887 to retrieve $25,000 worth of Duncan's private goods in old Metlakatla when they were about to be seized by Canadian authorities. Marsden said Duncan at the time had publicly declared the people shared in the ownership of the property and issued certificates to that effect which he later took back. "Mr. Duncan has no right to claim the complete religious, moral and physical subjugation of his Indian converts today because he paid them wages in the past, any more than any other business corporation here in Alaska."

Petitions had become popular with the Metlakatlans. In March one was signed by 53 adult male supporters of Duncan, most of them heads of dependent families, asking him to operate the sawmill and cannery as usual in the summer. This provoked a reaction from the new mayor, Edmund Verney, a brother-in-law of Marsden, who protested to Secretary Lane that Duncan was going ahead with his businesses as if the new rules and regulations established by the Interior Department did not exist. Duncan, meanwhile, blithely wired Lane: "Time arrived operate sawmill and cannery. Many needy people applying for work. Require water power. Present waterpower insufficient run mill and serve village simultaneously. Ordered foreman use pipeline 8 hours a day, village use it 16. Jones objects and thus stops enterprises. Says he has full control pipeline. Has he full control? If so our operations must cease." Duncan was regaining his zest for battle.

Lane did not reply to the missive, even though he had been told by Beattie that the life of Metlakatla depended upon the industries —not the schools. The town had revived because the inhabitants thought the establishment of the school was an indication that they would be permitted to revive the industries.

288

Beattie was enraged by Duncan's intransigence. "He is the most tricky, revengeful, and merciless piece of humanity that I have ever had the misfortune to meet," he wrote Lopp in frustration. "I cannot but believe that the poor old fellow is insane." But Duncan's prickliness could not be explained away so easily. Dr. John L. Myers, not an unquestioning Duncan supporter, declared in 1916 that he had known Duncan for the last 12 years and had examined him on a number of occasions. "I have never seen anyone who has reached the age of Mr. Duncan who is so physically capable, and I might add that the same may be said about him mentally."

Duncan was sound enough in mind to carry on his exhaustive correspondence. There were fewer business letters to write these days, but many others. He graciously rejected Maude Cridge's suggestion that he retire and move into her father's old room in the family home in Victoria. She was worried that if Duncan became ill at Metlakatla there would be no one to care for him. Duncan wrote Robert Tomlinson Jr. at his new Methodist mission at Kispiox in the upper Skeena valley, asking him to return and help. Tomlinson replied that before leaving Metlakatla with his father in 1912 he had promised the natives he would come back some time if they called him, but he wanted to know specifically what Duncan had in mind. There was no further correspondence on the subject.

Duncan was also considering moving to a new site with 50 of his loyalists. Thomas Strong was enthusiastic. "It seems to me that the purchase of a tract of land somewhere in Alaska where he would have free scope for his own efforts without being dominated by the Government is the last chance that Mr. Duncan has to carry on his work," Strong wrote a friend. Earlier that year he had told Duncan the remedy for his plight was not in the courts. His fight was a political one and the only way to secure redress was through friends who could get action at Washington.

There was even an invitation of sorts to return to British Columbia. Duncan received a letter from W. Wymond Walkem, editor of the Victoria *Standard* and brother of former premier G. A. Walkem, an admirer of Duncan in the old days. Wymond Walkem said he was a member of the party with Lord Dufferin during the vice-regal visit to Metlakatla in 1876, and "I with many other of your friends would like to see your return to your first allegiance." After Minthorn replied for Duncan with tentative interest, Walkem said he had asked Premier Richard McBride for a crown grant of land. If that didn't work out, he said, a 160-acre homestead could be purchased at a moderate price in a good locality with water for industries and fruit growing. "I would consider it a great work in my life to be successful in bringing you all back to the land of your first efforts."

Walkem's next letter was less optimistic. He had buttonholed a number of members of the government but few remembered the old mission. Walkem complained they did not know their history and the memory of Metlakatla was already being erased from B.C. consciousness. It was a grim reminder for Duncan of the passage of time. The matter was quietly dropped.

Interior Secretary Lane was being pressured from many quarters to take action on Metlakatla's festering problems. James M. Condit, head of Presbyterian mission activities in Alaska, wrote that Duncan had "led the people further than he is willing that they should go and... in now doing his best to undo much of that which he has done." It was time, said Condit, for the government to act decisively. In April a temporary clerk in the department named Cragin submitted a report based on interviews with Bureau of Education officials and government lawyers. Cragin told Lane exactly what the secretary wanted to hear, since Lane now believed that Duncan was in fact demented. Because all the property on Annette Island belonged to the government, said Cragin, it could simply appoint itself successor to Duncan.

Quoting from Cragin's report, Lane advised Duncan on June 26, 1915, of the impending takeover. The secretary said he was satisfied that under the law all public buildings, dwellings, industrial buildings and machinery in the community belonged to the government. Only the stock of goods in his store, canned salmon in the warehouse and boats built or bought by him were exempted as Duncan's private property. Duncan would be allowed to stay if he co-operated with the government agents. "If you are not willing to give such co-operation it would be best for you to seek a home elsewhere," Lane told him.

The seizure was abrupt. On August 5 Commissioner Claxton tacked up documents on the main buildings of Metlakatla:

NOTICE: Know all men by these presents, that the building and premises upon which this notice is posted are the property of the United States for the use of the Metlakatlans under the direction of the Secretary of the Interior and are in the possession of the United States for that purpose; all persons are hereby notified of this fact and required to govern themselves accordingly.

(Signed) Franklin K. Lane, Secretary of the Interior.

The next day Commissioner Claxton advised Duncan that under orders of the secretary he had assumed control of the buildings on which notices had been posted. Duncan could retrieve his personal possessions at any time but must get Jones, who had the keys, to open up. He could operate his store until further notice.

The seizure order released the Bureau agents' pent-up frustration. They forced their way into the cannery, sawmill, schoolhouse, town hall, warehouse and carpentry shop, breaking doors and windows. The agents took over Dr. Minthorn's office and residence in an old dormitory and moved out medicine bottles, surgical, dental and optical instruments, medical books and journals. Minthorn was forced to move to the guest house, the only building left untouched by the agents other than Duncan's cottage. The stove, cupboards, tables, chairs and other furniture were taken from Minthorn's suite and tossed into an unused, leaky building nearby. Six new Bureau teachers left the native house they had been renting and moved into the renovated dormitory.

After viewing photographs of the carnage, Thomas Strong said they showed "a state of affairs that might be justified by war, but it seems to me by no other cause." Duncan protested that he would not have been treated in such a manner if he belonged to an established missionary society. "But dealing with an aged, independent man, it is different, it seems." The Bureau's actions caused alarm in the village. Lane had to reassure the natives the seizure notices did not endanger their right of ownership of houses and property, though none had title deeds in any case.

Beattie pressed for more punitive measures against Duncan, suggesting to Claxton that he should not be allowed to carry on with his store. "We frown upon any other missionary who attempts to carry on trade with the Indians and I believe that Mr. Duncan should be prohibited from trading with them." There were three native stores in Metlakatla and Beattie said Duncan should not be allowed to compete with them.

The sawmill was turned over to Rod Davis by six council members who held a special Saturday meeting which went ahead without a quorum. Davis prospered under the new Bureau regime. When one of his traps yielded 400,000 fish in 1915, some natives complained they were unable to catch their usual number of salmon in the bay for their own use.

Some of the Bureau actions against Duncan were clearly vindictive. Jones locked him out of the cannery where he went each day for exercising, and he was forced to hold school classes and Sunday school in the dining room of his cottage, taking meals in the kitchen. The agents also organized dances on Wednesday evenings across the road from Duncan's regular weekly prayer meeting. When restrictions were removed on alcohol and gambling, the lawlessness so common to other Alaska communities increased dramatically. Duncan's cottage was broken into twice. One Sunday evening $200 was taken from his office during the church service. Other homes were burglarized and some youths broke into a boathouse to steal brass fittings which they sold in Ketchikan.

In the face of all this, Duncan reached for his trusty pen. He told Claxton the cannery and sawmill had been shut down but work had already started on readying boats and nets for the fishing season before his telegram arrived. "Over $700 was spent in wages fruitlessly, and the timber at the sawmill is rotting, and the machinery and material for cannery purposes deteriorating for not being used. Worse than that, over 150 people—many being aged and feeble, who cannot well seek work—are disappointed. This question is being asked by all who have learnt the above facts. Why this action of the government?"

When Duncan told Thomas Strong what had happened, he replied that it was "the old British Columbia situation right over again. The right of yourself and your people on the Island was in the beginning and continued to be simply a permissive one." Strong said Duncan should consider moving from the island with his money and becoming a missionary at large to the Indians of Alaska. He could settle in Ketchikan, Seattle, Portland or even Victoria and make trips north whenever he felt up to it. "You are a good deal in the position of a man with a large family who has brought them up to such a state of education and capacity that they feel capable of looking out for themselves and so desert the old home and ways and you must bear seeing your people scattered up and down the coast of Alaska."

Strong was trying to let Duncan down gently, while admitting to Claxton that something had to be done about Metlakatla. His implied approval of government intervention caused Strong embarrassment in the future with the one formidable figure who was not prepared to see Duncan's lifetime of effort end in disgrace— Henry Solomon Wellcome.

Despite the outward appearances of success in business and a growing reputation as a philanthropist and archaeologist, life had not been kind to Wellcome. His marriage to Syrie Barnardo was a costly and humiliating mistake. Two years after the wedding, which had been boycotted by the father of the bride, a son was born. Mounteney Wellcome was a disappointment to his parents. He had suffered slight brain damage either during a difficult birth or in an early fall and was hard to control, especially for an aging, globe-trotting father and socially ambitious mother. The boy was sent to foster parents in the country at the age of 3, and never lived with his parents again.

Syrie grew restive at Henry's rigorous demands upon her. She confided to a friend that her husband frequently burst into her room wearing only a raincoat, which he would fling off with a flourish before leaping into her bed. This was not the sort of behaviour the sheltered, innocent young daughter of a religious family had expected. She was also mortified by reports in a London scandal sheet that one of Wellcome's greatest pleasures on his African expeditions was flogging the natives. Syrie began to look elsewhere for love. She formed liaisons with a number of Mayfair's leading men, including the American-born department store magnate, Gordon Selfridge.

In 1911 Syrie fell in love with author William Somerset Maugham, a successful playwright and man-about-town. She persuaded Maugham to have a child by her, even though she was still legally married to Wellcome. They had separated the previous year, with Wellcome agreeing to pay her $50,000 a year. He maintained custody of Mounteney.[30]

Liza was born September 1, 1915, and Maugham was soon after named co-respondent in a divorce action launched by Wellcome, who had set private detectives on their fashionable trail. Although he had already formed the first of a number of lifetime homosexual attachments, Maugham reluctantly married Syrie in 1917, partly out of a sense of responsibility to their child, but also because of his need for a glamorous party hostess. After spending 10 miserable years with Maugham, Syrie divorced again and began a successful career as an interior designer. She was later forced to endure a bitter attack from Maugham in his autobiographical writings.

---

[30] Biographical material on Henry Wellcome came primarily from *Maugham: A Biography*, by Ted Morgan. Simon & Schuster, 1980; and *The Scandal of Syrie Maugham*, by Gerald McKnight. W. H. Allen, 1980.

The effect of the scandal on Wellcome was devastating. Because of his obsessive secrecy about his private life, there has never been a published biography. Some information has leaked out, however, despite intense efforts by the present guardians of his business and philanthropic interests to protect his reputation. The Wellcome Foundation commissioned one of its employees to write a biography during the Second World War, but it remains tightly guarded in the firm's stately London headquarters on Euston Road. Portions have appeared in print, however, and it is difficult without contrary evidence to disagree with the conclusion of the author, A. W. Haggis, that Wellcome's failed marriage resulted in a "morbid misery." By his failure to let his better nature prevail, Wellcome was for the first time "defeated in a great struggle with himself, and in some respect it soured his character for the remainder of his life." He developed an "obstinate spirit of intolerance," Haggis concluded.

This was Wellcome's mood, then, when he received word of the troubles afflicting Duncan. He could not stand idly by while the name of the man he had sponsored, and attempted to bestow sainthood upon, was being dragged through the Alaska mud.

Chapter 26

Henry to the Rescue

THE FIRST CALL FOR HELP TO Wellcome arrived in September of 1915 from Edythe Macdonald Fleet, who said Duncan was too old to fight his own battle and had no faithful supporters left to do it for him. Wellcome sprang into action instantly. He cabled Duncan: "WRITE ME FULL HISTORY AND DETAILS ALL TROUBLES. URGENT."

The telegram "thrilled me with joy," Duncan responded, enclosing copies of his correspondence with the government over the past few years. Duncan said the United States was much worse than Canada, which at least had not seized the mission buildings and industries until they were abandoned. "Had we anticipated the treatment we are now suffering we should never have come to Alaska," he wrote Wellcome. The Metlakatlans had believed the Congressional Act of 1891 was enacted to protect them against hostile intruders, "whereas we now find it is being used as a trap to rob and degrade us."

Wellcome received Duncan's reply on October 5 and wired back: "Send copy all letters and documents and fullest details everything. Don't hurry and don't decide anything hastily. Rely upon me." Wellcome then asked Mrs. Fleet to write Duncan to advise him and his people "to petition me to take up the case, empower me to act for them, and then leave it entirely in my hands." It was important, Wellcome said, that he should be able to show the government he represented Duncan and the natives at their request and had full authority to act for them. Wellcome said he would bear all costs of an investigation. Duncan was not to write to anyone else about his troubles, especially the newspapers. Mrs. Fleet said Wellcome was a "brick" to help and she would do as instructed.

Wellcome received a letter from his old ally in Washington, John W. Foster, relaying the government's point of view in the Metlakatla dispute. Wellcome replied that the allegations were "a great shock, especially as they are so entirely contrary to all the known acts of Mr. Duncan during the 58 years of his mission work on the North Pacific Coast." He could not reply to them without first obtaining all the evidence from both sides because there appeared to be some mystery which he intended to unravel. Wellcome felt "a deep personal responsibility" for the conduct of Duncan's mission.

"Opinions may differ as to the most suitable methods of mission work," he told Foster, "but the supreme test is the result. Mr. Duncan has been successful in the highest sense." There was nothing in Duncan's letters indicating his mind was impaired. Wellcome tried to make light of that delicate topic. "The very fact that Mr. Duncan chooses at the age of 84 to continue his strenuous work and to suffer privations instead of seeking ease and comfort, as most men do in the autumn of life, might convince some men who hold different views that his mind is unbalanced."

Wellcome suggested that malice and intrigue were behind Duncan's difficulties. "Such missions ... are never free from internal troubles: there are liable to be black sheep in every flock and amongst natives intrigues are ever brewing." Some "crafty trouble makers" had misled the government into taking actions which were too severe. Wellcome conceded only that "years of constant isolation from the graces of social life do not tend to make a man 'worldly wise', or promote in him a deferential attitude towards official rank or official usages."

Then he pronounced the fateful words: "I am anxious to follow this matter up and to learn the whole of the facts from top to bottom. All the questions involved must be reducible to simple verifiable matters of fact." They were not, of course, but fine points or shades of grey never gave pause to Henry Wellcome. The Metlakatla Case was launched.

Foster was unmoved by Wellcome's impassioned letter. After further talks with Secretary Lane and Commissioner Claxton, he remained "much impressed with the government's view." There had been many complaints against Duncan over a long period, but the government had not acted hastily. It would not have intervened at all, Foster added, if Duncan had picked a competent assistant to help in the mission work and eventually take his place. Foster said his own health was too poor to pursue the matter further, but he would advise his attorney, Walter S. Penfield, of the points Wellcome had raised. Penfield later played a key role for Wellcome in the preparation of the case.

Wellcome pushed ahead. On October 28 he wrote Duncan with a further request for evidence which he could present in Washington. He wanted to know every allegation ever made against Duncan, as well as an outline of his methods of operation and the names of all his loyal adherents. Duncan was to take witnessed statements from the natives who had stuck by him, and record all the visits made by various government officials over the last six years. He should provide a breakdown of the exact numbers of supporters and opponents and recent population changes, as well as the number of children attending his school. Copies of all articles and books written about the settlement were required. Wellcome also asked for full information on the state of Duncan's health over the last three years.

He wanted "every scrap of letters and other written records or documents." These should include a full account of Duncan's finances, whether the natives received any of the profits, and with whom Duncan shared authority. How much property and money did he have at the time of the move? How much now? Duncan was to provide all information about the Walkem proposal to move back to Canada, "but carefully avoid making any promises or taking any steps in respect to this unless and until we should fail in our efforts to secure adjustment in Washington. Avoid making any statement, intimations or threats to anyone about any such removal." Wellcome knew his man, and wanted to avoid compromising their position. His list of questions and demands went on for 11 typewritten pages.

"If you have under any of the trying circumstances done or said any hasty or unwise things," Wellcome told Duncan, "it is very desirable that you should write me quite *frankly* and *privately* about it with full explanations so that I shall not be in the dark and embarrassed by any allegations which may be sprung upon me ... give light on both sides and don't hold anything back! I will treat such information with utmost discreetness." Wellcome was relishing his role of investigator. "You can rely on me to spare no effort to secure a fair and just reconsideration of your case." That was a promise Henry Wellcome would keep with a vengeance for the next 20 years, long after Duncan's death.

The year had begun with Duncan's arrest and ended on another bizarre note with allegations he was responsible for the death of a 6-year-old native girl. The Town Council issued a statement claiming that when Laura Dundas first became ill her father, Benjamin, called on Duncan and asked him to have Dr. Minthorn visit the child. Dundas claimed Duncan told him he was not one of "his people" and showed him the door, sneering that he should go to the government teacher for help, which Dundas did.

Jones, who had little medical training, gave the girl castor oil. When she failed to improve, Dundas went directly to Minthorn, who attended to the child immediately. But it was too late; the girl died soon after. Jones thought the cause of death was typhoid fever, but Minthorn diagnosed her illness as auto-intoxication. According to the council statement, Minthorn was furious that he had not been called sooner. "Mr. Dundas told him how it was and, of course, he understood, but said nothing. It is a standing rule that patients must get Minthorn's aid through Duncan."

Minthorn denied the council's version of the incident, and an investigation bore him out. There was no record of a council meeting at the time, and the statement, as one investigator put it, was written in "the telltale phraseology of Jones and Marsden." Minthorn denied he needed Duncan's permission to treat patients, and pointed out that he had gone immediately to the Dundas girl when he was called. He didn't believe Duncan had "any bitterness in his heart toward anyone, much less the sick." Minthorn said that when he returned to Metlakatla that spring, Duncan had told him Benjamin Dundas required treatment for an unhealed wound. Duncan's enemies, Minthorn charged, were "without compunctions of conscience or shame." They had no mercy and would leave no means untried to accomplish "their selfish ends." Whatever the facts of the case, it was another unhappy chapter in the history of Metlakatla.

Medical care did not have a high priority with the Bureau of Education. "We all took a hand in doping out pills and belladonna plasters whenever there was a call for them—which was very often," Jones wrote in a report to Claxton. "It is a big question, however, whether we did any real good or the patients got well in spite of our treatment."

Jones said the general attitude toward Indians was poor in Alaska. The hospital in Ketchikan was closed to natives or anyone with a strain of native blood. "A Hottentot, Greek or what not may go there and receive, if he has the money, all the courtesies and services of the place. Not so with the poor native. He may be operated upon there, but quick as scat thereafter—before anything can be contaminated—he must be trucked out to a cabin on the flats where there is neither trained skill nor sanitary surroundings to further his convalescence."

The year-end elections in Metlakatla in 1915 were once more the occasion for bitter divisions. Duncan loyalist Moses Hewson claimed the Marsden-led clique on the council sent constables around the homes to warn the natives that if they voted for church Elders who backed Duncan, the government would send a big warship to take them back to British Columbia. During the voting anti-Duncan forces stationed men at the church door to write down names. The Bureau took an active role in the election. Lopp addressed a public meeting for more than two hours on the night before the vote. He spared none, "not even the king," Lopp boasted. "They surely got a strong dose of anti-Duncan dope."

Marsden addressed a total of 15 election meetings during December. On January 1, 1916, he was sworn in as secretary of the council although he had been away from Metlakatla for 25 years. He crowed to the Presbyterian Board of Home Missions that under the new laws governing the community, "I am custodian of all the public buildings, the cannery, the sawmill, the town water works and the church building . . . the very building in which Mr. Duncan is preaching." He also warned Duncan not to conduct baptisms in the church or it would be closed to him.

On March 6 the interior secretary advised Duncan a number of natives had formed a co-operative store and his building was the only one suitable for it. Duncan was given three months to clear out his stock. The native firm opened its store in another building in May, however, and never did use Duncan's building, which remained closed. Duncan lost a ton of perishable food, and the salvageable goods were sold at a loss in Ketchikan.

The decision not to occupy Duncan's store was taken after a stormy council debate. Marsden's takeover motion brought forth an impassioned plea from Thomas Hanbury. "I don't think it is right to treat Duncan like that. Duncan is getting old and will be passing away pretty soon, and we ought to give him respect and remember the many good things he has done for our people for many years and not trample on him before he dies. You ought to have some mercy on him in his old age, so he may die in peace . . . in the winter when it is hard times here, lots of the poor old women find that Duncan passes out to them a sack of flour or some sugar or something like that from his store." The motion was defeated. Hanbury noted Marsden "got pretty hot and mad about it."

Marsden kept up his vendetta by writing more letters and articles for the Ketchikan *Progressive*. For many years, he said, the people had conducted all their financial affairs with Duncan, who acted as town banker. "But in a white man, be he saint or scoundrel, the love of money is the root of all evil. This got the best of him in spite of his great name. With the help of some shrewd lawyers in Oregon and Washington, he gobbled up the whole thing. We are left entirely penniless today."

Marsden as usual exaggerated the state of affairs, but the town *was* going to seed. Sidewalks were rotting and windows left broken in the town hall. Hanbury claimed that after the Bureau "interfered and claimed to own our homes the people don't know what to do, and they let the place grow up with weeds." The sawmill was idled after the water line burst and was left unrepaired. A log boom in the bay was allowed to drift away and break up. Fire gutted the cannery two weeks after it had been leased by the government to P. E. Harris of Bellingham. Marsden and some of the Bureau people hinted the fire had been deliberately set and Duncan was involved, but offered no evidence. Duncan actually lost more in the blaze than Harris, who was insured. Tinplate valued at $3,000 and a big lathe belonging to Duncan were destroyed. The cannery was rebuilt the following year and Harris was granted a new lease which included the fish traps. The operation was so profitable he renewed for the next 15 years.

The secretary of commerce, who had jurisdiction over the Alaska fishery, set aside a protected zone extending 3,000 feet off the Annette Island shoreline for the exclusive use of the Metlakatlans. A clause in his lease gave Harris first refusal on all salmon caught in these waters. His monopoly was resented not only by natives who thought they should be sharing in the trap and cannery profits, but also by competing canners in the area. Charles A. Burckhardt of Portland, president of Alaska Pacific Fisheries, complained bitterly to the Bureau over its deal with Harris, charging that "someone was certainly trying to do some grafting in the matter." Burckhardt also protested the natives were being induced to turn over their traps to Harris for a pittance. Permits for new traps were issued to natives acting as front men or "dummies" for Harris, he said. Burckhardt became so angered by the unfair competition that he erected his own trap in the restricted zone as a protest gesture. He fought the government all the way to the Supreme Court before losing in 1918.

Many natives were opposed to the use of traps by anyone. Jones reported to Beattie in 1916 the Indians were upset over the Bureau's manipulation of the traps. "Our fortress of native faith is being bombarded from every quarter, and I am frank to say Metlakatla is in the most critical condition it has been in the past three years."

Wellcome, meanwhile, despite being weakened by surgery, was busy at a hideaway in North Carolina building his case against the government. He was disappointed by a letter from Dr. Bluett. "To be quite truthful, and impartial," Bluett had written, "I must say that from what I had been told, especially by the late Robert Tomlinson, I had formed the opinion that the autocratic nature of Mr. D., which was of course one of his great advantages when as a young man he had to deal single handed with the then savage Indians, and also with the white men, as whisky smugglers, and to combine the offices of pastor, school-teacher, and magistrate, had, in late years, proved a hindrance rather than a help, in the work, especially when, of necessity, he had to work with others who naturally resented it."

At Duncan's advanced age, Bluett said, he did not have either the physical or mental powers to run the mission. It was impossible to prevent the young men mixing with the outside world and demanding a higher education than he could provide. Bluett expressed admiration for Duncan's early work, however, and said he was glad Wellcome was championing his cause. "It grieves me to think that such a noble life, and work, as his, should end under a cloud."

Wellcome set out to disprove allegations made by Marsden and others that Duncan had been sexually involved with native women in British Columbia. He elicited a statement from Senator George Vest of Missouri, who had visited old Metlakatla shortly before the exodus and been told by Bishop Ridley that Duncan had debauched the women. "I made some inquiries about that and found that it was a vile slander," Vest declared. "Not only the Indians themselves, but the neighbours said it was false."

Dr. John Myers wrote that he had questioned Robert Tomlinson on the subject when he was on his way home after his break with Duncan. Tomlinson said he had personally investigated the accusations against Duncan and found them to be untrue. Wellcome obtained another convincing letter from George F. Rounsfell, manager of a Ketchikan packing company, who said he had employed a large number of Metlakatlans for the past 16 years and in all that time had heard nothing about sexual misconduct that could be substantiated. "Some years ago I met a friend of mine, Mr. Charles Windsor," Rounsfell said, "who knew Mr. Duncan very well in his younger days and I asked him if there had ever been any reports against Mr. Duncan's character years ago. He told me that both he and the late Robert Cunningham had tried their best to discover some weakness in Mr. Duncan's character but failed to do so. Knowing the Indians as I do, there is no doubt in my mind that the slightest lapse with an Indian woman would have been known, in fact would have been impossible to keep secret. I have heard white men, usually newcomers, speak of Mr. Duncan's illegitimate children, but the fact is none of these persons knew anything on the subject and when cornered would talk vague generalities."

In November of 1916 Wellcome arrived in Metlakatla to investigate the situation firsthand. He found Duncan's health and mental state "remarkably good for one of his age." His memory was acute and he was able to provide details of events which had taken place 60 years before. However, "his distress of mind over the division in his flock is now undoubtedly aging him rapidly and hastening his end."

Wellcome met with the council on December 13. The session began cordially. Marsden and Mayor Alfred Atkinson thanked Wellcome for his past support, especially during the 1887 move. Wellcome said he had come seeking a way to restore harmony in the community and perpetuate Duncan's work.

In the opening address Marsden said he was being blamed for the trouble and hoped Wellcome did not believe that. "If you want to see harmony," Marsden said, "the wisest Christian and human course . . . is to retire him forcibly from the active work and let him end his days in peace away from Metlakatla. As for his means of support, that will not worry either you or ourselves for we know him very well, and we know how he has amassed a big fortune which he calls as his own when in fact the greater part of it lawfully belongs to this community."

When Marsden charged that Duncan's failure to provide an adequate education was holding the natives back in business, Wellcome responded weakly that "some of the greatest wrecks that have occurred in American and European commerce have been by men who have been overeducated." He was never very good at mathematics himself, Wellcome said, and was "pitifully ignorant"

302

of bookkeeping. The British had blundered in India by educating too many people, he said. "The lawyers were without briefs, the doctors too many for the patients, and the poets without readers and the result was an enormous discontent."

The natives pressed for a broad discussion of their needs and complaints against Duncan, but Wellcome insisted on pursuing the question raised by Marsden of why the sawmills owned by Mark Hamilton on Gravina Island and Edmund Verney at Saxman had failed. He tried to get the Indians to admit that Duncan was not to blame since he had provided a practical education for the men. Marsden said they lacked training that would have given them the judgement to make business decisions. That couldn't be taught in school, Wellcome retorted. The meeting continued in this vein for three hours, until it was adjourned for the day.

Opening the second session, Atkinson proposed the natives be allowed to complete their statements, after which Wellcome could question them. But Wellcome said he knew all about conferences and the correct way was to proceed point by point. He seemed to confuse a conference with a courtroom. An exasperated Marsden accused him of prejudging the issues. The debate went on for a time before it was adjourned again. The meetings were accomplishing nothing but to expose the great gulf between Wellcome and the natives. He remained inflexible and unwilling to defer to them on any issues. While priding himself on being an expert on native cultures, he neither respected nor understood their values.

The next day Marsden advised Wellcome by letter the council had decided to break off the talks because there were serious objections to Wellcome's methods. Any future discussions should be held before an official tribunal with binding powers. Marsden said Duncan was their minister at the natives' request and although there would be no move to oust him now, it must be understood that the mission would end with him. "I am requested to notify you that any attempt on your part to re-establish and finance the mission . . . would not only be the cause of a more bitter trouble but it would be wholly disapproved and resisted."

Marsden offered to meet Wellcome privately, but their talk did not take place until the following March. Wellcome began by saying his first interest in Metlakatla was the mission and his second ethnology. He had always been impressed by the skills of the Tsimshians, he said. Marsden squelched that approach by saying the people were not interested in totems and history anymore. Wellcome insisted cultural artifacts were valuable.

Marsden said he bore no ill-will toward Duncan and had never tried to establish a Presbyterian church in Metlakatla. He had been ordained as a Presbyterian only because he went to a Presbyterian school. "When I became a man myself I acknowledged that Mr. Duncan had given his time and his best for our sakes here and it was our duty to see that he was well cared for in our midst and that he was upheld in his work and all his efforts." The words hardly squared with Marsden's abusive treatment of Duncan over the last 15 years. His only regret, he said, was that Duncan had not used him as he had wanted in the Christian work at Metlakatla. He had been misinformed about Duncan by his relatives and wished he had seen Wellcome sooner so that he could have avoided "all those useless and misjudged words that I have misused."

But Marsden was not being candid. His true feelings emerged in subsequent exchanges with Wellcome when the subjects became more contentious, such as Duncan's honesty. Wellcome asked if the people would have followed Duncan to Alaska if he had been guilty of the alleged crimes. "Now, you have touched a part of our Indian ways, Mr. Wellcome," Marsden said. "The explanation of that is . . . although they knew some of those things, yet they were too dignified to stoop down to say them." Such dignity had seldom been a concern of Marsden. When he refused to retract the allegations of dishonesty, Wellcome cut him off and the interview ended abruptly.

During his stay Wellcome also met with Thomas Hanbury and Mark Hamilton. Hanbury told him Duncan's biggest mistake was failing to train the younger natives to take over the businesses when he died. Wellcome said when Duncan tried that the Indians got the account books into a mess. "He ought to send them to teachers," Hanbury retorted. "He ought to spend two or three years to train a boy, because if he don't train him right but begins calling him down for his mistakes the Indian loses heart and quits." Wellcome said some of the best bankers and businessmen never went to business college. "What is the use of having these colleges then and schools?" Hanbury asked. There was no reply.

Duncan wanted to do everything himself, Hanbury said, and that was why there was trouble. Now Duncan was living "in old Indian ways—he has got no cook and he has no wall paper on the wall or carpet on the floor . . . I don't know what he is saving his money for." Duncan was planning for perpetuity, Wellcome answered lamely.

After the interview Wellcome asked Hanbury to submit a written report on Metlakatla affairs. In it Hanbury took a tolerant view of the younger people and their modern ways which so upset Duncan. "You and I are growing old and we heed the whispering voice of caution that has no place in the heart of gaiety," Hanbury wrote Wellcome, "and I thank God when I look upon the young faces with bright shining smiles and the pink in maidens' cheeks, there is not yet young faces grown old from privation or sufferings." Such wisdom was too rare around Metlakatla.

Hanbury was also eloquent on the subject of salmon. Urging a ban on traps, he said the fishery was the only inheritance his generation could leave their children. "To me this subject is sacred and greater than life itself. When the salmon fisheries are exhausted, God only knows what will become of my children and my people. No mining or farming of the future Alaska can readjust the place that salmon has always taken in our lives."

Wellcome was hostile throughout his brief interview with Hamilton. When Hamilton said Duncan owed him $124, Wellcome wanted to know if he had ever asked for it. "I was like a little kid and Mr. Duncan was a big man," said Hamilton. "I am scared; I'm scared." Hamilton said many people in Metlakatla had big houses but little to eat. "The only thing I want to do," he said, "is do what is right between us and Mr. Duncan before he die. Let us make peace and join together and have good preaching... and everything will be all right in Metlakatla and we will love each other and obey the government law." Wellcome rejected the overture. He wasn't there to make peace; he was embarked on a crusade to vindicate Duncan.

When Wellcome left in mid-March of 1917, an aide, Charles S. Boren, stayed on for a time in Metlakatla. Boren was a court reporter from Portland hired by Wellcome to transcribe his interviews with Duncan and the natives. "Duncan just gave me a sermon," he wrote Wellcome later that month, "on the folly of going into all the details as you are doing and said it was God's work, not man's he was doing in Metlakatla." Boren added that one of the natives had suggested to him that the way to make peace and have good feelings all around was to have a big feast, "where everybody come and eat sweet things and have much sugar-wah-wah (sweet talk)."

Chapter 27

Grief for a Leader

Wellcome was not the only outsider snooping around Metlakatla that winter. After a number of Duncan supporters in Ketchikan complained about Marsden's conduct, the Presbyterian Board of Home Missions sent the Reverend James H. Condit to investigate. Condit reported that although Marsden had not always acted with discretion, as the most intelligent and best educated of the natives he had been called on to act for his people.

There was evidence of an organized campaign to discredit Marsden, Condit said, suggesting that racial prejudice was at the bottom of it. Racial intolerance was indeed rampant in Alaska at this time, but on all sides. In a report to the Presbyterian Board blaming bootlegged liquor for Saxman's problems, Marsden had said, "the influx of the lowest type of Filipinos, Koreans and Mexicans in this country is the curse to us today."

Condit's harsh verdict on Duncan was that he was "an old man feeble in physical strength and failing mental power, suspicious of everyone, taking counsel of none and hurling out his impotent maledictions against all who oppose him."

In contrast to his endorsement of Marsden to the Presbyterian Board, Condit's correspondence with the Bureau of Education was highly critical of the native preacher. "We have had long enough now the travesty of a Tsimshian native ministering to Haidas and Tlingits through interpreters," he told Lopp. It was also learned later that in a blunt talk with Marsden, Condit told him it would be best if he resigned from the Presbyterian mission service in the fall and accepted a Bureau offer to become a fulltime teacher in Metlakatla, with time off to deal with council and business affairs. That way the Bureau could keep a tighter leash on Marsden. He was confident Beattie could "manage him perfectly in all matters, whether spiritual or temporal."

In his letter of resignation to the Board, Marsden referred to the growing tension between natives and whites. "I believe we ourselves are to blame for this more than anybody else. We have permitted ourselves to become pets and victims of our white brethren . . . we have learned from them how to use two tongues and put on two faces."

One way for the natives to assert themselves was by competing with the whites in business. To succeed they would have to be persuaded to work together, which the Bureau discovered was easier said than done. When storekeepers Haldane, Brendible and Benson refused to merge their operations, Lopp conceived the idea of forming a co-op company to run a general store and other businesses. The natives were reluctant to invest, so the Bureau took $2,500 which had been subscribed by the natives for the operation of the cannery before it was leased out. Lopp held out the prospect of earning up to $14,000 annual profit from the store, although Duncan had never exceeded $3,000. Lopp also assured the people they would obtain regular employment in the cannery by investing in the new company, which would have a profitable contract to supply labourers each canning season.

Bureau auditor H. C. Sinclair came from Seattle for a promotional meeting. According to native John Hayward, Sinclair put a lot of figures on a blackboard painting a rosy financial picture, then erased the numbers as the meeting ended so they could not be examined. In succeeding years the annual balance sheet of the new Metlakatla Commercial Company was also seen only on a quickly cleaned blackboard.

Bureau agent J. C. Helwig admitted to Lopp that it had "almost come down to a proposition of forcing the natives into the company." Six natives and a Bureau representative were named to the board of directors, with the Bureau man in control of the funds. Brendible was named president and general manager, and Marsden secretary. Brendible's son-in-law, James Evans, was chosen as storekeeper. In 1916 Brendible and his family owned almost 60 per cent of the M.C.C. shares. Two years later, after more shareholders had been brought in, the Brendible and Marsden families still owned 53 per cent of the stock.

The Bureau and the Marsden-dominated council did all in their power to help the M.C.C. prosper. Beattie told Lopp he had "thrown practically all my energies in the Commerical Company's affairs this year . . . and have neglected work about the cottage and school because I feel that it is absolutely necessary that there be at least no loss." For the sake of appearances, the Bureau named Beattie "Industrial Director" of Metlakatla.

Lopp told Beattie it was essential that stock be placed only in "safe hands" and that none should be sold to Duncan supporters. Ed Benson was among the natives who tried to steer a neutral course between the two factions, but Beattie was berated by Marsden and Brendible for selling a share to him. The sale was rescinded. Shares were also refused Moses Hewson and Benjamin Haldane because they had argued strongly against formation of the company.

The M.C.C. began with a general store situated on a choice building lot generously supplied by the council. It was not long before the company, with more co-operation from council, took over Duncan's old sawmill. The mill had been allowed to run down by Rod Davis, who surrendered his lease to the council. The executive committee of the council—Marsden, Brendible and Atkinson—assessed the value of the mill at a mere $800. They were about to turn it over to themselves, in the guise of the M.C.C., when democracy unexpectedly reared its head in Metlakatla. A number of villagers had become concerned about the self-serving antics of the M.C.C. group and decided to oppose them in the year-end election. To almost everyone's surprise, they were successful. Alfred Atkinson was unseated as mayor by Harry Lang, who pledged that "all things must be done right while I am holding the chain... and no crooked work will be allowed to be done here-after."

The sawmill deal appeared to be dead, but Beattie moved quickly. Before Lang was installed he pushed Atkinson and the other members of the executive committee to complete the sale to the M.C.C. The company was not even required to put up the $800. Instead it issued 80 shares valued at $10 each which were turned over to the council. Paul Mather said later he had wanted to bid on the mill and valued it at $2,600. He pointed out that it had made an $1,800 profit the previous year under Davis. Mather offered to put up $850 but his bid was brushed off by Beattie. Another bid of $3,000 was also ignored. And so the evils which had been alleged against Duncan were now introduced to Metlakatla by his accusers.

The M.C.C. blacklist prevented some natives from getting work, and the store was accused of profiteering for the private gain of its principal shareholders. Brendible was reckless with the firm's money. Helwig told Lopp that if cash dividends were to be paid, the money would have to be borrowed because "Brendible's purchases in Seattle amounted to about $8,000 and were gotten from several Jew concerns who I never heard of and most of it is trash . . . if Brendible is to be manager . . . he'll certainly need a curb along the ordering line. Another break like that and we might as well kiss the Commercial Company good-bye."

Meanwhile, Henry Wellcome was laboriously assembling his case. "We cannot expect to make rapid progress and may have to wait long and patiently," he warned Duncan. Everybody in Washington was involved with the war in Europe, which the U.S. entered in 1916. When Duncan expressed despair at this news, Wellcome tried to reassure him: "I see no reason to be discouraged, or to doubt that with God's guidance right and justice will prevail."

That kept Duncan quiet for a time, but as the months dragged on he grew impatient. He picked a four-man native delegation to go to the capital to press for government action. Blaming the war for holding matters up was not good enough, he told Wellcome. "Fighting abroad is no excuse for neglecting to administer justice at home." But Wellcome tactfully persuaded him to forget about the delegation for the time being.

A diversion that fall took the minds of both men briefly from their troubles. On October 1, 1917, a small celebration was held in Metlakatla marking the 60th anniversary of Duncan's arrival at Fort Simpson and the start of his missionary career. Wellcome organized and presided over the affair after soliciting funds for a gold-plated, silver loving cup from Tiffany's in New York. Dr. Bluett protested that since Duncan was nominally a teetotaller, the cup was an inappropriate gift. He suggested a tray would be more suitable, but was overruled.

A congratulatory message from President Woodrow Wilson told Duncan the Indians' "advancement in education and in capacity for usefulness in the world should be your sufficient reward." There was also a letter from Maude Cridge and the Macdonald sisters. "We the children of your old friends are writing to you to express our esteem of your wonderful life and work. Our parents could have written much better, but there was one thing they never knew and that was the unspeakable happiness that we as children enjoyed from the visits of our dear Mr. Duncan."

There was one sour note. Mayor Atkinson said the celebration was inappropriate because the disputes over business, education, religion and representative government which had split the community remained unsettled. He also wondered why the whites didn't consult the natives before going ahead with the party. The official photograph of the loving cup presentation shows the snowy-haired Duncan surrounded only by whites, all of whom except Minthorn came from outside the community.

Minthorn was concerned about the old man's behaviour. Some days he was a pleasant and interesting companion, but on others he seemed "determined to start something." Duncan accused his supporters of fraternizing with the enemy. He fired his native cook, Maria Booth, then tried to get her back. He hired another who soon quit. Minthorn worried that Duncan was not eating any fats, just starchy foods, and would suffer for it in the winter. When he told Duncan that Moses Hewson had good butter in his store, Duncan went, found it cost 60 cents a pound, and refused to pay what he protested was an outrageous price.

A report from Minthorn to Wellcome summed up the bleak situation. The weather was bad, the church bell had not rung for 10 days, and last week he and Duncan were the only ones at Sunday service. Duncan had no coal and it was miserably cold in his room. "I offered to bring coal for him but he said no. The real truth is that his clothes, his bed, his food . . . are all insufficient." Duncan would do nothing to make himself more comfortable, or allow anything to be done for him.

Minthorn finally gave Duncan an ultimatum. If he didn't hire a housekeeper, Minthorn would. Minthorn's wife had died the previous year. In November, Matilda Atkinson, who had written from Augusta, Maine, where she was director of a Children's Home Society, offering her services at Metlakatla, was sent for by Minthorn. The doctor told Wellcome that because General Pratt had been spreading gossip of immorality in Metlakatla, he thought it might be because he was living alone and had many Indian women patients calling on him. (He was 71.) That was why he had urged Miss Atkinson to come. They were married a month after her arrival. Minthorn was a practical and resourceful man.

Pratt visited Metlakatla in the fall of 1917 to spend three weeks fishing with Marsden. He reported to the Presbyterian Board that Duncan was "almost insanely vicious and denunciatory." Marsden, on the other hand, was "extremely modest and reluctant to even speak of his affairs." Pratt protested that the Board had left Marsden dangling after he had been cleared by Condit of the accusations against him.

310

But Marsden was running into increased opposition from some natives antagonized by his aggressive conduct on council and with the M.C.C. "Many of them think he is trying to do everything," Beattie noted. Despite his setback in the year-end election when Harry Lang was voted in as mayor, Marsden gloated that he had installed his slate of Elders "in the very church buildings in which old Duncan curses heaven and earth for the existence of the new order of things in Metlakatla." But when Condit went to Metlakatla in February of 1918 to see about establishing a Presbyterian church and installing Marsden as pastor, he was persuaded by Mayor Lang that Marsden did not have enough support on the island. As he left, Condit declared there would be no Presbyterian church as long as Duncan remained.

There was no room for mediators in Metlakatla. The Bureau's new school principal, C. D. Schell, attempted to fill that role and paid the price. Schell began by distributing seeds among the people. For the first time in years flowers and berries bloomed again in the gardens. Schell's daughter taught in the school and his wife helped with Duncan's housekeeping. This alarmed the Bureau agents, who feared Mrs. Schell would be spending too much time with Matilda Minthorn and might "unintentionally give... too much information." Lopp complained Schell was "a well-meaning man and fairly good teacher, but he is a man of no force or leadership." In other words, he wouldn't play ball with the Bureau officials. He was summarily fired.

An imposing figure stepped onto the Metlakatla stage about this time, and his goal was anything but mediation. As one biographer said of the Reverend Mark Allison Matthews, he was "never so happy as when in a fight of some kind."[31] The flamboyant Matthews, a lanky 6'5", was said to keep two loaded pistols in his office at Seattle's First Presbyterian Church. With a congregation of close to 9,000, including some of the city's most influential citizens, Matthews carried considerable weight in church and civic affairs. In 1912 he had been elected to the national post of Moderator of the General Assembly of the Presbyterian Church. At the same time, he was an active back-room participant in Seattle's boisterous

[31] Biographical material on the Reverend Matthews came from *Mark Allison Matthews: Seattle's Southern Preacher*, an unpublished thesis by Dale Edward Soden, University of Washington, 1980; and *Skid Road: An Informal Portrait of Seattle*, by Murray Morgan. Viking, 1960.

politics. Matthews once threatened to throw the mayor out of his window unless he agreed to take action against some wartime labour strikers.

Matthews liked fast cars, money and gambling, pursuits not likely to endear him to Duncan or Wellcome, but somehow he managed to ingratiate himself with both. He became an eager participant in "The Case." In 1917 Wellcome sent $500 to Matthews and urged him to say when he needed more, "so that I may always keep you in funds." No further encouragement was needed to bind him to their cause; that promise ensured Matthews' continued involvement.

Early in 1918 Matthews advised Dr. Myers he was sending a worker in his Sunday school, Bert Thompson, to Metlakatla to make an investigation. Matthews, who also had a law degree, was irresistibly drawn to the clandestine. "I am sending him to Alaska to find out about the infamous treatment which has been accorded Father Duncan," he wrote Myers. "Please give him instructions, show him how to get into the secrets of their diabolical conspiracy and help him in every way possible. I have told him to visit Alaska as a Sunday school worker interested in their work."

Thompson knew what his employer wanted. He found Duncan to be "a very impressive figure" who was forceful and vigorous in speech, although feeble in his movements. As for Marsden, Brendible and the Bureau agents, they had for selfish and ambitious motives conspired to defame Duncan, drive him from the community and spread unrest among the natives. There was not much surprising in those findings, but by the time they had been interpreted by Matthews and passed on to Wellcome, Thompson's report had taken on a sinister aspect.

"I spent considerable time and some money on an operator in Seattle trying to get a lead on the thing," Matthews wrote Wellcome. "This man has discovered, in my opinion, the key to the whole situation. You will see from this summary of reports that my suspicions were well founded. I am now convinced that the conspiracy between government officials—Lopp and others and Mr. Marsden, to establish different commercial companies, etc., was for the purpose of destroying Mr. Duncan, getting all commercial interests of this section of Alaska into their own hands in order that they might make fortunes."

Matthews proposed sending Thompson or another "operator" back to Metlakatla, ostensibly in the fishing business, to buy stock in the M.C.C. in order to see the company's books, records and incriminating correspondence. "When we get in we will not only save Mr. Duncan, but we will be able to expose a well laid plot to exploit the government in Alaska."

Wellcome replied tepidly that Thompson's report was "of considerable interest and adds material evidence." The ultimate object of the Bureau agents was a mystery that must be solved, Wellcome said. He was clearly not ready to accept Matthews' sweeping conclusions. And he proceeded to show that his own knowledge of Metlakatla's intrigues was far more exact and comprehensive than anything Thompson might have picked up during his short stay. Wellcome discounted the evidence given Thompson by Casper and Paul Mather because they were the sons of Edward Mather, "a devotee to the Sally Ann and very eccentric and unreliable." Herb Murchison, Ben Haldane and Ed Benson had all wavered, but Benson and Haldane had been ardent lately in support of Duncan. Murchison was unstable; Eaton too close to Marsden; Atkinson, Hamilton and Verney were "venomous"; and so on.

Age had long since begun to take its toll on Duncan's mental processes; now it was overtaking him physically. He became perceptibly weaker. There was one positive aspect of this decline, as Dr. Minthorn reported to Wellcome in February of 1918. Duncan was now letting others perform some of the responsibilities he had always shouldered himself. On their own, the natives had put new lights in the church, fixed the roof and kept it warm during the winter, which Minthorn said had helped increase attendance.

In March Duncan tumbled on a slippery sidewalk and suffered a chest injury. Bronchitis followed, as well as a weakened, irregular heartbeat. The Sunday after his accident Duncan missed his first church service since 1864. He was cared for by the Minthorns and spent most of the day in a large leather upholstered chair telling Matilda about the early missionary days. Shortly before his fall Duncan had adjusted Dr. Minthorn's salary to that of a married man, but at the same time stopped supplying medicines and increased his board, so the net result was a loss of income. The Minthorns didn't seem to mind.

Duncan's recovery was slow. He tried to resume work on a book he had started on the history of the two Metlakatlas. "I expect he will quit it soon as he has so often done before," Minthorn told Wellcome in July. The first 35 pages were good, he said, but then

Duncan launched into "strictures" against the government. Duncan also made an effort to gather together his records after being implored by Wellcome not to "allow a single scrap of your letters, papers, books or other documents to be destroyed...even some apparently unimportant papers may be helpful in meeting some of the many false statements which have been made." On the day he got word of Duncan's mishap, Wellcome told Dr. Myers to be ready if he died to seize all his books, papers and personal effects.

On Sunday, August 25, 1918, Duncan preached at both morning and evening services. In the afternoon he walked to the cannery to look at the boats tied up at the wharf. Matilda recalled later that his spirit was "as free as ever" and he made a jest about Thomas Hanbury's appearance. On Monday Duncan was unusually cordial, standing in his doorway and waving to passers-by.

There had been other signs of mellowing during his convalescence, even to the extent of forgiving John Arctander. After leaving Ketchikan, Arctander had visited some of Duncan's friends in Victoria. Edythe Fleet wrote that he was "heart-broken at having offended you of whom he was so fond and proud. I'm sure it was only impulsiveness and I am sure anyone mentioned in the book would never give it a thought. If only you forgave him—I am sure he has had his punishment." Duncan asked Matilda to find Arctander's address and said, "perhaps I was hard on him and rather hasty in my decision about the book. I should like to write to him and tell him so." There is no evidence, however, that he ever did.

After walking to the post office on the afternoon of August 27, Duncan was stricken. He was seen pulling himself slowly up the stairs to his house, where he locked the door behind him. Later that evening Minthorn entered the cottage by a window and let Maria Booth in with Duncan's dinner. She found him lying unconscious on the floor beside his bed. He had suffered a stroke. Dr. Myers came over from Ketchikan to attend him. Most of the natives were away fishing, but three women, Mary Hudson, Sarah Dundas and Agnes Buxton, took turns acting as nurses. Other natives came and went during the next three days, sitting in the kitchen waiting to be called upon to perform some task.

Matilda wrote in her diary: "Two things are on their hearts, one is that they will miss him sorely if he goes from their midst, and the other is, how they can get some thing from his house or belongings to keep for their own. Most of them would be glad of some little keepsake, some are after the goods, and one, Catherine Marsden, has actually laid claim to the real estate, saying that Father Duncan promised her the house when he was gone. She was his house keeper for many years and claims that he promised her all that he had at his death."

Duncan regained consciousness briefly but could not speak. He died at 1:15 a.m. on Friday, August 30, 1918. The church bell was rung to let the people know. The natives held a farewell service Saturday that lasted until 2 a.m. Sunday. Matilda wrote: "It is their custom at such a time to rehearse all the life history of the deceased and to tell of his deeds and character." The choir had been practising for two nights. They sang some Tsimshian songs that Duncan had written. Matilda observed the natives shed no tears during the choir practice or funeral service. They seemed instead to "put their tears and grief into their voices and told it in their song."

The main funeral service was held on Sunday, as warm and cloudless as the day Duncan arrived in New Metlakatla 31 years before. There were 1,000 people at the service, many from Ketchikan. A funeral procession through the town was led by Moses Hewson. The Reverend C. M. Van Marter of the Ketchikan Methodist Church gave the eulogy, speaking for almost an hour on Duncan's illustrious career. Beattie found the eulogy "tiresome" and added sourly that when he had offered his help to the Minthorns and the natives who had been caring for Duncan in his last days, he was called on only to supply government tools to dig the grave.

Duncan had asked to be buried in Victoria beside Edward Cridge. "Don't bury me in Metlakatla," he had pleaded. "It will be a deserted village some day." But the natives called a council meeting on the day he died and overruled his wish. According to Matilda, they decided that if the people saw the boat leaving the wharf bearing Duncan's body, "there would be no more heart left in them to live or to do any more work." And so Duncan was buried beside his church under a small, simple grave marker near a grove of young alders, "so that our children and our children's children will always know who it was who first brought the Gospel to us." A metal coffin was used, however, in the event it was decided in the future to move the body to Victoria for reburial.

Chapter 28

"The Case"

IF ANYONE THOUGHT Duncan's death would bring an end to Metlakatla's travails, he was sadly mistaken. New controversies were soon stirred into the old pot. On the day of the funeral Hawkesworth confided to Beattie he was afraid the Minthorns "might work themselves into the hearts of the people and endeavour to continue the church work." Although Mayor Lang had asked Minthorn after the service to keep the church keys and "hold the hearts of the people together," the Bureau agents made it known to the couple that they should depart. "They have made it very clear that we are not wanted here," Matilda wrote Wellcome, "because they do not want any vestige of the mission nor of Mr. Duncan's work to remain."

The day after the funeral, Matilda noted the people were coming to her door in greater numbers than before. "They are lonely and unsettled and seem to be looking for comfort from some source." Her husband added: "I feel sorry for the people, who are like sheep without a shepherd and exposed to wolves."

The wolves were closing in quickly. On September 15 government takeover notices were posted on the last remaining unseized buildings—Duncan's cottage, the guest house and the church. Minthorn protested in vain that it was unprecedented for the government to seize a church. But Commissioner Claxton had wired authorization to Beattie: "Duncan has no rights on the island which could be transferred by will and can have no successor which we will in any way recognize." Beattie allowed the Minthorns to hold services in the church for a time and also dropped his plan to use the guest house as a teachers' residence. He did not want it to appear the doctor and his wife were being unceremoniously tossed out. But the Minthorns were soon forced to turn over the church keys and leave. At Wellcome's request they took up temporary residence in Ketchikan and commuted at least once a week to Metlakatla.

As he departed in December, Minthorn expressed hope the natives would not be smothered with help. "It seems to me that with a start with such men as John Hudson and Tom Hanbury it would be possible to gradually select and add to the number until there was a community making their way as well as the ordinary white community." But with the determined Bureau agents on one side facing the uncompromising Wellcome on the other, there was little chance the Metlakatlans would be allowed to work out their own destiny.

Wellcome's staff began studying material in the eight boxes, one trunk and three handbags filled with Duncan's effects which were transported to Ketchikan by Myers immediately after the funeral. Mrs. I. G. Pruell, operator of a Ketchikan gift shop and secretary for the trustees, began typing copies of the letters, journals, bank books, ledgers and various records. Myers left a few books and articles of clothing in the cottage so that it would not appear they were deserting the place.

In his will Duncan named three trustees of his estate Dr. Ben Myers, Thomas N. Strong, now a judge in Portland, and Ketchikan businessman H. C. Strong. The will, rewritten in 1916 and witnessed by Wellcome, who dictated its wording, attempted to justify Duncan's money-amassing policy in Alaska.

It also harped on the old theme that students who went away to residential schools became puffed up with conceit and disdain for their parents. Duncan intended that the money in his estate would help keep them at home. But there was not enough left to carry that on for many more years. There was $138,679 on deposit in a Seattle bank when Duncan died, and the total value of the estate was placed at $146,159. That amount was reduced by $12,000 in estate duties which the trustees were ordered to pay after a number of unsuccessful court appeals claiming exemption.

What had happened to Duncan's fortune? His private ledger showed a balance of $207,000 as early as 1907. There were big profits from the cannery over the next six years and his account had almost doubled by 1913. But then followed a five-year period in which there were continuing expenses and little or no income from the store or cannery.

Wellcome repeatedly claimed that Duncan had lived like a pauper on 25 cents a day for most of his life. What he did not mention was that for years Duncan had been playing the role of a grandfatherly Santa Claus, dispensing hundreds of dollars in gifts each year to friends, relatives and charities. Every Christmas he sent a large sum to the Cussons in Beverley to be disbursed to his mother, assorted aunts and uncles and the widow and children of his old friend Stephen Hewson, as well as the poorhouse. By 1907 this donation alone had reached $500 annually. Each year he sent Edward Cridge at least $250 for his personal needs as well as contributing large amounts to Cridge's church. There were expensive presents for the Cridge and Macdonald children, which were increased to Maude Cridge as she grew older and in need of care. Money was sent to Minskinisht to support Tomlinson's mission and provide gifts for his children.

Some of this largesse was desperately needed. In 1904 Duncan received a letter from young Eleanor Tomlinson. "Thank you very much for the present of money. It was very kind of you to remember me. The only recollection I have of you is a dear kind man who used to carry me on his shoulder when I was very tired... I hope to spend your money on my teeth. They are in a very poor condition." Gifts to the wealthy Macdonalds are harder to justify. Questionable too were the $50 annual donations to funds for converting Catholics or Jews to Protestantism. There were also numerous gift subscriptions to Duncan's favourite religious publications for his friends.

Had these been strictly private funds there would be no issue over his generosity. But his profits were enhanced by paying the natives lower wages—50 cents a day was deducted from their earnings—on the grounds that he was supporting community services and improvements. Duncan also told the people that *all* the money he accumulated would end up in their pockets.

Duncan's last will and testament became as contentious as his life. The main fund and a designated $20,000 "Benevolent Fund" for the care of the aged and needy were tied up for years by litigation and Wellcome's demand that nothing be touched until the case was settled. "We see nothing but complete slavery under the terms of the will that dispose of our own money," Ed Verney declared in 1919. Earlier that year Joseph Hayward, James Howard and Silas Booth had collected 65 signatures on a petition urging acceptance of the will's terms before they were stopped by a constable under orders from Marsden.

Meanwhile, the uneasy partnership of Marsden and Charles Brendible continued to manipulate the operation of the Metlakatla Commercial Company in a manner that made Duncan's payroll deductions seem picayune. Under the terms of its contract with the cannery lessee, the M.C.C. took a one-third commission or "sweat out" from the payroll. Individual wage packets went from the cannery to the company store, which deducted for any outstanding bills before turning over their pay to the natives. Out of every $100 paid for cannery labour, $65 went to the worker and $35 to the M.C.C., with the largest portion skimmed off by Brendible and Marsden. Bureau agent Helwig said he was disgusted with the antics of the pair, but would "probably have to back down on some of the things which I believe are right in order to preserve harmony."

When some of the natives attempted to redeem their shares they were not only turned down but found themselves on the employment blacklist. The only way to get off the list was to switch from Duncan's church to the Presbyterians. "Everything here is run by bribery," John Hudson protested. Many natives chose to leave the island. Minthorn reported to Wellcome in 1920 that 50 natives had returned to B.C.

As it had been during his life, Duncan's church was the focus of controversy after his death. Interior Secretary John B. Payne told Mayor Andrew Usher in 1920 the non-denominational church was for the use of everybody. Payne suggested three trustees be elected to make "equitable arrangements" for each religious organization to have it at certain times. If an agreement could not be reached peacefully, Payne added, a U.S. marshal would enforce compliance with the decision of the estate trustees. Many natives were angered by this intrusion of government into their religious affairs, and the trustees voted not to disturb Duncan's "Christian Church" in its sole right to use the building.

A Presbyterian congregation was formed in October 1920, and Marsden was permitted by Bureau officials to preach in the Duncan church despite vigorous protests by the trustees. By 1922 there were an estimated 300 members of the Duncan church and only 60 Presbyterians. Nevertheless, Marsden began the construction of a church of his own that year, with volunteer labour and credit from the M.C.C. for materials. Wellcome wrote to the Church Elders in 1923 warning them of the danger of inroads by the Presbyterians. The Elders should respect the advice of the trustees, said Wellcome, who resorted to the white man's primitive witchcraft to enforce his wishes. "You have very sacred duties," he told them. "Duncan knows everything you do."

Moses Hewson wrote on his own initiative in 1920 asking Robert Tomlinson Jr. to come and take Duncan's place. Tomlinson replied that the best thing for the people was to join the Presbyterians and ask for a minister other than Marsden. He bore no ill-will toward Marsden, he said, but it would be better for Metlakatla if he left.

Marsden, however, was busy building the largest house in town for his family. Once again he got lumber on credit from his company, promising to pay later with shares. Bureau officials expressed concern that the house was beyond his means. They also complained about his attitude following Duncan's death. Frustrated at not automatically stepping into his shoes, Marsden became increasingly bitter, cynical, arrogant and domineering. He had waited so long.

As his personal bills mounted, Marsden also pushed the council to spend community funds as soon as they came into the treasury. As secretary he stopped keeping records of council meetings in 1919 and no accounting of payments could be found after that date. He had a falling out with Brendible, which resulted partly from personal animosity but was also a reflection of underlying tension between the Tlingits and Tsimshians in Metlakatla.

Despite his growing unpopularity, Marsden managed to hang on to his council seat through ballot-box manipulation. Besides allowing unqualified natives to vote, he had an ordinance passed declaring that only those paying poll tax could vote, then allowed his supporters to use promissory tax notes which he subsequently tore up. He sent his boat to outlying camps on election day to pick up his backers, leaving Duncan's people behind.

In April 1932, while travelling in a small boat through stormy waters to a Presbyterian meeting at Hydaburg, Marsden was hurled against the side of the vessel and suffered internal injuries. He died a month later in hospital at Ketchikan, aged 62.

On July 11, 1923, President Warren Harding stepped ashore at Metlakatla, the initial stop on the first presidential tour of Alaska. The President spent three hours in Metlakatla, twice as long as scheduled, listening patiently while the natives complained that proliferating salmon canneries were endangering their food supply. Harding promised to study the matter, but told the natives there could be "no return to primitive conditions because that is against God's law and the best interests of human society." To the staunchly conservative President, the practice of unfettered commerce was the first of God's laws.

Trustee H. C. Strong briefed Harding on "The Case." The President told him he should demand a thorough investigation, unaware that Henry Wellcome already had that well in hand. "Why, why did agents of the government seize the buildings and industries?" Harding asked. "It is beyond me," replied a flustered and inarticulate Strong.

Matilda Minthorn, who had returned to Metlakatla at Wellcome's request following her husband's death in Oregon the previous year, proved a more able advocate. She told Harding that after Duncan's death she and her husband were not allowed to hold a prayer meeting anywhere in the village, even in their own home.

"Do you mean to say that a government official so far interfered with a religious service as to forbid you to hold one?" the President asked. When Matilda repeated her charge, Harding turned to his entourage and said: "No government official of the United States under our constitution has any rights to interfere with any religious service in any manner whatever." Walking back to his ship, Harding noticed the two churches in town and commented: "Such things ought not to be, either here or anywhere. Churches ought to get away from those divisions and rivalries. It is not right that Christians should compete for souls, like rivals in commerce."

Interior Secretary Hubert Work and Secretary of Commerce Herbert Hoover had accompanied Harding—who died suddenly in San Francisco on the way home—and soon afterwards long-overdue changes were made in the administration of native affairs in Alaska. Lopp was ousted as Chief of the Alaska Division of the Bureau of Education and posted to Anchorage to work with his reindeer. The New York *Times* said Lopp's demotion was a direct result of the Harding visit, which had convinced government officials the Bureau was inefficient and the natives were lacking adequate educational and medical services. In denouncing previous policy for Alaska native schooling, Secretary Work said academic training without vocational instruction "cultivated the taste of the Indian for better living but left him without the ability to live as well as he had lived as a hunter, trapper or fisherman." The more education the native received, often the more unfortunate and unhappy he became, Work said. Those who had gone away to boarding school found it difficult to adapt to their former way of life when they returned home, while the ones who remained in the lower states were social misfits.

321

In 1931 Indian schools in Alaska were turned over to the Commissioner of Indian Affairs and the role of the Bureau of Education downgraded. The secretary of the interior at that time, Ray Lyman Wilbur, also conceded that Indian education had been a failure. It had not enabled the natives to go into the world outside the reservation and become self-supporting. Thousands of Indian students had gone back to a primitive, tribal existence "because they were still strangers to the white civilization." Although Duncan in his later years had failed to back up his theories in practice, his long-standing criticisms of the government's education policies were at last being acknowledged.

Metlakatla took on a ramshackle appearance as more families abandoned their homes to move to Ketchikan for work. The population fell below 500 for the first time. There was no resident doctor and medical care was provided through the Duncan estate using Ketchikan doctors.

Henry Wellcome's other interest in Metlakatla, as he told Marsden in their 1917 interview, was anthropological. That included the gathering of native myths, legends and other cultural information, but primarily the collection of artifacts. Wellcome hired as his agent an educated Tsimshian, William Beynon, a grandson of Duncan's language teacher at Fort Simpson, Arthur Wellington Clah. He paid Beynon $75 a month and travelling expenses at the same time that Beynon was on the Canadian government payroll as an interpreter for anthropologist Marius Barbeau. Barbeau, who also paid Beynon's travelling expenses, was collecting the same legends which Beynon was passing on to Wellcome. The contract was ended when Wellcome learned of Beynon's arrangement.

Before their rupture, Wellcome came close to acquiring 200 oil paintings by Emily Carr of Indian totems and villages in the Queen Charlotte Islands and along the Skeena and Nass Rivers. Carr told Beynon, who did not say he was an agent for Wellcome, that she would sell the collection for $6,000. She wanted to pay off a $5,000 mortgage on her Victoria home and have a bit left over to continue her painting. But the price was too high for Wellcome. He revealed a singular lack of art intuition when he told Beynon, "these kind of pictures have not much value. Unless the artist is a very great one the pictures will sell for a very small amount." He instructed him to wait until Carr was more desperate, but fortunately for Canadians she was able to hold out and sell her works individually within the country.

Wellcome could be generous at times. In 1927 he learned that Moses Hewson, a Duncan loyalist despite a brief flirtation with the Salvation Army, was in poor health after the death of his wife, who had woven a number of baskets for Wellcome on assignment. Wellcome told Matilda to provide at his expense anything that Hewson might need to recover. "Please see that he is comfortably clothed and has suitable bedding and is not lacking in fuel." That same year Wellcome sent a $500 cheque to Matilda to dole out to the neediest natives. Fishing had been poor in the summer and the people needed help to get through the winter. Wellcome sent money each Christmas for flour and canned milk and saw to it that funds were provided for the education of the brighter young people at colleges in Washington and Oregon.

But Wellcome could have done much more if he had spent in the community the thousands of dollars being squandered on the staff of lawyers, secretaries and investigators he had assembled in Washington in a futile effort to vindicate Duncan's career.

The government was also wasting thousands in responding to Wellcome's campaign. In 1927 the department of the interior produced a 489-page report reviewing the history of the Metlakatla dispute. Its author, department official Donald V. Hunter, concluded that Duncan's industrial activities were unauthorized by law and were a trespass on the Indian reservation. The fact these businesses were tolerated for years did not make them legal, said Hunter. He proposed legislation to enable the Metlakatlans to get title to their property, which they would be allowed to sell to whites so that Annette Island could be opened to commercial development. The Hunter report declared the Metlakatlans were "aliens to whom the U.S. gave assistance as an act of grace," even though by this time most had been born on the island and could vote in Alaska territorial elections.

Questions were also raised within the department on the legality or propriety of Henry Wellcome, a British citizen, playing such an active role in the dispute. When the government pressed Wellcome to say what action he expected it to take in respect to Metlakatla, he was always evasive. Restitution could not be fixed, he said, until all the facts had been "completely assembled, analyzed and determined."

In pursuit of this impossible goal, Wellcome assembled a staff of a dozen, including members of the Burroughs-Wellcome office, collecting and notating every scrap of information remotely relating to Duncan. The goal was to prepare a brief which would force the government to admit it had been wrong to intervene in the affairs of Metlakatla. Eventually the conglomeration of paper was filed in cardboard boxes occupying 105 cubic feet of space. There were 70,000 hand-written index cards containing innumerable cross-references. Thoroughness was transformed into fanaticism.

The zeal of Wellcome and his aides was fearsome. H. L. Scaife, the office manager, told Wellcome at one point: "I feel that the Brief when completed will smash everything they have done or can do." But at what cost and to what end? Nobody involved in all that feverish activity seems to have asked themselves those questions.

Duncan loyalist John Hudson wrote Wellcome from Metlakatla: "Dear Friend: We have been delighted to learn that you are still wasting your precious time in Washington for us poor people." The word "wasting" was circled by Wellcome, who wrote above, "He means sacrificing, using." A humourless man, he was oblivious to the unintended irony.

By 1930 both Myers and H. C. Strong had grown impatient at the lack of tangible results from all the detective work. Strong told Myers the government could not go into all the past history and it wanted simply to deal with the existing situation. The trustees should act while there was a friendly President (Hoover) in office. "I do not think we are doing right in permitting Dr. Wellcome to prolong it further." Myers and Strong told Wellcome the following year the Indians were critical of the long delay, and said the trustees were being forced to act as buffers between the natives and Wellcome's obscure purposes. More should be done to help them. Fish prices were down and the church was in need of repairs. Although they were the official trustees of Duncan's estate— Thomas Strong was too old and ill to take an active role but could not be replaced because of a Wellcome edict—it was Wellcome who ran the show.

Despite the grumbling, Wellcome's air of authority—not to mention his money—carried the day in every instance. He told Myers that "there should be no talk or thought of making any changes at the mission or of the trustees. Nothing should be done to change the status quo, or that would lead to complications... the prospects for a successful termination of the case have never been greater."

So Metlakatla stood still for a decade, waiting for its fate to be decided by outsiders. Each week Matilda Minthorn reported to

Wellcome on the minutiae of village life—who was remaining loyal, who had defected, who had left town. Nothing was too trivial to be recorded. Matilda, who used "thy" and "thou" in her letters, criticized the white teachers for dancing with the natives. Mrs. Hudson was sending her daughters to Portland to escape the influence of the Metlakatla dance halls, she said. There had been a time when Metlakatla was considered a refuge from the dance halls of the outside world.

But the world beyond Metlakatla was a fast-changing place. Not even Henry Wellcome's stern edicts could hold back the future from the little settlement. In 1928 government surveyors arrived to resurvey the village and mission grounds, causing fearful memories among those who were present during similar activities in old Metlakatla. By 1932, as the great depression began to be felt, a number of expatriate Metlakatlans drifted back to the village, where they could receive free water and electricity. Many brought with them the roisterous habits and ways of life picked up in the cities, causing more turmoil in the town.

Matilda felt it was time for her to leave, and Robert Tomlinson Jr. was officially invited to return. This time he accepted. He said he had felt an obligation to the people for the past 20 years. Tomlinson tried to be a unifying force in the community but soon ran afoul of Wellcome's insistence that Duncan loyalists always came first. Mrs. Tomlinson, a nurse, was reprimanded for distributing powdered milk to *all* the children, even those from the outcast Presbyterian families.

The government was equally capable of such pettiness. In 1933 some 200 natives petitioned the secretary of the interior to give the cannery lease to Trustee H. C. Strong, who had experience in the business and would take no profit. The government instead gave a five-year lease to a private operator who pocketed half the profits.

Despite his erratic behaviour, the Reverend Matthews was kept on staff by Wellcome. The reason was not hard to find. Wellcome wanted a prominent Presbyterian to lend credibility to the case against the government, to use his name on the formal brief. Matthews also had a self-righteous manner that Wellcome could identify with, and a charisma he could only envy. Wellcome was impressed by Matthews' "forceful, vigorous" sermons.

Matthews was always begging money from Wellcome. He lost heavily with investments in the 1920's and the strain brought him close to a mental breakdown. He insisted that "assassins" were

325

after him. In 1934 he wrote Wellcome in London to complain he had not heard from him for some time. Socialists and atheists were overrunning the U.S. He was fighting a great battle against communism. "As you know, the communists have their murder bureau, their kidnapping, racketeering, blackmailing, and government wrecking departments. Have recently been notified they have their Chicago gang represented here for the purpose of giving me a ride." Two years earlier Matthews had wired Wellcome that he was sick from the tremendous pressure he was under. Wellcome sent $2,000 to ease his strain. The next year Matthews asked for and received another $5,000. Over the years frequent sums of money were sent in answer to Matthews' fawning "My Dear Brother..." pleas.

Staff members preparing the report that was to bear Matthews' name and be called an "Independent Report on the Metlakatla Case" became exasperated with his wild inaccuracies. Scaife complained to Wellcome that Matthews was often "confused as to the facts" and was overconfident of the results that would follow his muddled suggestions. At one point Matthews asserted that Duncan's mission buildings were worth $1 million when they were built in 1885 (he was not much on dates) and told Wellcome to present that exaggerated figure to the government in order to get a favourable settlement.

Matthews also succeeded in alienating President Hoover with one of the numerous bombastic letters on the case he dispatched to the White House. Hoover replied angrily that Matthews had been "entirely misled in many things," particularly his accusation that the interior department had been destroying key documents. The President also revealed his impatience with Wellcome when he added, "this is just an indication of the oversuspicious attitude of your friends, when the Department, on my instructions, is endeavouring to find out what is wrong and what Wellcome's idea of remedy is."

The so-called "Matthews Report" is a tedious, overwritten, repetitious blend of fact and opinion that talks of plots and conspiracies and is nastily racist. Marsden's role in the anti-Duncan movement is chronicled in a vicious manner which was approved by Wellcome. One of Wellcome's memos told the staff to "use diplomatic language, but make it as strong as you care to. Discredit Marsden wherever possible."

One passage was especially lacking in subtlety: "True to the instincts of the untrained savage, after all these years of stoical waiting, Marsden knew that if the final spring on his victim were made stealthily there would be less danger of an outcry that would bring rescue." All that was needed to complete the image was a swirling tomahawk and Duncan's scalp dangling from Marsden's belt. Marsden was described as "cunning" and likened to the treacherous Iagoo in Longfellow's *Song of Hiawatha*. It is noteworthy that Sheldon Jackson, who was accused in the report of masterminding the early plotting against Duncan and whose "adroit and flattering plans appealed to Marsden's vanity and crafty mind," was treated far less harshly in the report than his protege.

The theme of the report was that the government, specifically a succession of secretaries of the interior, had been "misled and deceived" into taking action against Duncan by the reports of Bureau of Education agents. The Indian agitators other than Marsden were merely a few natives who Duncan "had been obliged as pastor to rebuke, or as magistrate punish." The report also hinted darkly of communist plots. "From the day the Bureau of Education entered Metlakatla it preached the doctrine of Bolshevism—everything belonged to the workers."

The report attempted to discredit Duncan's critics by dredging up their peccadilloes. Bishop Rowe of the Episcopalians was said to have a drinking problem. Marsden had once attempted on his boat to force his attentions on a young Metlakatlan woman who fought him off with kicks and slaps.

In a burst of hyperbole, the report referred to "a series of outrages and acts of frightfulness, committed under the Bureau of Education, which will not only horrify the American people but shock the conscience of the civilized world." It was not to be. The Congressional committee to which the report was submitted in 1934 was no more sympathetic than had been the department of the interior. The stalemate continued until Sir Henry, who had belatedly received a knighthood in 1934 for his philanthropic and scientific works—it would have come sooner had it not been for his messy divorce—became ill. He had suffered from colitis for many years and died on July 25, 1936, aged 83.

At last "The Case" was ended. There was no one left with the desire to carry on the crusade, the purpose of which had long been forgotten. The government quietly closed its voluminous file.

In his will Wellcome left annual bequests of $500 for Matilda

Minthorn and $1,000 for Reverend Matthews for the rest of their lives. Matthews didn't enjoy his legacy long, dying in 1940. Matilda reached the age of 92 before her death in 1954.

Metlakatla was now free to work out its future. The influence of the Duncan estate trustees diminished as the fund ran down. It was eventually depleted in the 1960's. Some $30,000 had been spent to build a new church after the original building burned down in 1949. The rest was used for church upkeep, the minister's salary, and student loans, most of which were never repaid.

The schisms opened in Duncan's declining years that festered during the long years of "The Case" healed slowly. Some scars are still evident today. Perhaps that's not surprising. As Dr. Minthorn observed in 1921: "I do not think there is any hope of the Metlakatla people ever being united. Such a state of affairs is impossible of realization even among white people." He might have said, *especially* among white people.

Duncan had always stressed the importance of unity in the community but, like many of his plans and goals, it was never achieved. Perhaps the idea of Metlakatla itself was an impossible dream. The forces arraigned against Duncan and his Tsimshian followers were formidable. The opposition of the white settlers against his efforts to make the Indian self-supporting on his own land was unrelenting. The resistance of some Tsimshian chiefs to the changes Duncan was attempting to introduce was also a considerable factor in his difficulties. Their objections are understandable, but it is an inescapable fact that the rank and privileges they enjoyed in the traditional Tsimshian society were doomed by the onslaught of the white man's culture. Change was inevitable, and Duncan attempted to make the transition as easy as possible for the Indians.

That he did not completely succeed was more his fault than theirs. Despite his humble origins, Duncan was a brilliant innovator. The wisdom of the policies he urged has been validated by time. His quick grasp of the Tsimshian language and perception of their thinking was astounding. In many ways he understood them better than he did himself. Time and again, the contradictions of his combative, frustrated personality tripped up his plans.

Toward the end, in Alaska, he became a victim of the infirmities of age. In her classic study on the subject, Simone de Beauvoir points out that money often becomes synonymous with power. The old father revenges himself upon his children by refusing to help them financially, or forcing them to live at a poverty level. "It is the only kind of power left to him, and he takes an ill-natured pleasure in making them feel it." The aged often refuse to listen and become sly and secretive about their financial resources. They forget how to live among men. "All they do appears to them virtuous; all they cannot do they rank as vice." The new generation arouses the old man's fury because he comes to believe they are dispossessing him.[32]

The words may describe Duncan in his later years, but it is not how he should be remembered. Rather, it must be acknowledged that he was a man ahead of his time. Only now are governments grudgingly coming to recognize the validity of the Indians' cause which he championed. In doing so, "he left a deeper mark than any other single person on North Pacific coast Indian history."[33]

[32] Beauvoir, Simone de. *Old Age*. Andre Deutsch, 1972.

[33] Drucker, Philip. *Cultures Of The North Pacific Coast*. Chandler, 1965.

Epilogue

DESPITE THE TURMOIL THAT preceded and followed Duncan's death, the modern community of Metlakatla, Alaska, remains his most tangible legacy. Its proud and independent citizens have created what has been recognized as the outstanding native community in Alaska and one of the most unique in North America.

Still operating under its 1891 Congressional charter, the town runs its own affairs and is self-supporting. A modern fishing fleet and cannery are owned and operated by the town council. The sawmill and timber on the island generate revenue through a lease to outside interests. A new $16-million hydro-electric plant financed with federal funds is planned to provide more power for industries. A computer system installed in the municipal hall in 1982 has been extended to the cannery. The population in 1983 was about 1,500, of whom 200 were non-natives. The original Tsimshian stock has been considerably altered through intermarriage.

When Alaska used some of its new oil wealth in the early 1970's to settle native land claims, the Metlakatlans alone opted to forego the cash offer. They saw there were strings attached and wanted to preserve their long history of independence. Annette Island is the only reserve in the state. Other Alaska natives who surrendered their land rights 10 years ago now are seeking to undo the settlement and get them back.

The Metlakatlans possess exclusive fishing rights around their island up to 3,000 feet offshore and are still using the much-debated salmon traps after a battle that went all the way to the U.S. Supreme Court. During the Second World War the U.S. Army built a large air base on Annette Island and 10,000 men were stationed there at one time. After the war the Army turned the field over to the Federal Aviation Agency, which granted landing rights to commercial airlines for Ketchikan-bound passengers. The Metlakatlans were forced to go to the Supreme Court a second time to win compensation for the use of their land. The fighting spirit of William Duncan obviously lives on.

The airliners are gone now and the runways abandoned since the opening of a large new airport nearer Ketchikan in 1973. Four years later the Coast Guard Air Station for Southeastern Alaska was moved from the island to Sitka. Despite these setbacks, the economy has continued to thrive. Tourism may be added to the community's revenue as the Alaska cruise ships add Metlakatla to their list of stopovers.

The athletics which Duncan introduced continue to flourish, and two descendants of the pioneers have gained national renown. Wally Leask was an All-American basketball player at the University of Washington who returned to Metlakatla to skipper a fishboat. John Smith was an All-Alaska centre in high school, was captain of the fishing fleet's "top-boat" seiner for many seasons, served as mayor for 12 years, and as an adviser to the North Pacific Fisheries Commission travelled to conferences as far away as Tokyo. Trim and fit in his 70's, the distinguished-looking Smith wintered with his wife Ruth each year in southern California. For those who stay at home during the long wet months, a modern Olympic-size swimming pool was completed in the early 1980's.

In Metlakatla, B.C., where 120 people live, the atmosphere is different. It is quiet, almost sleepy, but far from the run-down, dispirited village one had been led to expect. Many of the houses are freshly painted and have well-tended gardens. A new water and sewage system had recently been installed, as well as a satellite TV dish. The population is growing slowly as more natives become disillusioned with life in Prince Rupert and return to the tranquil home of their ancestors. In 1956 Metlakatla was the first native community in Canada to seek enfranchisement under new federal laws.

Not surprisingly, there is a lingering resentment against Duncan among the Tsimshians in the area because he is held responsible for dividing the people and their families. But links are maintained between the two Metlakatlas. The mayor of the Alaskan community in 1982 was Casey Nelson, a B.C. Tsimshian who visited Annette Island on a sports junket and decided to stay. The elders of both communities are attempting to spark a cultural renaissance by gathering information on the old Tsimshian legends, customs and artistic skills to pass on to the younger generation.

332

Acknowledgements

I OWE A SPECIAL DEBT TO Imbert Orchard, who generously turned over research material which he had gathered on William Duncan, particularly in Beverley, and whose enthusiasm for the project spurred my efforts. I am grateful for the encouragement and help provided by David Piff, who guided me through the labyrinth of the Henry Wellcome Collection in Seattle; to the staff of the Provincial Archives of B.C., particularly Jean Southey for her cheerfulness and patience in assisting a novice find the materials he needed; to George P. Brown of the Beverley Public Library for kindly help in tracing Duncan's well-buried family roots; to Les Yates for acting as boatman and guide to Metlakatla, B.C.; and to Horace Leighton of that community, a warm and gentle man who took two strangers into his home and talked about his past and that of the trim little village; to Russell Hayward, Solomon Guthrie, Sol Atkinson, John Smith, Eleanor Booth and others who made me feel at home in Metlakatla, Alaska; and especially to my wife Pat for her encouragement, helpful editorial suggestions and painstaking proofreading.

Lest anyone assume from the above that a researcher's path is always strewn with daisies, it should be noted that my reception at the august Wellcome Institute of London was in stark contrast to that in both Metlakatlas. The determination to conceal information about the life of its benefactor had to be experienced to be believed. I take some comfort from the fact I am not the first author to run up against the unyielding granite walls of 183 Euston Street. Wellcome was a remarkable man, and some day his biography will be written, but not until enlightenment and common courtesy penetrate within.

PETER MURRAY

I WILL NOT ATTEMPT to list all the other books, articles and manuscripts studied during the research for the book but only those that were drawn upon in the writing. These include:

Bancroft, H. H. *History of Alaska 1730-1885*. Antiquarian Press reprint, 1959.

Beynon, William. *The Tsimshian of Metlakatla, Alaska*, an article in American Anthropologist, 1941.

Black, C. E. D. *Dufferin and Ava*. Toronto, 1903.

Bruce, Miner. *Alaska*. 1895.

Brooks, Alfred H. *Blazing Alaska's Trails*. University of Alaska Press, 1953.

Cail, Robert E. *Land, Man, and the Law: The Disposal of Crown Lands in British Columbia.* University of British Columbia Press, 1974.

Church Missionary Intelligencer, A Monthly Journal of Missionary Information. London, 1857-1887.

Colonial Correspondence, Public Archives of B.C.

Crosby, Thomas. *Up and Down the North Pacific Coast*. Toronto, 1914.

Doig, Ivan. *The Tribe That Learned the Gospel of Capitalism*, article in The American West, March 1974.

Duff, Wilson. *The Indian History of British Columbia, Vol. 1: The Impact of the White Man*. Provincial Museum of B.C., 1964.

Fisher, Robin. *Contact and Conflict: Indian-European Relations in British Columbia, 1774-1890*. University of B.C. Press, 1977.

French, Harold. *Duncan of Metlakatla Deserted*, an article in Overland Monthly, 1913.

Gruening, Ernest. *The State of Alaska*. Random House, 1954.

Helmcken. J. S. *Reminiscences*, edited by Dorthy Blakey Smith. University of B.C. Press, 1975.

Hinckley, Ted C. *Alaskan John G. Brady: Missionary, Businessman, Judge, and Governor.* Miami University Press, 1982.

Kohlstedt, Edward D. *William Duncan.* William Duncan Trust, Palo Alto, 1957.

LaViolette, F. E. *The Struggle for Survival: Indian Cultures & the Protestant Ethic in B.C.* University of Toronto Press, 1961.

Maud, Ralph. *A Guide to B.C. Myth and Legend.* Talonbooks, 1982.

Moorehouse, Geoffrey. *The Missionaries.* Lippincott, 1973.

Nichols, Jeanette Paddock. *Alaska: A History of Its Administration, Exploitation, and Industrial Development During Its First Half Century Under the Rule of the United States.* Russell, 1963.

Peake, Frank A. *The Anglican Church in British Columbia.* Mitchell Press, 1959.

Pethick, Derek. *James Douglas: Servant of Two Empires.* Mitchell Press, 1969.

Sage, Walter N. *Sir James Douglas and British Columbia.* University of Toronto Press, 1930.

Shankel, George Edgar. *The Development of Indian Policy in British Columbia.* Unpublished Ph.D. thesis, University of Washington, 1945.

Sherwood, Morgan B. *Ardent Spirits: Hooch & the Osprey Affair at Sitka,* an article in Journal of the West, July 1965; and editor, *Alaska and Its History.* University of Washington Press, 1967.

Usher, Jean. *William Duncan of Metlakatla, a Victorian Missionary in British Columbia.* National Museums of Canada, 1974.

Warren, Max. *Social History and Christian Mission.* London, 1967.

Zaslow, Morris. *The Opening of the Canadian North 1870-1914.* McClelland and Stewart, 1971; *The Missionary As Social Reformer: The Case of William Duncan,* an article in the Journal of the Canadian Church Historical Society, 1966.

335

Index

336

340